Consumer Survival

Consumer Survival

AN ENCYCLOPEDIA OF CONSUMER RIGHTS, SAFETY, AND PROTECTION

Volume Two
H–Z

Wendy Reiboldt and
Melanie Horn Mallers, Editors

 ABC-CLIO

Santa Barbara, California • Denver, Colorado • Oxford, England

Copyright 2014 by ABC-CLIO, LLC

Library of Congress Cataloging-in-Publication Data

Consumer survival : an encyclopedia of consumer rights, safety, and protection / Wendy Reiboldt and Melanie Horn Mallers, editors.

    pages cm

  Includes bibliographical references and index.

  ISBN 978-1-59884-936-3 (hardback) — ISBN 978-1-59884-937-0 (ebook)
1. Consumer protection—Law and legislation—United States—
Encyclopedias.   I. Reiboldt, Wendy, editor.   II. Mallers, Melanie
Horn, editor.

  KF1607.5.C66   2014

  343.7307'103—dc23   2013023279

ISBN: 978-1-59884-936-3
EISBN: 978-1-59884-937-0

18   17   16   15   14   1   2   3   4   5

This book is also available on the World Wide Web as an eBook.
Visit www.abc-clio.com for details.

ABC-CLIO, LLC
130 Cremona Drive, P.O. Box 1911
Santa Barbara, California 93116-1911

This book is printed on acid-free paper ∞

Manufactured in the United States of America

Contents

List of Entries

Guide to Related Topics

Federal Reserve

FHA (Federal Housing Administration)

Fair Isaac and Company (FICO)

Freddie Mac

Gift Cards

Hazard Analysis and Critical Control Point (HACCP)

Health and Healthcare

Home Equity Loans

Insurance

Investing Regulations

Malpractice

Minimum Wage

Mortgages

Pawn Shops

Penny Stocks

Prepaid Cards

Producer Sovereignty

Social Networking

Government Agencies

Administration on Aging (AoA)

Attorney General Office (AG)

Bureau of Consumer Protection (BCP)

Bureau of Labor Statistics

Centers for Disease Control and Prevention (CDC)

Commission on Civil Rights

Commodity Futures Trading Commission (CFTC)

Congress

Consumer Financial Protection Bureau

Consumer Product Safety Commission (CPSC)

Customs and Border Protection (CBP)

Department of Agriculture (USDA)

Department of Commerce (DOC)

Department of Defense (DOD)

Department of Education (ED)

Department of Energy (DOE)

Department of Health and Human Services (HHS)

Department of Homeland Security (DHS)

Department of Housing and Urban Development (HUD)

Department of Justice (DOJ)

Department of Labor (DOL)

Department of State

Department of the Interior (DOI)

Department of Transportation (DOT)

Department of the Treasury

Department of Veterans Affairs (VA)

Departments of Consumer Affairs (DCA)

Departments of Insurance

Environmental Protection Agency (EPA)

Equal Employment Opportunity Commission (EEOC)

FDIC (Federal Deposit Insurance Commission)

Federal Aviation Administration (FAA)

Legislation

Movements

Organizations

H

HAACP. *See* Hazard Analysis and Critical Control Point (HACCP)

Hazard Analysis and Critical Control Point (HACCP)

The Hazard Analysis and Critical Control Point (HACCP) is a food safety management system that analyzes biological, chemical, and physical hazards in all segments of food industry, including production, procurement, handling, manufacturing, distribution, merchandising, and preparing food for consumption. HACCP systems are a preventive measure in the food safety control system that identifies points to monitor and control in the entire process throughout the farm-to-table food continuum. Although producers have incentives to adopt HACCP to satisfy downstream clients or to sustain reputation and market share, the use of HACCP systems is mandated for food industries in many countries.

HACCP Mandate

Initially, the prototype of HACCP was developed by Pillsbury Corporation when Pillsbury was assigned the task of producing first astronaut meals for NASA during the 1960s. Prevention of disease-producing bacteria and toxins through a nondestructive safety verification system in space food programs was a crucial and challenging task. The first food products ever manufactured under the HACCP system went abroad Apollo spacecraft.

The first legal mandate of HACCP for the commercial food industry in the United States was in 1994 through regulations for seafood. The mandate was subsequently expanded to other raw and unbranded food products marketed directly to consumers, such as meat and poultry, dairy, fish, and fresh fruit and juice. Regulations mandating a written HACCP plan as well as regulations regarding minimum HACCP training requirements for those who handle food are contained in the Code of Federal Regulations. The HACCP mandate is an example of *process* standards of government food safety regulation.

For food products other than those listed earlier, implementation of the HACCP system is left voluntary and works through third-party certification and labeling. The HACCP system is recommended by the National Advisory Committee on Microbiological Criteria for Foods, and voluntarily adopted by many food processing plants, retail food stores, and commercial and noncommercial food service operations.

The U.S. Department of Agriculture Food Safety and Inspection Service (USDA-FSIS) provides guidelines to set up a HACCP system, which can be tailored to customized HACCP plans for any food production, food retail, and food service operations. The guidelines include five planning steps and seven principles to follow. The seven principles are conduct a hazard analysis; determine the critical control points; establish critical limits; establish monitoring procedures; establish corrective actions; establish record-keeping and documentation procedures; and establish verification procedures.

Despite the legal mandates, compliance rates vary by industry. Particularly low compliance rates are found in seafood industry. Some argue that poor administrative coordination resulting from the Food and Drug Administration (FDA), not the USDA, being the enforcement agency for seafood HACCP may be part of the problem.

Merits and Issues of HACCP

Besides its scientific reliability, it is believed that HACCP's preventive focus makes it a more efficient and cost-effective alternative to testing of end products. It is considered to save time and money for the producers as well as for the regulatory agencies. Increasing distancing of food-making, difficulty of traceability in food production, and resultant concerns for global food safety and quality issues can also make HACCP a more viable international trade standard than product testing. In fact, HACCP replaced the old, more elaborate, and less flexible Good Manufacturing Practices (GMP) standards in European Union countries.

However, several controversies question the merits of HACCP. Some argue that HACCP can reinforce the two trends in food industry: greater industry concentration and increased vertical coordination. Some are concerned about the difficulty to measure the benefits of HACCP. Ensuring equivalence and consistency in HACCP standards across different regulatory units or across the world may also be a challenge. For those reasons, HACCP is sometimes used in conjunction with direct command and control (CAC) standards for end product performance to verify its effectiveness. For example, certain meat and poultry processors are required to perform laboratory tests to detect fecal bacteria, *Escherichia coli* O157:H7, and salmonella in addition to implementation of the HACCP system.

HACCP and Consumers

HACCP has the potential to alleviate uncertainty among consumers regarding the quality and safety of food products because the revelation of the measures taken to improve the quality and safety status is formal part of the HACCP principles. Research finds that consumer awareness and knowledge about safe food handling practices have increased and consumer confidence in the safety of meat and poultry has increased as a result of the 1996 U.S. Pathogen Reduction/HACCP farm-to-table initiatives. However, despite the increased knowledge and awareness, many consumers do not follow recommended safe food handling methods themselves.

Yunhee Chang

See also: Department of Agriculture (USDA); Food and Drug Administration (FDA); Food Labeling; Food Safety; Warnings

References and Additional Readings

Hong, C.H., Todd, E.C., & Bahk, G.J. (2008). Aerobic plate counts as a measure of hazard analysis critical control point effectiveness in a pork processing plant. *Journal of Food Protection, 71*(6), 1248–1252.

Hooker, N.H., Nayga Jr., R.M., & Siebert, J.W. (2011). The impact of HACCP on costs and product exit. *Journal of Agricultural and Applied Economics, 34*(01).

Health and Health Care

The definition of "health" has been debated for decades. According to the World Health Organization, health is "a complete state of physical, mental and social well-being and not merely the absence of disease or infirmity." Another definition is that health and disease is determined by "a dynamic state of well-being characterized by a physical, mental, and social potential, which satisfies the demands of life commensurate with age, culture, and personal responsibility" (Bircher, 2005, 336). If the potential is insufficient to satisfy these demands, the state is disease.

In 1974, Blum developed a model that proposed four major inputs influencing health. These inputs include the environment (physical, socioeconomic, sociopolitical, and sociocultural factors), lifestyle (behavioral and attitudinal factors), heredity (predisposing genetic factors), and medical care (preventive, curative, rehabilitative factors); all of which should be

The American Medical Association (AMA) has been in existence since 1847, founded by Nathan Smith Davis, a young doctor in New York who had a vision to elevate American medical education. Today, their mission is "to promote the art and science of medicine and the betterment of public health." They promote the following core values: (1) leadership; (2) excellence; and (3) Integrity and ethical behavior. Their vision is to be an essential part of the professional life of every physician.

They promote their vision by assisting doctors by promoting sustainable safe practices that lead to improved health outcomes for all patients, accelerating change in medical education, and enhancing physical satisfaction and practice sustainability by shaping delivery and payment models. The AMA website offers resources for physicians, as well as a variety of other resources.

For more information, see http://www.ama-assn.org

considered together when determining health status. The four determinants of health function simultaneously, but in different intensities

According to the model, environment is the most important force, followed by lifestyles and heredity, then medical care. These health inputs have ascertained that no singular focus on healthcare delivery will significantly improve health status. However, medical care services are a vital component and driving force for health production. Healthy People 2020 concurs that health and well-being can be affected by determinants such as policymaking, social behavior, individual behavior, physical environment, health services, or genetics. Lifestyles, both healthy and unhealthy, are often a result of the interrelationships of the aforementioned categories and are rarely determined by a single factor.

In health production, each individual is viewed as both a producer and a consumer of health, wherein the flow of inputs and the flow of outputs are specified over a period of time. Generally, outputs are measures of health status and inputs to health include health care, environment, education, lifestyle, genetic factors, and income. Health inputs include several other commodities in terms of resources, effort, and time; however, medical care services have been viewed as the most important input that is critical to health production function. Consequently, healthcare services have contributed significantly to improved health status and enhanced quality of life.

Health Care

Health care in the United States is an intricate system comprised of various different institutions, individual practitioners, resource networks, and other health-related organizations. Through this intricate system, providers, organizations, and institutions must work together to achieve an increased quality of life for the consumer. Health care involves the prevention, treatment, and management of illness as well as the preservation of mental and physical well-being through medical services and allied health professions.

The U.S. healthcare system involves four key players: (1) employers, (2) patients, (3) payers, and (4) providers. Although these major players function in the same healthcare system, each group has its own specific interests. Employers supply funding for healthcare coverage for their employees. Therefore, employers' main concern is to keep the costs down as well as maintain the health of employees to maximize work productivity. Patients want quality care with clear communication and the best possible healthcare coverage. Payers include health plans and health providers who focus on cost-effectiveness. Providers supply systematic healthcare services, and focus on accurate and appropriate diagnosis and therapy to improve health outcomes.

For patients, employers are expected to offer diverse healthcare options for the various needs and fund the majority of the health insurance costs. Employers, on the other hand, intend to minimize cost contributions, and prefer that employees use care when it is needed, oblige to doctors' recommendations, and return to work as soon as possible. However, some employers offer incentives, subsidies, and monetary reimbursements options to their employees who practice healthy behaviors and join to health promotion programs.

Health providers can fall under two broad categories: (1) health institutions and (2) healthcare personnel. Health institutions include hospitals, clinics, community health centers, and so on. Healthcare personnel include physicians with various specialties, nurses, nurse practitioners, physician assistants, many therapists, and pharmacists.

Quality and preventative healthcare services for patients are the main interests of healthcare providers. However, these best practices, such as latest technology and treatment, are often not covered by payers. Instead, providers prefer to follow clear treatment plans using the least amount of resources possible.

The Government and Health Care

Although the healthcare system functions through the interaction of patients, employers, providers, and payers, the government plays a major role in the delivery and financing of health and health services. The federal government interplays with social and economic entities in order to create health policies and authoritative bodies that affect health and health care for its citizens. Specifically, the government makes authoritative decisions through the branches of government that determines the fiscal responsibilities and resources to be allocated to the healthcare system. The roles of the three branches of government are all inclusive in regards to health care. The legislative branch creates laws. This includes funding health programs and maintaining a balance between health policies and other policy domains. The executive branch is responsible for policy implementation, approval, veto, and promulgation of rules and regulations. Lastly, the judicial branch interprets health policies, ensures rights, and resolves disputes.

Although the government holds a significant role in health care, the majority of resources used in health production in the United States are dominated by the private sector. The U.S. healthcare system is composed of both private and public insurers. This system contrasts many developed countries that have national health insurance programs and provide routine basic health care, which is government-controlled and financed through federal taxes. Instead, the U.S. healthcare system has no central governing agency and funded by the public and private industry with significant control held by the private sector. Furthermore, diversification in payment, insurance, and delivery methodologies is complex and interacting.

The public insurance sector consists of Medicare, Medicaid, VA Health Care, and other public systems. Medicare is a federal program funded by federal income taxes to insure individuals aged 65 and older, including some disabled persons. Medicaid is designed for low-income and disabled persons. Funding of this program is financed jointly by taxes from the states and federal government. Other public systems include the State Children's Health Insurance Program (S-CHIP) and the Veteran's Administration (VA) program. S-CHIP was implemented to cover children whose families make too much money for Medicaid, but too little to purchase private insurance. The VA is funded by taxpayer dollars to provide coverage for veterans of the military.

Private health insurance encompasses employer-sponsored insurance and private nongroup insurance (individual market). Employer-sponsored insurance is financed through the employers and employees, wherein a contracted third-party administers the company's health insurance plan. More specifically, employers will pay all or a percentage of the premium and the employee will pay for the remainder of the premiums and/or deductibles. For private nongroup insurance, the individual market pays for a percentage of the population that is self-employed, retired, or do not obtain insurance through their employer. Financing of the individual market occurs through individuals who pay their own premiums out-of-pocket.

Health Care and the Economy

The U.S. healthcare system is a fiscally driven entity. Furthermore, the United States spends more on health care than any other developed country in the world. Despite the limited access to basic health care and the millions of uninsured, costs continue to rise at exponential rates. In 2009, annual national health expenditures totaled $2.5 trillion in comparison to $27.3 billion in 1960. Other estimates predict that by 2018, the United States will spend more than $4.3 trillion per year, or 20.3 percent of the gross domestic product.

The increasing trend of healthcare expenditures is a major concern, which disproportionately reduces access to services and insurance. These increases cost more for employers to provide health coverage for their employees, resulting in decreased wages. Moreover, some employers have chosen to abstain from providing coverage to their employees because of high costs. The resulting effect of these increases places substantial pressures on federal budgets. In other words, the large fiscal consumption of health services detract from providing federal support to other national priorities such as education and homeland security.

Healthcare industries function differently than traditional economic markets due to the existence of information asymmetry and the third-party payment system, quality measurement issues, and market failures. The patient's lack of knowledge of illnesses and treatment alternatives created information asymmetry that tilted the patient–doctor relationship in favor of the provider. This information problem required a strict licensure practice for practitioners. The third-party payment system is related to insurance companies paying the large portion of the patient's health care, which results in a massive amount of moral hazard in the form of overutilization of health services by both patients and doctors. This requires extensive regulations like Certificate of Need or rate regulations that are not uncommon in health care. Insurance companies (and HMOs) developed their own practices to lower utilization such as copayments, coinsurance, and deductibles imposed on patients.

Quality measurement issues in health care are also related to asymmetric information problem and the difficulty of standardizing care provided to each patient. When patients cannot judge whether the quality of care they receive is good, there must be some regulation to protect the public in the form of accreditation standards, government regulations, and purchaser requirements. For instance, the healthcare industry created the Joint Commission on Accreditation of Healthcare Organizations (JCAHO) or systems like the Healthcare Effectiveness Data and Information Set (HEDIS), that is a tool used by more than 90 percent of America's plans to measure performance on important dimensions of care and service in order to monitor the quality of health care provided by doctors, hospitals, and HMOs.

Finally, market failures such as the existence of large number of uninsured people or the extensive use of health and health-related services without a payment (public good) are quite common in healthcare industry. For instance, following the Great Depression in the 1930s and the World War II, a private insurance sector that was created to fund healthcare markets failed to provide healthcare coverage to the low-income groups and elderly. That is why the federal government established Medicare and Medicaid programs in 1965 to provide healthcare coverage to individuals in the categories mentioned earlier.

Patient protection and consumer advocacy laws are not new to the healthcare industry. Patient's access to quality health care, right to fair compensation in malpractice cases and quality of care, and protection against rising healthcare costs are only few examples of these types of regulations. On March 23, 2010, President Obama signed the reform bill, known as the Patient Protection and Affordable Care Act (PPACA), proposes many regulations to improve consumer protection. The Patient's Bill of Rights outlines the consumer protections and provides the knowledge needed for consumers to make their own health decisions. The Consumer Assistance Programs (CAPs) will educate consumers about their rights and responsibilities to request an appeal when coverage is denied for a service or treatment. The CAPs will also provide information about insurance coverage and assist consumers in purchasing desired insurance plans. Preventative Care, such as screenings, vaccinations, and counseling, will be available to consumers who purchased a health plan after March 23, 2010. Prevention coverage is dependent upon age, gender, and health status. Children under the age of 19 who exhibit preexisting conditions will not be denied insurance coverage due to their disease or illness.

Another protection is the Preexisting Condition Insurance Plan (PCIP), which will be available until the Affordable Insurance Exchanges take effect in 2014. The PCIP will provide coverage for any legal U.S. resident who has been denied insurance coverage due to a preexisting condition and who has been uninsured for at least six months. Under the PPACA, consumers can choose their own in-network doctor and will not be subject to referrals from primary care for OB-GYN appointments. Consumers will no longer be required to apply for approval from their insurance companies before using out-of-network emergency room services. These are the primary regulations set forth in the PPACA to protect the consumer and to increase the access of healthcare information, services, and insurance coverage.

In the last 20 years, there has been an increase in demand for consumer protection as well as in "fraudulent practitioners." Because the quality of life for healthcare consumers is heavily dependent on the quality of services provided by healthcare physicians, a strict licensure process for practitioners is paramount to overall health. Since 1914, the Federation of State Medical Boards (FSMB) of the United States has aimed to "improve the quality, safety and integrity of health care" in order to ensure the protection of U.S. healthcare consumers (Healthcare Licensing Services, 2012). Each U.S. state has its own medical board, supported by the FSMB. Medical boards are government agencies that believe "the practice of medicine is . . . a privilege granted by the people of a state" (Healthcare Licensing Services, 2012, n.p.). Their primary function is to facilitate proper licensing and disciplining of medical doctors. All states require "proof of prior education, training, and . . . completion of all three steps of the United States Medical Licensing Examination (EUMLE)" (American Medical Association, 2012, n.p.). To ensure the protection of the consumers, medical boards provide "public-record information about licensed physicians" as well as "investigate complaints against physicians" (The Medical Board of California, 2010, n.p.). Each state also creates its own Medical Practice Act to ensure the medical board regulates the integrity of medical practice. Medical Practice Acts are constantly revised with the progression of education and medical advancement.

The U.S. Food and Drug Administration (FDA) has an important role for protecting the health of the American people. In 1906, the first Food and Drug Act was enacted, becoming the first law to show concern for consumer protections. In 1938, the Federal Food, Drug, and Cosmetic Act passed, which "authorized the FDA to demand evidence of safety for new drugs, issue standards for food, and conduct factory inspections" (FDA, 2011, n.p.). Under the Food, Drug, and Cosmetic Act, the Center for Drug Evaluation and Research produces the "Orange Book," updated daily, to provide healthcare consumers with information about new generic drugs. In 1962, the Kefauver–Harris Amendments "strengthened the rules for drug safety" by requiring manufacturers to prove the effectiveness of drugs as well as requiring full disclosure of benefits and side effects of drugs used in clinical. In 1976, the Medical Device Amendments "applied safety and effectiveness safeguards to new [medical] devices" (FDA, 2011, n.p.). The Center for Devices and Radiological Health uses regulatory science to test medical devices for "safety, effectiveness, quality and performance" (FDA, n.d.). Currently, $1 trillion of health-related products are regulated for safety each year, including food, drugs, biological products, medical devices, animal drugs, cosmetics, and radiation products.

The Emergency Medical Treatment and Active Labor Act (EMTALA) is a provision that requires most hospitals to provide examinations and stabilizing treatment to all patients who present themselves to an emergency room for medical emergency conditions. The primary purpose of this statute is to prevent hospitals from rejecting or refusing to treat patients or transferring patents to charity or county hospitals due to their inability to pay for healthcare services. The EMTALA was passed as part of the Consolidated Omnibus Budget Reconciliation Act (COBRA) of 1986 in order to ensure access to emergency services despite inability to pay. Hospitals are mandated under Medicare to offer emergency services for medical screening examinations (MSE), including pregnant women in labor, regardless of health insurance coverage. Consequently, this statue obligates hospitals to provide stabilizing treatment or ensure appropriate transfers for treatment if a hospital is incapable of stabilizing a patient within its capacity.

The EMTALA applies to hospitals in provider agreements under Medicare, which includes nearly all U.S. hospitals except for the Shriners' Hospital for Crippled Children and several federal military hospitals. Although the majority of EMTALA statutes apply to hospitals, some terms apply to physicians. In both cases, responsible parties (receiving hospital or on-call physicians) are subject to penalties for violations. Hospitals who violate EMTALA statues may receive a civil money penalty without criminal implications of up to $50,000 per violation. For hospitals with 100 or fewer beds, the maximum fine is $25,000 per violation. Physicians can be subject to these monetary penalties as well, but in different amounts and situations, which may include misrepresentation of patient's condition or refusal to provide services. The COBRA also protects employees by requiring employers with a group health plan to provide the opportunity to employees to continue temporarily with their group health coverage if their coverage otherwise would cease due to termination, layoff, or other change in employment status. Employees and their spouses and dependents are covered up to 18 months; up to 29 months if they are disabled.

The Health Insurance Portability and Accountability Act of 1996 (HIPAA) was established as a set of national standards to protect health information of patients. The HIPAA was implemented as part of the "Privacy Rule" (Standards for Privacy of Individually Identifiable Health Information) that was issued by the U.S. Department of Health and Human Services (HHS). The primary purpose the privacy rule is to ensure the protection of patient health information, while allowing the need for dissemination and flow of health information to promote quality healthcare services and well-being. Within the HHS, the Office for Civil Rights (OCR) is the governing body responsible for implementing and enforcing the privacy rule in regards to compliance activities and civil money penalties.

Tony Sinay

See also: Department of Health and Human Services (HHS); Drug Safety and Clinical Trials; Medicaid; Medicare; Patient Protection and Affordable Care Act (PPACA); Social Services

References and Additional Readings

Agency for Healthcare Research and Quality. (2012). Health services research core competencies: Final report. Retrieved from http://www.ahrq.gov/fund/train ing/hsrcomp08.htm

American College of Emergency Physicians. (2012). Emergency Medical Treatment and Labor Act (EMTALA) Interim Guidance. Retrieved from http://www.acep.org/search.aspx?searchtext=emtala

American Medical Association. (2012). Medical licensure. Retrieved from http://www.ama-assn.org/ama/pub/education-careers/becoming-physician/medi cal-licensure.page

Bircher, J. (2005). Towards a dynamic definition of health and disease. *Medicine, Health Care and Philosophy, 8*(3), 335–341.

Blum, H. (1981). *Planning for health* (2nd ed.). New York: Health Sciences Press.

Census Bureau. (2013). People quick facts. Retrieved from http://www.quickfacts .census.gov/qfd/states/00000.html

Center for Drug and Health Plan Choice. (2012). Centers for Medicare & Medicaid Services. Retrieved from http://www.cms.hhs.gov/CMSLeadership/05_Of fice_CPC.asp#TopOfPage

Centers for Medicare and Medicaid Services. (2013a). Overview EMTALA. Retrieved from https://www.cms.gov/EMTALA/

Centers for Medicare and Medicaid Services. (2013b). Overview ERISA. Retrieved from https://www.cms.gov/hipaageninfo/

Congressional Budget Office. (2009). The budget and economic outlook: Fiscal years 2009–2019. Retrieved from http://www.cbo.gov/doc.cfm?index=9957

Department of Health and Human Services. (2012). Summary of the HIPAA privacy rule. Retrieved from http://www.hhs.gov/ocr/privacy/hipaa/under standing/summary/index.html

Department of Labor. (2012). Employee retirement income security act—ERISA. Retrieved from http://www.dol.gov/dol/topic/health-plans/erisa.htm

Department of Veterans Affairs. (2012). Retrieved from http://www.va.gov/health/default.asp

Food and Drug Administration. (2011a). Orange book: Approved drug products with therapeutic equivalence evaluations. Retrieved from http://www.accessdata.fda.gov/scripts/cder/ob/default.cfm

Food and Drug Administration. (2011b). Regulatory information: Legislation. Retrieved from http://www.fda.gov/RegulatoryInformation/Legislation/default.htm

Food and Drug Administration. (2013). Regulatory science in CDRH. Retrieved from http://www.fda.gov/downloads/AboutFDA/CentersOffices/OfficeofMedicalProductsandTobacco/CDRH/CDRHReports/UCM274162.pdf

Grossman, M. (1972). On the concept of health capital and the demand for health. *Journal of Political Economy, 80*(2), 223–255.

Healthcare Licensing Services. (2013). Overview of state medical boards. Retrieved from https://www.healthcarelicensing.com/state-medical-license-requirements

HealthCare.gov. (2013). The healthcare law and you. Retrieved from http://www.healthcare.gov/law/index.html

HealthyPeople.gov. (2012). Determinants of health. Retrieved from http://www.healthypeople.gov/2020/about/DOHAbout.aspx

Hollingswort, B., & Wildman, J. (2002). The efficiency of health production: Re-estimating the WHO panel data using parametric and nonparametric approaches to provide additional information. *World Health Organization.* Retrieved from http://chpe.buseco.monash.edu.au

Longest, B. (2010). *Health policymaking in the United States.* Chicago, IL: Health Administration Press.

McKee, M. (2001). Measuring the efficiency of health systems. *British Medical Journal, 323*(7308), 295–296.

The Medical Board of California. (2010). What does the medical board do? Retrieved from http://www.mbc.ca.gov/board/role.html

Organisation for Economic Cooperation and Development. (2008). *OECD Health Data Law 22(3),* 721–788.

Purcell, P., & Staman, J. (2012). Summary of the employee retirement income security act (ERISA). Retrieved from http://aging.senate.gov/crs/pension7.pdf

World Health Organization. (1948). *Preamble to the constitution of the world health organization as adopted by the international health conference.* New York: International Health Conference.

World Health Organization. (2005). What is a health system? Retrieved from http://www.who.int/features/qa/28/en/

World Health Organization. (2012). Retrieved from http://www.who.int

World Health Organization. (2013). *Re-defining health.* Retrieved from http://www.who.int/bulletin/bulletin_board/83/ustun11051/en/

HIPAA (Health Insurance Portability and Accountability Act)

The Health Insurance Portability and Accountability Act (HIPAA) of 1996 (PL 104–191) was enacted into the U.S. Congress and first signed by President Bill Clinton in 1996. It was sponsored and supported by Senator Edward Kennedy (Massachusetts/Democrat) and Senator Nancy Kassebaum (Kansas/Republican).

The HIPAA law is twofold; it is a law with two Titles. Title I: Health Care Access, Portability and Renewability. Title II: Preventing Health Care Fraud and Abuse; Administrative Simplification; Medical Liability Reform. To explain the titles in lay terms, Title I offers insurance coverage for people who change careers or lose their jobs. Title II sets security and privacy standards for how doctors, hospitals, health insurance companies and employers handle private health information.

HIPAA Resolution Agreement

In 2011, the U.S. Department of Health and Human Services (HHS) Office for Civil Rights (OCT) announced a resolution agreement regarding potential violations of the Health Insurance Portability and Accountability Act (HIPAA). The complaints involved two celebrity patients of the University of California at Los Angeles Health Systems (UCLAHS), who claimed the employees repeatedly and without cause viewed the patients' protected electronic health information. Investigations performed by the OCT revealed repeated viewings of the electronic protected health information during the years 2005–2008. Furthermore, the violating employees were not sanctioned, in accordance with the law. The UCLAHS paid $865,500 to settle the two complaints and has promised to implement a corrective plan that will address gaps in employee compliance. Corrective action includes, according to the OCT, regular training of employees, sanctioning of employees who violate the Act, and identifying an independent monitor to review the UCLAHS plan every three years.

Because the HIPAA states that patient information must be restricted to employees with a valid reason to access the protected electronic health information, any employee not complying (i.e., seeking information that is not warranted) must be sanctioned. It is the responsibility of the employer to make sure the employees are in compliance.

Source: U.S. Department of Health and Human Services. (July 7, 2011). University of California settles HIPAA Privacy and Security case involving UCLA Health System facilities. Retrieved from http://www.hhs.gov/

Medical offices ensure the rights of consumers by keeping patient records private and levying fines from $100 to $250,000 for non-compliance. (AP Photo/Bebeto Matthews)

Section I of HIPAA is intended to prevent people from being discriminated from employment due to health conditions. Prior to HIPAA, Individuals feared that leaving their job could jeopardize valuable health insurance coverage and that they could be excluded from benefits with a new employer's health plan because of preexisting conditions. Title I primarily involves group health insurance plans and employee's access to them. The first intention of the HIPAA law is to ensure that no employee be denied coverage and prevent the premium being based on an individual's health status or health history. This means that a young healthy employee may have the same monthly premium as an older, diabetic employee. Title I also establishes rules on how group health plans treat preexisting conditions. Before HIPAA employees could be declined for health coverage if they had chronic conditions.

Under the new HIPAA guidelines, the maximum amount of time that an employee must wait for full coverage cannot exceed 12 months (18 months for late enrollees who did not enroll during "open enrollment"). HIPAA established a term called "credible coverage," which means that an employee does not have a break without insurance coverage for more than 63 days. Most people who transition between jobs will move out of one health plan to another. When this happens there is no break of coverage and therefore no waiting period for any preexisting conditions. If an employee has a break of coverage for more than 63 days then the new health plan may exclude that employee's preexisting conditions, usually for up to six months. If an employee moves from an individual plan to a group employer sponsored plan the same provisions apply under "credible coverage." Upon leaving employment an employee is offered COBRA, Medicare, or Medicaid.

Limitations of HIPAA Title I: HIPAA cannot force an employer to offer or pay for health insurance coverage. It does not force group health plans to offer specific benefits or how much a company may charge for the insurance. It also cannot determine which employees in the work force will qualify for the health plan. Some health plans are exempt from Title I requirements. Examples are long-term care plans and ancillary medical products such as vision, dental, infertility, and so on. However, if the ancillary product was offered as part of the general health plan then the HIPAA still applies to such benefits.

Section II: The U.S. Department of Health and Human Services (HHS) issued the privacy rule to implement the requirement of the HIPAA. The Standards for Privacy of Individually Identifiable Health Information became the privacy rule. This privacy rule was added to the HIPAA Legislation and was published on December 28, 2000. In March 2002, modifications were made to the privacy rule. The entire regulation with the modifications can be found on the HSS's website.

The Standards of the Privacy Rule address the use and disclosure of people's health information (called protected health information) by entities that are subject to this rule (covered entities). Entities regulated by this rule are obligated to comply with all of its requirements and disclosures. Such covered entities are health plans, healthcare providers, and healthcare clearinghouses.

Health plans: Individual and/or group plans that provide or pay the costs of medical care. Health plans include health, dental, vision, and prescription drug insurers, health maintenance organizations (HMO), Medicare, Medicaid, and Medicare Supplement providers. Health plans include employer-sponsored health plans, government- and church-sponsored health plans. An exempt entity is a small business health plan insuring less than 50 employees administered solely by the employer. Other exempt entities are insurance companies selling only workman's compensation coverage, automobile, and property and casualty insurance policies.

Healthcare providers: Any healthcare provider that electronically submits health information relating to transactions is a covered entity.

Common providers are doctor offices, hospitals, and so on. Examples of transactions are processing claims, benefit eligibility inquiries, and referral for authorizations. Electronic technology includes the use of e-mail, facsimile, or third-party copy services.

Healthcare clearinghouses: Nonstandard processors of information that transact from another entity or vice versa, as a means of a business relationship and dealing with personal, private health information. Examples of clearinghouses are third-party billing services, community health management information systems, and pricing companies.

The primary purpose of the privacy rule is to publish the circumstances an individual's private health information may be used by covered entities. A covered entity may not use or disclose protected information unless the privacy rule permits or with written authorization from the individual. Two important rules apply with the privacy laws: disclosures and authorizations. The covered entities must disclose that they protect health information on behalf of individuals and provide the information only with proper authorizations. A covered entity must obtain the individual's written authorization for any use of the protected health information that is not for treatment or payment or otherwise permitted by the privacy rule. This authorization must be written in specific terms and in plain language. Each covered entity must provide a notice of its privacy practices. The notice must describe the ways that the entity may use protected health information and it must state their duties to protect privacy (privacy practices).

A covered entity must have a procedure for individuals to complain about its compliance with respect to the privacy of their patients/customers. This complaint process must be explained in the privacy practices notice. HHS may impose civil monetary penalties on a covered entity of $100 per failure to comply with the privacy rule requirements. The penalty may not exceed $25,000 per year for multiple violations by one entity per calendar year. A person who intentionally uses protected information and knowingly violates the HIPAA law can be fined up to $50,000 and serve one-year-term imprisonment. Criminal penalties can increase up to $250,000 and up to 10 years of imprisonment if the act involves the intent to sell the personal health information for personal gain or malicious harm.

The privacy rule permits the use of protected health information without the consent of the individual for national priority purposes. Some examples of such use are required by law (court ordered), in cases or neglect, abuse, or domestic violence. Law enforcement has six special circumstances that they may use to obtain private medical information without the knowledge of the individual. Some examples of these six exclusions are to solve a crime, solve a missing person case, when health information is evidence relating to a crime or to locate a suspect, fugitive, or missing person.

Aleta Ostlund

See also: Department of Health and Human Services (HHS); Health and Health Care

References and Additional Readings

Centers for Medicare and Medicaid Services. (n.d.). HIPPA. General information. Retrieved from http://www.cms.hhs.gov/HIPAAGenInfo/

Department of Health and Human Services. (n.d.). The Health Insurance Portability and Accountability Act of 1996 (HIPAA) Privacy and Security Rules. Retrieved from http://www.hhs.gov/ocr/privacy/

OCR (Office for Civil Rights). (2011). Summary of the HIPAA Privacy Rule. In *Privacy brief: United States Department of Health & Human Services*. Retrieved from http://www.hhs/gov/ocr/hipaa

Home Equity Loans

For most consumers, a home is their most valuable asset. This is true for those consumers who have built up equity in their home. To have equity in one's home refers to the increased value of the home in excess of the balance on a mortgage. For example, a homeowner may own a home that is valued at $300,000 but has a mortgage balance of $200,000. In this case, the homeowner has equity in the amount of $100,000. Home equity loans are a means by which a homeowner may extract 75–90 percent of the home's value minus the amount owed on the first or primary mortgage. In this instance, the homeowner would be able to take a potential loan for $40,000 [($300,000 × 0.80) ?200,000]. It might be tempting for some to tap into this equity to pay for home improvements, credit card debt, medical bills, an education, or reoccurring household expenses during periods of unemployment. The 2001–2002 monthly survey of consumers (SOC) revealed that the uses of liquefied home equity went toward consumer purchases (16 percent), home improvements (35 percent), repayment of other debt (26 percent), and the remainder to stock market and business ventures (Cooper, 2010).

Consumers may access the equity in their homes through a second mortgage in one of two ways, through a home equity loan (HEL) or a home equity line of credit (HELOC). These are referred to as second mortgages because they are a second lien on the mortgage. When one solicits and agrees to a HEL or HELOC, the home is used as collateral as is the case with the primary mortgage. Second mortgages are a riskier venture for lenders but can still be profitable. In the event of default, a primary mortgage is paid first, whereas a second mortgage would be paid second with the possibility of none payment or a settled payment (smaller than the original amount). Second mortgage lenders offset this risk by charging interest rates of 2–5 percentage points higher than first mortgage rates.

There are differences between a HEL and a HELOC. The differences are related to the form in which the consumer has access to the cash drawn from their equity, type of interest, repayment period, and other costs and fees related to the origination of the loan. With a HEL, cash is available in a lump sum with fixed interest and principal monthly payments. A HELOC is a line of credit that may be used in the form of checks or an actual credit card. The credit may be used periodically which gives the consumer flexibility in the use of their credit; similar to that of a credit card. The interest rates are typically variable with some lenders allowing for conversion to a fixed rate. However, there is a fixed period of time during which the credit can be borrowed referred to as the *draw period*. A consumer may have a 10-year draw period and a 15-year repayment period. Some lenders may allow a renewal, but it is important to inquire on this option.

In today's market, HEL and HELOC are easy to apply for and may be a less expensive alternative to refinancing and extracting cash, a personal loan, or using a credit card. Additionally, the interest on these loans is tax deductible. However, consumers must read and ask questions regarding the HELOC contracts that they agree to. HELOCs have limitations in regard to how often the line of credit is drawn and minimum balances. The payment options may include interest-only payments or a percentage of the balance owed (www.FederalReserveBoard.gov). Some may require a *balloon payment* or payment in full of any outstanding balance. The inability to make the balloon payment or to refinance at this point, may lead to foreclosure and the loss of one's home. The Federal Trade Commission warns consumers about this practice by some lenders as a hidden loan term.

Instead of relying on the equity of one's home as a means for cash, homeowners should engage in prudent planning. Additionally, establishing an emergency fund, investing in a college fund, and considering other alternatives to repaying debt should also be considered. It is a good idea to explore other methods of acquiring cash that involve less risk. If however, using home equity is part of one's plan, then careful consideration and selection of the equity extraction method is essential.

Dolores Robles

See also: Banking; Federal Trade Commission (FTC); Foreclosures and Short Sales; Mortgages

References and Additional Readings

Cooper, D. (2010). Did easy credit lead to overspending? Home equity borrowing and household behavior in the early 2000's. *Federal Reserve Bank of Boston Public Policy Discussion Paper*, 09–7, 1–47.

Federal Trade Commission. (2012a). Home equity loan: Borrowers beware. Retrieved from http://www.ftc.gov/bcp/edu/pubs/consumer/homes/rea11.shtm

Federal Trade Commission. (2012b). Home equity credit lines! Retrieved from http://www.ftc.gov/bcp/edu/pubs/consumer/homes/rea02.shtm

The Federal Reserve Board. (2012). What you should know about home equity lines of credit. Retrieved from http://files.consumerfinance.gov/f/201204_CFPB_HELOC-brochure.pdf

Garman, T., & Forgue, R.E. (2010). Obtaining affordable housing. In *Personal Finance*. Mason, OH: South-Western Cengage Learning, 271.

Home Ownership and Equity Protection Act (HOEPA)

During the 1990s, the mortgage finance industry began to transform and became liberalized to cater to previously underserved populations, such as minorities, recent immigrants, and single females. While homeownership opportunities were being extended to millions of new households, the lending community also grew to include several "subprime" lenders, a term that referred to lenders that provided credit to would-be borrowers that were considered below "prime" status. These borrowers usually had a credit score and history that were considered less than desirable by most lenders, sometimes due to either a lack of sophistication with the banking process or an inability to establish a credit history in the first place. As a result, subprime lenders would provide loans to these previously underserved borrowers, but would charge a set of fees that would compensate them for assuming the risk involved with the transaction. Whereas the subprime industry largely filled a void previously absent among low- and moderate-income consumer borrowing options, a number of subprime borrowers routinely stained the reputation of the industry by charging exorbitant fees over and above sensible risk-based pricing strategies. Because of the lack of familiarity that many of these potential borrowers had with the home buying experience and with the lack of financial literacy among the American population in general, an alarming number of borrowers became enmeshed within financing schemes that ultimately led them to default on their mortgages over time.

The Homeownership and Equity Protection Act, often referred to as HOEPA, is a federal consumer protection legislative act that addresses these high-cost mortgage lending practices that can be termed as "predatory." In many ways, it helped to codify what sort of threshold exists that separates a legitimate subprime loan from one that is predatory. The law was part of a set of amendments to the Truth in Lending Act, and specifically addressed the issues of points, fees, and the interest rate that mortgage borrowers would be charged, as reported to the borrower through the annual percentage rate (APR). The law applies largely to mortgages on primary residences, and exempts those related to commercial property, investment property, and second homes. Its primary focus is to protect consumers from both egregious up-front and ongoing costs. Whereas a risky borrower should be expected to pay a higher interest rate than a "prime" borrower, HOEPA distinguishes a threshold at which a borrower's interest rate can be considered to be egregiously high. As a result, the HOEPA threshold for so-called "high-cost" loans was codified as being 8 percentage points above the applicable treasury index. In the case of most U.S. mortgage holders, that equates to the equivalent of the prevailing interest rate for the 30-year U.S. Treasury bond. Because new home borrowers are often vulnerable to lender tactics at the closing table, HOEPA also protects consumers by forbidding consumers from paying more than 8 percent of the actual loan amount toward points and fees.

Once a loan becomes classified as a HOEPA, or high-cost loan, there are a number of provisions to which it must adhere. If the mortgage has a term of less than five years, then a balloon payment is not acceptable. A HOEPA loan can also not be subject to negative amortization, in which the borrower's outstanding principal balance is actually growing over a period of time. This unique type of situation can normally occur in some situations involving either adjustable-rate mortgages or graduated payment mortgages. In addition, a HOEPA loan cannot have an interest rate adjusted in the event of loan default that is higher than the note rate. Finally, HOEPA alleviated, but did not altogether eliminate, some of the most onerous prepayment penalties that borrowers were subject to during the life of the loan.

Not surprisingly, the criticism from the lending community upon the passage of HOEPA was harsh, and the ripple effects from within the mortgage finance industry were substantive. In 2000, Fannie Mae and Freddie

Mac, the two giant secondary mortgage marketing agencies, stated that they would no longer purchase HOEPA-triggered mortgages, threatening to drive up the cost of lending to low- and moderate-income borrowers in the process. Meanwhile, the primary lending industry lobbied against the strengthening of HOEPA over time, claiming that regulatory costs would be passed through to consumers, thereby slowing the efficiency of the mortgage finance process and adding even more burden to that population that could least afford such added regulatory costs.

Because of the burgeoning subprime lending industry and also questionable enforcement of predatory loans by the federal agencies, many states decided to enact their own predatory lending statutes, sometimes referred to as "mini-HOEPAs." Several of these states also felt that the federal definitions for so-called predatory loans were not stringent enough, and that high fees and interest rates were only two of several types of predatory practices to which low- and moderate-income borrowers succumbed. As of 2008, more than half of U.S. states had enacted their own predatory lending statutes, which sought to go beyond the original intentions of HOEPA. These laws went beyond the issue of up-front costs and APR calculations to include such loan provisions as prepayment penalties, balloon payments, loan flipping, and the actual allowance of financing of points and fees. Enforcement provisions differ by state, with some government agencies providing their own enforcement to the state court system allowing private redress cases to be brought forth by aggrieved borrowers, with relief and damages coming from either the loan originator or through securitized trusts. Meanwhile, several studies that followed the passage of such "mini-HOEPA" laws throughout the states suggested that the increased regulation did not cause a dampening effect on overall mortgage loan volume, as had been predicted. One potential impact, however, is that lenders compensated for these laws through creative structuring of their mortgage loan products or by providing pricing just high enough that it would not trigger the loan as being HOEPA-eligible, but which still provided a high degree of burden to the borrower.

Andrew T. "Andy" Carswell

See also: Banking; Foreclosures and Short Sales; Department of Housing and Urban Development (HUD); Mortgages

References and Additional Readings

Bostic, R.W., Engel, K.C., McCoy, P.A., & Wachter, S.M. (2008). The impact of state anti-predatory lending laws: Policy implications and insights. *Joint Center for Housing Studies at Harvard University*, 1–37.

Ho, G., & Pennington-Cross, A. (2006). Predatory lending laws and the cost of credit. Federal Reserve Bank of St. Louis Working Paper No 2006–022A. Retrieved from http://research.stlouisfed.org/wp/2006/2006–022.pdf.

Holder, K., & Manuel, K. M. (2007). *Predatory lending: A comparison of state laws to the federal home ownership and equity protection act.* Washington, DC: Congressional Research Service.

Staten, M. E., & Elliehausen, G. (2001). *The impact of the Federal Reserve Board's proposed revisions to HOEPA on the number and characteristics of HOEPA loans.* Washington, DC: Georgetown University.

HUD. See Department of Housing and Urban Development

I

Identity Theft

Identity theft involves stealing someone else's identity, including someone's name, driver's license, social security number, driver's license number, any financial instrument number (such as a credit card or debit card number), or any other useful personal identifying information without permission. Generally, these items are taken to commit fraud by using them to procure a monetary benefit of some kind. Identity theft, also known as identity fraud, provides identity thieves the ability to use another person's identifying information for financial gain or other illegal purposes.

Often, persons committing identity theft use the personal data, especially a victim's social security number, and/or date of birth, to withdraw funds from bank accounts or other financial institutions. Commonly, the use of another person's identity provides financial gain to the perpetrator as he or she pretends to be the victim and run up large credit card debts or withdraw money from the victim's bank accounts. Perpetrators also use a victim's identifying information to create new financial institution accounts (usually credit card accounts) that a victim may not know about, thereby building up large credit card charges on these new accounts. Once the credit limit is reached on these new accounts, the perpetrator will abandon the account, but the victim may still be responsible for the charges associated with the newly created account. Not only may identity thieves wreck credit limits or create new accounts that hurt a victim's credit, but there will likely be substantial financial costs to repair the victim's financial reputation as well.

Increasingly, the Internet provides identity thieves an easy venue to obtain personal identifying information, including passwords and financial institution data. Victims often respond to "spammer" e-mails (unsolicited e-mail) that might request identifying information, thereby allowing identity thieves to use this information for further criminal activity. Either by way of computer, or other methods, the identity thief can virtually take over a victim's identity to conduct a wide range of criminal activities.

A sample identity card used by victims of identity theft to prove their identities to law enforcement, government agencies and other third parties. (AP Photo/Rogelio Solis)

Case Study: Identity Theft and Assumption Deterrence Act

Cases like the one below show how the act is utilized and why it is so important.

In 2008, the U.S. attorney general announced that 11 perpetrators had been identified and captured in the single largest and most complex identity theft case ever charged in this country. The case, one on an international level, involved criminals from the United States, China, Estonia, Ukraine, and Belarus. Law enforcement officials estimated that the group stole and sold up to 130 million credit and debit card numbers between 2006 and 2008. One technique used by the group is "wardriving," literally driving around searching for unsecure wireless networks to capture data at major chains such as Dave & Buster's, Sports Authority, Barnes and Noble, TJ Maxx, Office Max, to name a few. The group also managed to install "sniffers" (a computer code to capture credit debit card data) on cash registers. In one location at one chain, experts estimated that this technique created a loss of over $600,000.

Moreover, the group encoded and sold the stolen credit and debit card numbers to other international criminals and "cashed out" the cards, withdrawing tens of thousands of dollars from ATMs. The "ring leader," Albert Gonzalez, is a former informant for the U.S. Secret Service, who previously helped the service hunt down hackers. Agents discovered that he was double-crossing the service by alerting some of the very people the agency was trying to investigate. While consumers did not personally and directly incur financial losses, the credit card companies lost tens of millions, according to best guess estimates from the Department of Justice.

Source: U.S. Department of Justice. (2008, Aug 5). Retail Hacking Ring Charged for Stealing and Distributing Credit and Debit Card Numbers from Major U.S. Retailers. Retrieved from http://www.justice.govw

There are numerous methods by which identity theft can be committed:

- Theft of material from burglaries or breaking into vehicles.
- Pretexting: obtaining material and identity information through false pretenses
- Skimming: utilization of electronic devices that capture credit card or debit card information in the public sphere
- Thefts of wallets or purses
- Theft of garbage and recycling material, both at residential and commercial vicinities (also known as dumpster diving)
- Mail theft, primarily of solicitations from financial institutions
- Misappropriation of credit card/debit card information, sometimes through compromised point of sale servers
- Information sharing through eavesdropping or looking over one's shoulder
- Data breaches in computer repositories or large scale electronic data servers, or digital device theft

The Department of Justice (DOJ), Federal Bureau of Investigation (FBI), and the U.S. Attorneys' Offices (USAO), along with many other agencies, work tirelessly to combat identity theft. In 1998, the Identify Theft and Assumption Deterrence Act was passed and made identify theft, for the first time, a federal crime. In a 2000 statement by the Federal Trade Commission (FTC), it is articulated that the act strengthens criminal laws and makes is a federal crime to "knowingly transfer or use, without lawful authority, a means of identification of another person with the intent to commit, or to aid or abet, any unlawful activity that constitutes a violation of Federal law, or that constitutes a felony under any applicable State or local law" (18 U.S.C. § 1028(a)(7)). Also, the act focuses not just on institutions, but on the consumer as a victim, including the right to restitution.

Once the personal identifying information is obtained, the perpetrators of the crime then use that identifying information to seek a benefit from a financial institution, the state, or federal government, or the marketplace at large. Many large financial institutions do not have the ability to screen the use of personal identifying information to ensure that the provider of that information is actually the person to whom it belongs. Thus, with the proliferation of Internet banking and procurement of credit and debit cards online, it becomes much easier for identity thieves to ply their trade without alerting authorities. As such, identity theft and its attendant crimes have proliferated as the Internet has grown.

Identity theft is a crime. The Department of Justice (DOJ) prosecutes certain types of identity theft, including unlawful production of a document (18 U.S.C. § 1028(a)(1)), possession of five or more documents with intent to transfer or use them (18 U.S.C. § 1028(a)(3)), possession of a stolen document (18 U.S.C. § 1028(a)(6)), and aggravated identity theft (18 U.S.C. § 1028A). The DOJ also prosecutes access device crimes and computer hacking crimes, both of which often have an element of identity theft associated with them.

Identity theft generally also involves the commission of other crimes. Certain schemes to commit identity theft will encompass these other crimes, including credit card fraud (18 U.S.C. § 1029), computer fraud (18 U.S.C. § 1030), mail fraud (18 U.S.C. § 1341), wire fraud (18 U.S.C. § 1343), or financial institution fraud (18 U.S.C. § 1344). The federal government punishes each of these attendant criminal violations as a felony, and some of them carry substantial penalties like imprisonment, fines, and criminal forfeiture.

Several bureaus in the federal government deal with identity theft. The Federal Trade Commission (FTC) provides resources to educate consumers about identity theft and offers information about how to detect and defend against identity theft. Under the Identity Theft and Assumption Deterrence Act, Congress assigned the FTC to receive and process complaints from victims relating to identity theft. It is required to refer complaints to the appropriate entities, including both major credit reporting agencies and the relevant law enforcement agency.

The Social Security Administration and the Internal Revenue Service also investigate identity theft crimes, given the ability of persons to procure benefits from both agencies through identity theft. For instance, a number of identity theft rings have developed in the last decade using the social security numbers of recently deceased persons to continue to claim fraudulent social security benefits and/or fraudulent income tax refunds. The later, known as stolen identity refund fraud, involves a fraudulent claim for a tax refund using personal identification information that has been stolen or unlawfully used to make the claim. In 2012, the IRS issued an Inspector General Report noting that the IRS may issue $21 billion in fraudulent tax refunds resulting from identity theft over the next five years. Accordingly, the IRS and the DOJ have instituted new stolen identity refund fraud task forces throughout the country to deal with this heightened issue.

Overall, numerous studies demonstrate that annual monetary losses from identity theft, including out-of-pocket expenses by victims, number in the billions of dollars. These losses come from new account fraud—wherein the identity thief creates a new account and uses that account, as well as from misuse of existing accounts. While studies demonstrate that businesses suffer the majority of the direct losses from identity theft, individual victims collectively spend billions of dollars recovering from the effects of identity theft.

For additional information, refer to the Primary Source Appendix: Identity Theft and Assumption Deterrence Act.

According to most recent statistics from the Department of Justice (DOJ), "a Federal Trade Commission report estimated that 8.3 million Americans were victims of identity theft in 2005, resulting in losses of $15.6 billion. In June 2009, a Deputy Assistant Attorney General for the DOJ's Criminal Division testified that a more recent estimate suggested that identity theft was the fastest growing crime in 2008, victimizing more than 10 million Americans."

Source: U.S. Department of Justice. (March2010). The Department of Justice's efforts to combat theft. Audit report 10–21 (p. i). Retrieved from http://www.justice.gov

---

Stewart M. Young

See also: Department of Justice (DOJ); Federal Trade Commission (FTC); Identity Theft: Child; Privacy: Online; Privacy: Offline; Social Security; Website Security

References and Additional Readings

Anderson, K. B., Durbin, E., & Salinger, M. A. (2008). Identity theft. *The Journal of Economic Perspectives, 22,* 171–192.

Federal Trade Commission. (2000). Identity theft. Retrieved from http://www.ftc.gov/os/2000/09/idthefttest.htm

GPO. (n.d.). Identity Theft Penalty Enhancement Act of 2004, Pub. L. No. 108-275. Retrieved from http://www.gpo.gov/fdsys/pkg/PLAW-108publ275/pdf/PLAW-108publ275.pdf

IT Law. (n.d.). Identity Theft Enforcement and Restitution Act of 2008, Pub. L. No. 110-326. Retrieved from http://itlaw.wikia.com/wiki/Identity_Theft_Enforcement_and_Restitution_Act_of_2008

Kahn, C.M., & Roberds, W. (2008). Credit and identity theft. *Journal of Monetary Economics, 55*(2), 251–264.

Public Law. (n.d.). REAL ID Act of 2005, Pub. L. No. 109-13. Retrieved from http://www.uscis.gov/ilink/docView/PUBLAW/HTML/PUBLAW/0-0-0-30238.html

The President's Identity Theft Task Force Report (2008). Retrieved from http://www.idtheft.gov/reports/IDTReport2008.pdf

Richey, M. (2010). Identity theft. Retrieved from http://www.fd.org/docs/select-topics-common-offenses/oct-2010-update-final-x.pdf?sfvrsn=8

Sabol, M.A. (1999). The identity theft and assumption deterrence act of 1998: Do individual victims finally get their day in court? 11 Loy. *Consumer Law Review, 165*, 169.

Identity Theft and Assumption Deterrence Act. *See* Identity Theft

Identity Theft: Child

Identity theft occurs when personal information is stolen and is used for the thief's gain. A child's identity can be used in the same ways an adult's identity can: for financial gain, to receive medical benefits, and to avoid an arrest record. Any child with a social security number is vulnerable to becoming a victim of identity theft. Given that children's identities are often used for financial gain, this is in part due to credit grantors not verifying the applicant's age on credit applications. As a result, identity thieves can potentially use a child's identity for many years without the threat of being caught. A child's identity appeals to thieves because children have clean credit histories; a child typically does not have established credit. The Identity Theft Resource Center projects that cases of child identity theft will rise in the future.

Parents are the most common perpetrators of child identity theft. Parents have used their children's identities to establish utilities and obtain employment. Child identity theft can be committed by individuals unrelated to the child as well. Typically, if not parents, a child's identity is stolen by individuals who have access to the child's personal information including his/her social security number and birth certificate. These individuals may be school employees or healthcare workers. In cases where a thief unrelated to the child has stolen his/her identity, the identity has been used to obtain employment, apartments, and medical procedures.

Two categories of child identity theft victims, based on when the theft is discovered, are identified: (1) child victims and (2) adult/child victims. Child victims' a relative, such as a parent, discovers the crime before the child turns 18 years of age. In these cases, the efforts to restore the child's identity fall to the adult who discovered the crime. Adult/child victims are adults (age 18 years or older) who find out that their identity was stolen before they turned age 18. Adult/child identity theft victims typically do not find out about the identity theft until they apply for credit. Typically, at the time of discovery, fraudulently opened accounts have been placed with collection agencies and the victim's credit rating has been damaged. As a result, many adult/child victims are denied loans, including student loans, and apartment leases as they emerge into adulthood. These rejections continue until the victim's credit report is cleared of fraudulent information.

To protect a child's identity, parents or guardians should minimize sharing the child's social security number. If someone asks for a child's social security number, the parent or guardian should ask why it is needed, how it will be stored, and how it will be disposed of when it is no longer needed. If a parent or guardian suspects his/her child has been a victim of identity theft, he or she should request a "minor credit file check" from each of the three credit bureaus—Equifax, Experian, and TransUnion. If a child's identity has been stolen, the first step in recovering their identity is filing a police report. With child identity theft, "each individual case is unique and there is no single path to recovery—it takes a tremendous amount of work and persistence" (Betz, 2009, 53–54).

Axton Betz and Laura B. Lucas

See also: Credit Reporting Agencies; Federal Trade Commission (FTC); Privacy: Offline; Privacy: Online; Public Safety; Social Security

References and Additional Readings

Betz, A. E. (November 2007). Living with my invisible shadow: The experience of being a child identity theft victim in central Iowa. Poster session presented at the Iowa State University Extension to Families In-Service. Ames, IA.

Betz, A. E. (2009). Child identity theft and the need for consumer education. *Journal of Consumer Education 26*, 45–57.

Betz, A. E. (2012). The recovery experiences of child identity theft victims (unpublished doctoral dissertation). Iowa State University, Ames, IA.

California Office of Privacy Protection. (2006). When your child's identity is stolen. Retrieved from http://www.privacy.ca.gov/sheets/cis3bchild.htm

Collins, J. (2006). Investigating identity theft: A guide for business, law enforcement, and victims. Hoboken, NJ: John Wiley & Sons.

Collins, J., & Hoffman, S. (2004). Identity theft victims' assistance guide: The process of healing. Flushing, NY: Looseleaf Law Publications.

Foley, L., & Nelson, C. (2009). ITRC fact sheet 120: Identity theft and children. Retrieved from http://www.idtheftcenter.org/artman2/publish/v_fact_sheets/Fact_Sheet_120.shtml

Identity Theft Resource Center. (2010). ITRC forecasts black ice ahead in 2011. Retrieved from http://www.idtheftcenter.org/artman2/publish/m_press/ITRC_Forecasts_for_2011.shtml

Identity theft victims getting younger. (2006). Retrieved from http://www.consumeraffairs.com/news04/2006/03/identity_theft_babies.html

Sealey, G. (2003). Child id theft can go unnoticed for years. Retrieved from http://abcnews.go.com/us/story?id=90257page=1

Segall, B. (2012). Targeting children: The young victims of identity theft. Retrieved from http://www.wthr.com/story/16690002/targeting-children-the-young-victims-of-identity-theft

Sullivan, B. (2004). Your evil twin: Behind the identity theft epidemic. Hoboken, NJ: John Wiley & Sons.

IIPPA (Insurance Information and Privacy Protection Act). *See* Insurance Information and Privacy Protection Act (IIPPA)

Inspector General (IG)

The role of an inspector general (IG) is to oversee and assure efficiency and effectiveness of an organization, including preventing waste, fraud, and abuse. In the U.S. Federal government, federal offices have IGs who provide progress reports to Congress. For example, the Department of Housing and Urban Development, the Small Business Administration, the Social Security Administration, the Department of Health and Human Services, to name just a few, all employ an IG. The more high level departments' IGs are appointed by the president (with Senate approval), others are appointed by the head of the respective agency. Currently, there are 73 IGs in throughout the federal government. Moreover, following in the steps of the federal government, states and many state agencies utilize IG.

The Inspector General Act of 1978 established office of IGs at the federal level, while the 2008 amendment expanded and enhanced their role and purpose. The 2008 amendment also created the independent Council of Inspectors General on Integrity and Efficiency (CIGIE) under the executive branch, which allows the IGs to share information and ideas with one another. The mission of the CIGIE is to oversee governmental agencies to assure integrity, economy, and effectiveness. The CIGIE also seeks to enhance professionalism and effectiveness and develop policies and approaches to assist in the IGs' workforce.

To accomplish the mission mentioned earlier, the CIGIE will:

- continually identify, review, and discuss areas of weakness and vulnerability in Federal programs and operations with respect to fraud, waste, and abuse;
- develop plans for coordinated, Government wide activities that address these problems and promote economy and efficiency in Federal programs and operations, including interagency and interentity audit, investigation, inspection, and evaluation programs and projects to deal efficiently and effectively with those problems concerning fraud and waste that exceed the capability or jurisdiction of an individual agency or entity;
- develop policies that will aid in the maintenance of a corps of well-trained and highly skilled Office of Inspector General personnel. (CIGIE, 2013)

The CIGIE website has a list of job openings and tools that can help IGs. It also lists "What's New" and links to other related and useful websites.

Wendy Reiboldt

References and Additional Readings

Council of the Inspectors General on Integrity and Efficiency. (2013). Retrieved from http://www.ignet.gov/cigie1.html

Light, P.C. (1993). *Monitoring government: Inspectors general and the search for accountability.* Washington, DC: Brookings Institution Press.

Insurance

Insurance is defined as the equitable transfer of the risk of a loss, from one entity to another in exchange for payment. An insurer is a company selling the insurance; the insured, or policyholder, is the person or entity buying the insurance policy. The insurance transaction involves the insured receiving a contract, known as an insurance policy, which details the conditions and circumstances of the agreement in exchange for the premium, which is the amount charged for the amounts of insurance purchased.

Health insurance covers medical costs related to accidents, illness, and medical conditions. Many consumers are uninsured or underinsured, especially children and older adults. (Photo-Disc, Inc.)

From a social economic standpoint, insurance is a device for reducing and or eliminating risk through the process of combining a sufficient number of exposures into a group to make the losses predictable and bearable on the group as a whole. Insurance cannot prevent losses nor can it reduce the cost of these losses to society. Insurance can be accused of increasing the losses to society as a whole since the temptation of insurance fraud exists.

There are certain principles that must exist for insurance to function. The first and most important principle is "insurability." Insurability requires that certain conditions are met for the insurance policy to be valid.

There are many types of insurance and insurance companies. Insurance can be classified into two categories: public and private. Public insurance (or social insurance) is a device for pooling risk by a transfer to an organization such as a government that is required by law to pool risk on behalf of the citizens to effectively cover personal losses.

The first social insurance program was the worker's compensation system that was adopted in the early 1900s. Today some of the other social insurance programs include Social Security (Old Age, Survivors, Disability, and Health Insurance Program), railroad retirement, disability, unemployment, and the largest: Medicare. Medicare is a federal health

---

Conditions Necessary for Insurability:

- Large numbers: Insurance works by pooling risk across a large number of individuals in order to make risks more predictable.
- Definite loss: The loss that is being insured must be (1) measurable and (2) difficult to counterfeit. The loss must be measured by a value.
- Accidental loss: The loss event must be outside of the control of the insured.
- Large loss: The loss must not be catastrophic but the value of the loss must be incentive for the insured to insure.
- Affordable premium: The payments made must be manageable for the insured.
- Calculable loss: The probability of loss must be measurable.

Insurance also operates within a certain number of legal restrictions. Examples include:

- Indemnity: The insurance company must compensate the insured in case of loss but only up to the insured's interest.
- Insurable interest: Economic or financial loss must be proven at the time the contract is entered. The insured must have a "stake" in the loss or damage to the life or property that is being insured.
- Utmost good faith: The insured and insurer are bound to a contract based on honesty and fairness.
- Subrogation: The legal right of the insurer to pursue recovery of their losses if the losses were caused by another party. For example, the insurance company has the right to sue on behalf of their injured party.
- Causa Proxima (proximate cause): The cause of the loss must be covered under the policy.

---

insurance program for persons age 65 or older, individuals with kidney failure, and others with permanent disabilities.

Private insurance is sold to individuals by private firms and usually is specialized into three areas: life, health, and property/liability.

Life Insurance

Life insurance is designed to prevent against two risks: superannuation (living too long) and premature death. The event insured against is an eventual certainty, no one lives forever. The risk in life insurance is not "if" the death occurs, but "when"; and the risk increases each year as the person ages. Life insurance provides a monetary benefit to the descendant's family, or beneficiary, and provides money for funeral expenses, or other living expenses. Life insurance proceeds are paid out in a lump sum or as an annuity. An annuity is a stream of income that is categorized as insurance because it is issued by an insurance company, is regulated like insurance and requires the same actuarial management to determine risk. Some annuities can pay a benefit for life and insure a retiree will not outlive his/her financial resources.

There are several types of life insurance that a consumer can purchase. They fall into two categories: term or whole life (insurance including a savings or investment element). Over time, several variations of each of these types of insurance have spun off into combinations of the two.

Term or "pure life insurance" is the simplest type of insurance and is known as yearly renewable term. This insurance contract provides protection for one year but provides a renewal provision for the next year at a slightly higher premium rate. The underlying concept of how life insurance is priced is that the mortality rates increase with each older age so the premium payment is based on a insured's age at the time of contract and their health status. As the insured ages, the premium increases. Term insurance pays out a face amount (contract amount purchased) if the insured passes away during the term of the policy. Term insurance is sold in fixed amounts to last several years such as 10-, 15-, or 20-year term. Term insurance is also portable and can be converted into one of the other types of life insurance contracts.

The other type of life insurance is known as whole life which incorporates the insurance with a savings or investment tool within the one contract. The concept of whole life is that the insured can have life insurance coverage throughout their life without the contract expiring if they choose. Whole life contracts have varying payment methods and thus variations of whole life have emerged. An insured can have the option of paying a predetermined premium each year known as a straight whole life. The savings aspect of the contract accumulates, known as "cash value" and offsets the additional costs of insurance as the insured ages.

A consumer can also opt to buy a limited-pay policy where they pay for a set amount of years and the policy should last for their whole life based on the concept that the interest earned on the savings within the policy begins to pay the cost of insurance.

In the early 1980s a new type of life insurance contract was introduced called universal life. Universal life is a flexible premium that adjusts based on the performance of the cash value in the savings account. The cash value account earns interest on a tax deferred basis at either a guaranteed set interest rate or a market rate. This type of contract offers a possibility of higher earnings, offsetting the premium and has caused much attention.

A new spin off of this policy called variable universal life emerged. With variable contracts the excess cash that does not need to pay for the cost of the insurance is placed in an investment account. The policyholder can use these funds to invest in various market or fixed investments and somewhat control the savings potential within their life insurance contract. Some of these investment accounts are linked to the consumer price index (CPI) which has led to investors using the life insurance contract as an investment. This has resulted in a controversy that makes purchasing life insurance tricky. Does one buy the less costly term coverage and invest the difference or buy the variable life contract with both an insurance and investment element but costs much more?

Health and Disability Insurance

The field of health insurance is confusing to the average consumer due to the enormous amounts of health insurance contracts available in the market. Health insurance is a generic term that encompasses different types of insurance for accident, sickness, and disability. Disability income insurance is purchased to provide financial support in the event the policyholder becomes unable to work because of an injury or illness. The contract will provide monthly income payments to help with financial obligations. Consumers can purchase short- or long-term disability contracts. Because the cost of long-term policies is expensive, usually individuals earning more than six figures can afford to buy them. Short-term policies usually cover a term of about six months whereas long-term policies can cover a person up until they are considered permanently disabled. Disability income policies are sold through life insurance companies as well as property and liability insurers.

Health insurance is purchased to attempt to protect against risks of incurring medical expenses by an individual and transferring the risk to an organization that is private, government, private business, or not-for-profit entity. A health insurance policy is a contract between an insurance provider (as mentioned earlier) and an individual or his/her sponsor (employer or association/community). The contract can be renewable (annually), or mandated in the case of national mandated plans. The type and amount of healthcare costs that are covered by the policy are outlined in the contract which is known as "evidence of coverage." Several terms are common in all health insurance contracts and have become a standard in the industry. The differences amongst the following terms determine the cost of the policy to the consumer as some policies are more beneficial than others.

- Premium: The dollar amount the policyholder or his/her sponsor pays to the health plan for the purchase of the health insurance policy.
- Deductible: The dollar amount the insured must pay out of pocket before the health plan begins contributing their share for claims. For example, if a member has a $500 deductible then that member is solely responsible for the bills until the total up to $500 and after that the insurance carrier will contribute their share, referred to as coinsurance.
- Coinsurance: A percentage that insurance company agrees to pay toward the member's healthcare bills. For example, once a member meets his or her plan deductible, the coinsurance of 80/20 will begin, which means that the insurance company pays 80 percent of the bill and the member will pay 20 percent up to a maximum.
- Out-of-pocket maximum: The dollar amount that a member is responsible for before the insurance company pays 100 percent of the healthcare costs. For example, once a member meets the plan deductible and pays his or her share of the coinsurance, he or she will hit a maximum that he or she is expected to pay. Any additional bills are paid at 100 percent by the carrier.
- Co-payment: A fixed dollar amount that is paid up front by the insured for services such as a doctor office visit. For example, a co-payment of $30 is required to be paid for each and every visit the insured incurs with the plan.
- Coverage limits: Some health plan policies have placed a specified limit on the dollar amount they are willing to cover and if this dollar amount is met, the insured must pay any of the additional charges out of their own pocket. This arrangement is not common with employer-sponsored programs. Some individual policies that do have limits can be in the amount of $2,000,0000 and more.
- In-network provider: A healthcare provider will distribute a list of providers that the health plan has networked with to offer better rates and benefits to the members.

The two systems of healthcare providers that exist in the private healthcare marketplace are known as health maintenance organization (HMO) and preferred provider organization (PPO). An HMO is regarded as an organized system of health care that provides comprehensive medical services on a prepaid basis to enrolled members that are within a geographic location of that HMO. HMOs are usually run for a profit and believe in keeping costs manageable through promoting preventative care, which means requiring their members to have an annual physical exam. Another key feature of the HMO is the use of a "gate keeper" or a primary care physician, general a family doctor who monitors the member's health care and will refer that member to a specialist. The members will only receive their covered benefits and services by utilizing the HMO's facilities, doctors, and pharmacies. If an HMO member does not utilize this network then the charges will not be covered, which causes some limitations on choices.

A PPO is an arrangement with a selected group of independent hospitals, surgery centers, and medical personnel to offer services at a prearranged cost. Unlike the HMO where the fees are a flat fee per month, the PPO utilizes a fee-per-service approach where the fees are discounted for staying in the provided network. If a member opts to use an out-of-network provider they pay a higher rate for that care but have the choice and freedom to do so. A PPO does not utilize the gate keeper approach so members have access to several doctors of all specialties with no need for a referral to see them which offers more flexibility. In the past the cost of the PPO exceeded the cost of the HMO; however, the costs have flattened out between the two. Both HMO and PPO offer coverage for the usual needs but the differences lay with the deductible, coinsurance, and max-out-of-pocket.

Most health plans offer additional coverage for dental and vision. Both offer routine examinations at a co-pay and coinsurance for any additional needs that may arise with a cap on the benefit amount offered.

Long-term care (LTC) insurance is a relatively newer type of health insurance that was introduced to help with the increased costs of care for the aging. With the "babyboomers" aging along with increased life expectancy and improvements in medical care, long-term care has become a value. Senior citizens, people age 65 and older, are now the largest in terms of size and percent of the population in the United States. This age group has grown at a faster rate than the total population between 2000 and 2010, according to a 2010 Census brief. More of these individuals are living in nursing homes or extended care facilities with annual costs from $40,000 to $100,000. Long-term care is different from other types of health insurance in that the insured may not be sick or injured. However, with old age comes a need for help with everyday living. The elderly do have some benefits with Medicare, however, they are very limited and usually only last a short period. The benefit of long-term care insurance is for the everyday needs of the elderly whether they are confined to a nursing home or remain in their own home.

Travel insurance can be purchased to protect two things: travel arrangements and health while traveling outside the country. The elderly should be aware that Medicare does not provide coverage outside the United States so additional supplemental travel insurance can be obtained to help in the event of illness or accident while outside the United States. Some travel insurance policies include as a bundle coverage for trip cancellation (due to illness or emergencies), interruption, and travel delay, travel medical expenses and emergency medical evacuation, lost, stolen or damaged luggage, and other travel assistance. Most health insurance policies do cover medical needs outside the country but for extended vacations a supplement is wise.

Property and Liability Insurance

Property insurance provides protection against risk to one's property and includes insurance on auto and home, for example. Liability insurance covers legal claims others make against the insured. Some insurance policies include liability coverage such as on auto and home. Liability can be purchased to cover specific areas such as professional liability insurance or environmental liability insurance.

Automobile Insurance

Automobile insurance is a contract that assists paying for certain types of financial loss that result from the use of a personal automobile. A personal auto policy (PAP) is a packaged policy that protects against three types of losses: legal liability (bodily injury and property damage to others), medical coverage (injuries of the insured and/or people insured is responsible for), and property (damage or theft of the auto itself). The purpose of an auto policy is to protect the policyholder against financial loss in the event of an incident involving an automobile they own. By purchasing a PAP, a consumer agrees to meet a financial responsibility. The Department of Motor Vehicles outlines limits that must be present in these PAPs under state vehicle codes.

The PAP is issued only to the owner of the standard type of automobile and/or members of the owning family. There are commercial policies available to businesses that offer different coverage than the PAP.

Most PAP policies are divided into six sections: Part A: liability; Part B: medical payment coverage; Part C: uninsured motorist; Part D: damage to one's auto; Part E: duties following an accident/loss; and Part F: general provisions.

Each part of the policy has its own issuing agreement and exclusions. For example, in the state of California, the minimum limits of liability insurance are as follows: bodily injury liability: $15,000 for death or injury for any one person in any one accident; $30,000 for all persons in any one accident; and property damage liability: $5,000 for any one accident.

Comprehensive coverage (other than collision), uninsured motorist, medical payments, medical payments, and collision insurance are not required by law.

Homeowners Insurance

A home can be the most expensive asset most Americans will come to own so protecting the home is essential. The purpose of a homeowner's (HO) policy is to protect not only the dwelling but also any liability that comes with owning the dwelling. The HO policy comes in a standardized format in all states: HO2: Homeowners Broad Form; HO3: Homeowners Special Form; HO4: Homeowners Contents Form; HO5: Homeowners Comprehensive Form; HO6: Homeowners Unit Owners Form; and HO8: Homeowners Modified Coverage Form.

Most policies are divided into sections: Section I provides coverage on the insured's property and Section II provides coverage for liability and medical payments should an accident occur on the insured's property. Section I is further divided up into sections of coverage: Coverage A provides protection on the dwelling and is included in HO2, HO3, and HO5; Coverage B provides coverage to a specific amount of insurance on other related structures (garages, maid's quarters, barns, and even swimming pools) and is equal to 10 percent of the amount of the dwelling; Coverage C provides protection on personal property—contents. Under Forms 4 and 6 the minimum coverage on personal property is $6,000. Under the other forms, it is 50 percent of the amount insured on the dwelling; and Coverage D protects against loss of use and indirect loss. This benefit is in the form of monetary reimbursement for alternate living arrangements while the property is inhabitable. If the property is a rental and loss of income occurs, then fair market rental value is given.

Each coverage is categorized as one of two types of loss: named-peril loss and open-peril loss. Under the named-peril loss the specific perils (loss) are outlined in the policy and is the coverage is limited to only those losses specified. Most modern policies utilize the open-peril loss approach where most all losses are covered, except those specifically excluded. These more modern policies usually come with three levels of coverage. The first is the basic coverage, which offers minimal protection with named perils (fire, theft, vandalism, etc.). The second is the broad form, which offers more perils covered. The third is the special coverage, which offers coverage on an open-peril basis, thus being the most comprehensive policy.

HO policies have a deductible that works the same as health insurance. The HO must pay the first determined amount of the loss before the HO policy begins to pay for losses. The premium is tied to the deductible so the larger the deductible, the lower the annual premium.

Most policies also have a long list of exclusions that the HO needs to be aware of such as earth movement (earthquake), certain types of water damage (flooding or overflowing from sewage drains, etc.), power failures (interruption of power), neglect (a HO cannot collect on a claim that could have prevented due to lack of care), war or terrorism, nuclear hazard, and intentional loss. Intentional loss can be proven when the HO intentionally causes a loss, as in the case of arson. Intentional loss is fraud and is punishable by fine and/or imprisonment.

Fraud

Because most people insure their property, and themselves, fraud is a big concern for the insurance companies. Fraud is any malicious attempt to profit or benefit from someone or a company when not entitled. Insurance fraud unfortunately has existed since the inception of insurance in the marketplace. Fraudulent claims account for a significant amount of claims the insurance companies handle and cost society billions of dollars annually. Fraudulent activity ranges from exaggerating the severity of a claim to intentionally causing a loss or accident with hopes of a large financial gain.

These crimes affect innocent people by means of harm and increased insurance premiums. The main motive behind insurance fraud is financial gain. Insurance companies sometimes cannot differentiate between legitimate and fraudulent claims and the most common type of fraud is inflating the loss.

It is hard to estimate the actual annual cost of insurance fraud, but according to the Coalition Against Insurance Fraud, in 2006 the loss due to insurance fraud was about $80 billion in the United States alone. The National Health Care Anti-Fraud Association estimates that about 3 percent of the industry's annual expenses are due to fraud, which is about $51 billion, annually.

There have been reported cases of life insurance fraud where individuals purchase life insurance on the lives of homeless victims and then after their death they collect the death benefit and have no real insurable interest on their victims. In regards to the Medicare system, fraud often occurs by doctors themselves who double bill for treatments or bill innocent elderly for visits or treatments they did not actually have. It is said that the most prevalent perpetrator for healthcare fraud is the healthcare providers themselves. Doctor offices have been known to bill for different services than what was rendered to get the highest dollar amount paid back to them. The patient usually does not know this is going on since the insurance company pays the doctor or hospital direct. This procedure is known as "upcoding" or "upgrading," which involves billing for treatments that are not medically necessary, scheduling extra visits for patients, referring patients to other physicians for treatments that are not necessary, or for outright billing for services that have not been rendered, also known as "phantom billing."

In regards to automobile insurance, it has been estimated that one-third of all auto claims that take place each year have some element of fraud to them. There is a wide variety of schemes that are used to defraud the auto insurance companies. Examples range from billing for higher repairs than those actually received to staging automobile collisions, filing completely false claims, reporting stolen automobiles falsely, or creating injuries. "Rate evasion" occurs when an automobile owner files his or her registration in an area that yields lower insurance rates than the area he or she actually lives in. Another mild fraud known as "fronting" takes place when someone other than the actual driver of the car is actually registered as the owner. More serious auto fraud occurs when individuals scam insurance companies out of money by involving innocent civilians in auto accidents by staging the classic "rear-end stunt." A con artist will slam on their breaks causing an innocent person to rear-end them and file claims for not only the damage to their automobile but also medical expenses for their injuries. There is organized crime set out to defraud insurance companies from the individuals who steal cars all the way up to dishonest doctors and hospitals that diagnose false injuries in hopes in sharing in the profit from the claims.

Because of the concerns for insurance fraud that exist, personnel in the medical field must purchase medical malpractice insurance. For the honest doctors and nurses that work in the industry, malpractice insurance protects them against claims made against them for lack of care or outright neglect they may have caused the patient. Again, this area of insurance leads to a temptation for fraud since a patient can make claims against a doctor knowing they must carry a malpractice policy. Malpractice insurance and Errors and Omissions (E&O) are types of liability insurance that are purchased by working professionals. In the event of a professional, in the position to cause bodily harm, malpractice insurance is used. In a profession where property could be damaged where lack of care could lead to financial strain, E&O is utilized, such as for architects, real estate agents, attorneys, insurance agents, and for others.

The insurance industry has created an insurance policy called "umbrella policy" to protect the liability of individuals whether personal or professional. This policy provides catastrophic liability protection where their other insurance policies, such as homeowners, may be maxed out. The liability limit with an umbrella policy may be in the range of $1 million to $5 million of coverage.

As a licensed health insurance agent, I have seen a change in the Health Insurance Business as a result of the HIPAA legislation. Protecting ones privacy is necessary and the abuse of such information should be punishable. However, unforeseen consequences can be harmful to consumers. Some healthcare "entities" use the HIPAA regulations as a means to avoid providing consumers with personal information that, in fact, individuals are entitled to. I know, firsthand, that consumers do not like the obstacles they face to get a copy of their own medical file. A healthcare provider can utilize a 30-day waiting period and ask for compensation of up to $50 to copy and provide medical files. In situations where crucial medical information is needed by a family for the care of an incapacitated patient these regulations can cause a serious problem. No information is released unless the patient names related family members as being authorized to receive the personal information. In cases of individuals trying to obtain information for purposes of buying Life or other types of insurance, this process has increased the fees involved and the time it takes the company to process, due to the added regulations imposed.

Aleta Ostlund

Aleta Ostlund

See also: Consumer Price Index (CPI); Departments of Insurance; Frauds and Scams; Health and Healthcare; Insurance Commissioners; Malpractice; Social Welfare; Workers' Compensation

References and Additional Readings

American Academy of Actuaries. (2008). Fundamentals of insurance: Implications for health coverage. Retrieved from http://www.actuary.org/files/coverage_ib_08.4.pdf/coverage_ib_08.4.pdf

Coalition Against Insurance Fraud. (2010). Annual report. Retrieved from http://www.insurancefraud.org/downloads/Annual_Report_2010.pdf

Hallman, V., & Hamilton, K. (1994). *Personal insurance: Life, health and retirement.* Malvern, PA: American Institute for CPCU.

Hungelman, J. (2009). *Insurance for dummies* (2nd ed.). Hoboken, NJ: Wiley Publishing.

Hyman, D. A. (2001). Health care fraud and abuse: Market change, social norms, and the trust. 'Reposed in the workmen.' *The Journal of Legal Studies, 30*(2), 531–567.

Lyke, B. (2009). Health care reform: An introduction. CRS Report for Congress. Congressional Research Service 7–5700. Retrieved from http://assets.opencrs.com/rpts/R40517_20090414.pdf

National Health Care Anti-Fraud Association. (n.d.). The problem of health care fraud. Retrieved from http://www.nhcaa.org/resources/health-care-anti-fraud-resources/the-problem-of-health-care-fraud.aspx

Insurance Commissioners

The 50 states in the nation, the District of Columbia, and five U.S. territories each either elect or appoint an Insurance Commissioner to serve as chief watchdog over insurance activities that take place within their respective jurisdiction. The commissioner is the head of the state insurance department or division. Most are appointed positions, selected by the governor of the given state, with about 25 percent of the states in 2012 being represented by an elected commissioner. The standard-setting professional membership nonprofit organization for the collective body of insurance commissioners is the National Association of Insurance Commissioners (NAIC).

Benjamin Franklin and his fellow firefighters helped found the insurance industry in the United States in 1752 with the formation of the Philadelphia Contributionship for the Insurance of Houses from Loss by Fire. The company formed was a mutual insurance company. Policyholders came together to share the risks, with a focus on prevention and inspection of a property prior to accepting it for insurance, and establish a solvent pool of funds from which a property owner could have a safety net in case of disaster. The original company adapted its operating model from the Amicable Contributionship of London. Today, the Philadelphia Contributionship Mutual Holding Company remains as an umbrella for several other insurance companies.

New Hampshire appointed the first state insurance commissioner in 1851, giving way to the current structure of state-based regulation. Over the next two decades, a growing network of state insurance commissioners and the complexities encountered by multistate insurers illuminated the need to pool resources, to discuss issues of common concern with one another, and to align their oversight of the industry. Each state would ultimately continue to hold independent authority to determine the actions, legislation, or approaches that suit its population; however, a national association of elected or appointed state insurance officials along with their departments and staff, it was thought, would offer a useful forum for thoughtful consideration, technical support, agreement on relative regulatory continuity, and professional networking among its members.

Created in 1871, the National Association of Insurance Commissioners' (NAIC) first order of business was to coordinate regulation of multistate insurers. The commissioners, supported by the NAIC structure, initially developed a uniform financial reporting system that would make interstate comparisons and transactions possible by adding continuity. NAIC today operates from offices located in Kansas City, Missouri, New York, and Washington, D.C. All concerns relating to the operation of the insurance industry in America have an avenue for vetting at NAIC. NAIC receives and analyzes legislative concerns, conducts data collection, generates aggregated reports relating to all aspects of the operation of the insurance business. A strong set of legal and actuarial professional assistance among NAIC offices is tapped to make the views, the work, and the impacts of insurance commissioners easier, more detailed, relevant, and substantial than ever before.

Through the NAIC, its voting membership, the executive committee, standing committees, and special committees contribute to the establishment of standards, best practices, peer reviewed publications, and regulatory decisions. The paid staff of the NAIC supports these efforts and actively represents to the public the views and policies of the American Insurance Commissioners both within the United States and in the international community. Essentially, the commissioners and the NAIC's resources are the whole of insurance regulation in the United States.

The main goals of the NAIC, which are inextricably tied to the appointed or elected charge of each individual commissioner, are to protect public interests, promote healthy competitive markets within the insurance industry, facilitate just treatment of insurance consumers, promote the financial stability and reliability of insurance institutions, and streamline and ensure quality in the state regulation of insurance.

Within each state or territory, the office of the individual commissioner is a respected executive office. There are slight differences state to state. In some states the insurance department or division stands alone as an independent government agency; in other states it is part of a larger body.

No matter the method of identifying the insurance commissioner, once seated, he or she fairly consistently across the nation provides a collection of needed and valuable services to its constituency. The office of the insurance commissioner generally provides free information and assistance to the public, business community, and insurers to help them make best decisions relating to all aspects of provision and consumption of insurance products. The commissioner's office makes available educational materials, bulletins, and news briefs for citizens to help them understand facets of the insurance industry and consumers' rights and methods of recourse if they have a problem or complaint relating to any kind of insurance, including those relating to the federally funded Medicare insurance program for seniors. The commissioner's office is responsible for investigating and assisting in the prosecution of property and casualty, auto, life, health, workers compensation, provider and agent insurance fraud. The commissioner regularly dispatches financial examiners to audit an insurance company's accounting methods, procedures, and financial statements to validate whether it is in good enough financial standing to pay claims. The insurance commissioner's office reviews and approves or disapproves rates submitted by insurance companies in an effort to make sure fair and reasonable prices are made available to consumers. The commissioner's office issues licenses to, and conducts continuing education with, companies, agents, and brokers, and actively promotes current industry knowledge and professionalism among the community of licensed practitioners. The commissioner's office, through publishing rate comparison guides, directly helps individuals and businesses research and obtain best-value insurance premiums for their needs. The commissioner's office is the authoritative voice of the insurance industry in that state or territory, issuing news releases and opinions about current issues affecting the people and companies in their jurisdiction.

Protection for the consumer and advocacy for best quality, informed choices, and the upholding of rights and laws relating to insurance are the underpinning and the greatest challenge of the office of the insurance commissioner. The premise for government oversight and regulatory control of the insurance industry is to inform and protect American consumers of insurance products and services. States have been aggressive in seeking to established hotlines, interactive methods for consumers to report inappropriate actions or suspected fraud on the part of insurance industry personnel. Conduct reviews are routine and ongoing, but also can be initiated as a result of such complaints.

The overarching role of an insurance commissioner, which propels all the activity in state insurance offices and in the professional membership organization that coordinates and communicates with them, is to ensure that data-driven, high-quality and high-value insurance products, reports, services, and educational materials are readily available to constituents, customers, and to those engaged in legislative policy considerations.

Megan J. O'Neil

See also: Departments of Insurance; Insurance; Licensing

References and Additional Readings

National Association of Insurance Commissioners. (2011). Bylawas. Retrieved from http://www.naic.org/documents/members_bylaws.pdf

National Association of Insurance Commissioners. (2012). About the NAIC. Retrieved from http://www.naic.org/index_about.htm

The Philadelphia Contributionship. (2012). Company history. Retrieved from http://www.contributionship.com/history/index.html

State Insurance Regulation (2012). History, Purpose and Structure. Retrieved from http://www.naic.org/documents/consumer_state_reg_brief.pdf

Insurance Information and Privacy Protection Act (IIPPA)

The Insurance Information and Privacy Protection Act (IIPPA), while not a federally mandated law on its own, was adopted by the majority of states in the 1980s. Each state's version may vary slightly; however, all are intended to regulate the collection and use of personal information by an insurance provider. This is a consumer protection, safeguarding a policyholder, or a policy applicant's privacy rights.

Each respective state's IIPPA provides protection over the collection and use of sensitive and personally identifiable information by an insurance agent, broker, or insurance company. The law was adopted as a way of protecting consumers and ensures safeguards particularly when applying for insurance or when submitting a claim. Provisions of the IIPPA include requiring a "privacy notice" be given to the consumer that describes practices and policies regarding privacy, the kind of information collected in connection with the transaction, how and with whom personal information will be shared, and rights to restrict that sharing, and the right to "opt out" of information sharing for marketing purposes. IIPPA applies to all types of insurance products such as vehicle, home, business, life, and health-related policies. A federal law called the Health Insurance Portability and Accountability Act that more specifically applies to the healthcare industry and health insurance was passed in 1993 that may, in some instances, supersede and offer more protection and guidance than IIPPA. Unlike IIPPA, HIPAA pertains to all states.

HIPAA's set of patient privacy rules are that which healthcare facilities, health insurance companies, physician's offices, hospitals, and pharmacies are required to follow. These entities are under threat of serious sanction if HIPAA's guidelines are not carefully followed. In some cases, HIPAA includes more stringent rules to protect medical information than IIPPA and would thereby become the default regulation, offering greater privacy to the consumer.

Megan J. O'Neil

See also: Departments of Insurance; Health and Healthcare; HIPAA (Health Insurance Portability and Accountability Act); Patient Protection and Affordable Care Act (PPACA)

References and Additional Readings

Albert, P. (2012). Gramm–Leach–Bliley Act Privacy Rule, 16 CFR Part 313—Comment. Retrieved from http://www.ftc.gov/privacy/glbact/comments/albert.htm

Karr, G. J. (n.d.). The regulation of health information privacy—HIPAA and other relevant laws and legal actions—the impact on insurance agents. Retrieved from http://www.forc.org/pdfs/vol14-ed2-art2.pdf

International Trade Commission

International trade plays a critical role in the U.S. economy and, thus, the work of the U.S. International Trade Commission (USITC) has and will continue to have a significant impact on industry, economic, legal, and international expertise in this country. The agency was established on September 8, 1916, as the U.S. Tariff Commission, and then in 1974, the name was changed to the U.S. International Trade Commission. Throughout the years this small federal agency has always operated independently with broad investigative responsibilities on matters of trade. The commission maintains high standards and a commitment to objectivity and transparency in support of its customers.

The agency has three important mandates that contribute to the development of a comprehensive U.S. trading policy. The first mandate, as written on their website, consists of (1) administering U.S. trade remedy laws in a fair and objective manner; (2) providing the president, the U.S. trade representative, and the Congress with independent analysis, information, and support on matters relating to tariffs, international trade, and U.S. competitiveness; and (3) maintaining the Harmonized Tariff Schedule of the United States. The commission performs these duties through its import injury investigations, intellectual property-based import investigations, industry and economic analysis program, tariff and trade information services, and trade policy support. Strategic goals also help to define the work of the commission. These include investigating the effects of "dumped and subsidized imports on domestic industries and also conducts global safeguard investigations" (USITC, 2011). The commission serves as a key federal resource for analysis of international trade matters that supports the U.S. international trading system based on specific rules and agreements. This agency also gathers and analyzes trade data and other trade policy-related information

Table 26 Office-level organizational chart

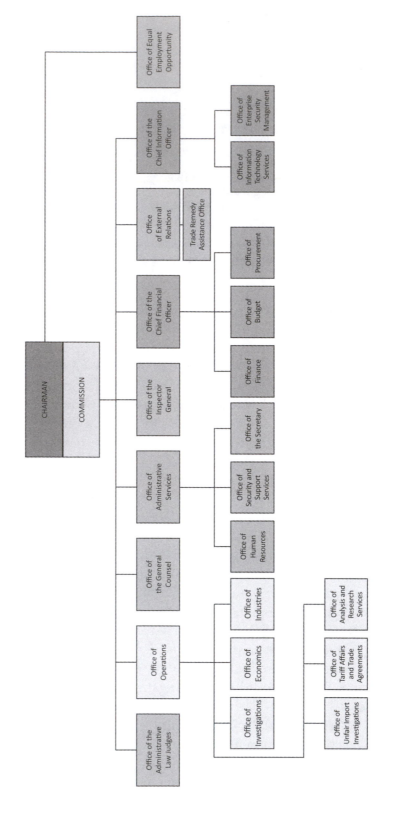

UNITED STATES INTERNATIONAL TRADE COMMISSION

Office-Level Organizational Chart

for federal and general consumer requests to help promote understanding of international trade issues.

The USITC annual performance report explains that "The six Commissioners who lead the agency are nominated by the President and confirmed by the U.S. Senate. No more than three Commissioners may be of any one political party. The Commissioners serve overlapping terms of nine years each, with a new term beginning every 18 months. The Chairman and Vice Chairman are designated by the President from among the current Commissioners for two-year terms. The Chairman and Vice Chairman must be from different political parties, and the Chairman cannot be from the same political party as the preceding Chairman. The Commission staff of about 365 individuals includes investigators, auditors, industry and tariff nomenclature analysts, international economists, attorneys, and support personnel" (USITC n.d.). See Table 26 for the office-level organizational chart of USITC.

Sandra L. Poirier

See also: Congress; Fair Trade; United Nations; World Trade Organization (WTO)

References and Additional Readings

USITC. (2011). United States International Trade Commission annual performance report. Retrieved from http://www.usitc.gov/press_room/documents/USITCFY2011APR.pdf

USITC. (n.d.) Strategic plan. Retrieved from http://www.usitc.gov/press_room/documents/strategic_plan_2009-2014.pdf

Investing Regulations

Consumers work hard, live on a budget, and save so they can invest for the future and for retirement. But who is watching out for the money that has been saved and invested? Who makes the laws that are intended to protect consumers from scammers and illegal schemes? The SEC, or U.S. Securities and Exchange Commission regulates securities at the federal level, meaning they protect the investors, and make sure that the market is fair, orderly, and efficient. The concept is simple, yet very important as more and more U.S. citizens invest their money to pay for homes, save for a comfortable retirement, and send their children to college, vacations, or other goals they may want to achieve either before or after retirement.

Basic household transactions such as deposits made into savings accounts in banks are protected by the Federal Deposit Insurance Corporation

(FDIC). Checking accounts, saving accounts, certificate of deposit's (CDs), and money market accounts with amounts up to $250,000 per depositor are protected by the FDIC. These are deposits made into accounts with a set interest rate, and easy to insure because banks have rules that control what percentage of deposits can be used for loans. However, nondeposit investments such as mutual funds, insurance policies, annuities, and stocks and bonds are not covered by the FDIC. These investments are covered by the SEC, and if the SEC finds there has been fraud in any of these areas by anyone, the FBI will investigate.

In October 2000, the SEC ratified Regulation Fair Disclosure, requiring publicly traded companies to make all information available to all investors and potential investors. The amount of the investment does not matter, the regulations are there to protect everyone equally regardless of the size or number of investments a person may have. All investors should have access to full information about a company or stock before making an investment, and the SEC requires that all public companies make all their financial information available to the public. Having all the information about a company allows all investors to make a decision to buy, sell, or hold based on the same pool of information. No one has access to information because of who they know, who they are, or how much they have invested. Without access to complete and honest information about a company, investors would not be able to sound financial decisions. Investments are divided into levels of risk: low risk, medium risk, and high risk, with low-risk investments having a low return, and high-risk investments having a much higher possible return, but also with a higher degree of risk. All investments have a risk, and there is no guarantee the investor will see the return they are hoping for, or possibly any return at all on their investments. Not only they may not see a return on their investment, they may lose their initial investment and end up with nothing. In order to provide as offer as much protection as possible, investment companies that sell stocks, bonds, insurance, mutual funds, and other securities are required to follow strict rules to ensure all information about the companies and is disclosed.

Affordable, yet tricky, stocks are Penny stocks. Penny stocks are stocks that sell for $5 or less per share, and can be stocks of private companies, foreign stocks, or securities, or over the counter stocks. Even though the price per share is cheap, they are still considered a high-risk investment. Penny stocks do not have a proven track record of returns that the investor can use to make an informed decision. Because all of these stocks and securities are considered high-risk investments, the SEC requires the firm or broker to approve the customer for the transaction, have the customer agree to the purchase in writing, and provide the investor with documentation that explains the risk of these stocks. Every month the broker or firm must send the investor a monthly account statement showing the current value of the stocks. Penny stocks do not trade on regular basis because of their high risk, and it may be difficult to find information. The investor must be prepared for the possibility that they will lose all of their investment.

While Penny stocks do not represent investment fraud, per se, investment fraud is prevalent in the industry. Investment fraud and scams can financially destroy individuals, families, and businesses. Ponzi schemes are the most common fraudulent investment scheme. Investors are promised a higher than average rate of return on investments, and the scammer tells them they have inside information that will make them a lot of money. To make the scheme seem real they will provide the investor a pay off that is the promised rate of return. This is for show to get other investors to invest their money in the scheme. The scheme continues until no more returns are paid to the investors, the scammer leaves town, and many people have lost their life savings. Because of schemes like this, the SEC sets rules and regulations that protect the investors. The best advice when handling money and investments is that "if it seems too good to be true, it probably is . . . walk away."

Elowin Harper

See also: Commodity Futures Trading Commission (CFTC); FDIC (Federal Deposit Insurance Commission); Securities and Exchange Commission (SEC)

References and Additional Readings

Beatty, R., & Kadiyala, P. (2003). Impact of the penny stock reform act of 1990 on the initial public offering market. *JL & Econ.*, *46*, 517.

Jo, H., Saha, T., Sharma, R., & Wright, S. (2010). *Socially responsible investing vs. vice investing*. Retrieved from http://www. aabri. com/LV2010Manuscripts/LV10107. pdf.

J

The Jungle

Upton Sinclair's 1906 novel *The Jungle* tells the story of a family of Lithuanian immigrants working in the Chicago meat-packing industry. The incredible hardships faced by inhumanely treated packing district workers and the vivid descriptions of workrooms filled with rats and rotting meat, touched the minds, thoughts, and stomachs of its readers. The resulting uproar over food safety concerns led to legislation regulating the production, advertising, and sale of foods and other products.

To write the book, Sinclair spent seven weeks researching the meat industry in Chicago. talking "not merely with workingmen and their families, but with bosses and superintendents, with night watchmen and saloon keepers, and policemen, with doctors and lawyers and merchants, with politicians and clergymen and settlement-workers" (1906, 593). Sinclair claimed that he "spared no pains to get every detail exact" (p. 593) as he intended the book to illustrate the problems with capitalistic businesses and the plight of the workers within the system. As a socialist, he felt that the abuses perpetuated against the workers represented a serious situation in need of redress, and in fact those he interviewed seem to largely have felt the same, since he gained access to the industry through his socialist connections. However, readers were less interested in the plight of meat industry workers and much more incensed by the food safety issues Sinclair brought to light (Wright, 1992). For example, one prominent passage discussed how workers would ". . . sweep off handfuls of the dried dung of rats [from piles of meat]. These rats were nuisances, and the packers put poisoned bread out for them, they would die, and then rats, bread, and meat would go into the hoppers together" (Sinclair, 1906, 136). It must be said that Sinclair was dismayed by this reaction; he would lament that "I aimed at the public's heart and by accident I hit it in the stomach" (p. 594). *The Jungle* sold a million copies in the first year after its publication and caused a short but notable decline in meat sales in the United States. But arguably the most important long-term consequence of the book was the examination of the way meat and other products were processed, handled, prepared, and sold in the United States.

A poster advertising Upton Sinclair's *The Jungle*, a muckraking novel published in 1906 that exposed the seamy underside of America's meat industry. (Library of Congress)

Legislation of this genre had been under consideration off and on for more than 20 years, spearheaded by "public-spirited and fearless friends of the consumer" such as Dr. Wiley, Professor Ladd, the American Medical Association, the National Association of State Dairy and Food Departments, and various farmer organizations. With public opinion strongly in favor of regulation, Congress quickly passed several pieces of food safety legislation, including the Pure Food and Drug Act of 1906 and the Meat Inspection Act of 1906.

These acts required that certain additives, among them alcohol and opium, be listed on an item's packaging, and forbade misleading or false claims from being listed on the packaging. They also introduced penalties for selling adulterated foods and drugs across state lines.

In 1938, a more comprehensive law was passed, the Federal Food, Drug, and Cosmetic Act, extending the authority of the Food and Drug Administration (FDA) to "demand evidence of safety for new drugs, issue standards for food, and conduct factory inspections" (FDA.gov, 2011). Later amendments made in 1962 and 1976 (the Kefauver–Harris Amendments and the Medical Device Amendments) strengthened drug safety regulations and extended the FDA's authority to cover medical devices (ibid.).

Over a 100 years after its publication, *The Jungle* is still read today and is considered a classic work in the area of food purity, food safety, and workers' rights in the food and meat packing industries.

Cynthia R. Jasper

See also: Activism; Department of Labor (DOL); Food and Drug Administration (FDA); Food, Drug and Cosmetic Act (FD&C Act); Food Labeling; Food Safety; Wiley, Harvey

References and Additional Readings

Barber, R. J. (1966). Government and the consumer. *Michigan Law Review, 64*(7), 1203–1238.

Corbett, J. F. (1933). The activities of consumers' organizations. *Law and Contemporary Problems 1*(1), 61–66.

Dudley, S. C., Dudley, L. W., & Phelps, L. D. (1987). Consumer reactions to walk-behind power lawn mower safety features. *Journal of Public Policy & Marketing, 6*, 181–191.

Food and Drug Administration. (2011). *Regulatory information: Legislation.* Retrieved from http://www.fda.gov/RegulatoryInformation/ Legislation/default.htm

Friedberger, M. (1994). Cattlemen, consumers, and beef. *Environmental History Review, 18*(3), 37–57.

Herrmann, R. O. (1970). Consumerism: Its goals, organizations and future. *The Journal of Marketing, 34*(4), 55–60.

Keller, D. (2000). Upton Sinclair: His book on meatpacking plants shocked the nation. *Progressive Farmer, 30.*

Pickavance, J. (2003). Gastronomic realism: Upton Sinclair's *The Jungle,* the fight for pure food, and the magic of mastication. *Food & Foodways: History & Culture Of Human Nourishment, 11*(2/3), 87–112.

Sachs, B. R. (2009). Consumerism and information privacy: How Upton Sinclair can again save us from ourselves. *Virginia Law Review, 95*(1), 205–252.

Sinclair, U. (1906). *The Jungle.* New York: Doubleday, Jabber & Company.

Sinclair, U. (October 1906). What life means to me. *Cosmopolitan Magazine, 41*(6), 591–595.

Schaffner, D. J. (1992). Review of *food trends and the changing consumer* by Ben Senauer, Elaine Asp, and Jean Kinsey. *American Journal of Agricultural Economics, 74*(3), 846–847.

Sobel, R. S. (2002). Public health and the placebo: The legacy of the 1906 pure food and drug act. *Cato Journal, 21*(3), 463–479.

The Consumer and Federal Regulation of Advertising. (1940). *Harvard Law Review, 53*(5), 828–842.

Wright, A. (1992). Gut reaction: Upton Sinclair's *The Jungle* and progressive-era America. *Melbourne Historical Journal, 22*, 39–56.

K

Kallet, Arthur. *See One Hundred Million Guinea Pigs*

Kennedy, John F.

President John F. Kennedy's signal contribution to consumer protection was articulating a specific list of consumer rights, a list that inspires consumer advocates to this day. Of less enduring significance was Kennedy's establishment of a Consumer Advisory Council as a means of institutionalizing the voice of consumers within the federal government. Kennedy's contributions to consumer protection might have been greater had he not been assassinated on November 22, 1963, after less than three years as president.

Kennedy wasn't the only force behind consumer protection in the United States during the early 1960s—far from it. When Kennedy delivered his stirring inaugural address on January 20, 1961, the pot of consumer protection was already simmering due to the actions of several U.S. senators.

Senator Estes Kefauver (D-TN) had been pursuing reform in the pharmaceutical industry since 1959, efforts that were rewarded with the passage in 1962 of the Kefauver–Harris *Drug amendments* to the Federal Food, Drug, and Cosmetic Act. (The amendments included the requirement that new drugs be effective, not just safe.) Senator Paul Douglas (D-IL) began a campaign in 1960 to improve consumer understanding of the terms under which credit offers are made. Although Douglas left office in 1966, Senator William Proxmire (D-WI) carried the ball across the goal line when he secured passage of the Truth-in-Lending Act in 1968. A final champion of consumer protection in the U.S. Senate was Philip Hart (D-MI). His ire against dishonesty in the marketplace—misleading claims on labels, unpredictable package sizes and weights, and slack-filled containers—led him to introduce truth-in-packaging legislation in 1962. His efforts resulted in the Truth in Packaging and Labeling Act of 1966.

At a rally in Springfield, Ohio, during his 1960 campaign for the U.S. presidency, Kennedy promised to stand up for the consumer: "The consumer is the only man in our economy without a high-powered lobbyist. I intend to be that lobbyist." Senators Kefauver, Douglas, and Hart had done the hard work of putting consumer issues on the policy agenda. The White House had to figure out a way to add its weight to their efforts and to use the right language to frame his support. President Kennedy settled on sending a Special Message on Protecting the Consumer Interest to the U.S. Congress, emphasizing the concept of "consumer rights." The term "rights" had ample precedent in such landmark statutes as the National Labor Relations Act, the Social Security Act, and the GI Bill of Rights, but it had not yet become an overused rhetorical device.

On the morning of March 15, 1962, the president recorded his consumer message in the White House for later use on television. He then sent his written message to the U.S. Congress. After describing consumers as "the only important group in the economy who are not effectively organized [and] whose views are often not heard," he moved swiftly to the enumeration of four consumer rights:

(1) The right to safety—to be protected against the marketing of goods which are hazardous to health or life.

(2) The right to be informed—to be protected against fraudulent, deceitful, or grossly misleading information, advertising, labeling, or other practices, and to be given the facts he needs to make an informed choice.

(3) The right to choose—to be assured, wherever possible, access to a variety of products and services at competitive prices; and in those industries in which competition is not workable and government regulation is substituted, an assurance of satisfactory quality and service at fair prices.

(4) The right to be heard—to be assured that consumer interests will receive full and sympathetic consideration in the formulation of government policy, and fair and expeditious treatment in its administrative tribunals.

To realize these consumer rights, the president stated that it was necessary to both strengthen existing government programs and, where necessary, enact new legislation.

The right to be heard was particularly controversial. The business community worried that this right might mean a new Department of Consumers, an idea that been around since the Great Depression and had a new champion in Senator Kefauver. Stopping short of proposing a new department, Kennedy himself to reforms he could put into place immediately within the executive branch. Specifically, he asked "the head of each federal agency whose activities bear significantly on consumer welfare [to] designate a special assistant in his office to advise and assist him in assuring adequate and effective attention to consumer interests in the work of the agency, to act as liaison with consumer and related organizations, and to place increased emphasis on preparing and making available pertinent research findings for consumers in clear and useable form." Also in pursuit of the right to be heard, the president committed himself to creating, within his Council of Economic Advisors, a Consumers' Advisory Council "to examine and provide advice to the government on issues of broad economic policy, on governmental programs protecting consumer needs, and on needed improvements."

The 12 appointees to the Consumers' Advisory Council were a who's who of the consumer leaders of the time. Five of the members were associated with the large and powerful Consumers Union, including its president Dr. Colston E. Warne. In addition to Warne, the appointees included three other members of the academic community; there were also three members of community organizations and two government officials. The council had the potential to be a powerful voice for consumers.

President Kennedy convened the first council meeting in July of 1962. At the meeting, the president told the council members that he wanted them to "come forward with as many important decisions and proposals as you can, and bring them to my attention." Kennedy told the council that they were not "windowdressing" and that he hoped, well beyond his administration, that it would be "a definite part of our governmental structure."

The council outlived Kennedy, but barely. It issued a report on September 30, 1963, less than two months before Kennedy's assassination. At the end of 1963, Kennedy's successor, President Lyndon Johnson, took the bold step of establishing the first White House Special Assistant for Consumer Affairs. Johnson chose Esther Peterson for the position, someone who had risen in stature within the Kennedy administration's Department of Labor. The Consumers' Advisory Council was folded into a new entity, the President's Committee on Consumer Interests that reported to the new Special Assistant. The overall arrangement appeared to lift consumer representation to a new high-water mark, but the President's Committee of Consumer Interests never became an influential body. In February 1971, the committee was abolished when the Office of Consumer Affairs was created.

President Kennedy's articulation of a consumer bill of rights was his most important achievement for consumers. Later U.S. presidents and consumer organizations outside the United States have added to Kennedy's list. These additions, far from indicating any inadequacies in the original list, are a testament to the enduring and inspirational power of Kennedy's vision of consumer rights.

Robert N. Mayer

See also: Activism; Congress; Consumer Bill of Rights; Consumers Union; Departments of Consumer Affairs (DCA); Petersen, Esther; Social Security; Social Services; Social Welfare; Warne, Colston

References and Additional Readings

Kennedy, J. F. (1960). Speech by Senator John F. Kennedy, Wittenberg College, Springfield, Ohio. Retrieved from http://www.presidency.ucsb.edu/ws/index.php?pid=74079

Kennedy, J. F. (1962a). Special message to the Congress on protecting the consumer interest. Retrieved from http://www.presidency.ucsb.edu/ws/?pid=9108

Kennedy, J. F. (1962b). Remarks at a meeting with the Consumers' Advisory Council. Retrieved from http://www.presidency.ucsb.edu/ws/?pid=8776

Lampman, R. J. (1998). JFK's four consumer rights: A retrospective view. In E. Scott Maynes (ed.), *The frontier of research in the consumer interest* (pp. 19–36). Columbia, MO: American Council on Consumer Interests.

Nadel, M. V. (1971). *The politics of consumer protection.* Indianapolis, IN: Bobbs-Merrill.

King, Martin Luther, Jr.

Dr. Martin Luther King Jr. worked for racial equality and civil rights in the United States. He was born on January 15, 1929, in Atlanta, Georgia, to Martin Luther and Alberta Christine Williams King. Dr. King had a brother and sister, named Alfred and Christine, respectively. His father and his grandfather were both ministers and his mother was a public school teacher. His mother ensured that young Martin had learned to read before he began school.

Martin Luther King Jr. was known to be an excellent student when he was a young man. As a result, he was able to skip grade levels at both his elementary and high schools. At the age of 15, Martin Luther King began studying at Morehouse College in Atlanta, Georgia. Like most African Americans in the United States at that time, he experienced racism early in his life. Many surmise that these experiences were part of what motivated his desire to do to something to make the United States a more just place to live for people of color.

In 1948, during the final semester of his senior year at Morehouse College while earning a Bachelor of Arts in Sociology, Martin Luther King Jr. was ordained as a Baptist minister. He went on to complete a Bachelor of

Divinity from Crozer Seminary in Chester, Pennsylvania, in 1951. Upon completing that degree, he enrolled in the doctoral study of systematic theology at the School of Theology at Boston University. Dr. King married Coretta Scott on June 18, 1953, in Alabama, where he went on to become pastor of the Dexter Avenue Baptist Church in Montgomery in 1954.

It was during the 1950s that Dr. Martin Luther King engaged in the civil rights movement, striving for racial equality. King's commitment to peaceful protest and advocacy for others was greatly influenced by the precepts of Mohandas Gandhi. King likened Gandhi's ideas with the Christian social gospel, to which Dr. King was committed. In Alabama in 1955, Dr. King was selected to lead the

Reverend Martin Luther King Jr. led the African American struggle to achieve full rights of U.S. citizenship; he eloquently voiced the hopes and grievances of African Americans and the poor before he was assassinated in 1968. (Library of Congress)

Montgomery Improvement Association (MIA). The MIA was organized to protest the arrest of Rosa Parks, an official of the National Association for the Advancement of Colored People (NAACP), after she refused to relinquish her seat on a public transit bus to a Caucasian man. A successful bus boycott in Montgomery, Alabama, helped bring the struggle of African Americans to the public's eye, but it also brought Dr. King and his work to notoriety and began to set him apart as a voice protesting the unfair treatment of people of color.

In 1957, Dr. King helped found what would eventually become the Southern Christian Leadership Conference, which protested racial injustice and racism through marches, boycotts, and political action. Dr. King was the first president of the organization.

In 1958, Dr. King was the victim of the first attempt to assassinate him. During the Montgomery bus boycott, his house had been bombed on several occasions, but later he was stabbed in the chest with a letter opener by Izola Ware Curry, an African American woman, during a book signing. Dr. King was signing copies of his first book, *Stride Toward Freedom: The Montgomery Story* (James, 2003). King was seriously wounded and it took several months for him to recuperate. During this time he was forced to give up all protest activity.

Dr. King was also drawn to the ideas related to peace and nonviolence promoted by the Quaker movement of the American Friends Service Committee. The influence of the Quakers, combined with Gandhi's success with nonviolent activism, inspired much of King's approach to social justice issues (The Martin Luther King, Jr. Research and Education Institute). Dr. King expressed a deep desire to visit Gandhi's birthplace in India and he did so in 1959. The trip inspired Dr. King in significant ways, including an expansion of his understanding of nonviolent resistance and how these ideas might shape his own commitment to the struggle for civil rights.

Dr. Martin Luther King Jr. had a unique ability to focus national attention on well-organized confrontations with racist and discriminatory authorities. He was also able to combine his skills as an organizer with his unique oratory skills, one of his most notable presentations being the 1963 civil rights march in Washington, D.C. The 1963 march in Washington, D.C., was designed to challenge many inequities. These included racial segregation in public schools, discrimination in employment decisions, protection from police brutality, enforcement of a minimum wage, and self-governance for Washington, D.C. Over a quarter of a million people attended the march and they were represented by various ethnicities. At the time, it was the largest gathering of protesters in Washington, D.C.'s, history and Dr. King's speech, "I Have a Dream," was given during the event.

Dr. Martin Luther King Jr. was named *Time* magazine's "Man of the Year" in 1963, and in December, 1964 he became the youngest individual to be awarded the Nobel Peace Prize. Dr. King's speeches and writings have been called oratorical masterpieces that formulated a multicultural vision that inspired diverse audiences, especially white moderates, to accept the urgent need for racial reform. These factors made him one of the most influential African American spokespersons of the 20th century.

Soon after winning the Nobel Peace Prize, Dr. King began to seriously speak out against America's involvement in the Vietnam War. In a speech given one year before his assassination, he suggested that the U.S. government may be one of the greatest purveyors of violence in the world. He suggested that America was involved in a type of colonialism in Vietnam. Dr. King also argued against the Vietnam War based on the costs of the conflict. For King, the Vietnam conflict utilized funds that might have been better spent on resources like the War on Poverty or other social welfare programs. He challenged the Congress of the United States with the notion that taxpayer dollars were contributing to the build-up of the military industrial complex instead of programs designed to assist those who need it the most. Dr. King charged that these skewed priorities might lead to what he called the spiritual death of the country. It was his opposition to the Vietnam War that cost him the support of many Caucasian Americans, most notably President Lyndon Johnson, but also many labor union leaders and some leading publishers.

Dr. Martin Luther King Jr. also received criticism from other African American civil rights leaders. Nation of Islam leader, Malcolm X, suggested that Dr. King's commitment to nonviolence made him weak and not enough of a concern to the dominant white leadership in the country. Stokely Carmichael, who was considered a separatist, often disagreed with Dr. King's attempts to integrate the races because he considered it to be a threat to the unique nature of the African American culture.

Dr. Martin Luther King Jr. went to Memphis, Tennessee, in March of 1968 in an attempt to assist African American sanitary public works employees in their effort to secure fair wages. King delivered his well-known "I've Been to the Mountain Top" speech at the Masonic Temple on April 3, 1968 (The Martin Luther King Jr. Research and Education Institute). He was standing on his motel balcony the next day when he was shot by an assassin. Waves of violence and riots followed Dr. King's assassination. President Lyndon Johnson, though sometimes considered a foe of Dr. King, declared April 7, 1968, to be a national day of mourning.

There has been some controversy regarding the arrest, confession, conviction, and sentencing of James Earl Ray, the assumed assassin of Dr. King. Ray made accusations that his confession was forced and that he had been contacted by a man with the name "Raoul" in Montreal, Quebec and that the assassination of Dr. King was the result of a conspiracy. None of Ray's accusations were ever validated.

Further controversy followed Dr. King related to potential marital infidelities. Because the Federal Bureau of Investigation (FBI) developed concerns that he might have communist ties, Dr. King was under regular surveillance in hopes of finding information that might discredit him. Regardless of the source or the rationale for gathering the information, there have been a number of suggestions that Martin Luther King Jr. might have been involved in affairs outside of his marriage.

It seems, however, that the potential controversies surrounding Dr. King have not had any significant negative impact on his legacy as one who was a leader in the quest for civil rights in the United States. In order to commemorate his life as an important leader, the United States celebrates Martin Luther King Day every year on the third Monday of January. The month of January was chosen because Dr. King was born on the 15th. Dr. King's 1963 famous "I Have a Dream" speech is remembered as "Dream Day" each year on August 28, the anniversary of the event (Proclamation 6401).

James R. Ruby

See also: Activism; Commission on Civil Rights; Discrimination; Kennedy, John F.; Social Welfare

References and Additional Readings

The American Presidency Project (1992). Proclamation 6401—Martin Luther King, Jr., Federal Holiday. Retrieved from http://www.presidency.ucsb.edu/ws/index.php?pid=47329

Fairclough, A. (1995). *Martin Luther King, Jr.* Athens, GA: University of Georgia Press.

James, J. (2003). *Imprisoned intellectuals: America's political prisoners write on life, liberation, and rebellion.* Lanham, MD: Rowman & Littlefield Publishers, Inc.

Johnson, D. (2007) Martin Luther King Jr.'s 1963 Birmingham campaign as image event. *Rhetoric and Public Affairs, 10,* 1–26.

Ling, P.J. (2002). *Martin Luther King, Jr.* New York, NY: Routledge Publishing.

Manheimer, A.S. (2004). *Martin Luther King Jr.: Dreaming of equality.* Minneapolis, MN: Twenty-First Century Books.

The Martin Luther King, Jr. Research and Education Institute. (2013). Retrieved from http://mlk-kpp01.stanford.edu/index.php/encyclopedia/encyclopedia/enc_martin_luther_king_jr_biography/

Robbins, M.S. (2007). *Against the Vietnam War: Writings by activists.* Lanham, MD: Rowman & Littlefield Publishers, Inc.

Sidey, H. (February 10, 1975). L.B.J. Hoover and domestic spying. *Time Magazine.*

Kyrk, Hazel

One of the first women to receive a doctorate in economics, Hazel Kyrk was instrumental in developing the field of family and consumption (aka consumer) economics. In particular, her dissertation in economics at the University of Chicago, completed in 1920, laid the groundwork for the development of the field of consumption economics. Her later work laid the foundation for the field of family economics.

Background

Hazel Kyrk was born in 1886 in a small house on her paternal grandfather's homestead near Ashley, Ohio. She was the only child of Elmer and Jane (Benedict) Kyrk. Her mother died when she was three years old. After graduating high school at the age of 17, Kyrk became self-supporting. As a student at Ohio Wesleyan, Kyrk worked for the family of Professor Leon Carroll Marshall as a "mother's helper." In 1906 Marshall joined the economics faculty of the University of Chicago, and in 1908 Kyrk moved to Chicago and again worked for the Marshall family while attending the University of Chicago. She earned a BA in economics in 1910 and was elected to Phi Beta Kappa. She went directly on to graduate study in economics at the University of Chicago.

In 1914, after completing her coursework for the PhD, Kyrk joined the faculty at Oberlin College. In 1920, she received her PhD in economics, one of only a handful of women at the University of Chicago around that time to actually do so. In 1921, a panel that included distinguished economists awarded her dissertation, "The Consumer's Guidance of Economic Activity," first place "in Class A, which included any American without restriction" of the Hart, Schaffner and Marx annual contest of economic essays. In 1923, her dissertation was published as a book, *A Theory of Consumption*, by Houghton Mifflin Company, Boston.

In 1925, after a few years in several other positions, Kyrk finally secured a faculty appointment as Associate Professor at the University of Chicago, but a promised joint appointment in the Economics Department did not materialize until the 1929–1930 academic year. Promoted to Full Professor in 1941, Kyrk remained there until her retirement in 1952.

Research Contributions

In the tradition of Institutional Economics, Kyrk's book on consumption economics drew upon an interdisciplinary body of literature, including anthropology, sociology, and psychology, as well as economics. It began by defining "consumption" and pointing out the past neglect of the subject by economists. It went on to place the consumer in his/her economic and social environment, including industrial organization, the economic system, and income distribution. Further, it shed light on such topics as how consumers choose what products to purchase and how to use them; the reasons why producers might take advantage of consumers and the need for state intervention to protect consumers; and standards of consumption and living. She appears to have identified consumer protection as an issue well before Ralph Nader began his work.

Throughout her career, Kyrk worked on defining the field of family economics and shaping the development of the field of home economics. She became an advocate for incorporating the insights of economics into the field and was instrumental in creating the Division of Family Economics in the then American Home Economics Association, serving as its first chair. Together with Elizabeth Hoyt and Margaret Reid, Kyrk's most prominent student, who joined her later, she is credited as a founder of the field of family economics. Kyrk's last book, *The Family in the American Economy* (1953), was actually an extensive revision of *Economic Problems of the Family* (1933), her first textbook.

The Family in the American Economy was an analysis of the economic position of families "in terms of incomes, prices and standards of living" (p. v). It dealt with the relationship between "the larger economy and family economic welfare as affected by its nature and functioning" (p. vi). The book, which had evolved over many years of teaching, addressed such issues as women in the labor market, racial differences in family characteristics, and family structure as a key determinant of the economic position of the family.

Further, the book was innovative in beginning to focus on families in their income-generating roles, along with their roles as consumers, with attention to maximizing and maintaining the flow of income to the family. Important topics of concern to this day, Kyrk analyzed the income distribution, poverty, and public policies designed to address "the income problem."

One of the most important ideas stressed by Kyrk was that the family is the decision-making unit with respect to consumption, and it is the family rather than the individual that allocates resources to alternative uses. It also covered household production (citing her student Margaret Reid's book) and the division of labor in the family and examined family time use data. These ideas were to become major features of Nobel Laureate Gary Becker's and subsequent work in what came to be known as "the new home economics."

In addition to these two books and a monograph, Kyrk was a coauthor of the book *Food Buying and Our Markets*, had several articles in periodicals and proceedings, and authored four government bulletins. In her work for the Federal government, Kyrk was associated with two significant studies. A pre-cursor of the Consumer Price Index, "the cost of living index," resulted from a landmark study of consumer purchases while another landmark study, the "Worker's Budget Study," resulted in a yardstick of family economic well-being that was quoted for many years.

Teaching, Mentoring, Government and Professional Service

Kyrk's research in consumption and family economics made her one of the intellectual pioneers in these developing fields. Over a period of several years, through pieces published in the *Journal of Home Economics*, Kyrk elucidated her vision of the role economics and social science could—and should—play in home economics research and its curriculum. During her years at Chicago, Kyrk supervised 15 PhD students and at least 20 master's students.

Kyrk also regularly engaged in government work. Initially she served as Principal Economist with the U.S. Bureau of Human Nutrition and Home Economics (April 1937–June 1942) and then, during World War II, as the Chair of the Consumer Advisory Committee in the Office of Price Administration (1943–1946). Later she was a member of the Consumer Advisory Panel in the Office of Price Stabilization. In 1937, she worked as a consultant for the New York Department of Labor and in 1947 and 1952 she was a consultant for the U.S. Bureau of Labor Statistics. Her professional service included being a charter member of the American Council on Consumer Interests (ACCI), an organization still active today.

Conclusion

Kyrk was recognized as a leader in the field of home economics. In 1953, Ohio Wesleyan University awarded her the degree of Doctor of Humane Letters. The citation emphasized her accomplishments as an inspirational teacher, as a scholar who made "unusual and outstanding contributions to the field of home economics," and as a government advisor.

Andrea H. Beller

See also: American Council on Consumer Interests (ACCI); Consumer Price Index (CPI); Nader, Ralph; Peterson, Esther; Warner, Colston

References and Additional Readings

Beller, A. H., & Kiss, D. E. (2001). Hazel Kyrk. In R. Lunin Schultz & A. Hast (Eds.), *Women building Chicago 1790–1990: A biographical dictionary.* Indiana University Press, 482–485.

Dye, M. (1972). *History of the Department of Home Economics, University of Chicago.* Home Economics Alumni Association.

Folbre, N. (1998). The sphere of women in early-twentieth-century economics. In H. Silverberg (Ed.), *Gender and American social science: The formative years.* Princeton, NJ: Princeton University Press.

Kiss, D.E., & Beller, A.H. (2000). Hazel Kyrk: Putting the economics into home economics. *Kappa Omicron Nu Forum, 11,* 25–42.

Libby, B. (1984). Women in economics before 1940. In E.J. Perkins (Ed.), *Essays in economic and business history: Vol. 3 Selected papers from the Economic and Business Historical Society, 1980–1982* (pp. 273–290). Los Angeles: Economic and Business Historical Society and History Department, University of Southern California.

Nelson, E. (1980). Hazel Kyrk. In B. Sicherman, & C. Hurd Green (Eds.), *Notable American women. The modern period: A biographical dictionary* (pp. 405–406). Cambridge, MA: Belknap Press.

Reid, M.G. (1972). Miss Hazel Kyrk. In M. Dye (Ed.), *History of the Department of Home Economics, University of Chicago* (pp. 184–186). Home Economics Alumni Association.

L

Legal Aid

Legal aid societies offer free or low-cost legal representation to indigent individuals for whom legal services would remain financially out of reach. Cases that might be brought to legal aid societies include denial of government benefits, immigration issues, domestic violence, home evictions, employment, or other forms of discrimination, access to health care, and family and custody issues. Most legal aid offices have lower-income thresholds that must be met before services can be rendered.

The first legal aid society was established in New York in 1876 to help defend rights of German immigrants. The national legal aid movement began in 1920, when Reginald Heber Smith, an attorney just a few years out of law school, published the landmark book *Justice and the Poor*. Charles Evans Hughes, later a Supreme Court justice and at the time the head of the New York society, read the book and was won over by Smith's cause. Hughes championed the legal aid cause at the American Bar Association, the largest association of American attorneys, today numbering about 400,000. Large-scale development of legal aid services arose in the turbulence of the 1960s, and in 1974, Congress created the Legal Services Corporation (LSC) as a private, nonprofit corporation, funded through congressional appropriations.

The oldest legal aid service in the United States, the Legal Aid Society of New York, is also the largest, employing over 900 attorneys and providing criminal, civil, and juvenile justice services. It receives funding from major New York law firms at the rate of $600 per attorney. In 2011, the society reported an annual caseload of 300,000 individual cases and legal matters. In the United States, there are legal aid societies or services in every state, funded through a variety of methods. One source estimated the number of these resources at about 500 nationally.

Legal aid services can include both civil and criminal assistances. In 1963, in the landmark Supreme Court case of *Gideon v. Wainwright,* the court said that accused individuals have the right to counsel in their criminal cases even if they cannot afford it, at both the state and federal levels. Some states have public defender offices to provide this service, while others rely on *pro bono* (free) services from private law firms.

In addition, the Innocence Project is dedicated to providing free legal assistance to exonerate those wrongly convicted of crimes. To date, the Innocence Project has resulted in the exoneration of 260 individuals, many through DNA testing and some of whom had been sentenced to death. In 2010, the project represented 289 individuals from 38 states. Criticisms have been leveled against the Innocence Project, including one that suggests "innocentrism" as a flaw—the idea that those who participate in innocence projects are somehow better or more righteous than criminal defense attorneys, who must pursue their clients' interests even if the client is clearly guilty. In the civil arena, there are public service law firms and legal clinics that offer free or reduced-cost legal services. Some of these firms and clinics receive supplemental funding from LSC, and funding can also come from state budgets and Interest on Lawyer Trust Account (IOLTA) programs. Funding for LSC is often dependent on the political party in power; the organization's most serious threat, President Ronald Reagan, attempted to do away with it by allocating it no money, but attorneys from the American Bar Association and others rallied to save it, and although its budget was slashed, the organization survived.

Funding for legal aid services is always an issue. LSC receives a budget from Congress; in 2011, it was $420 million. Total legal funding for civil legal aid alone in the United States is estimated to be about $1.3 billion. However, the major complaint of legal aid offices is that there is a severe lack of funding for the numbers of people who request services, resulting in many deserving individuals going unserved. In a 2009 report from LSC, entitled "Documenting the Justice Gap in America," it was estimated that for every person served by LSC, one had to be turned away. Moreover, the study suggested that only one legal aid attorney was available for every 6,415 low-income individuals (compared with one private attorney for every 429 people in the general population above the LSC poverty threshold).

There are regular calls for reform, including drafting model state legislation to fund legal aid services, ensuring those services are both publicized and made available to the individuals who most needed them, engaging the legal profession, including judges, courts, and attorneys, about the essential services provided by legal aid, and providing full ranges of services and education for the legal aid clientele (including support for those who are capable of representing themselves). The American Bar Association suggests a goal of each attorney providing at least 50 hours of *pro bono* service per year, and a 2008 study found that of 1,100 attorneys, 27 percent made that goal, but 73 percent did engage in some *pro bono* work for people of limited means. Yet more support can come from other means, from encouraging law students to participate in legal aid societies and clinics to creating partnerships between professions, such as partnering attorneys with medical practitioners to help indigent people navigate the complex world of medical law.

There are challenges for the legal aid system. Sometimes sharp distinctions between indigent individuals and attorneys, including class, race, cultural, and socioeconomic differences, serve to distance the parties—and some individuals may feel sufficiently disenfranchised that they do not make their preferences known. This makes the job challenging for the legal aid attorney, as not only are the resources of the organizations slim, but the caseload is daunting.

However, it remains clear that legal aid societies are critical for serving the legal needs of a significant portion of the American population. Many believe that access to qualified legal services and professionals is not unlike many other essential and fundamental rights that should be extended to all Americans, regardless of income. As retired California appeals court justice Earl Johnson Jr. puts it, "The time has come to give poor people the resources necessary for truly effective access to justice and truly fair hearings. Saving a fortunate few from injustice and the resulting deprivations they are doomed to suffer is no longer enough. It is time for the few to become the many and ultimately the all—the 'all' we have long promised will have justice in this land."

Genelle I. Belmas

See also: Department of Justice (DOJ); Social Welfare; Supreme Court

References and Additional Readings

Carrington, W. T. (2011). A house divided: A response to professor Abbe Smith's 'In praise of the guilty project: A criminal defense lawyer's growing anxiety about innocence Projects.' *University of Pennsylvania Journal of Law and Social Change, 15,* 1–24.

Gideon v. Wainwright, 372 U.S. 335 (1963).

Green, B. A. (1999). Rationing lawyers: Ethical and professional issues in the delivery of legal services to low-income clients. *Fordham Law Review, 67,* 1713–1748.

Houseman, A. W. (2009–2010). The future of civil legal aid: Initial thoughts. *University of Pennsylvania Journal of Law and Social Change, 13,* 265–293.

Johnson Jr., J. E. (2009). Three phases of justice for the poor: From charity to discretion to right. *Clearinghouse Review: Journal of Poverty Law and Policy, 42,* 486–491.

Legal Aid Society of New York. (2011). Annual report. Retrieved from http://www.legal-aid.org/media/151373/legalaidsocietyannual2011.pdf

Lemon Laws

There are a myriad of consumer protection laws at the local, state, and federal levels ranging in topics from unfair and deceptive trade practices, banking, and identity theft laws. These laws generally serve three purposes: (1) to protect companies from "unfair competition"; (2) to protect consumers; and (3) to protect society against business behavior with high unassumed social costs, such as pollution.

One consumer law, the Lemon Law, was created to protect buyers of defective automobiles from sellers who would otherwise do nothing to rectify the defective product. The Lemon Law was of particular interest to state regulators because it typically represents one of the largest household expenditures for consumers, and it was reported to be the leading cause of consumer complaints. Both the White House Council for Consumer Affairs and the U.S. Council for Better Business Bureaus in 1981 reported dissatisfaction with automobile purchases and repairs as the leading consumer complaint nationwide. Thus, the Lemon Laws that focus on the automobile industry were passed in all 50 states beginning with Connecticut in 1982 and ending with Alaska passing state legislation in 1994. Though there may be some specific additions that each state has chosen to put into effect, the general outline of the law remains the same.

Case Study: A Lemon Law Success Story

Wisconsin has an effective and stringent lemon law, and one customer, reaped the benefit. After buying a new Mercedes E320 for $56,000 in 2005, Mr. Marquez started having problems right away. The car did not start, so the dealership replaced the battery on several occasions. The problem was never correctly identified and so Mr. Marquez applied for a refund. Because Mr. Marquez did not receive his refund within 30 days, after he was promised a refund, he sought legal help. The attorney requested double damages and attorney's fees. Though it took 2 years, Mercedes Benz was ordered to pay $482,000 to Mr. Marquez, to cover twice the cost of the car, plus legal fees. Because Mercedes appealed with interest and additional attorney fees, the award likely approached $850,000. Experts agree that this sends a strong message to auto manufacturers to take lemon laws and customer complaints seriously.

Source: Associated Press. (May 24, 2012). Supreme Court upholds Lemon Law verdict.

Origins of the Lemon Law

Previous to the Lemon Law legislation, other more general warranty protections were available through state Uniform Commercial Codes (UCC), the federal Magnuson–Moss Warranty Act, and various state consumer protection statutes. Beginning in the 1960s with the UCC, this legislation changed how car warranties worked, afforded more protection to a consumer who was buying the product, and bound a manufacturer and seller to certain obligations. The UCC's traditional contract law response to defective products was—"let the buyer beware." With this law the burden was on the automobile dealer, with the manufacture often shielded by the doctrine of privity (i.e., the manufacturer has no contract with the ultimate purchaser of the automobile, only with the dealer).

A federal law, the Magnuson Moss Warranty Act, is often referred to as the "Federal Lemon Law." The act stipulates that consumers spending $25 or more on a product that cannot be repaired by the manufacturer is entitled to a free replacement product or a refund of the purchase price. A replacement or refund is not always the solution in warranty cases; sometimes a cash refund is calculated on the decrease in value of the vehicle due to the defects. This act offers solutions to the warranty problems that created the majority of consumer dissatisfaction.

In 1982, the first state Lemon Law was passed in Connecticut to further supplement the provisions in the UCC by creating another layer of buyers' remedies directed at compelling manufacturers to comply with express warranties. This legislation created by Connecticut was used as a template for many other states in designing Lemon Law legislation for their state. This law differed from the UCC in that the legal burden shifted from the auto dealer to the manufacturer. The law guarantees, if a car becomes classified as a lemon, then the buyer has the right to return the car and either receive a replacement from the manufacturer or receive a full refund. An auto would be classified as a lemon if the new car remains "substantially impaired" after four attempts to fix a problem, or 30 days in the repair shop. Lemon Laws were passed between 1982 and 1992 in the order shown in Table 27.

Each state has specific provisions to the law; however, all indicate that the vehicle must be a new automobile covered under the original manufacturers warranty—generally 18 months or 18,000 miles, whichever comes first. Extended warranties are not considered. In addition, most state Lemon Laws do not apply if the owner has been accused of abuse. Abuse includes such things as failure to maintain and service the vehicle according to the factory

Table 27 Lemon Laws

1982	Connecticut
1983	California, District of Columbia, Florida, Maine, Minnesota, Montana, Nebraska, Nevada, New Jersey, New York, Texas, Wisconsin, Wyoming
1984	Arizona, Colorado, Hawaii, Illinois, Iowa, Louisiana, Maryland, Massachusetts, Oregon, Pennsylvania, Rhode Island, Tennessee, Vermont, Virginia, West Virginia
1985	Delaware, Kansas, Mississippi, Missouri, North Dakota, Oklahoma, Utah
1986	Michigan, New Mexico
1987	North Carolina, Ohio
1988	Idaho, Kentucky
1989	South Carolina
1990	Alabama, Georgia, Washington
1991	New Hampshire
1993	Arkansas, Indiana, South Dakota
1994	Alaska

recommendations. Keeping detailed records of all work and the mileage of when the work was completed will serve to verify warranty repairs.

To make a Lemon Law claim, consumers will need all receipts for warranty repair work, a copy of the purchase or lease contract, a copy of the vehicle registration, and payment coupon (if financed or leased). Generally if the vehicle has been back to the dealer for repair of a reoccurring problem more than three times, the consumer must then notify the manufacturer again of the complaint through a certified letter and be given a final opportunity to repair the vehicle. Generally the address of the manufacturer is present in the owner's manual. Any vehicle that is out of service for 30 days or more, the consumer can file a complaint using a state-specific motor defect notification form and be eligible for a purchase price refund or a replacement vehicle.

If the manufacturer has another informal dispute settlement process that complies with the regulations of the Federal Trade Commission, the consumer must follow the specific manufactures procedures and the Lemon Law regulations will not apply. After a manufacture's decision has been made, the consumer is not bound by the decision and can still seek other legal remedies. This may include asking a court to award a replacement vehicle or reimbursement of the potential purchase price (less reasonable allowance for use), plus attorney fees and court costs.

Sandra L. Poirier

See also: Arbitration; Auto Purchasing; Corporate Social Responsibility; Department of Transportation (DOT); Mediation; National Highway Traffic and Safety Administration (NHTSA); Small Claims Courts; Supreme Court

References and Additional Readings

Clark B., & Davis, M.J. (1975). Beefing up product warranties: A new dimension in consumer "protection." *University of Kansas Law Review, 23*, 567.

Dahringer, L.D., & Johnson, D.R. (1988). Lemon laws: Intent, experience, and a pro-consumer model. *Journal of Consumer Affairs, 22*(1), 158–170.

Lemon Law Information. (2006). Retrieved from http://Lemonawinformation.com.

McDaniel, S.W. & Rao, C.P. (1982). Consumer attitudes toward and satisfaction with warranties and warranty performance-before and after Magnuson–Moss. *Baylor Business Studies, 12*(4), 47–61.

Shaffer, B., & Ostas, D.T. (2001). Exploring the political economy of consumer legislation: The development of automobile lemon laws. *Business and Politics, 3*(1), 65–76.

Woodcock, J. (1983). The lawyer vs. the lemon. *Barrister, 1*, 23–32.

Levies

A levy is an action to seek payment for a debt, typically the sale of property. Levies are more powerful than liens that are a claim against property without forcing a sale for repayment of the debt. A levy forces an action on the part of the consumer to satisfy the debt owed following a judgment. After a judgment is issued by the court, a writ of execution is created allowing property seizure on behalf of the creditor (typically a credit card company or other creditor). In some cases a Sheriff may physically seize the property.

Tax levies from the Internal Revenue Service (IRS) are a common example of a levy. According to the IRS, a levy is a "legal seizure of property to satisfy a tax debt." When taxes are owed to the IRS, property can be seized and sold to recompense the debt. The IRS may also levy against future earnings such as wages, or investments such as bank accounts, life insurance. The IRS follows specific procedures (see their website) before specific liquidation actions are taken; consumer appeals are allowable as part of the process.

Wendy Reiboldt

See also: Contract Law; Debt Management; Foreclosures and Short Sales; Liens; Small Claims Courts

References and Additional Readings

Barro, R. J. (1997). Optimal management of indexed and nominal debt (No. w6197). National Bureau of Economic Research.

Bohn, H. (2001). Retirement savings in an aging society: A case for Innovative Government Debt Management. Retrieved from http://www.econ.ucsb .edu/~bohn/papers/agingdebt.pdf

The Internal Revenue Service. (2013). Retrieved from www.irs.gov

Licensing

Licensing is an important control mechanism in ensuring that businesses and their operations are legitimate and fair to consumers. As noted in the definition section later, licenses are an official declaration of permission to operate. Such permissions provide assurances that oversight exists. Services made available to consumers by individuals, businesses, and associations must comply with applicable law and standards. Business and service providers must meet qualifications mandated by law when providing the public with a service or product. The consumers using the service or product are protected in the form regulatory laws that provide the public with safety and protections specific to use of the service or product.

Licenses provide the holder of the license with certification in the act or delivery of services. Documentation complies with appropriate laws, and permits the license holder to legally operate or provide public services in accordance with law. Depending on the business, type of service or privilege granted, licensure can be granted at the federal, state, or local level. Regulations vary by industry, state, and locality, so understanding licensing rules where the business is located is important.

The license itself generally acts in accordance with legal decisions and judgments made by the determined authority. Licenses are subject to jurisdiction based on the necessary requirements related to the activity, consumption, or trade of the related license. Government plays an important role in not only regulating licenses, but also in providing information to educate consumers, service providers, and the public about ways to support and protect their safety.

Licensing functions occur at multiple levels of government, and the appointed offices are primarily responsible for regulating the market for the product or service being licensed, defining requirements for legal operation, and enforcing licensing standards. The processes used for licensure will vary from state to state, using a variety of enforcement methods.

In the United States, state, local, and federal governments serve a number of roles in regulation of licenses by defining minimum requirements for the legal operation of programs made available to the general public. The following terms apply to general license information:

- License: A license is official authorization, formally protecting the public, the license holder, and license provider. Licenses give permission from an authority or governing body to own or use something, do a particular thing otherwise unlawful, and engage in trade or exchange.
- Licensee: Defined as the one who applies for the license, the holder of the license, or one that is licensed (http://www.merriam-webster.com/). The licensee can be an individual, organization, business provider, or other entity. Obtaining a privilege, like driving a truck or owning a gun, will require a license from the state or provincial government.
- License maintenance: While a few licenses may be lifelong privileges, the majority of licenses relevant in our society require scheduled review in order to renew the license. Obtaining the license does not grant the holder indefinite authority to practice the activity, and will require updates and provisions to continue certification.
- Licensing statute: The licensing statute establishes the scope of facilities subject to licensure and the scope of authority, responsibilities, and enforcement methods for the licensing agency.
- Federal licensing agencies: The Code of Federal Regulations (CFR) is the codification of the general and permanent rules and regulations and administrative laws published by the Office of The Federal Register (OFR). The OFR, National Association for Regulatory Administration (NARA), and the U.S. Government Printing Office jointly administer the Federal Register.gov site, which allows citizens and communities to access and understand the regulatory process by making information available to the public.
- Licensing requirements: The NARA defines the body of licensing requirements as the established regulatory prescriptions and proscriptions mandated by the licensing agency.

In order to legally drive a motor vehicle one must obtain a driver's license after demonstrating they can drive while adhering to traffic safety laws. A standard driver's license can be granted after reaching the required minimum age, completing traffic school, and a driving test. Drivers are normally required to obtain a license from their state of residence, and all states recognize each other's licenses for visitors. A state may also suspend an individual's driving privilege within its borders for traffic violations.

Human Care Licensing

Changes in the American family, increased maternal labor participation, and the advancement of society have accompanied the rapidly growing need for human care services. Today's working families need childcare and adult care for dependent family members who cannot stay home alone.

- National Association for Regulatory Administration (NARA): The NARA is a professional organization dedicated to human care licensing and regulation through leadership, education, collaboration, and services. NARA represents human service provider licensing, and is dedicated to promoting consumer protection through prevention strategies, such as reaching public audiences, care providers, consumers, employers, and sponsoring agents. Concepts developed by researchers, practitioners, and consumers of human care licensing make up the licensing professionals, and colleagues in allied professions form the body of accumulated knowledge about human care regulation.

The licensing function is established by state legislatures, creating offices that regulate child and adult care facilities by defining requirements for operation.

- The Child and Adult Care Food Program (CACFP): This is a federal entitlement program that reimburses providers for serving meals and snacks to children and adults in their care (NAEYC, 1998). The state agency is responsible for administering the program, often through the department of education or the health department. CACFP requires eligible family and group care providers to have current state or local licensing approval in order to participate. To ensure that programs benefiting from the CACFP meet basic safety requirements, the license ensures that the government doesn't support programs that fail to meet basic health and safety requirements in their state.

Child Care Licensing

Quality child-care is essential for the nation's economic well-being but there are no mandatory federal standards that govern the quality of licensed child care. The only existing law relative to child care licensing program standards is the Child Care Development Block Grant (CCDBG); this federal legislation necessitates unlicensed or unregistered care programs to meet the state's health and safety standards.

The child care licensing office within each state monitors adherence to the program's prescribed requirements: what each state considers to be essential in order to protect children's health and safety; how a program operates; qualifications of caregivers or practitioners; and experiences available to children in the licensed care environment. The measures states put into place to keep children safe range from background checks to preventative program standards that reduce the transmission of disease, injury, and death, to ensure children's safety.

When licensing programs fail to ensure proper practice, children's health and safety are compromised. In one case, the failure to enforce background check on a caregiver led to tragedy, resulting in the death of an infant under the care of a licensed child care provider in Georgia who had been previously charged with Child Protective Services violations.

Adult Care Licensing

Today families need adult care for dependent family members who cannot stay home alone due to illness or age. Adult care licensing is fundamental in public safety, and promoting a public understanding of how adult care licensing protects customers, families, and providers will help the public access quality services. This issue is becoming increasingly important as the U.S. population ages and the baby boomers approach old age. The National Administration on Regulatory Administration (NARA) represents human service licensing, including adult residential and assisted living, and adult day care providers.

- Administration on Aging (AoA): The AoA was created with the Older Americans Act in 1965, and is a partner of the National Aging Network. In the U.S. Department of Health and Human Services, the AoA is the nation's leading provider of home and community care for older adults. Assistance with services such as locating quality adult day care aim to protect the safety and health of elders in care facilities.

The licensing, certification, and regulation of adult care facilities remain the responsibility of state legislature. Variations between states will exist, but under the AoA the Elder Rights Services program administers prevention strategies that safeguard older persons from abuse and consumer fraud within the community and in adult care facilities. Other regulatory enforcement measures should be ongoing, and consumers should confirm that adult care facilities are licensed by the state.

Nicole Kelly

See also: Activism; Departments of Consumer Affairs (DCA); Public Safety; Social Services; Social Welfare

References and Additional Readings

Department of Health and Human Services. (2009). *Administration on Aging: FACTS.* Washington, DC: GPO.

The Federal Register. (2012). The Office of the Federal Register United States. Retrieved from https://www.federalregister.gov/

Garnett, S. (2007). Child nutrition division. Retrieved from http://fns.dpi.wi.gov/files/fns/pdf/07_02farm.pdf

Gigliotti K. (2005). Addressing hunger and nutrition: A tool kit for positive results. Child and adult care food program. National Conference of State Legislatures; Hunger and Nutrition Partnerships.

Lapp-Payne, A. (2010). National association for regulatory administration, NARA. *Strong licensing: The Foundation for a quality early care and education system.* Lexington, KY; NARA's Call to Action, pp. 1011–1108.

Merriam-Webster Dictionary. (2013). License. Retrieved from http://www.merriam-webster.com/medical/license

NAEYC. (1998). *Licensing and public regulation of early childhood programs.* Washington, DC: National Association for the Education of Young Children.

National Association of Child Care Resource & Referral Agencies. (2011). NACCRA supports the National Association for Regulatory Administration's recommendations for strengthening child care licensing regulations. Retrieved from http://www.naccrra.org/news-room/press-releases/2011/1/naccrra-supports-the-national-association-for-regulatory-administrat

QRIS National Learning Network. (2013). QRIS resource guide. Retrieved from http://qrisnetwork.org/category/author/nccic

Liens

Liens have been in existence since around 1791 when Thomas Jefferson and other legislators promoted and enacted them. They modeled the lien process after similar laws in Europe in an effort to stop the chaos of commerce in Washington, D.C. The government did not approve of consumers seeking services for construction and not paying when services were rendered. They saw this practice as weakening the economy and sought to insure builders from potential loss. Liens have since evolved to provide protections for service providers.

A lien is a claim on property (real or personal) as a result of payment owed. A lien is sought when a debt is owed and collection of payment has been unsuccessful. There are several types of liens, including the mechanic's lien, contractor's lien, tax lien, judgment lien, and attorney lien, depending on the origin of debt owed. Liens are usually classified as specific (specific property) or general (seeking debt repayment, but not only on a specific property).

When a person or company is not paid for work performed, after seeking payment in other ways, they may file a lien. Most commonly, contractors file liens for payment of work done but not paid (e.g., expensive remodeling projects). This is typically done in cases where a large amount of money is owed. If a smaller amount of money is owed (typically under $15,000), small claims court is a cheaper and more expeditious (normally 45–60-day resolution) alternative. State laws govern the lien process, so it is important to review specific state laws. Typically, the lien must be filed no more than 90 days after the work is completed. A lien is filed in the county courthouse (county where the property exists), identifying the owner of the property, a description of the property, name of the person ordering the work, and amount owed. A copy is also sent by certified mail to the property owner. If the debt is not paid (usually within one year), the creditor can file for foreclosure to recoup the money owed.

The lienee (person who owes the money, aka debtor) holds interest in the property of the leinor (person who is seeking payment, aka creditor), but only when the asset is sold, can the interest (i.e., the money) be claimed. A lien is different from a levy in that a lien is only resolved if payment is made or if the property is sold and the debt is paid. A levy is more powerful than a lien because it forces a sale to allow the creditor to collect the debt.

Wendy Reiboldt

See also: Contract Law; Debt Management; Levies; Small Claims Court

References and Additional Readings

Davidson, C. E. (1922). *The mechanic's lien law of Illinois: A lawyer's brief on the topic.* The Greenville Illinois Bar. St. Louis Law Printing Company.

Patel, N. (2010). Lien times: Use liens sparingly and carefully. Retrieved from http://www.remodeling.hw.net/legal-issues/lien-times.aspx

Long-Term Care

Long-term care services include personal care, social support, and medical services to assist people with physical and/or mental disorders. The goal of these services is to enable people to maintain independence for as long as possible while navigating through the aging process. It is a common misconception that many elders enter nursing homes. In reality, only 14 percent of those needing long-term care services receive them in nursing homes. Additionally, among long-term care service users, 42 percent are under the age of 65. In fact, aging, or even co morbidity, does not trigger the need for long-term care services.

To support those that do utilize long-term care services, three long-term care categories are available. These are (1) community-based service providers, (2) quasi-institutional providers, and (3) institutional providers. An individual's acuity level will dictate which service provider he/she will need.

Community-Based Service Providers

Community-based service providers enable people to live in a less restrictive environment by helping them manage the day-to-day responsibilities of living at home or with the family. Examples of such agencies include Meals on Wheels, home health, and homemaker/personal care providers. If desired, end-of-life care can also be offered at home through a company offering hospice services. Adult Day Care is a community-based provider offering daytime activities for elderly people and/or handicapped individuals living at home or with the family. This service, provided in a nonresidential facility, offers socialization, independence, and a break for family caregivers. It is governed by the Department of Social Services, Title 22, Division 6, Chapter 3 regulations. The advantages of community based services are numerous, including that they provide safety and security, enjoyable, educational activities, opportunities to improve mental and physical health; enhanced or maintained levels of independence; socialization and peer support; and nutritious meals and snacks. On the other hand, there also exist disadvantaged. These oftentimes include that daily costs are approximately $56 per day and that the majority of funding comes from the consumer/family or other options such as Medicaid, Medicare, long-term care insurance. Additionally, several regulations exist. Per regulations, Section 82065.5, Staff–Client Ratios: There shall be an overall ratio of not less than one staff member providing care and supervision for each 15 clients present. Therefore, this level of care does not give one-on-one supervision and interaction.

When a consumer is deciding if he/she or a loved one should live at home and utilize community-based services, many other considerations need to be addressed. For example, there are many advantages of living at home, including the ability to maintain independence for as long as possible; stay near or with loved ones; keep life's worth of belongings nearby; maintaining dignity; and ward off depression. In fact, research shows that most people prefer to age-in-place and that doing so can offset morbidity and mortality. On the other hand, the following should also be asked: How safe is the individual when home alone? Is there a feeling of isolation when home alone? What is the risk of a stranger hired for day care (abuse, theft)? Are the responsibilities of managing the home too high? A full portrait of a person's needs will allow for the most effective decisions to be made regarding housing options.

Quasi-Institutional Providers

Another option for consumers is quasi-institutional care, which includes residential facilities such as independent living/retirement centers, board and care homes, and adult foster care homes. The care provided in these facilities consists mainly of personal care and none or very limited medical assistance. Therefore, both mental and physical functions should be fairly intact and the intent is to maintain an individual's functional abilities rather than improve them. Funding sources include Medicaid, insurance, and private funds.

Institutional Providers

Many adults require more extensive care. The following three types of residential facilities are included in the institutional provider category: (1) assisted living, (2) nursing homes, (3) continuing care retirement communities.

Assisted Living

Assisted living facilities are governed by the state Department of Social Services and primarily provide custodial care. Medical care is offered but not on a continuous basis as in skilled nursing facilities. The environment is that of an apartment building where individuals live in their own homes under the care of the facility. This provider offers a safe environment where people can maintain a level of independence with the option of assistance with meals, laundry, medical care, and transportation. Socialization, planned activities, on-site medical care, and the relief of daily chores are some of the greatest benefits of assisted living. The cost of assisted living can range from $3,000 to $10,000 per month depending on the facility and additional services requested. Funding sources include private pay and in some states, Medicaid.

Nursing Homes

The following are types of facilities within the nursing home category:

1. skilled nursing facility
2. sub-acute facility
3. specialized facilities include psychiatric lock-down, Alzheimer's care, intermediate care facility/mentally retarded and inpatient rehabilitation.

Residential facilities require specialized training, administration, and staff to meet the mental and/or medical needs of its residents. Skilled nursing facilities governed by the California Department of Public Health provide both 24 hours a day skilled medical care and custodial care. Skilled care requires active involvement of professionals such as nurses and therapists.

Custodial care requires assistance with activities of daily living (ADL) (bathing, dressing, eating, toileting, bowel/bladder control, ambulation, transfer). Reasons for placement include decline in physical and/or mental function, need for "step down" care after an acute care hospitalization, rehabilitation, and respite care. Per Section 483.75 of the State Operations Manual, Appendix PP, "A facility must be administered in a manner that enables it to use its resources effectively and efficiently to attain or maintain the highest practicable physical, mental, and psychosocial well-being of each resident." These regulations are enforced from the time of admission to discharge. The cost of care can range from $3,000 to $10,000 per month depending on services required and type of facilities. Sources of financing include private pay, Medicare, Medicaid, Medicare supplemental insurance, third-party contracts, long-term care insurance.

The traditional model for nursing homes includes a clinical environment and approach to care that left residents feeling lonely, helpless, and bored. In 1996, the National Citizens' Coalition for Nursing Home Reform (NCCHNR) convened a panel to engage in transformational change to address the negative impact on nursing home residents. The pioneers from that meeting formed a national movement now referred to as "Culture Change." The goal of Culture Change is to move care from an institutional approach to an individualized approach making relationships the foundation for care. The environment of the nursing home should be more homelike by incorporating warm colors on the walls, pillows in the lobby area, curtains in the shower room, and photos of loved ones in rooms. Activities, bed time, and food preferences enhance the resident's living experience. Consistent assignment of staff allows for relationships to build so that trusted employees are responsible for intimate care. Culture change is important because it improves the quality of life and is supported through national regulations. It should be noted that regulations are in place to make sure the quality of administration and care is maximized. Administrators must train and test to qualify them as provider leaders. State and national regulations must be followed in the operations of the facility to ensure quality of care which ultimately ensures quality of life.

Continuing Care Retirement Community

The Continuing Care Retirement Community combines independent living, assisted living, and skilled nursing on one campus which allows for easy transition when care needs change. Socialization, planned activities, meals, medical care, and relief from household chores are benefits to using this provider. In addition, partners living together can easily cross campus to visit one another when a different level of care for one is required. Costs for this provider include an entrance fee and monthly charges. Financing is achieved through private funds. Placement with an institutional provider may garner guilt and depression from family members. The pros must be weighed against the cons. The pros include 24-hour nursing care (depending on type of facility); team of trained professionals attending to daily care needs; presence of state and national surveyors and local ombudsman as resident advocates; daily enforcement of resident rights; structured daily activities; relief from cooking, cleaning, and laundry; socialization with residents who may have common history and experience. On the other hand, several disadvantages can exist. These may include initial feelings of isolation; unfamiliar environment; intimate care conducted by unfamiliar caregivers; living away from loved ones; exposure to other conditions (infections, abuse, neglect); loneliness, and/or depression.

Overall, decisions regarding long-term care services are critical for one's well-being. As the population continues to "grey" it is critical that individuals advocate for themselves and their loved ones. Knowing options for housing and living arrangements are essential to one's dignity.

Rebecca Perley

See also: Administration on Aging (AoA); Americans with Disabilities Act (ADA); Health and Healthcare; Medicare; Older Americans Act (OAA); Ombuds Offices; Social Security; Social Services; Social Welfare

References and Additional Readings

Buchbinder, S. B., & Shanks, N. (2007). *Introduction to healthcare management (2nd Edition)*. Burlington, MA: Jones & Bartlett Learning.

California Code of Regulations, Title 22, Division 5, Chapter 3.

California Culture Change Coalition. (2013). Retrieved from http://www.calculturechange.org/

Centers for Medicare and Medicaid Services. (2013). State operations manual, Appendix PP. Retrieved from http://www.cms.hhs.gov/manuals/downloads/som107ap_pp_guidelines_ltcf.pdf

Day, T. (2012). Guide to long term care planning about adult day care. Retrieved from http://www.longtermcarelink.net/eldercare/adult_day_care.htm

Reinholz, A. (2011). www.suite101.com. In pros and cons of adult day cares. Retrieved from http://suite101.com/article/pros-and-cons-of—adult-day-cares-a344115

Robinson, L., Segal, J., & White, M. (2012). In adult day care centers finding the best center for your needs. Retrieved from http://www.helpguide.org/elder/adult_day_care_centers.htm

Science Daily. (2011). Adult day care services provide much-needed break to family caregivers. Retrieved from http://www.sciencedaily.com/releases/2011/07/110718121607.htm

Singh, D. A. (2010). *Effective management of long-term care facilities*. Sudbury, MA: Jones & Bartlett Learning.

M

Made in USA

Made in USA is a "country of origin" label showing that a product was made in the United States. The label is required by the Federal Trade Commission (FTC). Established in 1914, the FTC was charged with preventing deception and unfair actions in the marketplace. Originally the purpose of the FTC was to prevent unfair methods of competition in commerce (e.g., to bust the trusts).

In 1938, the Wheeler Lea Amendments articulated the role of the FTC in regard to unfair acts or practices. This gave the FTC jurisdiction over deceptive advertising. In 1975, the Magnuson–Moss Warranty Act added warranties and other trade regulations to the FTC's jurisdiction. In the 1980s, the FTC established the Office of Consumer and Competition Advocacy.

FTC Definition of Made in USA Label

If a product is advertised as Made in USA, the FTC requires that the product must be "all or virtually all" made in the United States. The FTC does not offer review and preapproval of advertising or labeling claims, therefore a manufacturer can make a claim given that it is truthful and substantiated. The term "all or virtually all" implies that all significant parts and production processes must be of U.S. origin; the product should contain no, or negligible, content from another country. The product's final assembly must take place in the United States.

The U.S.-made content must be clearly delineated on cars and textiles, including wool, and fur products. There is no law requiring other products sold in the United States to be marked or labeled "Made in USA" not disclosing the amount of U.S. content. The Made in USA standard applies to products advertised or sold in the United States; however, there is an exception for products who fall under specific country-of-origin labeling from other laws. Other countries often provide their own country-of-origin requirements. As a result, exporters must determine which countries imposes requirements.

Made in USA

There is a movement, even devoted websites, seeking and finding products that are still "Made in America". Manufacturing in the United has taken a nose dive in the last decade because companies are moving their production to China and India where labor costs are cheaper and labor laws are more lenient. It is becoming more difficult to find goods that are "Made in USA." In fact, ABC World News with Diane Sawyer launched a short series in which they visit a "typical American families" and canvas their homes for American made products. The families agreed that everything not made in America could be removed from their home and put into a storage container outside. They left the home and movers went to work. All kitchen furniture and appliances were taken out, and in the living room, only one vase with fake flowers remained. The show ran several interesting facts during the series, including the following statistic: in the 1960s, about 90 percent of products were made in the USA while today, over 50 percent are foreign made. Economists project that if Americans spend 1 percent more on American made products, approximately 18 cents per day, it would create 200,000 jobs in America. It is a powerful projection, and one that appears easy to do. However, the show portrayed it to be quite difficult to find even a coffee maker made in America when reordering furniture and household items for the family's home. To complicate matters, while some products appear to be "Made in the USA," some of the components used in production are made abroad. Several companies maintain that all or a vast majority of their products and components are truly American made, including Duraflame Fire Logs, Weber Grills, Harley Davidson, KitchenAid, Oreck, Big Wheels, Pyrex, Spanx, 3M post-it notes, and Intel chipmakers.

Laws on Labeling Fibers, Wool, Furs, and Automobiles

The Textile Fiber Products Identification Act and Wool Products Labeling Act both require a Made in USA label on most clothing and other textile or wool household products when the final product is manufactured in the United States from textiles manufactured in the United States, regardless of the origin of materials from previous stages in the manufacturing process. Imported textile products must be labeled, according to the Customs Service. A textile or wool product that is partially manufactured in the United States and in another country, it must be labeled accordingly. The Fur Products Labeling Act stipulates that the country of origin of imported furs must be clearly disclosed on labels and in any related advertising.

The American Automobile Labeling Act (AALA) requires that automobiles sold in the United States and manufactured on or after October 1, 1994, be labeled with information regarding where the car was assembled, the percentage of equipment from the United States and Canada, and the engine and transmission's country of origin. The FTC's standards will apply when and if advertising claims go beyond the AALA requirements.

The Future of American Manufacturing and Made in USA

The economic recession and the high unemployment rate in the United States are major concerns for many business leaders and policymakers. In February 2012, Strauss and Wang (2012, 1), economists for the Federal Reserve Bank in Chicago, wrote that the "U.S. economy continues to recover from the longest and deepest drop in economic activity since the Great Depression . . . But employment losses that had begun in February 2008 have continued to mount (even after the recession officially ended in June 2009) through February 2010."

In September 2012, forecasts from 79 economists surveyed by *Bloomberg Business Week* indicate a continued slowing of the U.S. economy. They noted that in July 2012, U.S. exports fell and in August of the same year, factories cut more than 15,000 jobs, the biggest drop in two years. At least one American entrepreneur and a former president of the United States are determined to restore American manufacturing.

Returning Manufacturing Business to the United States

Todd Lipscomb is an entrepreneur and s the president of MadeinUSAForever.com. After spending 15 years in the technology industry including seven years in Asia, he moved back to the United States and started MadeinUSAForever.com. His firm sells only high-quality American-made goods. To gain supporters, he has written a book about his beliefs and his work. The title of the book is *Re-Made in the USA: How We Can Restore Jobs, Retool Manufacturing, and Compete with the World.* In the book, he explains the challenges that America faces, how America's competitors are taking advantage of the United States and his recommendations for rebuilding American manufacturing.

To support his argument, Lipscomb explains his concerns about foreign labor standards, the fact that jobs shipped overseas almost never return, polluting practices of foreign manufacturing, lack of minimum wage restrictions in foreign countries, and low safety standards for foreign products. He points out that a service economy (e.g., the United States) is less productive than a manufacturing economy because service jobs pay less, they are easier to eliminate, and they add less value to the economy. He discusses in depth the loss of independent manufacturers and retailers in the

United States because they were not able to compete with lower prices for goods manufactured overseas and sold in large chain stores.

Lipscomb presents a list of conditions that would make a community appealing to a manufacturing business that was "shopping" for a location in the United States. His list of recommended conditions includes good schools, safety, availability of skilled labor, tax levels that represent a balance between the level of services and the payout, quality of wages and employees, a good standard of living, state and local leadership, financial stability, and finally the "whole package." He believes that community leaders and state and federal governments should work with businesses to rebuild the USA.

A Former President's Perspective on Back to Work and Returning Manufacturing to America

Former President Bill Clinton has written a book that presents ideas similar to Todd Lipscomb's plan to return manufacturing to the United States. Clinton's book is titled *Back to Work: Why We Need Smart Government for a Strong Economy*. Clinton explains his proposals to increase bank lending and corporate investment, to create more jobs that pay well, and to make sure that there are enough people trained to fill those jobs. He believes that local and state government policy makers could initiate and implement the recommended actions.

Clinton's first proposal included remedial actions to end the mortgage mess as quickly as possible. For example, for delinquent homeowners, the mortgage principal should be written down or the mortgage terms extended at a lower interest rate enabling the homeowner to make smaller payments. Clinton's second proposal stated that people with government-guaranteed mortgages who were not delinquent should have the opportunity to refinance their mortgages at current low interest rates.

Clinton's third proposal was for the Federal Reserve Board to give banks an incentive to lend. Clinton described a similar situation taking place in Sweden. Banks had plenty of capital but were reluctant to lend. When the central bank in Sweden started charging banks a small fee to hold their money, the banks became more involved in lending. As a result, the Swedish economy is growing at about 5.5 percent.

Clinton's fourth proposal was to provide incentives to corporations to bring more money back to the United States. Clinton (2011) noted that "Among wealthy nations, we (the US) have the second-highest corporate tax rate in the world . . . " (p. 132). Clinton's fifth proposal was to allow companies to repatriate the cash with no tax liability if it was reinvested to create new jobs. In summary, Lipscomb's active involvement in business (MadeinUSAForever) and former President Clinton's ideas to get Americans back to work could reinvigorate American manufacturing. These actions and recommendation would promote the manufacture of more products that could be labeled Made in USA.

Sharon A. DeVaney

See also: Counterfeiting; Fair Trade; Federal Reserve; Federal Trade Commission (FTC); Food Labeling; Magnuson–Moss Warranty Act

References and Additional Readings

Clinton, W. J. (2011). *Back to work. Why we need smart government for a strong economy*. New York: Alfred A. Knopf.

Federal Trade Commission. (1998). Complying with Made in USA Standard. Federal Trade Commission. BCP Business Center. Retrieved from http://business.ftc.gov/documents/bus03-complying-made-inusa-standard

Federal Trade Commission. (2013). Retrieved from http://ftc.gov

Garman, E. T. (2006). Chapter 9 government regulation of economic interests. *Consumer Economic Issues in America* (9th ed.), pp. 222–245. London, UK: Thomson.

Goldsmith, E. (2009). Chapter 5 government protection, nongovernmental proconsumer groups, and the media (pp. 131–160). *Consumer Economics: Issues and Behaviors,* 2nd Edition. Upper Saddle River, NJ: Pearson Prentice Hall.

Lipscomb, T. (2011). *Re-made in the USA: How we can restore jobs, retool manufacturing, and compete with the world*. Hoboken, NJ: John Wiley & Sons, Inc.

Made in USA Forever (2013). Retrieved from http://madeinusaforever.com

Phillips, M., & Coy, P. (2012). Global economics. *Bloomberg Business Week* (pp. 13–14).

Strauss, W. A., & Wang, N. (2012). Economic outlook symposium: Summary of 2011 results and 2012 forecasts. *Chicago Fed Letter*. Chicago, IL: The Federal Reserve Bank of Chicago.

Madoff, Bernie

On June 29, 2009, Judge Denny Chin sentenced Bernard L. Madoff, 71, to 150 years in prison for the largest fraud case in history, a $65 billion Wall Street Ponzi scheme. Madoff's sentence for his approximately 20-year scheme was one of the stiffest ever for white-collar crime. It was the statutory maximum for the 11 criminal counts he pled guilty to. Bernard Madoff was once a highly respected Wall Street investor who opened his firm, Bernard L. Madoff Investment Securities LLC, in 1960 with money he had earned from working as a lifeguard on the beaches of Long Island and from installing sprinkler systems. His firm was recognized for being a pioneer in market making where a firm acts as a middle man between buyers and sellers of stock.

Madoff was a prominent member of the securities industry throughout his career. His service included extensive involvement with the National Association of Securities Dealers (NASD). In addition, he was involved in the development of NASDAQ, served on its board of governors and its executive committee, and at one time was chairman of its trading committee.

Madoff served on the boards of several nonprofit corporations which helped to build his clientele base. His principal clients were charitable foundations. These organizations tended to withdraw very little of their funds annually.

Madoff's investments consistently provided higher returns than other investments which caused some of the financial publications to question his methods of success, but they did not question whether his methods were fraudulent as Bernard L. Madoff Investment Securities LLC was one of the biggest securities firms in the world. Eventually Madoff's methods did come into question. In 2000, Harry Markopolos, a Massachusetts financial

Bernard Madoff arriving at federal court for his hearing in New York on January 14, 2009. (AP Photo/Frank Franklin II)

analyst, asked the US Securities and Exchange Commission (SEC) to investigate his firm.

Despite repeated efforts, Markopolos' requests were mostly ignored. Six substantive complaints were filed with the SEC beginning in 1992, but the investigations weren't properly handled by the SEC. In 2006, one of these investigations came close to disclosing the fraud, but did not.

In the end, it was the stock market plunge in 2008 that unraveled Madoff's Ponzi scheme. Although Madoff claimed that his funds were earning money, investors began requesting to withdraw funds by November 2008. As things began to unravel, the Madoff's sent jewelry and other valuable items to family and friends. In addition, Madoff's wife, Ruth, withdrew $15 million from a brokerage firm that Madoff was affiliated with. On December 9, 2008, Madoff admitted to his two sons, who were employees of his firm, that his business was a fraud, a Ponzi scheme. He admitted that his losses from the fraud were at least $50 billion. Losses were later figured to be closer to $65 billion. Madoff's sons alerted the Federal Bureau of Investigation of their father's fraudulent business dealings and on December 11 the SEC charged him with securities fraud for his Ponzi scheme. Madoff surrendered to authorities and was released on a $10 million bond, but was placed on house arrest the following week when he was unable to find anyone outside his family to guarantee his bail money. In addition to criminal charges, the SEC filed a civil complaint against Madoff requiring him to pay a fine and return funds to investors. The Securities Investor Protection Corporation (SIPC) selected Irving to serve as Trustee for the liquidation of Bernard L. Madoff Investment Securities LLC. The Madoff Recovery Initiative can be found at www.madoff.com. On March 12, 2009, Madoff was jailed after pleading guilty to all 11 counts including investment advisory fraud, mail fraud, wire fraud, international money laundering, domestic money laundering, false statements, perjury, false filing, and theft from an employee benefit plan. In addition, the SEC filed a civil complaint against Madoff requiring him to pay a fine and return funds to investors. Madoff's hundreds of thousands of investors were from all over the world and included investors from Europe, Asia, and the Middle East. They included international banks, the owners of the New York Mets, charitable organizations including one set up by director Steven Spielberg, and celebrities such as Elie Wiesel, publisher Mortimer B. Zuckerman, actor John Malkovich, and Hall of Fame pitcher Sandy Koufax. The fallout from Madoff's Ponzi scheme also led to suicide for several individuals. Thierry Magon de la Villehuchet, a prominent French hedge fund manager whose firm Access International Advisors lost $1.4 billion, was found dead just 10 days after Madoff's arrest. William Foxen, an investor who was unable to bear the shame of the loss also committed suicide. On December 11, 2010, on the second anniversary of his father's arrest, Madoff's older son Mark was found dead in his New York City apartment.

Lisa J. Amos Ledeboer

See also: Ponzi Schemes; Securities and Exchange Commission (SEC)

References and Additional Readings

American Law Yearbook. (2010). Fraud. *American Law Yearbook 2009: A Guide to the Year's Major Legal Cases and Developments, 114–116*

Nawaw, D. (2012). Timeline: Key dates in the Bernard Madoff case. Retrieved from http://www.telegraph.co.uk/finance/financetopics/bernard-madoff/5650615/One-big-fraud-several-lawsuits-Bernard-Madoff-timeline.html

Securities and Exchange Commission. (2012). SEC charges Bernard L. Madoff with multi-billion dollar Ponzi scheme. Retrieved from sec.gov/news/press/2008

Washington, R. (2011). Bernard L. Madoff. *The New York Times*. Retrieved from Topics.nytimes.com

Magnuson–Moss Warranty Act

Congress enacted the Magnuson–Moss Warranty Act in 1975. In the House Report accompanying the bill, the first-listed purpose of the act is "to make warranties on consumer products more readily understood and enforceable" (House Report). To that end, much of the act is geared to enabling consumers to learn warranty terms before purchase and to standardize warranty terms to enable comparison shopping for warranties. In addition, the act limits the use of disclaimers of implied warranties, and provides for enforcement provisions. It is probably fair to say that the act's limits on implied warranty disclaimers and the enforcement provisions have had more of an impact on consumers than the attempt to facilitate comparison shopping.

Warranty Disclosure

Standardization

The act divides consumer goods warranties into full and limited warranties. Sellers are not obliged to offer full warranties, but if they choose to do so, they must meet the act's requirements. Full warranties are to be captioned "full (Statement of Duration) warranty" while limited warranties are headlined "limited warranty" (§ 2303). The goal was to enable consumers to identify which product carries a better warranty, and to purchase that product if they prefer the better warranty. In fact, it appears that most consumer goods carry only a limited warranty and so consumers are rarely able to choose a product with a full warranty over an item carrying only a limited warranty. In addition, it is not clear how many consumers know the differences between full and limited warranties, and are in a position to determine how much they value full warranties; indeed, it is not even certain how many consumers notice that most of the goods they purchase carry only limited warranties, if they have an express warranty at all.

What are the differences between full and limited warranties? To qualify as offering a full warranty, the warrantor must: promise to remedy defects in the product within a reasonable time and without charge; not limit the duration of implied warranties, and may not limit consequential damages for breach of warranty unless the limitation appears conspicuously on the face of the warranty. In addition, if the full warrantor is unable to fix a defect "after a reasonable number of attempts," the warrantor must allow the consumer to choose either a refund or replacement, again without charge (§ 2304). The Act also bars full warrantors from imposing any unreasonable duties (other than notice to the warrantor) upon the consumer as a condition for obtaining a remedy under the warranty.

A limited warranty is defined simply as an express warranty that does not meet the requirements for a full warranty. As explained later, under the act, sellers making limited warranties may not disclaim the implied warranties, though they may limit their duration. Accordingly, at a minimum, limited warrantors must make implied warranties.

Presale Disclosure

The act directs the FTC to promulgate rules providing that warranties shall be available to consumers before sale, again in an attempt to enable consumers to comparison shop for warranties. The commission's rules require sellers either to display the text of the warranty "in close proximity to the warranted product" or to make it available upon request before the sale and to place "signs reasonably calculated to elicit the prospective buyer's attention in prominent locations in the store or department advising such prospective buyers of the availability of warranties upon request" (FTC Regulations, § 702.3(a)). It is not clear how many retailers actually comply with this rule, or how many consumers take advantage of the right to inspect warranty texts prior to purchase. It seems likely that these particular provisions have benefited few consumers.

Warranty Text

The act also requires that warrantors "fully and conspicuously disclose in simple and readily understood language the terms and conditions" of the warranty (§ 2302).

Implied Warranties

Under certain circumstances, the Uniform Commercial Code, enacted at least in part in every state in the country, obliges sellers to make implied warranties of fitness for particular purpose and of merchantability. Before Congress enacted the act, some sellers had provided consumers with a document headed "Warranty" which actually disclaimed the implied warranties, leading some consumers to believe they had received a warranty when in fact they had been provided with less protection than they would have had if the seller had merely remained silent. Congress wished to prevent that practice, and so included what has turned out to be one of the more significant provisions of the act: a prohibition on the disclaimer of implied warranties if the warrantor makes a written warranty. One effect of this provision is to bar sellers providing limited warranties from disclaiming the implied warranties, though they may still limit the duration of the implied warranties "to the duration of a written warranty of reasonable duration, if such limitation is conscionable and is set forth in clear and unmistakable language and prominently displayed on the face of the warranty" (§ 2308(b)).

Enforcement Provisions

Warranty claims brought in the United States have traditionally been subject to the so-called "American Rule" under which each party, whether victorious or not, bears its own attorneys' fees. That rule has functioned as a disincentive to consumers contemplating a lawsuit because, given the small stakes involved in the typical consumer law suit, the cost of such litigation often exceeds the amount of the judgment, making victory for the consumer pyrrhic. To address this problem, the act provides that prevailing consumers in actions under written or implied warranties, or who are damaged by the failure of a warrantor to comply with the act, can recover attorneys' fees, "based on actual time expended" if the fees were "reasonably incurred" by the consumer, unless the court determines that an award of fees would be inappropriate (§ 2310(d)(2)). This represents a sharp departure from traditional contract law and at least theoretically enables consumers to assert warranty claims that would otherwise be pointless to bring.

Normally, breach of warranty claims are heard in state courts, and claims under the act can also be heard in state court, but the act provides federal courts with jurisdiction over claims under the act or for failure to comply with a warranty. Nevertheless, the act provides significant roadblocks to plaintiffs seeking to sue in federal court. Because the act confers federal jurisdiction only over cases in which the plaintiffs seek at least $50,000 in damages, and because few consumer warranty claims reach that amount, few consumers can bring claims in federal court, except as a class action. But the act also makes it difficult to bring class actions in federal court by requiring at least 100 named plaintiffs (as opposed to the more common unnamed plaintiff members of the class). The hardship of finding 100 consumers willing to serve in such a role, and the case management issues created by so many named plaintiffs, may deter plaintiffs from bringing Magnuson–Moss class actions in federal courts. Nevertheless, some such cases have made it to federal court.

The act also provides for informal dispute resolution procedures for warranty adjudication. The FTC has promulgated regulations regulating these informal procedures, which mandate that the procedures must be "fair and expeditious" (FTC Regulations, § 703.3). If a warrantor has established an informal dispute resolution procedure, it can require a consumer to use the procedure before commencing a lawsuit, as long as the procedure complies with the FTC requirements. According to one commentator, few warrantors have established such informal dispute resolution systems, perhaps because of the cost of doing so and the fact that consumers dissatisfied with the results can still seek a remedy in court.

Scope of the Act

The act applies only to consumer products. Consumer products are limited to "tangible personal property . . . which is normally used for personal, family or household purposes" (§ 2301(1)). Thus, the act would apply to consumer products even if the particular product is being used by a business, if it is the type of product that is normally used by consumers. The FTC regulations while giving the examples of automobiles and typewriters, note that they are used for both personal and commercial purposes, and state that they come within the scope of the act. This is an unusual feature of the act; consumer protection statutes more commonly apply only to consumer uses of products. The regulation also states "Where it is unclear whether a particular product is covered under the definition of consumer product, any ambiguity will be resolved in favor of coverage" (FTC Regulations, § 700.1).

The act's warranty provisions are limited to products carrying a written warranty. Theoretically a seller could evade the act's limits by making only oral warranties, but the practical difficulties in doing so have generally prevented use of this loophole.

Criticisms

Full Warranty

Suppose a warrantor wishes to offer a full warranty for six months. That warranty will be captioned "Full (Six Month) Warranty." But because the warrantor may not limit the duration of the implied warranties, the implied warranties may last longer than six months, depending on the nature of the product. If the product breaks down in the seventh month, a consumer may be misled into thinking the product is out of warranty. The express warranty will indeed have expired, but the implied warranty may well still be in effect and would give the consumer a remedy if, for example, the breakdown occurred because of a manufacturing defect. That means the consumer would still have warranty rights, but the label may cause the consumer not to assert them. That seems an odd result for a statute intended to inform consumers of their rights.

Comparison Shopping

While the act has made comparison shopping for warranties easier, little evidence suggests that consumers have taken advantage of the opportunity to comparison shop for warranties. So few sellers offer full warranties that consumers rarely have a chance to choose one over a limited warranty. Because limited warranties can vary, the mere fact that a warranty is captioned as limited tells consumers little. And few consumers seem to read through warranties before making purchases. In short, it appears few consumers have accepted Congress's invitation to comparison shop for warranties.

Successes

By making warranties more readable, the act has probably enabled consumers to determine more easily their rights under warranties. It has also aided consumers in recovering for breach of warranty by providing prevailing plaintiffs with attorneys' fees. In addition, the act has likely eliminated some deceptive warranty practices, including the former practice of disclaiming warranties in a document that appeared to be conferring warranties.

In short, the act's reach may have exceeded its grasp, but it did indeed grasp some consumer protections.

Jeff Sovern

See also: Extended Warranties; Federal Trade Commission (FTC)

References and Additional Readings

Federal Trade Commission. (1977). Regulations, 16 C.F.R. Parts 700-03. Retrieved from http://law.justia.com/cfr/title16/16cfr700_main_02.html

Magnuson–Moss Warranty Act of 1975, 15 U.S.C. §§ 2301–11 (1975) (the "Act"). Retrieved from http://www.law.cornell.edu/uscode/text/15/chapter-50.

Pridgen, D. (2011). *Consumer protection and the law,* Section 14.18.

United States. Cong. House (1974). 93th Cong. 2nd Session. *Report of the interstate and foreign commerce committee*, H.R. Rep. No. 93–1107.

Malpractice

Negligence is defined as an act that is below the standard of care in the community. There are many different types of negligence. There are areas of strict liability where a manufacturer may make an item that by its very nature is dangerous and harmful. There are forms of negligence that are the result of failing to drive carefully and causing an accident when failing to stop at a stop sign. Again, negligence comes in many forms and can have a serious effect on the consumer.

Of all types of negligence, the one that has the most potential impact on the public at large is medical malpractice. Medical malpractice is negligence that occurs in a medical environment. Malpractice involves failure on the part of a healthcare provider and can have disastrous consequences for the victim, such as injury or even death. According to recent research, medical errors caused approximately 195,000 accidental deaths and 1.14 million patient-safety incidents in the Medicare population between the years 2000 and 2002 (*Medical News Today*, 2012). The costs associated with such errors are enormous.

For medical malpractice to exist there are four elements that must be shown, (1) a duty to provide care was owed: this is a very complicated concept and requires that a legal duty existed at the time a hospital or healthcare provider agrees to take on the care or treatment of a patient, (2) a breach (failure) of that duty or responsibility by the provider either as a result of mistake or omission to perform to what is termed the standard care in the community, (3) the breach (failure) caused an injury: the breach of the duty

A doctor explaining consent forms to a patient prior to surgery. Strong doctor-patient communication is essential for consumer safety and malpractice avoidance. (Monkey Business Images/Dreamstime.com)

of care was a cause of the injury, and (4) there must be a damage (some form of loss that can be measured either as a financial loss or an emotional loss) to the individual. There is a limit to the amount of time between when the injury was inflicted on the patient and when an action against a medical provider can be filed in court. This is called a statute of limitations.

Medical malpractice can take many forms. Some are proactive and the healthcare professional has done something to cause the injury. In other cases the injury is the failure to act quickly, in a timely and appropriate manner to protect the well-being of the individual. What follows are examples of different medical malpractice events due to either an act or a failure to act.

A very common area of medical malpractice is where patients are misdiagnosed. The result of these missed diagnoses can result in a wide variety of injuries including but not limited to some of the following events: healthy organs being removed due to a misdiagnosis, failure to follow up on the patient's complaint and not providing the correct care in a timely manner resulting in damage or even death, and failing to read the lab and other results that have been performed and therefore making the incorrect diagnosis. Often a problem in cancer cases exists because several experts are working on the patient's case and there is a breakdown in communication and follow up.

Another common area of malpractice is child birth. A number of birth-related injuries can occur during the birthing processes. Very serious and severe injuries can be the result of medical malpractice. Also, medication, either related to prepregnancy or not, that is the wrong medication or the wrong dosage, can cause a wide variety of malpractice claims that often are the result of a failure on the part of the healthcare provider to consider the mother and the pregnancy in the decisions that are being made and the meds that are being prescribed. Some examples are errors made during a birth that lead a variety of issues including but not limited to a lack of oxygen to the brain, possibly resulting in cerebral palsy, paralysis due to a forced birth, or a failure to perform a caesarian when indicated causing the mother or her unborn child ongoing problems.

Another major example of medical malpractice is the found in the hospital setting. Hospitals have an abundance of medical malpractice opportunities in large part due to the size and scope of the practice issues related to the ongoing care of an individual. The problems and injuries can vary greatly from failing to give adequate treatment to a patient being exposed to and contracting another illness while in that hospital. Examples include using equipment that hasn't been properly sterilized, giving a patient the wrong medicine, giving the patient the wrong dosage of a medication, leaving instruments inside a patient following an operation, or a doctor or nurse failing to follow up or follow through on orders that have been written and placed into the care of that patient.

Common hospital mistakes often result in instances of someone being operated on unnecessarily. Very common events found in hospital settings include but are not limited to a lump or cyst being misdiagnosed as cancer, a simple stomach upset being misdiagnosed as appendicitis and the appendix being removed unnecessarily, or minor illness that could have been managed by medicine being operated on unnecessarily.

Lastly a very large problem in the arena of medical malpractice and one that is finding great growth in the "baby boomers" is the wrong medicine being either prescribed or provided. Common claims fall into several categories. Keep in mind that the baby boomer generation is growing at 10,000 baby boomers retiring each and every day for the next decade. As their numbers increase so does the number of potential medical malpractice claims that will grow out of the following types of mistakes: medicine dosage is too strong and causes side effects that would not have occurred if the correct dosage had been given, the wrong medicine is causing additional problems, and the wrong medicine is given and fails to resolve the existing problem.

Medical malpractice is really set to bloom over the next several years. The primary reason for that is a growing (10,000) baby boomers per day into the system that need care and medicine. The fact that this group is getting older and dementia and the ability to follow doctors' orders will become more and more difficult with time will also provide a fertile ground for mistakes and errors that will be severe.

As consumers, much of the malpractice can and will be avoided by consumer education as well as the further education of the medical professionals that will need to deal with a very large and growing population of elders that will come complete with a variety of limits on both ability to understand as well as to comply.

Zoran K. Basich

See also: Confidentiality; Health and Healthcare; Small Claims Courts; Supreme Court

References and Additional Readings

Hyams, A. L., Brandenburg, J. A., Lipsitz, S. R., Shapiro, D. W., & Brennan, T. A. (1995). Practice guidelines and malpractice litigation: a two-way street. *Annals of Internal Medicine, 122*(6), 450–455.

Jena, A. B., Seabury, S., Lakdawalla, D., & Chandra, A. (2011). Malpractice risk according to physician specialty. *New England Journal of Medicine, 365*(7), 629–636.

Medical News Today. (2012). In hospital deaths from medical errors at 195,000 per year USA. Retrieved from http://www.medicalnewstoday.com/releases/11856.php

Paik, M., Hyman, D. A., Black, B., Sage, W., & Silver, C. (2012). How do the elderly fare in medical malpractice litigation, before and after tort reform? Evidence from Texas. Retrieved from http://ssrn. com/abstract=1605331.

Mandated Reporters

Though several entries in this encyclopedia discuss the privacy rights of consumers, it is important to note that consumer safety is also ensured under some situations when information needs to be breeched. For example, situations that has the potential to inflict serious hard or cause destruction need to be revealed. "Since the passage of the Child Abuse Prevention and Treatment Act in 1974, all states have been required to set up standards for the identification, treatment, and prevention of child abuse" (Kanel, 2008, 312). These standards, known as mandatory reporting standards, are for professionals who engage in the care of treatment of minors. Similarly, after the passage of the Older Americans Act and Elder Abuse and Dependent Adult

Civil Protection Act, states also have mandates that require professionals who work with, provide support, or intervene on behalf of older adults or disabled persons to report suspected instances of abuse or neglect to the appropriate agency. Such professionals, who work with children, elders, or disabled persons, are known as mandated reporters, and include teachers, social workers/counselors, healthcare providers, child care providers, medical examiners/coroners, law enforcement officials, and even bank tellers (due to financial abuse of older adults). Some other professionals frequently mandated across the states include substance abuse counselors, probation or parole officers (Child Welfare Information Gateway, 2010), animal control or humane officers, court-appointed special advocates, and members of the clergy. Some states also mandate commercial film or photograph processors. These mandates are critical to protecting the overall welfare of people who are oftentimes vulnerable and unable to defend themselves. At the time of the writing, a former Los Angeles-area elementary school teacher has been charged with lewd acts on children; he was turned in to the police by a local film processor who gave authorities over 40 photographs of the man engaged in illegal actions with several children.

The circumstance under which a mandatory reporter must make a report does vary from state to state. Typically though, the report must be made when the reporter suspects or has reasons to believe that abuse or neglect has occurred or has knowledge of such abuse. Through the U.S. Department of Health and Human Services, (via the Administration for Children & Families, and U.S. Administration on Aging, via the National Center on Elder Abuse) state statutes can be individually researched.

In addition, the U.S. Food and Drug Administration (FDA) mandate's the reporting of industry regarding adverse events associated with nonprescription (over the counter) drug products and dietary supplement, as dictated by the Dietary Supplement and Nonprescription Drug Consumer Protection Act, signed by President Bush in 2006. On a side note, the FDA encourages consumers to be proactive participants in their safety and protection and offers the MedWatch website where consumers and health professionals can voluntarily file reports related to serious adverse events, product quality problems, product use errors, or therapeutic failure suspected to be associated with the use of an FDA-regulated drug, medical device, dietary supplement, or cosmetic.

Melanie Horn Mallers

See also: Consumer Product Safety Commission (CPSC); Department of Health and Human Services (HHS); Estate Planning; Food and Drug Administration (FDA); Older Americans Act (OAA); Social Services

References and Additional Readings

Child Welfare Information Gateway. (n.d.). State statutes search. Retrieved from http://www.childwelfare.gov/systemwide/laws_policies/state/

Kanel, K. (2008). *An overview of the human services.* USA: Wadsworth, Cengage Learning.

National Center on Elder Abuse. (2011). Analysis of state adult protective services laws. Retrieved from http://www.ncea.aoa.gov/Main_Site/Find_Help/APS/Analysis_State_Laws.aspx

Mann, Horace

Horace Mann is known as one of the most dedicated and aggressive educator reformers in America. He was born on May 4, 1796, in Franklin, Massachusetts. He was the youngest son of a farming family and did not start attending school regularly until he was 20 years old. Horace had no intentions of attending college when he first began his schooling. A teacher was able to motivated him and help him see that college was a possibility for him. At the age of 23 Horace graduated from Brown University as the class valedictorian and at 25 he attended law school in Connecticut. In his career as a lawyer Horace focused on issues that were the most important to him, education and public charities. He felt that America's greatest need was to educate children and young adults. Horace believed that the best way to set children on positive pathways and to become productive members of society was to provide them with education. In 1827, is began to serve in the Massachusetts House of Representatives and in 1834 moved to the Massachusetts State Senate. He led the movement that desired to create an organized and common system of education across the state of Massachusetts. He hoped by having a more uniform and standardized public schooling system would help even out the chances of men to move up in society. Horace believed that children were being left out of education and public schools were not receiving the financial help that is required to provide a quality education. In 1837, Horace was elected to be the first secretary of the new board of education. While serving as secretary he took a trip visiting all the schools in Massachusetts. While on this trip he noticed the lack of uniformity among the curriculum being taught to children and the lack of training and education teachers had. Horace developed schools for teachers so they could receive professional training and have better methods for maintaining a classroom. In the later years of his life Horace Mann served in the U.S. Congress and became the president of Antioch University. He died on August 2, 1859, at 63.

Horace Mann is one of America's first and most aggressive education reformers. He placed value on the education of children and setting them on paths to become productive members of society. Current influences that resulted from Horace's work are the value of public education for children, the value of professionally trained and educated teachers, and state-directed curriculums that are uniform from school to school in a state.

Jayna Seidel

See also: Activism; Department of Education (ED); Social Services; Social Welfare

References and Additional Readings

Groen, M. (2008). The Whig party and the rise of common schools, 1837–1854: Party and policy reexamined. *American Educational History Journal, 35*(2), 251–260.

Peterson, P. (2010). *Saving schools: From Horace Mann to virtual learning.* Cambridge, UK: Belknap Press of Harvard University Press.

Winship, E. (2006). *Horace Mann: The educator.* Boston, MA: Kessinger Publishing.

Material Safety Data Sheets (MSDS)/ Safety Data Sheets (SDS)

The Hazard Community Standard (HCS) of the Occupational Safety and Health Administration (OHSA) requires that Material Safety Data Sheets (MSDS), soon to be Safety Data Sheets (SDS), be provided by the manufacturer of chemicals to purchasers. These sheets are the beginning of a chain of information, including training and labeling, designed to inform users of chemicals or personnel who may encounter the chemicals in an emergency situation (accidental release/spills, fires, etc.) of safety and health hazards. The chain may include manufacturers and employees making products from chemicals, those transporting the chemicals or the products, and consumers, whether in a commercial, institutional, or home setting. Workers manufacturing a cleaning product or transporting tons of a cleaning product from manufacturer to retailer encounter different levels of health and safety hazards because of the quantity of chemical exposure compared to the consumer purchasing a single container or package of the product.

The SDS, training to work safely with the chemical, and product labeling for safe use are the three components reflected in the HCS. The information from the SDS is communicated to consumers via product labels indicating ingredients, uses, and warnings. Consumers have access to SDS on manufacturers' websites, which detail technical information and data not on the product label. A high level of consumer literacy is needed to understand the implications of concentration levels and exposure limits. (A drop in a swimming pool or a drop in a water glass? Does product testing on animals really apply to skin irritants in humans?) Consumers must recognize the information is dynamic as manufacturers change product ingredients and concentrations; manufacturers may have many different formulations of what is considered the same product (laundry detergent, tooth paste, deck/porch stain).

Though the final rule is in modification until 2015, information in the following categories are required by manufacturers:

- Identification—product; its uses/use restrictions; manufacturer's contact information
- Identification of hazards—classification of chemical (e.g., irritant); signal word (danger or warning); pictogram; toxicity
- Composition/ingredients—chemical and common name; percentages of ingredients classified as hazards
- First aid—necessary actions by route of exposure (skin contact, ingestion); acute and delayed symptoms; medical/treatment if necessary
- Fire-fighting—suitable and unsuitable actions; special gear/equipment
- Accidental release—precautions/actions if a spill/leak; containment and clean-up
- Handling and storage—precautions and conditions of safe storage (locked up, well ventilated)
- Exposure controls/personal protection—limits for exposure; protective equipment
- Physical and chemical properties—color; odor; boiling point; pH; flash point; etc.
- Stability and reactivity—possible reactions; conditions to avoid
- Toxicology information—likely routes of exposure (skin, eyes, inhalation, ingestion), symptoms; effects; measure of toxicity
- Ecological information (nonmandatory)—harm to water, soil, air; degradability
- Disposal (nonmandatory)—handling and disposal of waste, including contaminated packaging
- Transport (nonmandatory)—proper identification, hazard class
- Regulatory (nonmandatory)—safety, health, environmental regulations for the product
- Other information—including date of SDS or its last revision

In commercial and institutional settings where the product is manufactured or used, SDS are to be readily available to employees who are exposed or use the product. Training is to be provided.

The HCS was modified in March 2012 to conform to the United Nations' Globally Harmonized System of Classification and Labeling of Chemicals (GHS) to improve safety and consistency of standards (including labeling and pictograms). Besides the information indicated earlier, eight standard hazard pictograms are used—flame, flame over circle, exclamation point (irritant), exploding bomb, corrosion, gas cylinder, health hazard, and skull and crossbones. In addition, the diamond shaped signs with a pictogram depicting the hazards will appear on shipping containers, trucks, and railroad cars as part of the communication chain. The product label will include precautionary statements related to prevention of harm; response if exposed, storage, and disposal.

Products in everyday use as tooth paste, sanitizers, adhesives, degreasers, and others, are often perceived as safe, and may have an SDS. This is because one or more of the chemical ingredients are present in sufficient quantity to warrant precautions and/or the likelihood exists that the product may be used contrary to instructions (ingesting tooth paste, using a volatile cleaner in a nonventilated space, mixing products to get "better" results). SDS explain in more detail the hazards of product ingredients, which appear as chemical names on the product label. The SDS may provide information relevant to identifying allergens or sensitivities or safe disposal of a product. Thus, for the consumer who needs or wants to know about the products they use at home, on the job, or for a hobby, SDS provide vital information. SDS also are helpful in choosing products for particular uses consistent with objectives of avoiding certain chemicals (vinyl chloride), selecting for least toxicity (mercury), and reducing environmental hazards (low flammability).

Carole J. Makela

See also: Department of Labor (DOL); Environmental Protection Agency (EPA); Food Labeling; United Nations (UN)

References and Additional Readings

Nicol, A.M., Hurrell, A.C., Wahyuni, D., McDowall, W., & Chu, W. (2008). Accuracy, comprehensibility, and use of material safety data sheets: A review. *American Journal of Industrial Medicine, 51*(11), 861–876.

Ronald, J.W. (2012). Understanding a safety data sheet (SDS) in regards to process safety. *Procedia Engineering, 45,* 857–867.

McKinney–Vento Homeless Assistance Act

The McKinney–Vento Act was conceived through a series of events and circumstances concerning the homeless population. Beginning in 1986, the Homeless Persons' Survival Act was introduced to Congress. However, only a small portion of the act was enacted into law, which included long-term solutions, and preventative and emergency relief measures toward the homeless. In that same year, the Homeless Eligibility Clarification Act was adopted. This act removed permanent address requirements for Supplemental Security Income, Aid to Families with Dependent Children, Veterans Benefits, food stamps, and Medicaid. In addition, the act created an emergency shelter grant program as well as a transitional housing demonstration program. In 1987, the Urgent Relief for the Homeless Act was passed which aided emergency relief for shelter, food, mobile health care, and transitional housing.

In 2011 there were an estimated 636,017 people experiencing homelessness in the United States, and about 67,495 of them were veterans. The majority of the homeless populations live in emergency shelters or transitional housing but approximately 243,701 live unsheltered and on the streets. In 2003, about 39 percent of the homeless population is under the age of 18 while 25 percent of the population is between the ages of 25–34. Families with children are among the fastest growing homeless populations. A survey in 2006 on ethnicity found that 42 percent of the homeless population is African American, 38 percent is Caucasian, 20 percent is Hispanic, 4 percent is Native American, and 2 percent is Asian. This goes to show that people who are homeless do not fit just one specific description.

Source: National Coalition for the Homeless. (2009). Who is homeless? Retrieved from http://www.nationalhomeless.org/

Such events lead to the McKinney–Vento Act, which was signed into law by President Ronald Reagan on July 22, 1987. The act established the Interagency Council on the Homeless, now known as the Interagency Council on Homelessness, as well as 15 programs providing different services for the homeless. Before action from Congress, most programs that served the homeless were created, funded, and administered at the grassroots level.

Since then, the McKinney–Vento Act has been amended several times to address the increasing number of homeless women and children including added provisions for the rights to free and appropriate public education. Some of the changes allow children to attend their school of origin or the school of temporary residence. Children also received the right to transportation to the school and may enroll in the school without medical record or any of the like. Also children are automatically eligible for Title 1 services, which seek to improve academic achievement among those with disadvantages. School districts must also reserve a portion of Title 1A funds to make any adjustments to policies that may be barriers to homeless children, post information regarding rights of homeless children, and identify a McKinney–Vento Liaison to assist children.

The McKinney–Vento Act provided a foundation for the development of today's programs that provide interventions that minimize the nation's problem on homelessness. As an extension, on May 20, 2009, President Obama signed the Homelessness Emergency Assistance and Rapid Transition to Housing (HEARTH). HEARTH changed the definition of homelessness and chronic homelessness, increased resources and created an emphasis on performance. The Housing Choice Voucher Program Section 8 assists low-income families, the elderly, and disabled persons to afford decent, safe, and sanitary housing. Recipients of the voucher are allowed to choose any residence that fits the requirements of the program. Through its various efforts, the McKinney–Vento Act has opened a gateway to those less fortunate in our society.

Olivia Zavala

See also: Activism; Commission on Civil Rights; Department of Education (ED); Community Mental Health Centers (CMHC) Act; Department of Veterans Affairs (VA); Poverty Guidelines; Social Services; Social Welfare

References and Additional Readings

Department of Housing and Urban Development. (2013a). Homeless emergency assistance and rapid transition to housing (HEARTH) Act. Retrieved from http://www.hudhre.info/hearth

Department of Housing and Urban Development. (2013b). Housing choice vouchers fact sheet. Retrieved from http://portal.hud.gov/hudportal/HUD?src=/topics/housing_choice_voucher_program_section_8

Department of Housing and Urban Development. (2013c). McKinney–Vento Act. Retrieved from http://portal.hud.gov/hudportal/HUD?src=/program_offices/comm_planning/homeless/lawsandregs/mckv

Indiana Department of Education. (2012). McKinney–Vento Homeless. Retrieved from http://www.doe.in.gov/student-services/mckinney-vento-homeless

School of Education: Project Hope—Virginia (2012). *History of the McKinney Act*. Retrieved from http://education.wm.edu/centers/hope/resources/mckinneyact/index.php

Mechanic's Lien. *See* Contract Law

Mediation

Simply defined, mediation is any force outside of a particular conflict that assists with negotiation, resolution, or transformation of that conflict. For this introduction, mediation will be seen as facilitated discussion and problem solving that is fair to all participants.

If all parties to a conflict agree, a third-party individual, group, organization, or state, or the representatives of these entities not involved in the conflict and often described as impartial, can intervene. Party, or consumer self-determination, is the fundamental premise underlying contemporary mediation—at least as it is practiced and promoted within the United States. In other words, mediation is a voluntary and non-coercive process. Even when courts mandate mediation, most professional mediators agree that ethically no one can be forced to participate in mediation. Recommended in response to a court mandate is meeting with the mediator to educate oneself about the mediation process and that particular mediator. The consumer must decide whether participation would serve the consumer's interests.

Consumers can access the National Mediation Board, an independent U.S. federal agency, which in part provides programs for labor-management dispute resolution especially among railroad and airline industries. They oversee claims or charges regarding unions, government and other industries, as well as monitor union elections.

See the National Mediation Board at http://www.nmb.gov/

Consumers Beware

The growing popularity of facilitative mediation, whereby parties are empowered to come together, make their decisions through consensus building, and take responsibility for the consequences, is impossible to ignore. Consumers should be aware that when surveyed, corporations have picked mediation as their favorite dispute resolution mechanism as it is generally the least costly of responses to consumer complaint. It also is informal without legal requirements and allows corporations to resolve complaint behind closed doors without public record or scrutiny apart from the consumers intimately involved in the process. If parties to a mediation agree to confidentiality, all matters discussed in the mediation must be kept private.

Overseeing and Safeguarding Interests

On the other hand, a consumer is free to reject mediation and end participation at any point. Voluntary self-determination means that all parties to mediation, including the consumer, are the ultimate and deciding authorities for what happens during the mediation. Consumers should never feel pressured during a mediation. If consumers do not feel capable of strongly representing their interests and, for example, are prone to accommodating to more powerful parties or feel vulnerable to deceit or exploitation by the other party, mediation will not be the appropriate choice for resolving their complaint.

When consumers are not familiar with mediation and educated about its ethical and pragmatic ideals, they are ill equipped to safeguard their interests. Parties to mediation with the most power like corporate and government representatives often have the advantage of being familiar with mediation. Hopefully, they do not exploit consumer ignorance to their advantage by, as one instance, not sharing information vital to decision making that would be disclosed during a quality legal proceeding. The consumer cannot necessarily rely on the mediator to ensure party integrity. If legal rights are involved in a mediation, a consumer is well advised to consult with a trusted lawyer who has expertise in their respective unresolved issues.

Optimally, a consumer's mediation will honor the ethical principles of mediation described here. Unlike law, social work, medicine, and other professions, mediators are not licensed. Therefore, if a mediator fails to educate consumers about these ethical principles, or fails to exercise them, the consumer will not have the recourse present with the ethical code violations of licensed professionals. While there may be other legal grounds present in a particular situation, unless consumers are represented by lawyers in mediation, generally consumers who are parties to mediation must be prepared to scrutinize the ethical integrity of their mediation process by themselves.

Mediation can be abused and exploited due to its informal and private nature. If the mediator hired does not ask parties to sign an agreement promising good faith participation and disclosure of all information vital to making a sound and sustainable decision regarding a dispute's resolution, consumers are advised to propose and insist on such an agreement before agreeing to participate in a mediation.

Consumers must also be aware that once they sign an agreement made in mediation, they are bound by its terms like any contract. The consumer is free to contest the agreement in a court of law based on contract law. Nevertheless, if a consumer has any reluctance to sign a particular agreement, whether proposed by the mediator or a party, s/he must negotiate the requisite changes in the agreement. If this is not possible, consumers are advised to consult with trusted lawyers, once again with necessary expertise, before signing a mediation agreement.

True Impartiality

Ethically, mediators are asked to be truly impartial—a rarely seen or experienced role. Abraham Lincoln's role with slavery in the United States is a widely revered example that models requisite impartiality. If political friendship had been his priority, Lincoln may have allowed states to spread slavery. If he had seen the judicial system as sacred, slavery would have remained. Lincoln's ability to act with independent integrity under pressure from powerful interests provides an important example for mediators.

Key to impartiality and mediation's fairness is the mediator's ability and commitment to balance power between parties. Otherwise, the mediation is seen as unfairly showing preference toward the more powerful. Ethical mediators are advised to withdraw from unfair mediations. When a mediator is regularly employed by a more powerful party, at the very least they should be disclosing their past relationship and potential conflict of interest so the consumer party can decide whether the mediator is capable of acting impartially. One way parties to mediation can assess mediator impartiality is by noticing the particulars of how they treated. All parties should feel they are being treated equally when introduced, encouraged, and recognized. Parties should receive relatively equal opportunities to fully express concerns. All parties should hear the mediator address their concerns. Mediation, at its best, facilitates equal and inclusive decision making. Consumers must select mediators capable of doing this.

Nancy D. Erbe

See also: Arbitration; Freedom of Information Act (FOIA); Ombuds Offices; Small Claims Court; Whistleblowing

References and Additional Readings

Davies, J., & Kaufman, E. (2002). *Second track citizens' diplomacy: Concepts and techniques for conflict transformation.* Lanham, MD: Rowman & Littlefield.

Erbe, N. D. (2006). Appreciating mediation's global role in promoting good governance. *Harvard Negotiation Law Review, 11,* 355–419.

Erbe, N. D. (2011). *Negotiation alchemy.* Berkeley, CA: Public Policy Press.

Medicaid

Medicaid is a public insurance program that provides free or low-cost health insurance coverage for individuals with low income and resources who meet certain eligibility requirements, including children, pregnant women, parents, the elderly, and individuals with disabilities. As the largest program in the federal government's public assistance programs, Medicaid is the single largest healthcare program in the United States and provides services for about 60 million people at some point during the year. The Medicaid program was enacted in the legislation that created the Medicare program: the Social Security Amendments of 1965.

Before the law creating Medicaid was passed, healthcare services for the most vulnerable populations in society were mainly provided through a patchwork of programs sponsored by state and local governments, charities, and community hospitals. In 1965, Congress adopted several approaches to improve access to health care among the elderly, and also decided to provide coverage for other groups, such as families with children present, those who are blind, and disabled individuals.

Medicaid generally provides three types of healthcare coverage. The first type provides health insurance for low-income families with children present and those with disabilities. The second type provides long-term care for the elderly and disabled, and the third type provides supplemental coverage for low-income individuals who are Medicare beneficiaries so they can

President Lyndon B. Johnson signing the Medicare program into law on July 30, 1965. (Lyndon B. Johnson Library)

receive services not covered by Medicare. Since its inception, the enrollment and expenditures of Medicaid have grown significantly.

The Medicaid program is a joint federal–state program, and states are required to cover certain population groups, which are called mandatory eligibility groups, in order to participate. States have the option to cover additional groups (optional eligibility groups) and can apply to the Centers for Medicare and Medicaid Services to expand health coverage beyond these groups. Some states also have additional "state only" programs to provide medical assistance for certain low-income people who are not eligible for Medicaid.

The eligibility criteria for Medicaid are set by states within federal minimum standards. Individual states establish their own eligibility standards, benefits packages, payment rates, and program administration while following the broad federal guidelines. Thus, there are 56 different Medicaid programs in the United States, with one for each state, territory, and the District of Columbia. Many states have expanded coverage above the federal minimums, particularly for children. The eligibility for individuals in many groups is based on income in relation to a percentage of the federal poverty level (FPL), which is updated annually. In addition to income, most states also base eligibility on personal resources or assets. Some individuals with low income must spend down their assets in order to qualify for Medicaid. Income standards for some groups are based on the income or other nonfinancial criteria that are used as standards for other government programs, such as the Supplemental Security Income (SSI) program. Individuals must satisfy federal and state requirements regarding residency, immigration status, and documentation of U.S. citizenship in order to be eligible for Medicaid.

Benefits

The federal guidelines for administering Medicaid are broad, and include mandatory benefits and optional benefits. States are responsible for establishing and administering their own Medicaid programs, and determine the type, amount, duration, and scope of services provided for residents. States are required to cover the mandatory benefits established by the federal government, which include (among others): inpatient and outpatient hospital services; early and periodic screening, diagnostic, and treatment services; nursing facility services; home health services; laboratory and X-ray services; family planning services; and transportation to medical care. Optional benefits include (among others): prescription drugs, physical therapy, occupational therapy, podiatry services, dental services, dentures, eyeglasses, and hospice.

Eligibility Groups

All states are currently required to provide Medicaid coverage to certain eligibility groups. States are required to provide Medicaid to individuals who meet the requirements of the Aid to Families with Dependent Children program that went into effect in 1996. States must provide Medicaid to certain pregnant women and children defined in terms of family income and resources. Recipients of foster care and adoption assistance are also mandatory recipients of Medicaid. States must provide Medicaid to low-income Medicare beneficiaries, and are also generally required to provide Medicaid to recipients of SSI.

Pregnant Women

In the United States, only 60 percent of births are not financed by Medicaid. For pregnant women covered by Medicare, their coverage includes prenatal care as well as care throughout the pregnancy, labor, and delivery. Medicaid also provides coverage for perinatal care for 60 days postpartum. States can offer Medicaid coverage to pregnant women who are at or exceed 185 percent of the FPL and most states have elected to do so. Some states also offer programs allowing pregnant women who have income that exceeds the eligibility threshold to spend down to the eligibility limit if their healthcare expenses associated with the pregnancy are sufficiently high. Pregnant women are eligible for Medicaid until the end of the calendar month in which the 60th day after the pregnancy ended falls, even if their income changes. States may limit coverage for pregnant women to certain pregnancy-related services or can provide them with full Medicaid coverage.

Children

Children account for about half of those enrolled in the Medicaid program. The federal government has established minimum guidelines for Medicaid eligibility for children, with states having the option to expand coverage beyond the minimum threshold. Most states provide Medicaid to children in families with incomes above the minimum of 100 percent of the FPL. Children in families that have higher incomes can sometimes qualify for Medicaid if the children are in a mandatory Medicaid eligibility group or are in optional eligibility groups that a state may choose to cover. Infants born to pregnant women who are recipients of Medicaid on the date of delivery, called "deemed newborns," are automatically eligible for Medicaid. Coverage under the Medicaid program then continues until the child's first birthday. Citizenship documentation for the infant is not required. All children from birth to age 6 in a family with income up to 133 percent of the FPL and children age 6–18 with family incomes up to 100 percent are eligible for Medicaid. Also eligible are certain children in the foster care system or an adoption assistance program as well as certain children with disabilities. In the Medicaid system, all enrolled children are entitled to a comprehensive set of healthcare services that is known as Early and Periodic Screening, Diagnosis, and Treatment (EPSDT).

Parents and Caretaker Relatives

Parents or other caretaker relatives with low income are eligible for Medicaid coverage if their income meets minimum eligibility levels. The eligibility levels for parents and other caretaker relatives vary from state to state. Parents can also be eligible for Medicaid if they are medically needy or if they participate through Transitional Medical Assistance. States have the option to cover parents with incomes above federal minimum levels and many states do so.

Individuals with Disabilities

Medicaid provides healthcare coverage to nearly 9 million individuals under the age of 65 who have disabilities. This includes individuals who are employed or who wish to be employed. Federal law includes mandatory coverage as well as optional coverage for those who have disabilities. In most states, being eligible for the SSI program makes an individual automatically eligible to be covered by Medicaid, but some states are more restrictive in regards to eligibility than the guidelines used for SSI. Those who are not receiving SSI but seek Medicaid coverage because of a disability must show that their impairment does not allow them to perform "substantial gainful activity" for at least 12 months. After it is determined that there is a disability, specific income and asset requirements must be met in order to be enrolled in the program. Disabled individuals who meet the Medicaid eligibility requirements are able to receive all services that are considered medically necessary by a provider.

Other Adults Who Do Not Have Dependent Children

Currently, there is no federal requirement for states to provide healthcare coverage to adults who do not have dependents and are not disabled or elderly. About half of states do provide some coverage to these groups through federal waivers or programs funded by the state. States have the option to provide "medically needy programs," and many states do. Individuals who have significant healthcare requirements but do not meet the Medicaid income guidelines can become eligible for Medicaid by spending a proportion of their income that exceeds their state's "medically needy income standard." If eligible, Medicaid pays for services exceeding the amount spent to meet the medically needy income standard. More than one half of states use spend-down programs.

States can also elect to provide Medicaid healthcare coverage for some women who need breast or cervical cancer treatment. Qualifying under this option requires a woman to be screened by the Centers for Disease Control and Prevention's (CDC) National Breast and Cervical Cancer Early Detection Program, be found to have breast or cervical cancer, be under age 65, and be uninsured.

Some states also provide Medicaid healthcare coverage for low-income individuals infected with tuberculosis if they are not eligible for Medicaid based on other criteria. Individuals in this group are able to access services such as physician's services, laboratory and X-ray services, and case management services.

Dual Eligibility for Medicaid and Medicare

The Medicaid program provides healthcare coverage to nearly 5 million low-income elderly individuals, with almost all of these individuals also enrolled in Medicare. Medicaid also provides coverage to nearly 4 million people who have disabilities and are enrolled in Medicare. More than 17 percent of all Medicaid enrollees are enrolled in both Medicaid and Medicare. Elderly individuals with limited income and assets sometimes receive assistance from Medicaid to pay for medical expenses as well as services not covered by Medicare, such as nursing facility care for extended periods. If an individual has healthcare coverage through both Medicare and Medicaid, Medicare pays first and Medicaid pays the difference.

Prescription Drugs

Although coverage of prescription drugs is an optional benefit under federal Medicaid law, all states currently provide outpatient prescription drug coverage. The rules for Medicaid give states the ability to promote the cost-effective use of prescription drugs through out-of-pocket charges. For example, states can establish different copayments for generic drugs versus brand name drugs or for drugs on a preferred drug list in order to encourage the use of lower cost drugs. States can also establish different copayments for drugs sold in a pharmacy and mail order drugs. Copayments may also vary for different people depending on income.

Patti J. Fisher

See also: Americans with Disabilities Act (ADA); Health and Healthcare; Medicare; Poverty Guidelines; Social Security; Social Services; Social Welfare

References and Additional Readings

Department of Health and Human Services. (2000). A profile of Medicaid. Retrieved from http://www.cms.gov/Research-Statistics-Data-and-Systems/Statistics-Trends-and-Reports/TheChartSeries/downloads/2tchartbk.pdf

The Henry J. Kaiser Family Foundation. (2011). A Profile of Medicaid Managed Care Programs in 2010: Findings from a 50-state survey. In *Kaiser Commission on Medicaid and the Uninsured*. Retrieved from http://www.kff.org/medicaid/8220.cfm

The Henry J. Kaiser Family Foundation. (2013). Medicaid facts. In *Kaiser Commission on Medicaid and the Uninsured*. Retrieved from http://www.kff.org/about/kcmu.cfm

Medicaid. (2013). Program information. Retrieved from www.Medicaid.gov.

Medicare

The federal government has long had an interest in providing for those that are in need. In the health area it has established two major funds to assist Americans with their health needs. These two programs are Medicaid and Medicare. Medicaid is a federal–state health program for those with low income. Medicare insures older Americans (65 and older), as well as those with disabilities. The Department of Health and Human Services' Centers for Medicare and Medicaid Services (CMS) manages the Medicare program. Two trust funds, the Hospital Insurance (HI) trust fund (which pays for Part A benefits) and the Supplementary Medical Insurance (SMI) trust fund (which pays for Part B and Part D benefits) control the finances of Medicare. This entry covers Medicare as it is currently constituted.

A Brief History

Medicare was established in 1965 to provide affordable health insurance for the older adult population, regardless of income or health status. Before the creation of Medicare, approximately one-half of older adults (65 and older) had health insurance. The program has now expanded to include adults (under 65) with disabilities including those with end-stage renal disease.

Medicare funding has been an ongoing problem. This has lead to significant legislation in recent years. In 1997, the Balanced Budget Act of 1997 established the Health Care Financing Administrations that later were renamed the Centers for Medicare and Medicaid Services. These centers were charged to monitor Medicare so Congress would know if changes needed to be made to assure its financial viability. In late 2003, the Medicare Prescription Drug, Improvement, and Modernization Act was signed into law. This law again made some changes to the Medicare program to make Medicare more financially viable. However, this act also phased in Medicare Part D (officially starting January 1, 2006), the prescription drug portion of Medicare. Most recently, the Obama Administration orchestrated the passage of the Patient Protection and Affordable Care Act of 2010. Several provisions of the law were designed to reduce the cost of Medicare. One change was to decrease payments to privately managed Medicare Advantage plans to align their medical payment rates more closely to the medical payment rates of traditional Medicare. Congress also reduced annual increases in payments to physicians and to hospitals that serve low-income patients.

The Medicare Trustees submit a yearly report. The 2012 report predicts that the HI trust fund will be solvent through 2024. This means that in 2024, when HI trust fund reserves are depleted, current Medicare payroll tax contributions will still allow payment of doctor and hospital bills, but at a reduced rate of 87 percent.

Medicare is an expensive and controversial government program. With a significant portion of the American population aging (projected to be about 20 percent of the population by 2020), it is expected that ongoing legislative changes to Medicare will occur in an attempt to keep it financially viable.

Basic Features of Medicare

Medicare covers approximately 40.4 million older adults and 8.3 million Americans under 65 with disabilities. Around 19 percent of Medicare recipients also qualify for Medicaid. These Americans are called "dual eligibles." Table 28 summarizes the Medicare program.

Medicare Part A automatically enrolls Americans 65 and older if they or their spouse are entitled to social security benefits. Furthermore, those that are enrolled must have contributed payroll taxes on their wages for at least 10 years. The Medicare payroll tax is 1.45 percent on the wages from employers and employees (2.9 percent cumulatively). Unlike social security taxes, which are limited to income up to a certain level, Medicare taxes

Table 28 Medicare coverage and financing

Program Details	Hospital Insurance (HI) Trust Fund (Part A)	Supplementary Medical Insurance (SMI) Trust Fund (Part B and D)
Services covered	Inpatient hospital stays Skilled nursing facility stays Hospice care Home health visits	Part B: Physician visits, outpatient services, lab tests, medical supplies, home health services Part D: Prescription drugs
Major funding sources	Payroll taxes paid by workers and employers; interest earned on Trust Fund reserves; income taxes on part of social security benefits of upper income beneficiaries	Monthly premiums paid by beneficiaries; general revenues composed of federal income taxes; payments from states for premiums
Percent of Medicare spending in 2011	47%	Part B: 41% Part D: 12%

Source: Zainulbhai, S. and Goldberg, L. (2012, April). Medicare Finances: Findings of the 2012 Trustees Report. Retrieved from http://www.nasi.org/sites/default/files/research/Medicare_Finances_Findings_of_the_2012_Trustees_Report.pdf. Reprinted with permission from the National Academy of Social Insurance (NASI).

are collected on a worker's total wages. In 2011, the trustees disclosed that revenue from payroll taxes provided about 85 percent of the income for the HI trust fund. The remaining 15 percent is garnered from interest earned on the trust fund investments, as well as, income taxes on a portion of Social Security. Payroll taxes for Medicare are not levied against returns, dividends, or other passive investments.

The SMI trust fund consists of two separate accounts. The first account, for Part B, funds physician and other outpatient health services, while Part D pays for outpatient prescription drugs. Enrollment and monthly premiums are required for those beneficiaries who choose to participate in Part B or Part D. Part B premiums are fixed such that the total amount paid by beneficiaries covers approximately 25 percent of Part B expenditures. In 2012, beneficiaries pay a fixed monthly premium of $99.90. High-income enrollees (individuals with annual incomes more than $85,000 and married couples with annual incomes more than $170,000) pay a higher premium that ranges from $139.90 to $319.70 per month, depending on income. An additional premium (averaging $31) is required for Part D coverage (for prescription drugs). The cost of Part B and Part D not covered by premiums is funded by revenues from income taxes paid by taxpayers of all ages.

Cost sharing on selected benefits occurs in the form of deductibles and coinsurance for Medicare beneficiaries. Health services not covered by Medicare, which include routine dental care, eyeglasses, hearing aids, and most long-term services must be paid by Medicare beneficiaries. For dual eligible beneficiaries (those qualifying for Medicare and Medicaid), Medicaid pays for a portion of Medicare premiums and cost sharing. Medicaid also offers some benefits that are not covered by Medicare, such as long-term services.

Medicare Supplement Insurance (Medigap Policies)

Many, but not all, healthcare services and supplies are covered by traditional Medicare. A Medicare Supplement Insurance policy can help cover healthcare costs not covered by traditional Medicare, such as copayments, coinsurance, and deductibles. These Medicare Supplemental Insurance policies are sold by private companies, and often referred to as Medigap policies.

Certain Medigap policies will cover items not covered by traditional Medicare such as medical care when traveling outside the United States. If traditional Medicare is in effect, and a Medigap policy is purchased, Medicare will pay its share of the Medicare-approved amount for covered healthcare costs. Then, the Medigap policy pays its share. To get a Medigap policy, a consumer must first have Medicare Part A and Part B. Every month the consumer must pay the premiums for the Medigap policy in addition to the Medicare Part B premium. Also, a Medigap policy only covers one person so each spouse must get his or her own policy. It is also important to decide whether to get drug coverage from a private company that only sells Medicare Part D or through a Medigap company.

Each Medigap policy follows federal and state laws that protect consumers; policies must clearly indicate "Medicare Supplement Insurance." Insurance companies may sell consumers a "standardized" policy which, in most states, is identified by letters. All policies offer the same basic benefits, however, some companies offer additional benefits for consumers. It is wise to shop carefully for a policy that best fits individual needs.

Medicare Advantage Plans

A Medicare Advantage Plan is a type of Medicare health plan that is sold by a private company contracting with Medicare to provide all Part A and Part B benefits. Medicare Advantage Plans include Health Maintenance Organizations (HMOs), Preferred Provider Organizations (PPOs), Private Fee-for-Service Plans, Special Needs Plans, and Medicare Medical Savings Account Plans. Most Medicare Advantage Plans provide for prescription drug coverage. Medicare Advantage Plans also may offer additional coverage for programs relating to vision, hearing, dental, and overall wellness.

How Do Medicare Advantage Plans work?

Medicare pays a fixed monthly to the companies offering Medicare Advantage Plans, however, the companies must follow Medicare rules. However, a Medicare Advantage Plan may charge different out-of-pocket costs and have different rules for obtaining services (e.g., when a referral to see a specialist is needed).

Some consumers like Medicare Advantage Plans because these private plans take care of all the paper work. The elderly patients simply go to the doctor, show their Medicare Advantage card, and never see a doctor's bill. A drawback of Medicare Advantage Plans is that they can be more expensive than regular Medicare and they often have more extensive rules covering ability to get service. These rules often change each year. Also, Medigap policies can't work with Medicare Advantage Plans because the Medicare Advantage Plan services overlap with the services provided by Medigap programs. (Note: currently, about 75 percent of Medicare enrollees have traditional Medicare and about 25 percent of Medicare enrollees have a Medicare Advantage plan.)

Out-of-Pocket Costs for Medicare

While Medicare provides access to a variety of medical services, these are not "no cost" services to beneficiaries. For 2012, the per person costs for the Medicare Part A deductible was $1,156. For Part B, the per person standard monthly premium, covering physician and most other outpatient services, was $99.90 while the Part B deductible was $140. The monthly per person premium for Part D prescription drug coverage is approximately $40 on average; coverage varies depending on the drug plan selected. For couples, the standard Part B premium and an average-priced drug plan have premiums that total approximately $1,700 for an individual; $3,400 for a couple. For Medicare Parts A and B, the deductibles still equate to $1,300. There would also be a potential for greater costs from coinsurance costs for certain medical procedures. Medicare pays 80 percent of approved charges and the consumer pays the other 20 percent of the approved charges.

Premiums alone (for both Medicare and supplemental insurance) account for the largest share of a Medicare beneficiaries' out-of-pocket health spending. In 2006, Medicare enrollees spent roughly 16 percent of their income on out-of-pocket expenses (an amount that rises dramatically with age, poor health status, and low income). Furthermore, many seniors, even those with supplemental insurance, do not have any coverage for long-term services, dental care, and hearing appliances. This means that these services are unaffordable or that paying for them requires even larger out-of-pocket expenditures.

Conclusions

Paying for medical costs after retirement is an important financial decision and research is necessary to make an informed decision. The most basic parts of this decision have been discussed earlier, but additional education and research is always recommended.

David L. Schult

See also: Administration on Aging (AoA); Department of Health and Human Services (HHS); Health and Health Care; Medicaid; Older American's Act (OAA); Patient Protection and Affordable Care Act (PPACA); Social Services; Social Welfare

References and Additional Readings

Board of Trustees. (2012). 2012 Annual Report of the Board of Trustees, Federal Hospital Insurance and Federal Supplementary Medical Insurance Trust Funds. Washington, DC: Centers for Medicare & Medicaid Services.

Centers for Medicare and Medicaid Services (CMS). (2012a). Medicare Advantage Plans—How do Medicare Advantage Plans work? Washington, DC. Retrieved from http://www.medicare.gov

Centers for Medicare and Medicaid Services (CMS). (2012b). Medicare and you 2013. Washington, DC. Print.

Kaiser Family Foundation. (2010). Medicare chartbook. Washington, DC. Retrieved from http://www.kff.org/medicare/upload/8103.pdf

Komisar, H., Cubanski, J., Dawson, L., & Tricia N. (2012). Key issues in understanding the economic and health security of current and future generations of seniors. In *Policy Brief*. Washington, DC, Kaiser Family Foundation. Retrieved from http://www.kff.org/medicare/

National Academy of Social Insurance (NASI). (1999). Medicare and the American Social Contract. Washington, DC. Retrieved from http://www.nasi.org/sites/default/files/research/med_report_soc_contract.pdf

National Academy of Social Insurance (NASI). (2012). Medicare Finances: Findings of the 2012 Trustees Report. Washington, DC. Retrieved from http://www.nasi.org/sites/default/files/research/

Minimum Wage

The federal minimum wage provisions are contained in the Fair Labor Standards Act (FLSA). The first federal minimum wage was effective on October 24, 1938, in the amount of 25 cents. The federal minimum wage is currently $7.25 per hour effective July 24, 2009. The minimum wage does not increase automatically. Congress must pass a bill which the president signs into law in order for the minimum wage to increase.

Minimum Wage and State Laws

Numerous states have adopted minimum wage laws, with some of the state laws providing greater employee protections. Employers are required to comply with both state and federal laws. For cases in which an employee falls under both state and federal minimum wage laws, the employee is entitled to receive the greater minimum wage of the two. The highest minimum wage, as of January 2012 is in Washington, at $9.04, with Connecticut, District of Columbia, Illinois, and Nevada at $8.25, and California and Massachusetts at $8.00.

Employees

The U.S. Department of Labor reports that the minimum wage law is applicable to employees of businesses having gross volume of sales or business transactions of at least $500,000. The law also applies to smaller firm employees in cases in which the employees are engaged in interstate commerce or are engaged in the production of goods for commerce (e.g., workers in transportation or communications or who regularly use the mails or telephones for interstate communications). Interstate commerce is defined as work involving the movement of persons or things internationally or interstate. Employees also falling under the FLSA include, but are not limited to security guards and maintenance workers in close relation with the interstate activities; workers of agencies from the federal, state, or local levels;

and workers at hospitals and schools. The FLSA contains a number of exemptions from the minimum wage that may apply to some workers such as babysitters on a casual basis, newspaper delivery persons, and those who are paid on a salary basis. Some minimum wage exceptions apply in conditions surrounding workers with disabilities, full-time students, workers age 20 and younger in the first 90 consecutive calendar days of work, employees who receive tips, and student learners.

Workers with Disabilities

According to the U.S. Department of Labor, special wages may apply to workers with disabilities. Wages are required to be commensurate with individual productivity, regardless of limitations, and in proportion to wages paid to nondisabled employees performing essentially the same work (quantity, type, and quality) in the same geographic area.

Full-Time Students

The law also pertains to full-time students who are employed in retail or service stores, agriculture, or colleges and universities. The U.S. Department of Labor notes that an employer hiring a student may receive a certificate from the Department of Labor allowing the student to be paid not less than 85 percent of the minimum wage. This certificate provides limits on the hours that the student works (8 hours maximum per day, 20 hours maximum per week during school, and 40 hours maximum per week when school is out of session). The law also requires the employer to comply with all child labor laws. After the students graduate or leave school permanently, they must be paid $7.25 per hour effective July 24, 2009.

Young Workers Under the Age of 20

According to the U.S. Department of Labor (2012e), "a minimum wage of $4.25 per hour applies to young workers under the age of 20 during their first 90 consecutive calendar days of employment with an employer, as long as their work does not displace other workers. After 90 consecutive days of employment or the employee reaches 20 years of age, whichever comes first, the employee must receive a minimum wage of $7.25 per hour effective July 24, 2009."

Workers Who Receive Tips

In accordance with federal laws, an employer may pay a tipped employee not less than $2.13 an hour if that amount combined with tips equals at least the federal minimum wage, and the employee keeps all tips, and the employee regularly receives $30 a month or more in tips. If tips and wages (at least $2.13/hour) fail to equal the federal minimum hourly wage, the employer is required to make up the difference.

Student Learners

The law also applies to high school students (16 years old and older) who are participating in vocational education (shop courses). If an employer wishes to hire such a student, they must obtain a certificate from the Department of Labor allowing the student to earn wage of not less than 75 percent of the minimum wage, for the duration of time the student is enrolled in vocational education.

Violations

Every employer of employees subject to the Fair Labor Standards Act's minimum wage provisions must post, and keep posted, a notice explaining the act in a conspicuous place in all of their establishments so as to permit employees to readily read it. According to the U.S. Department of Labor employees may learn more information about filing an employer complaint by contacting the local Wage and Hour Division office, or by calling the program's toll-free help line. Furthermore, an employee is entitled to file a private law suit, typically for the past two years of back pay (three years of back pay is allowable for cases involving a willful violation). The law also provides for an equal amount as liquidated damages, court costs, and attorney's fees. Furthermore, it is a violation of the FLSA to fire, or discriminate against in any way, an employee for filing a complaint or for pursuing any legal action under the FLSA.

Martie Gillen

See also: Commission on Civil Rights; Department of Labor (DOL); Equal Employment Opportunity Commission (EEOC); Poverty Guidelines

References and Additional Readings

Department of Labor. (n.d.a). History of federal minimum wage rates under the Fair Labor Standards Act, 1938–2009. Retrieved from http://www.dol.gov/whd/minwage/chart.htm#.ULz99—I6Ag

Department of Labor. (n.d.b). How to file a complaint. Retrieved from http://www.dol.gov/wecanhelp/howtofilecomplaint.htm.

Department of Labor. (n.d.c). Fact sheet #14: Coverage under the Fair Labor Standards Act (FLSA). Retrieved from http://www.dol.gov/whd/regs/compliance/whdfs14.pdf

Department of Labor. (n.d.d). Minimum wages laws in the states. Retrieved from http://www.dol.gov/whd/minwage/america.htm

Department of Labor. (n.d.e). Wages and hours worked: Minimum wage and overtime pay. Retrieved from http://www.dol.gov/compliance/guide/minwage.htm

Mortgages

What is a mortgage? It really should be called a mortgage loan. It is a loan to purchase real estate in which the property itself serves as collateral. It is a very special loan that is larger and for a much longer period of time than any other loan that a consumer can have. In the current economic situation, the median home price for the country is just under $200,000 and a typical mortgage involves a 30-year repayment period.

A family in front of their new home. (iStockPhoto.com)

A Story about Unforeseen Mortgage Complications

A prospective homeowner moved to a new location to get a job. He rented at the new location and established himself in his new job (2 years). He checked out potential neighborhoods during this time period. He and his wife worked with one realtor but that person could not find anything they could afford. They found another realtor that was more interested in helping them. The realtor showed them several properties (4 months). They found a place that they liked and made an offer. The offer was rejected. They continued their search. They were surprised when two months later the first place contacted them saying their offer was now accepted. They entered the closing process (4 months). A few things in the house were found to be in error and the seller fixed those. They had several documents sent to them that they went through and had their lawyer go through. The day of closing arrived. Normally you just come in and sign everything and get the keys (about 1 hour). But there were a couple of documents that were presented at closing which were new. They reviewed these new documents (4 hours instead of the 1 hour expected). Near the very end of one of the last documents an extra $3,000 fee was mentioned. The people at closing reviewed the form and told this family why it was necessary. The family had been working on this transaction with a realtor and lawyer for several months and no one had ever mentioned that this home-to-be was not a townhouse, was not a condo (which is what everyone had called it), but was a PUD (Planned Unit Development) and would require some additional fees at closing. The couple could have walked away and would have had to start their long search process over. A lot of emotions were involved at this stage. Since the couple had done all the long hours of work on their finances they were able to understand the change and made a good decision, an informed decision, to go forward with the purchase. The point is that the perspective homeowner has the responsibility to do the investigative work and make an informed decision.

David L. Schult

A Brief History

To understand how mortgage loans have come to the point they are in now, it is helpful to review some history. From the beginning, the United States has had plenty of usable land for the population level. The first immigrants would earn or pay for their land and then they would build their own housing. As the nation was still expanding, there were several periods when the federal government offered settlers free land through Homestead Acts if the person would stay on the land and make improvements to the land. As the nation moved into the 1800s, a person might typically be required to make a 50 percent down payment and then have three to five years to pay off the mortgage. This system of 50 percent down and three too five years to pay off the mortgage continued with only minimal government intervention until the Great Depression. During the Great Depression the financial and mortgage systems collapsed and foreclosures soared. President Franklin D. Roosevelt promoted many policies to stimulate the economy. Several laws were passed during the 1930s to stem the number of foreclosures and stimulate the housing market. In 1934, the National Housing Act was passed. As a part of this act the Federal Housing Administration (FHA) was created to insure mortgage lenders against losses from default. This insurance would absorb the risk of the lenders so they were more willing to give people mortgages. FHA also developed the 30-year fixed-rate loan program, providing homeowners lower payments and more stabile payments for mortgage lenders. After World War II the government expanded this program to veterans. With this after-war stimulus the economy exploded with the housing market leading the way. The economy and the housing market did moderately well until the next "crisis." In the 1970s and early 1980s the economy experienced recession that had a harsh effect on the housing market. The government continued to support a system of federal involvement in buying up loans to put more money into the market and trying to relax the requirements for getting such loans. In the late 1990s there was a stock market crash and then in 2001, on September 11, there was a terrorist attack and the federal government and the Federal Reserve got very concerned that the economy might slip into a recession. Congress eased housing market regulations and the Federal Reserve took steps to keep interest rates low. After a mild slowdown, following the 9/11 attacks, the economy started a good recovery. These federal changes became especially beneficial to growth in the housing market, and it took off. By the mid-2000s these federal stimulus programs had gone too far. Too many high-risk loans had been written, too much deregulation had occurred, the Federal Reserve had propped up the market too much. By 2007, cracks in the mortgage market appeared and foreclosures started; the market unraveled. The credit markets were thrown into a tailspin and the housing market collapsed, causing the economy to fall into a recession.

What does this history demonstrate? There has always been enough land, feeding the American tradition of individual home ownership. The federal government promotes home ownership and if the housing market gets into trouble they often develop polices to promote more home ownership and intervene in the financial markets to prop them up. However, the federal government periodically over does their intervention and exacerbates problems.

Types of Mortgages

There are two major categories of loans. In the modern era the most common mortgage is the conventional mortgage. The conventional mortgage is a fixed-interest-rate, fixed-term, fixed payment mortgage loan. These types of loans are very popular because they are very predictable. Once the loan is written, the interest charge and the principle payment are the same each month for the entire loan. Very common loan periods that these mortgages come in are 15-year, 20-year, and 30-year lengths.

The next most common type of mortgage is an adjustable-rate mortgage (often referred to as an ARM). In this type of mortgage the interest rate fluctuates according to some specified financial index. As this index fluctuates, the mortgage interest rate is adjusted, usually only once a year. This means that when the interest rate adjusts, the monthly payment changes. Such loans usually start out with "teaser rates" 1 to 3 percentage points below the fixed mortgage rate. If it is a "good" ARM the mortgage would have interest-rate caps. This would include a cap on how much the interest rate could go up in one year (perhaps 2 percent) and a cap on how much the mortgage could go up over the life of the loan (perhaps 5 percent). This does not seem like a lot, but when considering a loan for $160,000 at 6 percent interest for 30 years, the monthly payment would start at $959.28 per month. If the interest rate over a 10-year period goes up the full 5 percent, the annual interest rate is nearly double. As a result, the new monthly payment is now nearly $1,300 per month. An additional $4,080 is paid per year under this scenario. Homeowners with ARMs should only sign up for such a loan after calculating the "worse case" scenario and making sure that the outcome is manageable.

Another "loan type" that is important to discuss is mortgage loans with special government subsidies. Governments do not really have money that they loan out but they offer insurance programs to encourage financial institutions to make additional loans. One of the important federal government programs is run by the Federal Housing Administration (FHA). FHA-insured loans can allow consumers to get a traditional mortgage for a good interest rate and with a lot less down. As of this writing, FHA loans require 3.5 percent down instead of current market down payments that could be anywhere from 10 to 20 percent.

Starting in 1980, there was financial market deregulation. Some of the laws allowing for financial market deregulation included specific standards for banks to increase banking services in poorer neighborhoods. The financial market deregulation has fostered an environment for the development of a wide variety of products. Most of these complicated alternative lending approaches were designed to keep monthly payments at the beginning of the loan as low as possible. Some of these additional types of loans are interest-only mortgages, graduated-payment mortgages, assumable mortgages, and growing-equity mortgages. A perspective home buyer should only take out a mortgage that they are very confident that they can repay.

"Reverse" Mortgages

A reverse mortgage, officially known as a home equity conversion mortgage (HECM), allows a homeowner who has turned 62 to borrow against the equity in a home that is fully (or close to fully) paid for. The elderly homeowner can borrow against the home's equity and receive the proceeds as a lump sum or a series of monthly payments. Unique with this loan is that the homeowner can continue living in the home. The mortgage does not have to be paid back until the last surviving owner sells the house, moves out permanently, or dies. When one of these events happens, the home becomes the property of the financial institution that loaned the money, not the owner or heirs. There are some traps with a reverse mortgage. To stay in the program consumers have to stay current on property taxes and homeowners insurance. HUD estimates that 8 percent of current reverse mortgages are in default. The amount of equity available depends on the homeowner's age, the property's value, and the current interest rate. Note that the financial industry controls two of these variables and the terms they control are not as good as the terms someone would get on a normal mortgage. Closing costs and other costs of writing these mortgages can be as high as $20,000. Many financial planners recommend renting a room in the house or selling the house and downsizing as better ways to take advantage of the home equity.

Personal Responsibility—Steps in Home Buying

As mentioned earlier, government agencies, since the 1930s, have been meddling in the housing market. Sometimes this interference was beneficial and sometimes (as in a recession) it had unfortunate results. As of this writing, the government was heavily involved in the housing market. It is the individual homeowner that must not take undue risks or follow inaccurate information that realtors, banks, or government officials might be promoting (Table 29).

Table 29 Home buying steps

1) <u>Get your finances in order:</u> This would include such things as cleaning up your credit history. Having a high credit score can save you thousands of dollars by helping you get the lowest possible interest rate. You also need to estimate all expected monthly housing costs. Online calculators and realtors can help you with such calculations. As you determine all of the monthly costs you need to make sure that you can make adjustments to your budget to accommodate these expenses.

2) <u>Prequalify for a mortgage loan.</u> You need to shop around among trusted financial institutions to find out who will offer you the best deal. You need to make sure, given your particular employment and financial situation, that you could afford the mortgage that you choose for the next thirty years. You should compare several lenders and mortgage brokers and weigh their offers carefully. When you have chosen the lender you wish to work with then they should tell you how much they would lend you for the purchase of a home (prequalification).

3) <u>Search for a home online and in person.</u> You need to decide on which features you want but which ones you could sacrifice. It is not just how many stories the house is or how many bedrooms it has. The old saying still holds. The three most important factors in buying a home are location, location, location. Is it in a safe place; is it in the right school district. Is it the right type of neighborhood for your family type. Is it in the rush of the city or the calm of a rural area. Is there plenty of room to expand the house in the future.

4) <u>Agree to terms with the seller.</u> Make an offer to the seller. You may offer the asking price or something less. Work with your realtor to help you with these negotiations. A realtor should know the market you are buying into and what prices similar houses sold for. When you have agreed on price, negotiate on closing costs and other issues. You need to have your lawyer go over the purchase contract to make sure it does not have any surprises and follows all local laws. Sign the purchase contract with the seller. Have the home inspected to assure that everything is in proper working order. You will need to put down some earnest money so that the seller knows you are serious. (If you or the seller later decide not to complete the transaction, you will get your earnest money back.) You may think that the house is now yours but not until your mortgage lender and several local government agencies have their say

5) <u>Formally apply for and obtain a mortgage loan.</u> You have already picked your preferred mortgage lender and they have prequalified you. When you formally apply for a mortgage loan the mortgage lender will look at all of your finances very completely. This process often takes one to two months to complete. They get in-depth employment and bank records to assure that you will be able to pay your mortgage each month. They also hire their own estimator and inspectors to make sure the house is worth what you are asking to borrow to buy it.

6) <u>Prepare for the closing.</u> Closing is the day you actually sign the paper work that will get you your mortgage money and complete all government paperwork needed for the change in ownership of the property. Preparing for this day is important. If the home inspectors found anything wrong, these problems need to be corrected before you move in. Normally it is the responsibility of the seller to make all corrections before you move in. You also need to make moving arrangements. You need to cancel any rental contract you might have as well as all of your utilities. You also need to set dates to have utilities activated at your new home. You need to make arrangements to have any upgrades (new carpets and drapes, etc.) made before you move in. And the new place. If you are moving to a new location across the country all of these arrangements may take weeks to arrange.

7) <u>Attend the closing.</u> At closing (or a week or two before) you need to look over all of the paperwork (and have your lawyer do the same) and correct any errors in the contract. You then sign you name and write the big checks and get the keys.

Buying a home is the biggest and most important financial decision consumers make in their lifetime. Consumers need to put in the work so that an informed decision is made. While this entry has outlined some of the most basic parts of mortgages, additional education and research is always suggested. Taking a personal finance class or reading a personal finance textbook can contribute to this education.

David L. Schult

See also: Banking; Debt Management; Department of Housing and Urban Development (HUD); Federal Housing Administration (FHA); Roosevelt, Franklin, D.; Foreclosures and Short Sales

References and Additional Readings

Department of Housing and Urban Development. (n.d.) Frequently asked questions about HUD's reverse mortgages. Retrieved from http://portal.hud.gov/hudportal/HUD?src=/program_offices/housing/sfh/hecm/rmtopten

Department of Housing and Urban Development. (2007). HUD historical background. Retrieved from http://www.hud.gov/offices/adm/about/admguide/history.cfm

Garman, E. T., & Forgue, R. E. (2012). *Personal finance* (11th ed.). Mason, OH: South-Western/Cengage.

Green, R. K., & Wachter, S. M. (2005). The American mortgage in historical and international context. *The Journal of Economic Perspectives, 19*(4), 93–114.

Reed, D. (2007). *Mortgage confidential: What you need to know that your lender won't tell you*. New York: American Management Association.

Multilevel Marketing and Pyramid Plans

Pyramids and Ponzi schemes are among of the most common and costly of consumer hazards. Millions of people are harmed each year. Pyramid fraud is seldom a one-time transaction. It more commonly involves ongoing payments by victims sometimes over years of time. Some victims become so entrapped in the fraud they take on the appearance and behavior of cult followers. Family members and friends of pyramid participants often report the continuous repetition of terms, words, and ideas that the scheme teaches or uses. These include slogans like "only losers quit and only quitters lose" or "fake it till you make it" or words like "exciting," "opportunity," or "unlimited." Some participants quit jobs and dropout of school, in the misguided belief in the wealth that has been promised by the fraud. By their design, pyramid and Ponzi schemes cause financial ruin to virtually all who join them. Yet, their promises to consumers of great rewards and profits have the power to win the fervent belief and loyalty of many victims. Some will divorce spouses who do not agree with their activity or neglect their children in pursuit of the fabled "success."

Yet, for all their power and widespread activity, few people understand even what pyramid and Ponzi schemes are, how they differ, how they operate, and how to identify them. This is not just a problem of public education. In the world of frauds, pyramid schemes occupy a special place. There are powerful reasons that consumers are lured by the millions into them, deceived and harmed when they are recruited and then dumbfounded as to the cause after they suffer losses.

- Pyramid schemes come in many disguises and under many different names.
- They are often introduced to victims by trusted friends or family members.
- The frauds employ confusing and misleading math projections regarding expansion and potential income, which many people cannot sort out or understand.
- There is no clear-cut legal *definition* of a pyramid scheme, beyond the basic elements. Therefore few people recognize a pyramid scheme even when they encounter them.
- Celebrities, politicians, and churches often are associated with schemes, giving them the appearance of integrity.
- Legality of pyramid schemes is an unsettled question. Companies that are accused of pyramid fraud argue they are legal. Lobbyists seek to weaken current laws against pyramid-selling schemes. Currently, there is no federal law in America that defines or outlaws pyramid schemes. Most state laws are seldom enforced.

One fact is clear and indisputable. Legal or not, and regardless of who promotes, supports or endorses the scheme, virtually all participants lose money in pyramid schemes. Only those at the very top can ever profit and only from the losses of all the others.

One law or one single court decision or one case study that would clarify consumer protection guidelines does not exist. A consumer's only true defense is to know and understand the nature and workings of pyramid schemes and Ponzis. Once the fundamentals of this form of fraud are grasped, a consumer can safely navigate the promoters' claims and denials, the solicitations by friends or relatives, the false testimonials of success, the claims of high income and miracle health products that blanket the Internet, and all the confusing rhetoric from lobbyists and lawyers.

Defining Pyramids and Ponzis

Pyramid and Ponzi schemes are frauds that make promises of profits or rewards to investors or participant that *cannot* and *will not* be fulfilled. The promised profits or rewards are claimed to be generated from sales or investments or the continued enrollment of new participants. Pyramids and Ponzis claim to offer the "opportunity" to make money, *a lot of money.* For that reason they are often called "opportunity" frauds. And because many pyramid schemes are disguised as businesses that offer an income opportunity by joining the business as a salesperson, they are usually included in the category of "business opportunity" fraud. In pyramid schemes, consumers are deceived into investing time and money into a business opportunity or an investment program that promoters claim is profitable and viable.

In fact, the promoters are merely transferring the investment money from later investors to earlier ones. They make exactly the same promise of income or reward to each new investor or participant, generating the continuous need for an ever-greater number of investors or salespeople, whose money will be transferred to the ones who joined earlier. Since it is impossible to recruit an unlimited number of investors, the promise of income cannot be fulfilled. The majority of participants will always be in the bottom ranks. Their money goes to the top but they do not have enough others below them whose money they could receive. The vast majority, therefore, never receive the promised rewards. For them, the "opportunity" becomes a lie. Only a tiny group at the top, usually the aggressive promoters, gain money, *fraudulently.* Pyramid schemes are called so because they are structured with large numbers of losing investors at the bottom whose money is siphoned to a small group at the peak.

Common Pyramid and Ponzi Schemes

The most famous and considered the largest Ponzi scheme in America was run by Wall Street financier Bernard Madoff. Madoff was among the most respected and trusted figures on Wall Street. He was also well known as a philanthropist. Individuals and investment funds had entrusted money with Bernard Madoff who claimed he invested their funds wisely and profitably, yielding a 12 percent return year after year. When it collapsed in 2008, Madoff's investment fund reportedly caused losses to investors of up to $60 billion. Madoff's fraud was called a Ponzi scheme after the famous Boston fraudster Charles Ponzi who ran a similar scam in 1920. He promised investors up to 50 percent return on their money and his name became synonymous with investment frauds. The Madoff fraud revealed that consumers cannot presume an investment program is legal and safe only because a famous or highly respected person manages the investment.

The FTC has prosecuted almost 20 major pyramid schemes in the last 20 years that were defined as "multilevel marketing" and claimed to be "direct selling" companies. Several of these schemes were members of a trusted trade group that touts a "code of ethics" for its members. The number of victims who signed up as salespeople for those pyramid schemes and others like them is in the tens of millions. The FTC estimated that one scheme alone that it prosecuted, known as Sky Biz International, caused losses of more than $175 million to nearly one-half million consumers. There are hundreds of multilevel marketing companies. Their solicitations to join them as salespeople are seemingly everywhere today. Many operate just like the schemes that the FTC had prosecuted. Therefore, a consumer cannot presume any multilevel marketing (network marketing, direct selling) companies is legal and viable. Only by understanding how pyramid schemes operate can a consumer determine that for themselves.

Describing another type of pyramid scheme known as gifting clubs, *Ladies Home Journal* reported that in the early 2000s as many as one-half million women in America invested between $500 and $5,000 each, with more than 90 percent losing all they invested. The schemes targeted women and used names such as "Women Helping Women" and "The Original Dinner Party." They were spread among friends, families, and within churches and social groups. Pyramid gifting schemes continue to operate throughout the United States and Canada under many different names. Some target ethnic groups, minorities or local communities, and churches. More than 30 states prosecuted or issued warnings to consumers about the fraudulence of gifting schemes.

The spread of these gifting frauds shows that a consumer cannot assume an income scheme is legal or safe because it was proposed by a trusted friend or relative or even within their church. Only with knowledge of how a pyramid scheme works can they spot the fraud.

Despite their recent prominence on Wall Street and their prevalence on Main Street, Ponzi and pyramid schemes are seldom recognized by consumer protection advocates. In fact, there is no national law in the United States that defines and specifically prohibits a pyramid scheme. Instead, this type of fraud is covered under the very broad language of the FTC Act referring to "unfair and deceptive trade practices." The lack of a defining law makes prosecutions costly and time consuming, sometimes taking years to settle.

Some states do have laws against pyramid schemes, but the various laws often contradict each other or are inconsistently enforced. And, given how many people fall into the schemes, it is evident that they are not well understood by the public. Victims range from the poor and the elderly to wealthy investors and educated professionals.

Difficulties in Detecting Schemes

A major reason that pyramids escape the notice of the media or the regulators is that this form of fraud is hidden between the two established areas of consumer protection—consumer products and consumer finances.

Most pyramid schemes involve purchases or sales of products. Many of the products are overpriced and falsely promoted, but pyramid fraud is not about faulty, overpriced, or deceptively advertised products. All pyramid and Ponzi schemes involve payments of fees and other financial investments, and some include monthly payments with credit cards. But the fraud is not in interest rates, transaction fees, or payment terms.

In addition to their somewhat hidden position somewhere between products and finances, pyramid and Ponzi schemes often escape scrutiny because they are disguised as legitimate businesses. In this camouflage, they enjoy the protection our society and laws give to businesses, which are the nuts and bolts of our economy. Consumers are also more likely to believe in propositions presented by what appear to be legitimate business operations.

In the disguise of businesses, pyramid schemes claim to offer an *income opportunity*. Millions of Americans are currently unemployed and are in desperate need of income. Though jobs may be scarce, "income schemes" are everywhere. They blanket the Internet with claims of six-figure incomes or "part-time" money "from your home." Many, perhaps most, of these solicitations to "make money from home" are actually pyramid schemes, that is, they are frauds, consumer traps, swindles, and scams.

Consumers encountering businesses that claim to offer "income opportunities" is a new phenomenon in America. Consequently most people are unprepared to recognize or avoid flimflam when they see it. In the past, when jobs were more plentiful and people remained on one job much of their lives, few people encountered any kind of proposition for self-employment or investments. But today, millions of people work from home, have several jobs, including part time, and during their lives move from job to job or career to career many times. Many people today buy and sell stock, speculate on real estate, or try to profit from online sales. Today, "income propositions" are very much a part of the average consumer's day-to-day life. The line between our consumer lives and our work lives is blurred.

Generally not recognized by consumer protection advocates, disguised as legitimate businesses and claiming to meet the greatest consumer need of our times—an income opportunity—pyramid schemes are finding easy prey among millions of consumers facing high debt, home foreclosures, unemployment, or underemployment. But the process is made even easier by another related factor, the inexperience of most people with business.

When consumers unwittingly join pyramid selling schemes they sign legally binding contracts that change their status from consumer to "contractor." In this new status they lose many protections and rights afforded to "consumers." The risks are higher in business and the protections are fewer. Though newly redefined as "business people" many consumers in fact, have little knowledge or experience with business, sales, profits, or market factors. They are therefore more easily misled or deceived. When they lose money in such schemes, as virtually all do, they can be misled to believe their losses were caused by normal market factors or perhaps by their own "failure," not by fraud. In confusion and shame, few realize how they were defrauded and, even if they suspect wrongdoing, are unlikely to report the schemes to the authorities or even to warn other consumers to avoid them.

Distinguishing Pyramids from Ponzis

Though they are fundamentally the same type of fraud—internal money transfers, disguised as legitimate income opportunities—there are some key distinctions:

- In the Ponzi, the scheme's organizer and promoter, for example, Bernard Madoff, finds the new investors. In the pyramid scheme, each new participant is told that gaining the promised rewards depends upon their bringing in new investors themselves. In a typical pyramid scheme, the investors are consumers who join as salespeople (sometimes called associates, coaches, consultants, business owners, etc.). To participate in the pay plan, they recruit other salespeople.

- Ponzi schemes are usually investment propositions. The consumer gives money to the scheme and is promised a profitable return. Sometimes the Ponzi scheme claims to be a retirement fund or an annuity or to guarantee a fix return monthly. The money invested by later investors is paid to earlier ones disguised as "interest" or "profit." Pyramid schemes, on the other hand, are typically disguised as sales companies. Each participant pays fees and buys products and is told to recruit others to do the same. Few actually sell the products to anyone who is not also another "sales" person. Money is transferred through the purchases of products or fee payments and is disguised as "commissions, royalties, or bonuses."

- In the Ponzi, the scheme must maintain total secrecy that the true source of the rewards is just other investors' money, not profits generated from business. In pyramids, the fact of the transfer from later investors to earlier ones and the reality that new investors, not sales, are the actual source of the reward money are not hidden. Rather they are *disguised* to lead the participants to believe this money transfer system is sustainable, legal, and viable. Enrollment of new salespeople is called "sales" and gaining some of the money the new recruits invest is called "commissions." In the gifting scheme programs, the pyramid investments and payments are called "gifts," which are said to be legal under the tax code. Though market factors and the limits of populations make it impossible for the scheme to expand *forever,* each new recruit is deceptively told that there will always be more people to recruit, making the income scheme sustainable and providing a real income potential to all and forever.

How Consumers Lose

Ponzis and pyramids differ also in how the losses to consumers occur. In a Ponzi, the losses happen to all participants at the same time when the scheme fails to bring new investors or the consumers discover that the source of the money is their own investments, triggering the scheme's collapse. When the consumers experience their loss, the scheme itself goes down as well.

Pyramid scams that are disguised as sales businesses cause losses to the majority on a *continuous* basis but the consumers' losses do not trigger a collapse of the scheme itself. For this reason, the pyramid is more destructive. It can operate longer and spread to more areas even as it inflicts enormous losses. Losses occur when the latest consumers to join inevitably do not find enough new recruits. Soon, they quit the scheme and lose their money. But the scheme does not collapse if it can replace those losers with new consumer investors. Though 90–99 percent who join each month may lose, the scheme itself can keep going for as long as it can find new recruits to replace them. This can go on for years or even decades. All victims suffer the losses alone, often believing they "failed" or in some other way caused their own financial loss. Few suspect that the scheme had misled them into a doomed and impossible proposition and that their lost investments and those of later consumers are the revenue that the scheme operates on. They do not realize that their losses were *inevitable* and were *predetermined* by the scheme's organizers.

How to Detect Scams

In the most recent and infamous Ponzi scheme, Bernie Madoff told investors that he made profitable stock trades to generate the 12 percent per year that he paid out, year after year. Fraudster Charles Ponzi told his investors that he was profitably trading international postage coupons in order to pay a 50 percent return to his investors. Both claimed that "outside" revenue was the source of their payments to investors, not just other investors' money. There had to be such revenue or the schemes would be obvious money-transfer frauds. If it were just the investors' own money, then more and more investors would have to be found, which would not be possible. Collapse was inevitable.

Pyramid schemes, disguised as sales companies, claim to pay their top-ranked recruiters based on salespeople selling products to retail customers. They usually claim they are "direct selling" companies. The "outside" revenue, which is required for the business to be viable, is the payments of retail customers. They are the ultimate source of the reward money. First, the customer pays the salesperson, who in turn pays the sales company. Next, the sales company pays the upper level salesperson who recruited the salesperson. If retail sales are not occurring or they are minimal, then the income proposition for rewards requires that each salesperson must recruit more salespeople, who would do the same, *ad infinitum*. That's a fraud. It can't deliver its promise of income. It dooms nearly all to fail.

So, to determine whether an investment scheme or multilevel marketing business is a pyramid fraud or not, the consumer just has to ask, "Where does the money for rewards come from?" If it is coming just from the purchases, investments, and fees of the salespeople/investors themselves, then more and more salespeople/investors will have to be found. Since that cannot happen, the company cannot deliver on its promise of income. The majority of salespeople/investors are doomed to fail and lose their time and money.

A common analogy has been offered to describe a fraudulent income plan that has no outside money. It goes like this:

If 10 people each put $10 into an income scheme, and there is no other outside money, there is only $100 available. If just one of the 10 investors is to get more than his original $10 as a return, all the others could gain no profit. For some to make money, others have to lose or at least make nothing. A promise to all that they could "potentially" make a profit would be a lie. It is not possible.

Pyramid schemes use this trick of making people think that if everyone puts in money, everyone can make money. When they are questioned as to where the profit would come from, they tell the consumers that everyone can still make a profit as long as more and more people join the plan.

So, all the investors put their own money into the scheme, and then all are promised they can make "unlimited" money as long as they can recruit more people. In fact, no matter how many join, the amount available is the amount the investors themselves put in. It is a closed system. For some to win, others still must lose or gain nothing. *Expansion does not change anything.* If more join, more will win but in proportion, more will also lose. The promise of "unlimited opportunity" is a calculated lie.

Many consumers do understand that the income in pyramid selling schemes is based on continuous expansion of the participating salespeople. But rather than seeing that as a hallmark of a fraud, they believe that everyone still has the potential for income as long as expansion continue and they believe it *can* continue. Surely everyone can find a few more to join, can't they? "Duplication" is described by the promoters as "explosive" and the key to "unlimited" income. They often show expansion with each person recruiting just two others who do the same for several cycles. Quickly the "down line" totals more than a thousand new investors, with money from each flowing up to "you" at the top.

In fact, such an illustration is a math trick and the belief that it can work is a delusion. What the consumers miss is how fast "duplication" would add up, if it really did continue beyond a few levels. In a very short time, there would not be enough new people. Recruiting would slow or stop. Those in the bottom would lose.

The fact of this rapid—and unsustainable—expansion is illustrated with the trick question, *"Which would you rather take, a million dollars in cash right now, or one penny today that would double each day for just 30 days?"* Best Answer: Take the penny. A penny doubled every day for 30 days adds up to over $5.3 million! (See Table 30.)

Similarly, if one person recruited just two others, and all who are recruited did the same and this continued each day for just 30 days, the number of "salespeople" would exceed one-half billion people! (third column). Where would they find enough new people? Just three more recruiting cycles would exceed the adult population of the earth! Four cycles more would require finding people on another planet!

Table 30 Power and delusion of duplication

Days	Dollars	People
1	$0.1	1
2	$0.2	2
3	$0.4	4
4	$0.8	8
5	$.16	16
6	$.32	32
7	$.64	64
8	$1.28	128
9	$2.56	256
10	$5.12	512
11	$10.24	1,024
12	$20.48	2,048
13	$40.96	4,096
14	$81.92	8,192
15	$163.84	16,384
16	$327.68	32,768
17	$655.36	65,536
18	$1,310.72	131,072
19	$2,621.44	262,144
20	$5,242.88	524,288
21	$10,485.76	1,048,576
22	$20,971.52	2,097,152
23	$41,943.04	4,194,304
24	$83,386.08	8,338,608
25	$167,772.16	16,777,216
26	$335,544.32	33,554,432
27	$671,088.64	67,108,864
28	$1,342,177.28	134,217,728
29	$2,684,354.56	268,435,456
30	$5,368,709.12	536,870,912

As the pyramid schemes reach a saturation points—long before the earth's population is exceeded—those in the bottom levels "fail" to find enough new people and they soon quit. The chain is broken, and the false promise of income potential is revealed as a fraud. But the scheme keeps making the promise to *new* people, who take their turns at investing, and then failing and quitting too. As long as the scheme can continue to find new and hopeful people, the fraud will continue to operate. Meanwhile, nearly all that are involved are losing their money. Only a tiny few at the top are "succeeding." They get the money that everyone else lost.

But, it does not even require that the math be extended into the millions and billions to prove that virtually all are doomed, *from the start*, to lose in a pyramid recruitment scheme. This is because no matter how long the scheme can keep recruiting and no matter how many are in the scheme, the majority will *always* be in a losing position. The promise of an income for all has a fatal flaw that is revealed long before it runs out of recruits.

The math in the typical pyramid recruiting system dooms the vast majority—as many as 99 percent—to financial losses. This is because more than 90 percent will *always* be in the bottom ranks where there are not enough recruits below to provide an income. This can be illustrated in a simple six-level chain in which each person recruits just five people. At least three levels of recruits (5 + 25 + 125=155) are needed for each participant to achieve a sustainable profit. See Figure 6.

Since only those with three levels below them are profitable, only the top person and the 30 other individuals in levels #1 and #2 qualify. Each of the people in next three levels below does not have enough "down line" to generate a profit. This means that only 31 out of 3,906, or less than one percent in the six-level chain, have as many as three levels below them and are profitable. The math dictates that more than 99 percent are unprofitable *based on their position*. This percentage will be true no matter how long the scheme runs or how large it becomes.

Conclusion: Recognizing and Avoiding

While Ponzi schemes gain most attention, when they collapse, pyramid schemes are the far more common financial trap that a consumer is likely to encounter. Masquerading as businesses and generally ignored by consumer protection professionals, a consumer needs the tools for unmasking the disguised scam. The following questions can reveal fraud versus legitimate income opportunities from pyramid plans (Table 31).

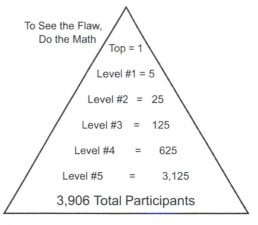

To See the Flaw,
Do the Math

Top = 1
Level #1 = 5
Level #2 = 25
Level #3 = 125
Level #4 = 625
Level #5 = 3,125
3,906 Total Participants

Figure 6. Another way to visualize the power of pyramid plans.

Table 31 Questions to ask yourself when considering a multi level marketing and pyramid plan

- Do you have to pay for your sales job?
- Beware of any scheme where you have to first pay money for the chance to make money from selling or recruiting.
- Key terms to watch out for: *Registration fee; renewal fees; "back-office" charges; website charges; certification test costs; "success system"; auto ship.*
- Is it *really* about selling?
- Could you sell enough of the products to customers – at the retail price – to earn a sustainable profit? Could you do it month after month, without recruiting other salespeople or making promises about "income"? *If not, then "endless" recruiting is required, not just by you, but all others too. Watch out!*
- Key terms to watch out for: *Anyone can do it; no selling required; no sales experience needed; our product sells itself; virtually no selling costs; make money while you sleep; just invest 3 hours a week.*
- Is it actually about *recruiting*?
- Does the company or your sponsor urge you to sign up new salespeople even before you have made any money from selling products to retail customers? Do they urge you to convert customers into salespeople? *If they do, run!*
- Key terms to watch out for: *fast start; fast track; customer acquisition bonus; build "structure"; right leg and left leg; 24 hour game plan*
- Are you *buying* or selling?
- Do the recruiters above you, as a group, make money when you, the salesperson, make a purchase (even if you don't make a sale)? *If they do, put your wallet in a safe place!*
- Key terms to watch out for: *Buy from your own store and find others to do the same; Gain points on your own purchases; earn rebates on your purchases; Be your own customer; You can't sell what you don't buy; Meet your minimum quota to start receiving commissions; Be a billboard for your products; 100% self-use; product loyalty.*
- Are you *paying* to be trained and "motivated" by the company (or upline) you work for?
- Do the company or your sponsors charge you for company-related training, rallies and meetings? If so, they may be profiting and you may be getting scammed.
- Key terms to watch out for: *You really need to attend this seminar; you need to get certified; learn from the masters; you have to invest to succeed; are you a winner or a loser; millionaires who can help you do what they have done, they have helped thousands become "free."*
- Does the company provide *enough* information for you to do your own "due diligence?"
- Does the company disclose enough information for you to honestly evaluate the "opportunity?" Do they disclose the true average incomes, competitive pricing of products, dropout rates of the salespeople, actual business costs for selling, all sources of income for the top people, and how much the upper people gain on each sale you make? *If not, beware of what they're hiding.*

Key terms to also watch out for: "Disclosures" that only count the "active" sales reps; disclosures that use percentages, not real numbers for counting sales people at each rank; "averages" that include the top 1 percent, skewing up the average for all; absence of data on business costs; data that omits dropouts; data that does not reveal how many are recruited each year, only how many are "active" at year end; data that does not disclose how much income comes from personal selling, and how much is based on sales and purchases of those recruited. Consumer should ask what the average net income is for all distributors after expenses, as well as what the attrition (drop out) rate is (as every company has these figures). Finally, a consumer should ask if he or she would invest in a franchise if it was known in advance that 99 percent of people earlier had lost money in the business.

Robert L. FitzPatrick

See also: Affinity Fraud; Federal Trade Commission (FTC); Frauds and Scams; Madoff, Bernie; Ponzi Schemes; Securities and Exchange Commission (SEC)

References and Additional Readings

Craig, B. (2012). An investor's guide to identifying pyramid schemes. Retrieved from http://seekingalpha.com/article/918831-an-investor-s-guide-to-identifying-pyramid-schemes

Federal Trade Commission. (1998). Prepared statement of Debra A. Valentine, general counsel for the U.S. federal trade commission on "pyramid schemes." Presented at the International Monetary Fund's Seminar on Current Legal Issues Affecting Central Banks, Washington, DC. May 13, 1998. Retrieved from http://www.ftc.gov/speeches/other/dvimf16.shtm

Postal Inspection Service. (2013). Multi-level marketing jobs (pyramid schemes). Retrieved from https://postalinspectors.uspis.gov/investigations/MailFraud/fraudschemes/employmentfraud/Marketing.aspx

VanderNat, P.J., & Keep, W.W. (2002). Marketing fraud: An approach for differentiating multilevel marketing from pyramid schemes. *Journal of Public Policy & Marketing, 21*(1), 139–151.

N

Nader, Ralph

Ralph Nader represents America's premier consumer advocate. He was the driving force for the consumer movement across the country and first came on the scene battling the car industry some four decades ago. Although well known for his work in protecting consumers, his highest notoriety come from his presidential bids in four campaigns spanning from the 1990s to 2008. He ran for president of the United States with the Green Party in both 1996 and 2000. Winona LaDuke, born in 1959, ran as his vicepresidential running mate in both the 1996 and 2000 campaigns. LaDuke is a Native American activist, economist, environmentalist, writer, and author. She founded and acts as the current executive director of both Honor the Earth and White Earth Land Recovery. Nader ran as an independent candidate in the 2004 presidential election. Although he fell short of securing the role of president, he outwardly battled corporations and their power over the political process. Known as an idealistic and modest man, Nader became known for his long working hours and unembellished and frugal lifestyle. His work as a consumer advocate and presidential candidate has helped countless consumers in the areas of information, safety, and financial fairness changing the way consumers and businesses operate in the open marketplace.

The Early Years

In 1912, Nathra Nader emigrated from Lebanon to the United States later to marry Rose Bouziane in 1924. Ten years later, on February 27 in 1934, Ralph Nader, the youngest of four children, was born in Winsted, Connecticut. In 1951, he went on to graduate from the Gilbert School in Winsted and entered Princeton University. In 1955, he graduated *magna cum laude* from Princeton and took an interest in attending law school. In 1958, Ralph Nader graduated from Harvard Law School and immediately served six months in the Army as a cook at Fort Dix in New Jersey. The following year not only did he publish his first article on automobile safety in the publication, *The Nation*, he also started his own law practice in Hartford,

Connecticut. From 1961 to 1964 Ralph Nader traveled throughout Europe, Africa, Latin America, and the USSR as a freelance journalist gaining insight of global issues.

Head-On with the Automobile Industry

In 1963, then 29 years old, Nader hitchhiked to Washington, D.C., where he served as a consultant under Assistant Secretary of Labor Daniel Patrick Moynihan and in the following year wrote a paper critiquing the federal highway and traffic safety program. *Unsafe at Any Speed,* one of his most notable writings is published and puts Ralph Nader on the map as a consumer advocate. The publication is a study by Nader claiming many U.S. automobile makers are producing structurally flawed products, particularly those of General Motors (GM). The publication incited the automobile industry, especially General Motors Corporation, as Nader clearly and publicly targeted the powerhouse in the publication. In 1966, GM tried to discredit Nader by digging in his past and attempting to trap him in a compromising situation. Vincent Gillen, a private detective, was summoned by GM to investigate Ralph Nader and followed Nader to intimidate him into pulling back on his attacks of the automobile giant. The effort by GM failed. Executives at GM appeared before the Ribicoff subcommittee and explained the company's investigation of Nader; eventually GM President James M. Roche publicly apologized for the tactic. *Unsafe at Any Speed* brought attention to the American government the automobile industry's unsafe practices of putting consumers at serious risk when operating a vehicle. On September 9, 1966, President Johnson signed the National Traffic and Motor Vehicle Safety and Highway Safety Acts allowing for the federal government to regulate the industry; a move that changed the automobile industry forever. Later that same year, Ralph Nader sued GM for $26 million for invasion of privacy due to the harassment of the investigator from GM.

Nader's Raiders

In 1967, Congress passed the Wholesome Meat Act as a direct result of Nader's efforts to clean up slaughterhouse practices. Subsequent years brought the passage of the Natural Gas Pipeline Act, Radiation Control for Health Safety Act, and the Wholesome Poultry Act, all a direct result of Nader's efforts. Nader was on the map and well established as a strong advocate for the American people. Hundreds of young activists and college students were inspired by Nader's efforts and consequently settled in Washington, D.C., to join Rader in the activist projects. A newspaper writer coined the term "Nader's Raiders" describing the mostly young college students supporting Nader's efforts and the large group of young citizens worked under Nader to investigate corruption in corporate America and government. The group published reports on varied consumer subjects including baby food, insecticides, mercury poisoning, radiation dangers, pension reform, and coalmine safety. *First Group,* a part of Nader's Raiders, investigated the Federal Trade Commission (FTC) and published a scathing report on the commission's activities accusing them of essentially being asleep at the wheel. The young energized group eventually completed many more publications including Nader's Raiders; the FTC, Vanishing Air (National Air Pollution Control Administration), the Chemical Feast (Food and Drug Administration), the Interstate Commerce Omission (Interstate Commerce Commission), Old Age (Nursing Homes), the Water Lords (Water Pollution), Who Runs Congress? (Congress), Whistle Blowing (Punishment of Whistle Blowers), the Big Boys (Corporate Executive), Collision Course (Federal Aviation Administration), and No Contest (Corporate Lawyers). An impressive feast of attacks by any standard existed as a direct result of Nader's Raiders and their ability to investigate and publish corruption and change needed in the American landscape.

Politics and Deepening Issues

In 1968, Nader established the Center for the Study of Responsive Law in Washington, D.C., and Ralph Nader became increasingly politically active. In 1969, Ralph Nader secretly discussed with Joseph A. Yablonski the idea to oppose W.A. "Tony" Boyle for the president's position for the United Mine Workers of America organization. Later that month, Yablonski announced his own candidacy for president of the United Mine Workers; a direct result of Ralph Nader's influence. That same year, the Coal Mine Health and Safety Act, which Nader advocated, passed Congress. Also in 1969, GM halts production of the Chevrolet Corvair due to the blatant safety issues brought to the attention of the federal government by Ralph Nader. By 1970, Nader's Raiders are fully functioning and investigating the Interstate Commerce Commission (ICC), the Food and Drug Administration (FDA), current air pollution, airline safety, nursing homes, the medical profession, and many other private and government entities. In Washington, D.C., the Public Interest Research Group was founded in 1970 with funding from Ralph Nader's GM settlement of $280,000. Other public interest research groups took root through student contributions in Oregon and Minnesota, a direct result of the advocacy of Ralph Nader. In 1971, Ralph Nader began Public Citizen, an entity that still serves as the people's voice in the nation's capital and accepts no government or corporate monies. Public Citizen served as an umbrella organization for projects and today boasts over 150,000 members and widespread researchers investigating governmental, health, environmental, and economic issues. They are credited with facilitating the passage of the Safe Drinking Water Act and the Freedom of Information Act. They also had a direct hand in the creation of the Occupational Safety and Health Administration (OSHA), the Environmental Protection Agency (EPA), and the Consumer Product Safety Administration. Divisions of these include the organizations of Buyers Up, Citizen Action Group, Congress Watch, Critical Mass Energy Project, Global Trade Watch, Health Research Group, Litigation Group, Tax Reform Research Group, and the Visitor's Center.

Nonprofit Organizations

Ralph Nader resigned as the director of Public Citizen in 1980 to allow work on other projects, particularly fighting the power of large multinational corporations through nonprofit organizations. An impressive list of nonprofit organizations grew from his efforts. These include Capitol Hill News Service, Corporate Accountability Research Project, Disability Rights Center, Equal Justice Foundation, Georgia Legal Watch, National Citizens' Coalition for Nursing Home Reform, National Coalition for Universities in the Public Interest, PROD for truck safety, Retired Professionals Action Group, the Shafeek Nader Trust for the Community Interest (named after Nader's elder brother), Congress Accountability Project, Citizen Advocacy Center, Pension Rights Center, Foundation for Taxpayers and Consumer Rights, and the Center for Auto Safety. Other entities and publications with Nader's influence prior to the 1980s included, but are not limited to the Center for Science in the Public Interest (1971), the Aviation Consumer Action Project (1971), Clean Water Action Project (1972), Center for Women's Policy Studies (1972), the *Multinational Monitor* (a magazine reporting on multinational corporations), Trial Lawyers for Public Justice (1982), Telecommunications Research and Action Center (1983), the Appleseed Foundation (for local change), the Resource Consumption Alliance (to conserve trees), the Center for Insurance Research (1995), Organization for Competitive Markets (1998), Congressional Accountability Project (2000), Citizen Works (2001—builds grassroots support), and Democracy Rising (2001—holds rallies to educate and empower citizens).

Presidential Bids

Ralph Nader has put in a bid for president of the United States six times starting with a write-in candidacy in 1992 in the New Hampshire Democratic primary. In 1996 and 2000 he ran on the Green Party ticket and then as an independent in 2004 and 2008. Many accuse Nader of handing George W. Bush the presidency in 2000, calling him a spoiler, due to drawing votes away from the Democratic nominee, Al Gore. Nader has defended himself on these claims. In 1990, Nader had considered starting a third political party focusing on citizen empowerment and consumer rights. Disenchanted with the Democratic Party he suggested a third party could address campaign finance reform, whistle-blower rights, and advocacy groups to oversee the banking industry, insurance agencies, and lawsuit reform.

In 1996, when Nader ran for president of the United States on the Green Party ticket, much of his platform rested on denouncing Democrat Bill Clinton and Republican Bob Dole over environmental issues. Nader managed to land on the ballot for some of the states but attained less than 1 percent of the American vote, though he did make significant gains for the party. Ralph Nader refused to spend more than $5,000 on his campaign. In 2000, Nader ran for president again with the Green Party. He was able to get on the ballot in 44 states and received support from well-known liberals such as Michael Moore, Phil Donahue, and Patti Smith. His platform included speaking out against the power of corporate America, the need for campaign finance reform, accessible healthcare for all, environmental issues, affordable housing, access to higher education by all socioeconomic levels, and an emphasis on higher taxes for corporations to alleviate the middle and lower tax levels.

Late in the race it was apparent Gore and Bush were in a tight fight to the finish and Nader had no realistic chance of becoming president. The Gore campaign realized every vote was needed and dispatched Gore supporters to put the word out to Nader supporters that a vote for Nader might actually be a vote for Bush, pulling support away from the Gore camp. Ralph Nader and his supporters admitted Gore was a better choice than Bush but argued the differences between the two front runners was not enough to secure support of Gore. When confronted with the dilemma of possibly spoiling the race, Nader stated he was trying to save the Democratic Party and at other times that he wanted to break it down in an effort to reform and make it better. After denouncing Al Gore and George W. Bush for their political views, he won about 3 percent of the national vote, falling short of the 5 percent needed to qualify for federal matching funds in the following election. Al Gore had received 48.4 percent of the votes and George W. Bush 47.9 percent. Ralph Nader received 97,000 votes in Florida where Gore and Bush had finished in a dead heat. Many believed Ralph Nader handed Bush the presidency due to distracting would-be Gore voters over to the Green party. Nader supporters rebutted many of the Nader voters who would not have voted at all if Ralph Nader was not on the ballot. Nader stated he was entitled to run for office as much as any other American citizen and that the public deserved more than two choices; and better choices than the two they got.

Nader supporters also proposed the Democrats could have won the election with a more competent candidate than Al Gore due to his inability to effectively debate George W. Bush. In 2004, Nader once again ran for president but this time as an Independent rather than on the Green Party ticket. Nader believed too much power and wealth was in the hands of too few people and wanted to change the way Washington ran. In May of 2004 Ralph Nader met with John Kerry in Washington, D.C., as the Democrats concerns heightened of Nader's factor in the 2004 election. Ralph Nader did not withdraw from the race as proposed discussing the importance of removing troops from Iraq. In the end, Nader received 463,655 votes giving him 0.38 percent of the popular vote and placing third in the election. In 2008, Ralph Nader ran for president as an Independent with Matt Gonzalez as his vice presidential candidate. He received 738,475 votes winning 0.56 of the popular vote and again a third place position in the election. In 2011, Nader called another independent run for president "very unlikely" and was not on the ballot for 2012.

Books by Ralph Nader (Include, but not limited to):

Getting Steamed to Overcome Corporatism: Building it Together to Win

The Seventeen Traditions

Only the Super Rich Can Save Us

The Good Fight

In Pursuit of Justice

Why Women Pay More, by Frances Cerra Whittelsley and Ralph Nader

Spices of Life, by Ruth Fort and Ralph Nader

Getting the Best from Your Doctor, by Ralph Nader and Wesley J. Smith

Ralph Nader has never been married citing he has been dedicated to his career as a life focus. In 2000, he stated he owned no real estate or an automobile and lived on $25,000 a year and is believed to be spending the rest of his million dollar investments on the nonprofit organizations he founded.

Zoe Bryan Engstrom

See also: Activism; Centers for Disease Control and Prevention

(CDC); Congress; Environmental Protection Agency (EPA); Federal Trade Commission (FTC); Food and Drug Administration (FDA); National Highway Traffic Safety Administration (NHTSA); National Traffic Safety Board; Peterson, Esther; Public Citizen; Whistleblowing; Wholesome Meat Act

References and Additional Readings

An Unreasonable Man: Ralph Nader—How Do You Define a Legacy? Dir. Henriette Mantel and Steve Skrovan. Production Company Two Left Legs. DVD.

Barabak, N. Z. (2011). Nader wants a primary challenge for president Obama. *LA Times.* Retrieved from http://articles.latimes.com/2011/sep/19/news/la-pn-nader-obama-20110919

Biography Base. (2013). Ralph Nader biography. Retrieved from http://www.biographybase.com/biography/Nader_Ralph.html

Biography.com. (2013). Ralph Nader. Retrieved from http://www.biography.com/people/ralph-nader-9419799

Citibank. (1973). *Citibank, Nader and the facts.* New York: Grossman Publishers.

de Toledano, R. (1975). *Hit and run: The rise and fall of Ralph Nader.* New Rochelle, NY: Arlington House Publishers.

Leinsdorf, D., & Etra, D. (1973). *Citibank: Ralph Nader's study group report on first national city bank.* New York: Grossman Publishers.

McCarry, C. (1972). *Citizen Nader.* New York: Saturday Review Press.

Nader, R. (2000). *The Ralph Nader Reader.* New York: Seven Stories Press.

Public Citizen. (2013). Retrieved from www.citizen.org

Whiteside, T. (1972). *Investigation of Ralph Nader: General Motors vs. one determined man.* New York: Arbor House.

National Consumer Law Center (NCLC)

The National Consumer Law Center (NCLC) is a nonprofit consumer advocacy organization (aka, the "Nation's Consumer Law Experts") that seeks to build economic security and family wealth for low-income and other economically disadvantaged Americans. NCLC promotes access to quality financial services and protects family assets from unfair and exploitive transactions that can wipe out financial resources and undermine self-sufficiency. It should be noted that NCLC does not provide direct con-sumer assistance and counseling to consumers but it is more of a "research organization" for community/government agencies and advocates who need assistance in consumer protection public policy, legal support, education, and training to assist their clients. NCLC is located in Boston, Massachusetts, and also has an office in Washington, DC.

Brief History

Since its inception 40 years ago, NCLC has used its legal and consumer protection expertise to write the rules of a fair and just marketplace. It was founded in 1968–1969 at the Boston College School of Law by Law Professor William Willier, with the support of then Father Robert Drianan who was the Dean of the Boston College Law School. Professor Willier was not only an accomplished commercial law professor but also a strong consumer advocate defending the consumer protection rights of the low-income consumer. He also served as its first executive director.

Richard Hesse followed William Willier as its second executive director. Mr. Hesse was formerly a legal services attorney from the State of Pennsylvania. During his tenure, NCLC was established as a "legal service" organization that focused on the issues impacting the low-income consumer. Other executive directors that followed included Mark Budnitz (1975), Robert Sable (1979), and current executive director, Willard P. Ogburn began in 1987. Mr. Ogburn was the former deputy commissioner of Banking for Massachusetts and also served as NCLC deputy director prior to his appointment as executive director.

Due to financial reasons and expansion of their work, NCLC incorporated as a nonprofit, tax-exempt organization in 1973. NCLC has an interesting funding history that has a nexus to the 1970s consumer protection movement and to the organizations that were created during this period of time. Its initial funding was provided by the Office of Economic Opportunity (OEO). OEO was the primary federal agency that funded many organizations that were part of the "War on Poverty" programs. In addition to funding the legal services offices throughout the country, OEO also funded "back up" or specialized research legal organizations to "assist" the local legal service offices throughout the country. Among the "specialized" organizations, OEO funded the National Consumer Legal Center (at Boston College School of Law), Center on Social Welfare Policy and Law at Columbia University School of Law, the National Housing Law Project (at Boalt Hall, UC Berkeley), and the Center for Law and Education (at Harvard Law School). Currently, NCLC has a budget of approximately 5 million dollars a year and it also receives funding from other sources, such as public and private grants, foundation support and contracts from public and private national and local organizations; private donations; *Cy pres* awards; and income from publications, conferences, and technical assistance services; and other sources.

Board of Directors

NCLC is governed by a volunteer national board of directors that includes bar association representatives from the private bar and clients from the communities it serves. Currently, there are 13 board members from throughout the country and Mr. Michael Ferry serves as president of the board. Mr. Ferry is an attorney and executive director of Gateway Legal Services, St. Louis, Missouri. In addition to the board of directors, it also has a Partners Council with representatives from various regions of the United States.

NCLC Staff

Mr. Willard P. Ogburn is the current executive director. The NCLC staff includes advocates, attorneys, administrative, development and publications support staff and a director of communications. NCLC has approximately 50 staff members that is engaged in and dedicated to legal research, advocacy, expert consumer protection knowledge, studies, and publications regarding current consumer protection issues impacting the marketplace, technical legal assistance, and much more.

Current Initiatives and Special Projects

NCLC has embarked on several initiatives and issues that significant impact low-income consumers and their role in the marketplace. These include Climate Change Justice, Domestic Violence Survivors, Military Personnel, Older Consumers, Racial Justice and Equal Economic Opportunity, Student Loan Borrower Assistance and State Initiative in states such as California, Massachusetts, and Washington. The Student Loan Borrower Assistance Initiative is of particular interest to students and college counselors. They provide information about student loan rights and responsibilities. NCLC seeks to increase public knowledge about student lending practices, as well as issues necessary for policy reform. The ultimate goal of their efforts is to reduce student debt burden and to increase the feasibility of repaying loans. The SBLA website has detailed information for borrowers who already have student loans and want to know more about their options and rights: (1) browse a wide range of questions and answers to find helpful information that may be needed; (2) a step-by-step guide to determine a strategy to solve a student loan problem; (3) hot topics—bankruptcy, rehabilitation and consolidation, and public service forgiveness. For information on other initiatives stated earlier, go to NCLS website or click on *Special Projects*.

Accomplishments

NCLC is recognized as a leading consumer organization and an expert in the areas of consumer credit, banking, home energy—home hear, utility services, home repairs and home mortgages, and other areas of special importance to low-income families. Additionally, it has a wealth of knowledge in areas of foreclosures and loan servicing and predatory mortgage lending.

Other initiatives that have been part of its effective consumer protection agenda are Consumer Financial Services Regulation, credit cards, debt collection, credit reporting, car sales and financing, refund anticipation loans and other high-cost, short-term loans, consumer bankruptcy, student loans, the Protection of Exempt Benefits (i.e., Social Security) from illegal seizure, energy efficiency improvements for low-income households, Affordable Home Utility Services, and more.

Legislation

In the area of credit card reform, "the Credit Card Reform Law" enacted in 2010 has brought consumers relief from years of abusive and confusing fine print on contracts, as well as, superfluous junk fees and penalties charged by the credit card industry. NCLC advised lawmakers and pushed for reforms relating to seeking reasonable penalty fees, and addressing retroactive interest rates, fee harvester charges, interest on payment balances. Congress sought advice from NCLC on what was best for vulnerable consumers. The final legislation was based on years of NCLC research that spelled out credit card abuses.

The 2003 Fair and Accurate Credit Transactions Act contained important amendments to the Fair Credit Reporting Act. Again, NCLC reported on ways to advance the accuracy of reports and educate consumers on risk-based pricing. They also sought to prevent debt collectors from ignoring requirements of the act. In the Truth in Lending Act and Regulation Z, NCLC made sure that the rights of consumers were defended by numerous attempts to undercut their consumer protection effectiveness.

Additionally, NCLC took a leadership role and prepared distressing report detailing examples of home improvement and second mortgage abuses. The report spurred the enactment of the Home Ownership and Equity Protection Act of 1994, including legal remedies for homeowners who risked losing their homes due to equity skimming scams.

Finally, on the legislative front, NCLC made sure the FTC's Credit Practice Rules abolished many of the most outrageous, commonplace creditor abuses consumers were experiencing. For other NCLC Legislative initiatives and activities, the reader can visit www.thomas.gov. Also, for more materials on a particular legislative subject area, visit their Issues page.

Publications and Studies

In the field of publications, NCLC is the leading resource in the nation on consumer protection issues. The 18-volume *Consumer Credit and Sale Legal Practices Series* (formatted like an encyclopedia) is an excellent resource, as are the books and guides for consumer advocates and consumers alike. The resources produced by NCLC are balanced, comprehensive, and state-of-the-art. The 18-volume series addresses various topics of consumer law—debt collection, credit reporting, unfair and deceptive acts and practices, utility customer service, bankruptcy, or sales of goods and service. NCLC is also widely cited by judges in the federal and state courts when they render their formal opinions. The books provide step-by-step advice and practical examples and documents that can aid consumers in their case, whether it is arbitration, fraud, or foreclosure.

NCLC published a revised edition of *Foreclosure Prevention Counseling* in 2009, an invaluable resource for foreclosure counselors. This is another example of a prominent and significant publication that was available, even before the National Housing and Foreclosure Crisis appeared on the radar screen in many communities.

Other publications include titles such as *Consumer Credit Regulations, Fair Debt Collection, Mortgage Lending, Student Loan, Surviving Debt, Truth in Lending, the Dodd–Frank Act* and more.

In the field of investigative reports, their aim is to expose marketplace abuses, propose legislative reforms, and propel action to correct marketplace problems. They are carefully researched, with facts and figures, real life stories, analysis, proposals for reform—all backed by NCLC's record of expertise. *Consumer Impact* (formerly known as *Outlook*), NCLC's newsletter, highlights the center's recent activities and is available free of charge on their website or by e-mail.

Conferences/Training

Another important field where NCLC has made a dramatic impact is its professional training programs and conferences. The primary aim of their training programs is to enhance the quality and accessibility of resources for consumers, attorneys, advocates, and service providers. Their training programs are appropriate for any experience level and beings with "nuts and bolts" for beginners and goes through cutting-edge practices for more advanced practitioners. In the spirit of technology, NCLC is offering regular webinars for attorneys and advocates in an effort to reach a broader audience, nationwide.

NCLC hosts the *Consumer Rights Litigation Conference (CRLC)* and the *Fair Debt Collection Training Conference* annually. The CRLC is one of the most well-attended and informative conferences for consumer protection advocates. The conference dispenses the latest on strategies in law from leading industry experts. Conference attendees acquire valuable knowledge on tactics, trends, and strategies for practice as well as participating in networking opportunities.

Summary

NCLC is committed to the consumer protection community, and their message is well summarized by Willard P. Ogburn, NCLC executive director:

> We remain as we began more than 40 years ago—when we were a legal services support center housed in a small office at Boston College—committed to justice for vulnerable consumers and with a passion and dedication to helping those in need. . . . speaking out on their behalf when others turned a deaf ear to the need for consumer protections. . . . We never forget the single mother, for example, who loses part of her hard-earned money to a rent-to-own store; the struggling family that faces homelessness because their home is being foreclosed; or the young student who hoped an education would lift her out of poverty, but is instead mired in insurmountable student loan debt. (NCLC, n.d.)

And the fight for justice in the marketplace continues.

Pastor Herrera Jr.

See also: Bankruptcy; Credit Cards; Debt Management; Debt, Student; Foreclosures and Short Sales; Long Term Care; Mortgages; Rent-To-Own (RTO)

References and Additional Readings

Harak, C., Wein, O. B., Saunders, M. F., & Colton, R. D. (2008). *Access to utility service: Regulated, de-regulated and unregulated utilities, deliverable fuels, and telecommunications*. Boston, MA: National Consumer Law Center.

Hill, C., Gonzales, H., & Colton, R. (1988). National Consumer Law Center, Inc. Clearinghouse Rev., 22, 146.

NCLC. (n.d.). Using expertise to rewrite the rules of a fair marketplace. Retrieved from http://www.nclc.org/images/pdf/about_us/NCLC%20Organizational%20Brochure.pdf

National Consumers League (NCL)

The National Consumers League (NCL) is America's oldest national consumer organization. It was founded in 1899 by Jane Addams and Josephine Lowell, two pioneers in charting new territory related to social reform and community change. During the 1930s, with the expansion of the social welfare movement and the Roosevelt administration, the league included focus on federal labor laws, as well as national health insurance, improved food and drug safety laws, federal pesticide monitoring, social security legislation especially for the elderly or disabled, and unemployment insurance. For the next 50 years, the league had several shifts in locations, as well as leadership. One thing remained consistent though: the commitment to spearhead efforts that would improve the quality of life for all people. Some of their work, for example, included programs to improve consumer education, food safety, workplace safety, health care, social security, Medicare, as well as increase the powers of the Federal Trade Commission (FTC).

Jane Addams was a leader of progressive reform in the United States around the turn of the 20th century. (Library of Congress)

The National Consumers League changes lived and fights for the well-being of all people. One of its special projects is to stop child labor. Some current challenges include:

- 18 countries produce gold with child labor and many children are exposed to toxic substances like mercury during the process.
- Over 60 million children around the world do not have access to basic education and of that number; almost 50 percent of them are expected to never enroll.
- Wage theft affects millions of blue-collar and white-collar workers each year, forcing them to choose between paying the rent or putting food on the table. It robs the government of taxes and puts ethical employees at a competitive disadvantage.

Source: http://stopchildlabor.org/

The league is led by an executive director whose key priorities are fraud, child labor, healthcare reform, and LifeSmarts (an educational program designed in 1994 to develop consumer and marketplace knowledge and skills of teenagers). NCL engages in campaigns, lobbying efforts, educational programs, and outreach to improve the living conditions and daily life of all people. For example, their Child Labor Coalition fights for the rights of children worldwide by getting involved with Congress, supporting educational programs, and fighting for the welfare of youth. NCL has also developed a medical adherence campaign called "Script Your Future," which partners with key healthcare providers, community members, government agencies, researchers, health insurance companies, and pharmaceutical companies to help consumers manage their health conditions. Another example of a current program is "Wage Theft" designed to raise necessary awareness to consumers about the fact that workers, oftentimes low-wage workers, are unpaid for overtime, or are misclassified in their position, resulting in lost wages.

Florence Kelly was the first general secretary of the National Consumers League (NCL). She exposed child labor and other scandalous working conditions existing at that time. She become one of the most influential and effective social reformers of the 20th century. As stated on the NCL's website, Kelly led the league in its original efforts to:

- issue a White Label designating products made under fair working conditions;
- protect in-home workers, often including whole families, from terrible exploitation by employers;
- promote the Meat Inspection Act of 1904 and the Pure Food and Drugs Act of 1906;
- write and then champion state minimum wage laws for women;

- defend and ultimately convince the U.S. Supreme Court to uphold a 10-hour work day law in the landmark Muller v. Oregon case of 1908;
- advocate for creation of a federal Children's Bureau and federal child labor restrictions.

Kelly spent 33 years as a leader in the league. During her time she worked closely with other reformers, including Franklin D. Roosevelt's Secretary of Labor Frances Perkins.

She is known for her motto: "To live means to buy, to buy means to have power, to have power means to have responsibility."

Source: National Consumers League. (n.d.). History. Retrieved from http://www.nclnet.org/

Currently, as written on their website, the NCL also:

- spearheads efforts to promote the safe use of medication, including convening a multifaceted, multistakeholder campaign to promote better medication adherence (ensuring that patients adhere to their medication regimen) in conjunction and with the support of a federal agency
- comments frequently on matters of concern to consumers and workers before the Department of Agriculture, Federal Communications Commission, Federal Trade Commission, Food and Drug Administration, and Department of Labor
- promotes better working conditions for migrant farm worker families and teen workers, both internationally and at home through the Child Labor Coalition
- is fighting to improve product safety, as well as misleading or confusing labeling on food and beverage products
- maintains several consumer-friendly websites, where consumers may download current publications and alerts on current issues ranging from avoiding fraud to maintaining one's mortgage, to understanding bloodthinners
- participates in the Safe Food Coalition, which promotes effective meat and poultry inspection
- distributes tens of thousands of publications annually, on topics including food and drug interaction, safe over-the-counter medication use, budgeting and credit, and telephone service
- convenes a consumer–labor coalition that meets regularly, bringing union and consumer groups together for discussions and joint activities of concern to workers and consumers.

On the NCL website, consumers can look up information on several categories. These are health, personal finance, worker's rights, food, and technology. They also provide a blog. A current example of a posting is about the U.S. sugar program reform, one that the NCL opposes because the current programs allow for increase in prices for foods that contain sugar. The current program is said to cost the average family of four about $40 per year, or $3.5 billion every year for all Americans. In addition, consumers can also find information for how to get involved via Facebook, twitter, newsfeeds, newsletters, and donations.

The league will continue to fight for consumer rights. As they continue to sponsor conferences, forums, and workshops, and develop policy and publications, as well as connect with other key players who fight for consumer rights, safety, and protection, the league will help to carry us successfully into the future.

Melanie Horn Mallers

See also: Americans with Disabilities Act (ADA); Activism; Administration on Aging (AoA); Commission on Civil Rights; Department of Labor (DOL); Discrimination; Dix, Dorothea; Equal Employment Opportunity Commission (EEOC); Federal Trade Commission (FTC); Food Safety; Frauds and Scams; Health and Health Care; Identity Theft; Insurance; Roosevelt, Franklin D.; Social Security; Social Services; Social Welfare

References and Additional Readings

Brobeck, S. (1997). *Encyclopedia of the consumer movement*. Santa Barbara, CA: ABC-CLIO.

National Consumers League. (2009). Retrieved from http://www.nclnet.org/

National Consumers League. (2013). Life smarts. Retrieved from http://www.life smarts.org/

Sklar, K. K. (1995). Two political cultures in the Progressive Era: The National Consumers' League and the American Association for Labor Legislation. *US history as women's history: New feminist essays*, 36–62.

Storrs, L. R. (2000). *Civilizing capitalism: The National Consumers' League, women's activism, and labor standards in the New Deal Era*. University of North Carolina Press.

Vose, C. E. (1957). The National Consumers' League and the Brandeis Brief. *Midwest Journal of Political Science*, 267–290.

National Credit Union Administration (NCUA)

The National Credit Union Administration (NCUA) is the federal agency responsible for chartering, supervising, examining, and insuring federal credit unions. NCUA also insures the accounts of those state credit unions that opt for (or that are required by state law) to become federally insured. NCUA is an independent agency financed by fees and assessments paid by the credit unions under its jurisdiction, an arrangement comparable to that of national banks and the Comptroller of the Currency. As an independent agency with a board appointed by the president of the United States, this supervisory authority gives credit unions the same status as other major financial institutions in relations with the executive and legislative branches of government. NCUA operates and manages the National Credit Union Share Insurance Fund (NCUSIF), insuring deposits of nearly 92 million account holders in all federal credit unions and the majority of state-chartered credit unions.

Organizational Structure

The NCUA is directed by a three-member board (chairman and two members). Each member is appointed by the president of the United States with the advice and consent of the Senate for specific terms. No more than two board members can be from the same political party, and each member serves a staggered six-year term. A provision in the Federal Credit Union Act requires appointees to the board to be people with a proven record of experience in credit unions.

NCUA differs organizationally from other federal financial institutions regulators in that the chartering, supervisory, examining, and insurance functions are vested in the one agency. There is no separate entity for insurance such as the Federal Deposit Insurance Corporation or the Federal Savings and Loan Insurance Corporation. Rather, share insurance for credit unions is provided through the Share Insurance Fund, a separate fund administered by the NCUA. In addition to the main offices in Washington, D.C., there are five regional offices. These regional offices are the operational bases for the field examination staff and the entry points for applications for chartering and insurance. These offices also handle on-site liquidation activities and conduct reviews of examination reports. Each office is supervised by a regional administrator.

Regulatory Responsibilities

NCUA also differs from other financial institution supervisory agencies in that it actually helps to organize federal credit unions. Supervisory activities focus on preventing and correcting operating problems. Through the issuance of regulations limiting or controlling certain practices or activities, the regulations attempt to prevent problems from developing. The Federal Credit Union Act allows NCUA to suspend or revoke charters or to place a federal credit union in involuntary liquidation if the credit union is insolvent or has violated the provisions of the Federal Credit Union Act, its bylaws, or any NCUA regulations.

Additional powers are provided under the share insurance provisions of the Federal Credit Union Act including the power to issue cease and desist orders, suspend or remove officers and directors, require additional reserves, and terminate insurance.

NCUA has other responsibilities including operations of the Central Liquidity Facility, the Community Development Revolving Loan Fund, and the Temporary Corporate Credit Union Stabilization Fund. The NCUA Chairman holds a voting seat on the Financial Stability Oversight Council, created in 2010 by the Dodd–Frank Wall Street Reform and Consumer Protection Act to monitor and ensure the stability of the U.S. financial system.

NCUA hosts a website and a toll-free line to help consumers locate credit unions. Additional services provide information regarding consumer protection and rights, resolve member complaints, and promote financial literacy.

National Share Insurance Fund

The National Credit Union Share Insurance Fund (NCUSIF) is the federal fund created by Congress in 1970 to insure member's deposits in federally insured credit unions. Administered by the National Credit Union Administration, the NCUSIF is backed by the full faith and credit of the U.S. government. The 1970 legislation required that all federal credit unions become insured and allowed the administrator (replaced by the NCUA board in 1978) to extend coverage to willing state-chartered credit unions that met the criteria established in the law. Several states have passed laws requiring state-chartered credit unions to become federally insured and many states require that they be insured by the federal government or a program approved by the state.

NCUA's standard maximum share insurance amount was permanently set at $250,000 in 2010 (individual accounts up to $250,000 and joint accounts up to $250,000 per member) by the Dodd–Frank Wall Street Reform and Consumer Protection Act. IRA and KEOGH retirement accounts are separately insured up to $250,000 by the NCUSIF.

The NCUSIF is financed with the premiums paid by the insured credit unions. By law, federally insured credit unions maintain one percent of their deposits in the NCUSIF and the NCUA boards can levy a premium if necessary. Taxpayer dollars are not used to fund the NCUSIF. No members have ever lost money from credit unions that are insured by the NCUSIF, according to NCUA.

History

The Federal Credit Union Act was signed into law in 1934, by President Roosevelt, which authorized the formation of federally chartered credit unions in all states. The federal agency that regulated federally chartered credit unions was first known as the Bureau of Federal Credit Unions, and was established in the Farm Credit Administration. Over the years, several federal agencies assumed regulatory responsibility for the Bureau of Federal Credit Unions, including the Federal Deposit Insurance Corporation, the Federal Security Agency, and the Department of Health, Education and Welfare. In 1970, the Bureau of Federal Credit Unions became known as the National Credit Union Administration. The NCUA's first assignment was to administer the National Credit Union Share Insurance Act of 1970, which provided, at that time, $20,000 coverage for share accounts of members of all federal credit unions and participating state credit unions.

A three-member board became the governing board of the agency in 1979 replacing the NCUA administrator. Congress created the Central Liquidity Facility also in 1979, which was recognized as the "credit union lender of last resort" (NCUA, 2012). For several years, credit unions operated in an arena of deregulation, greater flexibility in mergers and field of membership criteria, and expanded member services.

In the 1980s, higher interest rates and unemployment created insurance losses for many credit unions. With authorization granted by Congress, federally insured credit unions recapitalized the NCUSIF in 1985, to ease the financially stressed fund, by depositing 1 percent of their shares into the fund. Since then, credit unions have only been charged a premium by the NCUA board when the fund dropped to a 1.25 percent equity ratio.

Mary Jane "M.J." Kabaci

See also: Banking; Credit Unions

References and Additional Readings
Dublin, J. (1971). *Credit unions: Theory and practice.* Detroit, MI: Wayne State University Press.

Melvin, D.J., Davis, R.N., & Fischer, G.C. (1977). *Credit unions and the credit union industry: A study of the powers, organization, regulation and competition.* New York: The New York Institute of Finance.

National Credit Union Administration (NCUA). (2012). Retrieved from http://www.ncua.gov

Pugh, O.S., & Ingram, F.J. (1984), *Credit union management.* Reston, VA: Reston Publishing Company, Inc.

National Do Not Call Registry

The purpose of the National Do Not Call Registry (16CFR310.8) is to give consumers the option to limit telemarketing calls. Prior to its enactment in January, 2005, and the subsequent amendments in February, 2008, pesky telemarketing calls were a major intrusion into the lives of most Americans. Surveys indicate that consumers would receive approximately 30 calls a month prior to the rule's enactment. Since the National Do Not Call Registry became a regulation, calls have dropped at least fivefold.

Some argue that telemarketers should never be able to call unless specifically asked to do so by consumers and that the rule is too weak. Indeed there is a plethora of exceptions to the Registry Rule that cause consumers to continue to be irritated by such calls. Exceptions include, but are not necessarily limited to the following: (1) political representatives and political organizations, (2) charities, (3) telephone surveyors, (4) calls from companies with which the recipient has an existing business relationship, and (5) those to whom the recipient has provided express agreement in writing to receive their calls. It should be noted, however, that individuals may prevent calls from telemarketers who represent a company with whom an existing business relationship exists and from companies with which they previously provided express permission to receive calls from the company. An individual accomplishes this by informing the telemarketer to add their telephone number to the company's in-house do-not-call list. The company must honor the request.

The National Do Not Call Registry was an important piece of legislation protecting consumers from unwanted telemarketing solicitations. (Habrda/Shutterstock.com)

Further action can be taken by an individual to limit calls from legally exempt organizations, for example, nonprofits, political parties. Most companies and organizations voluntarily maintain such lists, including those that are exempt from the Do Not Call Registry. Still others are required to maintain their company-specific do-not-call lists. For example, companies with which the recipient has an existing business relationship, and those to whom the recipient has provided express agreement in writing to receive their calls as noted earlier. Thus, if contacted by a company that may be exempted from the National Registry, the concerned consumer should request to be placed on the company's in-house do-not-call list. Some entities are required to comply when requested; others comply as a courtesy.

Initially, the registry only covered those industries under the jurisdiction of the Federal Trade Commission (FTC), leaving out such industries as financial institutions, insurance companies, "junk" fax companies, and telecommunications companies. However, once the Federal Communications Commission (FCC) joined the FTC's registry the list of telemarketers required to comply with the National Do Not Call Registry substantially increased.

It is important to note that a major loophole in the rule exists because consumer inquiries are treated as exemptions. For example, an inquiry about or application for a service or product entitles a telemarketer to contact the inquirer up to three months after the contact. Examples such as calling a toll-free number about a product and inquiring or applying for a service on a website when the consumer provides a telephone number both constitute exemptions to the rule.

As noted on the FTC website, signing up for a contest or sweepstakes *is* not considered an inquiry or an application and should not result in telemarketing calls from those companies. However, if the form indicates that by signing and providing the home telephone number he/she has given express consent for a telemarketer to call, the rule no longer applies and the consumer may be contacted.

The telemarketing rules also prohibit telemarketers from blocking their calling numbers. That is they must transmit a telephone number and, if possible, the company name to caller ID devices and/or to those who use the *69 call-return feature. The company phone number must be one that can be called during normal business hours so that the request to be put on the company's in-house *Do-Not-Call List* can be easily accomplished. The law also requires telemarketers to provide their phone number when asked.

For some, fax transmissions can be as onerous as telemarketing solicitations. Federal law states that "no person may use a telephone facsimile machine, computer, or other device to send an unsolicited advertisement to a telephone facsimile machine 'without that person's prior express invitation or permission' " (47 USC 227 (a) (4)). The only companies that are allowed to send fax solicitations are those with which a consumer already has an existing business relationship (EBR) and only if they are given written consent with the recipient's signature.

The FTC and FCC will generally not take legal action against a telemarketer unless substantial and frequent violations of the rule have been determined. For the most part, complaints from consumers are the manner in which the federal and state agencies enforcing the law determine whom to investigate for possible noncompliance of the registry mandates.

Typical examples of violations include contact by a telemarketer who is not exempt from the rule, where previous requests to be placed on a company specific in-house *Do-Not-Call List* are ignored after the 30-day grace period is up, and also being in receipt of junk fax(es) without having an EBR with the sender.

Although the focus of this entry is the specifics of the National Do Not Call Registry, the prudent consumer should determine whether his/her state has its own no call registry and whether it is necessary to subscribe to both the state and federal do-not-call lists.

The success of the National Do Not Call Registry has given consumers a break from unwanted telemarketing calls, especially those that seem to arrive at dinner time.

Mel J. Zelenak

See also: Federal Communications Commission (FCC); Federal Trade Commission (FTC)

References and Additional Readings

Federal Communications Commission. (2011). Retrieved from www.fcc.gov/cgb/donotcall/Cached-Similar

Gupta, S. (2009). U.S. Patent Application 12/415,422.

Levy, R. A. (2012). The Do-Not-Call Solution: Turn the Ringer Off. *The Tea.*

National Do Not Call Registry. (n.d.). Retrieved from www.donotcall.gov

National Highway Traffic Safety Administration (NHTSA)

The Highway Safety Act of 1970 created the National Highway Traffic Safety Administration. Housed within the Department of Transportation, the newly developed administration assumed some of the functions of the Federal Highway Administration. These functions included highway and automobile safety. The Federal Highway Administration still oversees the infrastructure, design, construction, and maintenance of the national highway systems, including some federal and tribal lands.

National Traffic and Motor Vehicle Safety Act

The National Traffic and Motor Vehicle Safety Act of 1966 established the National Highway Safety Bureau which is now known as the National Highway Traffic and Safety Administration. The act, which was overseen by the first director of the administration, William Haddon, a physician, sought to reduce injuries in automobile accidents. The act allowed the federal government to create standards of safety for cars and highways. Some of the innovations in automobiles and roadways included:

- padded dashboards
- head rest restraints
- shatter-resistant windshields
- impact-absorbing steering columns
- dual braking systems
- seat belt restraints
- increased roadway lighting
- increased number of guardrails
- better signage on roadways
- break away poles and fixtures

The National Highway Traffic Safety Administration carries out safety functions provided by the National Traffic and Motor Vehicle Safety Act of 1966 (renamed the Motor Vehicle Safety), the Highway Safety Act of 1966 and the Motor Vehicle Information and Cost Savings Act of 1972 (also since restructured).

NHTSA is responsible for reducing deaths, injuries, and economic losses from motor vehicle crashes. They accomplish this by creating and enforcing standards of safety for motor vehicles and related equipment and via grants to local and state agencies to assist them in their highway safety programs. NHTSA is also responsible for several related tasks including investigating motor vehicle safety defects, setting and enforcing fuel economy standards, helping communities reduce drunk driving, promoting safety belts, promoting use of child safety seats, investigating odometer fraud, establishing and enforcing vehicle antitheft regulations, and providing education and information to consumers on topics surrounding motor vehicle safety. And, finally, NHTSA carries out research on traffic safety and driver behavior. This research assists them in developing effective techniques for auto safety improvements.

The mission of the NHTSA (2012) is to "save lives, prevent injuries and reduce economic costs due to road traffic crashes, through education, research, safety standards and enforcement activity." Core values include integrity, service, and leadership.

The administration conducts investigations, including the famous crash test dummy videos that are seen on the news and on the websites. As a result of their findings, they often issue recalls and can order repairs be made by manufacturers. They also monitor manufacturer recalls, initiated by manufacturers themselves. One of the more recent and highly publicized recalls involved Toyota and their steering relay rod recall. The Department of Transportation determined that Toyota did not do an adequate job in handling the recall and as a result, Toyota had to pay millions of dollars in civil penalties.

Through education and partnership with other organizations, the administration helps promote several activities that further its mission including national work zone awareness week, alcohol awareness month, national distracted driving awareness month, and national youth traffic safety month. Through these and other efforts, the department has been highly successful as part of the Department of Transportation in working to make America's highways safer.

Wendy Reiboldt

In October 2012, the National Highway Traffic Safety Administration announced seizure of fake air bags that are being sold by a Chinese manufacturer for between $50 and $75. The item typically retails for around $1,000, and the administration noted that approximately 2,500 fake airbags have been seized during the 2012 year. A video on the NHTSA website demonstrating the counterfeit airbags shows the devastating outcome that can occur if a fake airbag is in use. Fake air bags can fail to deploy, can explode, or send metal shrapnel into the driver.

Consumers who are at risk include those who do not have full knowledge of their vehicle's history, including the possibility of an after-market air bag installation, consumers who have had their air bag replaced within the last three years by a repair shop other than an automotive dealership, consumers who own a car with a salvage, rebuilt, or reconstructed stamp on the auto title, consumers who have purchased air bags from eBay or other noncertified entities, especially if the air bags' price was exceptionally low. While the risk of having a fake air bag is low, estimated to be about .1 percent, consumers can choose to have their air bag tested, at a cost to the consumer of between $100 and $200. The administration points out that some cars have up to eight air bags.

See also: Auto Purchasing; Department of Transportation (DOT); National Transportation Safety Board (NTSB); Public Safety

References and Additional Readings

Bradsher, K. (2003). *High and mighty: The dangerous rise of the SUV*. New York: Public Affairs.

Nader, R. (1972). *Unsafe at any speed: The designed-in dangers of the American automobile*. New York: Grossman.

National Highway Traffic Safety Administration. (2012). Core values. Retrieved from http://www.nhtsa.gov/About+NHTSA/NHTSA's+Core+Values

National Highway Traffic Safety Administration. (2013). Retrieved from http://www.nhtsa.gov

National Institute of Occupational Safety and Health (NIOSH). *See* Centers for Disease Control and Prevention (CDC)

National Minimum Drinking Age Act

The National Minimum Drinking Age Act was signed into law on July 17, 1984, by President Ronald Reagan. The act provided for withholding of federal highway funds from states that did not prohibit the purchase or public possession of any alcohol beverage by a person less than 21 years of age. By 1988, all states were in compliance with the act, although 19 states do not ban "underage" alcohol consumption outright. Many states permit underage consumption in some circumstances (religious ceremonies, supervised by family members). The intention of the act is to reduce alcohol use and associated problems among youth and young adults. By some accounts, the act saves 700–1,000 lives annually through reductions in alcohol-related traffic accidents. In addition, the National Highway System Designation Act of 1995 conditioned highway funds on adoption of a zero-tolerance law. By 1998, all states had adopted Zero Tolerance Laws requiring blood alcohol content (BAC) of less than 0.02 percent for drivers under the age of 21. Finally, in 2000, President William Clinton signed into law a transportation bill that required states to adopt a 0.08 BAC standard for adult drivers by October, 2003, or lose federal highway funds. Before this law was passed, only 19 states and the District of Columbia had a legal BAC limit of 0.08 percent.

Following the repeal of Prohibition in 1933, the individual states were given the authority to regulate the transportation, importation, distribution, and possession of alcohol beverages within their borders. Among many other provisions, this meant that each state could set its own minimum legal drinking age (MLDA). Since the age of majority at that time was 21, most states set the legal purchase age at 21 years. In 1971, the Twenty-Sixth Amendment lowered the minimum voting age to 18 and thereafter most states also set the age of majority at 18 years. During 1969–1976, some 30 states lowered the MLDA, generally to 18 years, but in some cases to 19 or 20. These actions were associated with increases in traffic fatalities among youth. During 1977–1982, a number of states increased their MLDAs. In 1982, President Reagan established the 30-member Presidential Commission on Drunk Driving. The commission's final report, issued in November, 1983, contained 39 recommendations including a presumptive BAC of 0.08 percent, prohibition of open containers in automobiles, and a uniform MLDA of 21 years. The report's commentary emphasized the lack of uniformity among state MLDA laws and the incentive for young person's to commute to border states if the drinking age was lower. Intense lobbying by several groups, such as Mothers Against Drunk Driving (MADD) and Remove the Intoxicated Driver (RID), led Senator Frank Lautenberg (D-NJ) to propose an amendment to the Surface Transportation Assistance Act. Ultimately, the amendment became known as the National Minimum Drinking Age Act of 1984.

During Congressional debates, several issues emerged regarding a federally mandated MLDA. One objection was that the act violated states' rights under both the Tenth and Twenty-First Amendments, and represented a form of blackmail by the federal government. Reflecting these concerns, 12 states unsuccessfully challenged the act's constitutionality in *South Dakota v. Dole*, 483 U.S. 203 (1987). A second objection is that the drinking age law is discriminatory, given that young persons between the ages of 18 and 21 years are legally adults for most other purposes. More recently, some have argued that the MLDA worsens the problem of underage drinking on college campuses. The Amethyst Initiative, a project of Choose Responsibility, calls for an "informed and dispassionate debate over the effects of the 21-year-old drinking age." More than 135 college presidents have signed the project's presidential statement supporting unfettered debate regarding the uniform MLDA, requiring as a first step the repeal of the highway funds "penalty." Another objection is that the MLDA-21 shifts alcohol problems to the 21–24 age group, so the net effect of the act is uncertain. Finally, some argue that the act merely reduced drinking by responsible youth and the decline in traffic fatalities reflects other key policies, such as safer automobiles or improved enforcement.

In 1982, there were 7,982 motor vehicle traffic fatalities involving 16–20-year olds, including 5,244 alcohol-related fatal accidents (any positive BAC). By 1991, alcohol-related fatalities had fallen to 3,013, but other fatalities rose from 2,738 to 3,144. During the period 1992–2001, alcohol- related fatalities averaged about 2,250 per year and nonalcohol fatalities were about 3,500 per year. During 2001–2009, alcohol-related fatalities among youth declined from 2,358 to 1,461. Nonalcohol related fatalities declined from 3,705 to 2,457. As a percent of total youth fatalities, accidents involving alcohol were 66 percent in 1982 and only 37 percent in 2009. This seems like a sure sign of progress, except that alcohol-related fatalities (any positive BAC) for all age levels also declined from 60 percent of all fatal accidents in 1982 to 38 percent in 2009. These changes occurred despite an 85 percent increase in vehicle miles traveled between 1982 and 2009.

There have been numerous attempts by researchers to parse the effects of the act on youth traffic fatalities and alcohol consumption. The variation in state MLDAs prior to 1988 represents a "natural experiment," but it is important to control also for state-specific heterogeneity, underlying time trends, and alcohol prices. A systematic review in 2002 of 132 analyses concluded that an inverse relationship exists between the MLDA and outcome measures for alcohol consumption and traffic crashes. However, the evidence for college-specific effects was weak. A high-quality analysis by Thomas Dee, reported in a 1999 issue of the *Journal of Public Economics*, found that the movement to a MLDA-21 reduced heavy drinking by high school seniors by at least 8 percent and traffic fatalities by 9–11 percent. Actual alcohol-related traffic fatalities for youth aged 16–20 declined by 55 percent between 1982 and 1992, so the higher MLDA accounts for about 20 percent of this change. The official figure used by the National High-way Traffic Safety Administration is that the act reduced all traffic fatalities (regardless of age) by 13 percent in those states where the drinking age was raised to 21.

Jon P. Nelson

See also: Department of Transportation (DOT); National Highway Traffic Safety Administration (NHTSA); Public Safety

References and Additional Readings

Amethyst Initiative. (n.d.). Statement. Retrieved from http://www.theamethysti nitiative.org/statement/

Carpenter, C., & Dobkin, C. (2011). The minimum legal drinking age and public health. *Journal of Economic Perspectives, 25,* 133–156.

Cook, P. J. (2007). *Paying the tab: The costs and benefits of alcohol control.* Princeton, NJ: Princeton University Press.

Nelson J. P. (2008). How similar are youth and adult alcohol behaviors? *Atlantic Economic Journal, 36,* 89–104.

National Traffic and Motor Vehicle Safety Act. *See* National Highway Traffic Safety Administration (NHTSA)

National Transportation Safety Board (NTSB)

The National Transportation Safety Board (NTSB) was created by Congress and the Air Commerce Act of 1926 to investigate aircraft accidents. The board consists of five board members, nominated by the president and confirmed by the Senate. Each board member's term is five years, with chairman and vice chairman terms of two years. The role of chairman requires separate and additional confirmation from the Senate.

The NTSB employs approximately 400 people across its headquarters in Washington, D.C., and regional offices in Gardena, California; Anchorage, Alaska; Ashburn, Virginia; Miami, Florida; Atlanta, Georgia; Chicago, Illinois; Denver, Colorado; Arlington, Texas; and Federal Way, Washington, D.C.

As stated on their website, the mission of the NTSB is to promote transportation safety by:

- Maintaining congressionally mandated independence and objectivity;
- Conducting objective, precise accident investigations and safety studies;
- Performing fair and objective airman and mariner certification appeals;
- Advocating and promoting safety recommendation;
- Assisting victims of transportation accidents and their families.

The NTSB operates as an independent federal agency charged by Congress to investigate and report on every civil aviation accident in the United States. Furthermore, the NTSB is required to investigate all other significant accidents in other modes of transportation including railroad, highway, marine, and pipeline. The NTSB investigates and reports on the probable cause of the accidents and follows up with safety recommendations aimed at preventing future accidents. Furthermore, the NTSB carries out special studies on transportation safety and then coordinates the resources of the federal government and other entities in an effort to provide assistance to victims impacted by major transportation disasters.

The NTSB publishes its "most wanted" list which is a list of the board's priorities for reducing accidents and keeping consumers safe. The current list of priorities, as of this writing, is as follows: addressing human fatigue, general aviation safety, safety management systems, runway safety, bus occupant safety, pilot and air traffic controller professionalism, recorders, teen driver safety, addressing alcohol-impaired driving, and motorcycle

---

Organizations within the National Transportation Safety Board
Office of Administration
Office of Administrative Law Judges
Office of Aviation Safety
Office of Chief Financial Officer
Office of Chief Information Officer
Office of Communications
Office of Equal Employment Opportunity, Diversity and Inclusion
Office of the General Counsel
Office of Highway Safety
Office of the Managing Director
Office of Marine Safety
Office of Research and Engineering
Office of Railroad, Pipeline & Hazardous Materials Investigations

---

safety. Each category has an explanation of the issue at hand, as well as, things that can be done to improve safety in that category. There are many things consumers can do to increase their safety and the safety of others.

Wendy Reiboldt

See also: Auto Purchasing; Department of Transportation (DOT); Federal Aviation Administration (FAA); National Highway Traffic Safety Administration (NHTSA); Public Safety

References and Additional Readings

Mintzer, R. (2002). *The National Transportation Safety Board.* New York, NY: Chelsea House Publications.

National Transportation Safety Board. (2013). Retrieved from www.ntsb.gov

New Deal. *See* Roosevelt, Franklin D.

No FEAR Act. *See* Whistleblowing

Nursing Home Rights

Nursing home residents have rights that are protected by both federal and state laws. Federal rights are supported by the Nursing Home Reform Law of 1987. This law requires nursing homes to "promote and protect the rights of each resident. Nursing homes must abide by these laws to be able to get funding from Medicare or Medicaid.

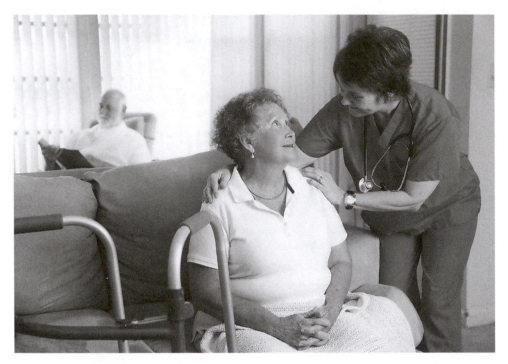

Senior citizens benefit from around-the-clock care when they choose to live in nursing homes. (Lisafx/Dreamstime.com)

These laws protect a person during the admission process, during transfer or discharge, and during the time that the person lives in the nursing home. In general, these laws aim to protect residents' rights including being treated with respect, being informed about fees, managing one's own money, maintaining privacy, and being informed about and involved in one's own health care.

Regarding admission to a nursing home, federal codes protect the right of the nursing home resident to be given the opportunity to complete an advance directive form, which allows the person to designate wishes about end of life care in the case that he or she can no longer communicate. Federal law also includes regulations about reimbursement from Medicare or Medicaid, including a rule that nursing homes may not require potential residents to waive their Medicare or Medicaid as part of being admitted to the nursing home [42 USC §1395i-3(c)(5)(A)(i)(I); 42 USC §1396r(c)(5)(A)(i)(I)]. State laws may cover what is allowable in an admission contract, such as requiring a detailed statement about what services are included in the monthly rate and how long a resident's bed must be held if he or she is admitted to the hospital.

Transfer (movement from one facility to another) or discharge (movement from a facility to a noninstitutional setting) is also regulated by federal law. Much of the federal law has to do with conditions under which it is legal to discharge or transfer a resident such as if the facility will close [42 USC §1395i-3(c)(2)(A)(vi); 42 USC §1396r(c)(2)(A)(vi)] or it is no longer safe to allow the person to live in that facility [42 USC §1395i-3(c)(2)(A)(iii); 42 USC §1396r(c)(2)(A)(iii)]. These laws also require that a resident is given proper notice before he or she will be transferred or discharged. The Nursing Home Reform Law of 1987 requires a nursing home to give a resident and his or her family member or legal representative notice at least 30 days in advance of the transfer or discharge.

During residence in a nursing home, the person is entitled to several rights under federal law. These laws aim to provide a resident with the highest quality care possible that attends to his biological, psychological, and social needs. It also aims to individualize the care as much as possible so that each resident's preferences for care and activities are met. Additionally, federal laws protect residents against elder abuse including verbal, sexual, physical, and mental abuse as well as corporal punishment [42 USC §1395i-3(c)(1)(A)(ii); 42 USC §1396r (c)(1)(A)(ii)]. Federal regulations address the rights of residents to make their own healthcare choices such as choosing a physician, participating in care, and having access to medical records. Informed consent, or agreeing to something after having full knowledge and understanding of it, is at the heart of these laws.

Involuntary seclusion and the use of chemical or physical restraints for the purpose of disciplining a resident or making care easier or more convenient are against federal law.

Federal law regulates a nursing home resident's right to make choices about participation in activities at the nursing home facility, communication with people both inside and outside of the nursing home, and involvement with the facility's residents' council. A residents' council is a group of nursing home residents that meet regularly to discuss concerns about life in the nursing home and make suggestions to staff and administration. These meetings are open to all residents, who may invite others, such as nursing home staff or administrators, to join the meeting.

The right to privacy is protected by federal and state laws. Under federal law, residents have the right to privacy to communicate with individuals or groups in a private setting. They also have the right to keep information about health and financial matters private.

Once living in the nursing home, a resident has the right to refuse being moved to another part of the nursing home and must receive the same care even if payment sources have changed. Further, residents cannot be treated differently according to the source of their payment (e.g., Medicare vs. Medicaid vs. private pay). Nursing homes must allow residents to manage their own personal funds and not require the deposit of funds at the facility.

Family members of nursing home residents also have rights. Under federal law, they must be able to visit any time and should be given the opportunity to participate in the resident's care, with the resident's consent, whenever possible.

Finally, an important part of the many rights afforded to nursing home residents is the law that residents can file a complaint if they think a law has been broken and that the nursing home may not retaliate in any way against a resident that has filed a grievance. Each state has a program that provides advocates to help nursing home residents and their families report and find solutions to situations in which nursing homes are not protecting the rights of its residents. The Long-Term Care Ombudsman Program is a requirement by federal law to protect the rights of residents in long-term care facilities.

The Affordable Care Act (health reform), which wasfully implemented in 2013, will further improve the care and safety of nursing home residents through its Nursing Home Transparency and Elder Justice provisions. These provisions will ensure that several steps be taken by nursing homes including more information to guide families in the choice of a nursing home for their loved one, public disclosure of nursing home owners and operators, increased accountability and oversight, a better consumer complaint system, better notification of closures for smoother relocation, elder abuse prevention training, ombudsman training, background checks on nursing home staff, mandatory elder abuse reporting, and increased coordination among agencies that deal with elder abuse.

Maria Claver

See also: Estate Planning; Health and Healthcare; Long-Term Care; Medicaid; Medicare

References and Additional Readings

California Advocates for Nursing Home Reform. (2010). Outline of nursing home residents' rights. Retrieved from http://www.canhr.org/factsheets/nh_fs/html/fs_outline_resrights.htm

Medicare. (2012). Nursing homes: Resident rights. Retrieved from http://www.medicare.gov/nursing/residentrights.asp

The National Consumer Voice for Quality Long-Term Care. (2007). *Residents' rights: An overview.* Washington, DC: NCCNHR.

The National Consumer Voice for Quality Long-Term Care. (2011). The Affordable Care Act. Retrieved from http://www.nursinghomeaction.org/public/50_156_455.cfm

Older Americans Act (OAA)

In 1965, Congress passed the Older Americans Act (OAA) in response to the concern by policymakers about a lack of community and social services for older adults. The original legislation gave authority for states to receive grants that would allow them to develop community planning and social services, as well as to develop and implement research projects, and training for aging-related personnel. OAA also established that the Administration on Aging (AoA) would administer this grant program and serve as the hub or focal point on all broad matters related to older citizens.

Today, the OAA is one of the major vehicles that assists in the organization and delivery of several programs for older adults and their caregivers, including social and nutrition services. It does this by overseeing individual state-based Offices on Aging or Area Agencies on Aging, service providers, tribal organizations, and Hawaiian natives. The OAA also oversees community service employment for low-income elders, ongoing education for professionals in the aging field, and activities related to elder protection rights.

In 2006, the act was updated and several amendments were made. Several new definitions, such as related to assistive devices, caregivers, and neglect were added. The amendments also strengthened the role of the AoA and Assistant Secretary for Aging, as well as expanded efforts to target services to older adults with limited proficiency in English. Several other amendments were made:

- Title I: Declarations of Objectives and Definitions—updates and makes consistent aging-related terms with other statutes and proposals, as well as introduces several new words related to assistive device/technology, elder justice, and principles of choices for independence.
- Title II: Administration on Aging—broadens the role of the AoA as it concerns to justice, elder abuse, and mental health. For example, it designates a federal staff person for elder abuse prevention and mental health services.

Then and now, the OAA has provided instrumental and critical support for older adults. (Creatista/Shutterstock.com)

- Title III: Grants for State and Community Programs on Aging—funds grants related to several issues affecting older adults, including nutrition, mental health, older adults with limited English-speaking skills, baby boomers and family care providers, volunteers in direct service to older adults, and disaster preparedness.

- Title IV: Activities for Health, Independence, and Longevity—this increases the type and nature of activities eligible to receive grant funding. This includes multigenerational activities, aging in place, transportation, and education and awareness for cognitive impairments.

- Title V: Community Service Senior Opportunities Act—within the Department of Labor, the amendment expands financial opportunities for low-income older adults who are unemployed to participate in a community service and work-based training program.

- Title VI: Grants for Native Americans—allows tribal organizations that were part of an earlier consortium to continue to apply for funding.

- Title VII: Vulnerable Elder Rights Protection—expands funding to activities that include public education on financial literacy, identify theft and exploitation, as well as elder abuse shelters, and provisions to underserved older adult populations.

As reported by the AoA, as of 2010, there were 40.4 million adults aged 65 and older. By 2030, this number is projected to increase to over 70 million. Given these projections, strong legislation and policy related to the rights of older adults are critical.

Melanie Horn Mallers

See also: Activism; Administration on Aging (AoA); Department of Labor (DOL); Frauds and Scams; Health and Health Care; Mandated Reporters; Public Safety; Social Services Programs; Social Welfare

References and Additional Readings

Administration on Aging. (2011a). A profile of older Americans: 2011. Retrieved from http://www.aoa.gov/aoaroot/aging_statistics/Profile/index.aspx

Administration on Aging. (2011b). Outline of 2006 amendments to the older Americans act. Retrieved from http://www.aoa.gov/AoA_programs/OAA/oaa .aspx

Hudson, R. B. (2010). The Older Americans Act and the aging services network. *The New Politics of Old Age Policy, 14*, 307.

O'Shaughnessy, C. (2011). The Basics: Older Americans act of 1965: Programs and funding. *National Health Policy Forum.*

Ombuds Offices

The position of ombuds was first created in Sweden in 1809. That original ombuds was to act as the people's agent or representative in the abducted royalty's absence. Today, ombuds encompass several distinct functions including the legislative, classical (or executive), organizational, and advocate ombuds. As Howard Gadlin, ombuds at the National Institutes of Health has observed, the proliferation of a variety of ombuds models in different sectors performing different functions and serving myriad constituencies lead to confusion in the general public about what an ombudsman is. The classical, or executive, legislative and advocate ombuds is a quasilegal role that fields complaints (consumer and other), conducts factual investigations and makes recommendations based on the results of its findings. The legislative is traditionally appointed by the legislative branch, to investigate poor administration of government. All classical roles tend to focus on maladministration and rule breaches. Thus, they serve a watchdog oversight role regarding the policies and procedures that govern their jurisdiction. The advocate ombuds, such as the Long-Term Care ombuds, actually advocates for the rights of particular constituencies. The organizational ombuds, in contrast, is employed by organizations, typically corporations, international agencies, and universities/colleges. It expressly distinguishes its role from those described earlier as an informal "soft" alternative to legal channels of redress.

Given the distinct ombuds roles just described, the first step to consumer protection is for the consumer to be aware and informed of the type of ombuds being used. Since the first contact with an ombuds typically involves expression of consumer complaint or concern, the actual ombuds may initially appear to be alike in how they represent themselves. Since their responses to consumer complaints are quite different, the ombuds should introduce themselves to consumers with a thorough and complete description of their approach, including the limits of their office and the code of ethics. Consumers should leave their first visit or conversation with any ombuds with the ability to identify whether the ombuds is classical or organizational and articulate their expectations of next steps.

Some organizations, like universities, ask faculty or staff to play a dual role. This creates a clear ethical dilemma that is beyond the scope of this introduction. During their initial conversations with an ombuds, consumers are advised to research whether the ombuds has a dual or competing role. Learning that an ombuds does hold another job within an organization in addition to acting as ombuds should serve as a red flag indicator that this ombuds office has been established without careful regard for professional ethical standards.

Whatever the ombuds' specific role, consumers need to know that no ombuds has the authority or power to mandate change. They can only present their recommendations and attempt to persuade those who do hold this authority. Some classical ombuds regularly refer concerns to attorney general offices, but a consumer should check on this relationship rather than assume it is present. Nevertheless, many, if not most, consumers may still be willing to explore this informal dispute resolution. Research has shown that most consumers are not interested in pursuing lawsuits against their doctors as one instance, even when they are undeniably harmed. The ombuds provides an alternative for addressing concerns.

All ombuds should share three essential characteristics. If any of these appear absent or questionable to consumers, they are advised to be cautious to ensure that they and their interests are not damaged. Ombuds should be entirely independent from the control of those who may be subject to complaint or investigation. They should be impartial, without bias, preference or conflict of interest favoring one party over another. They should keep all consumer information, including identifying data, confidential.

Classical

Classical ombuds can demonstrate fulfillment of their mandate to investigate, publicize, and confront legal concerns with data. Consumers can ask to see such data when deciding whether to use classical ombuds services.

Some classical ombuds derive their powers from legislation requiring cooperation with the ombuds when complaints are received. Consumers can ask to see authorizing legislation when acquainting themselves with a particular ombuds' mandate. As mentioned earlier, classical ombuds have investigatory powers and make recommendations after fact finding. Legislation may grant these ombuds the authority to recommend compensation or other remedial measures to consumers. Unlike legal action, however, the process will normally be confidential. Some classical ombuds office, however, like the Office of the Independent Adjudicator for Higher Education in Great Britain, have the ability to end confidentiality and name and shame institutions who fail to comply with ombuds recommendation.

Organizational

The term "Organizational Ombudsman" was first used by Mary Rowe (1995, 103–104) in the mid-1980s. She defined the term as "a confidential and informal information resource, communications channel, complaint-handler and dispute resolver, and a person who helps an organization work for change." Even though organizational ombuds are employed by their organizational leaders and laud their ability to help organizations avoid lawsuits and scandalous publicity, their ethical code still speaks of independence, specifying that ombuds should avoid the reality and the appearance of bias and conflict of interest. Impartiality regarding all perspectives is stressed.

Despite such encouraging and idealistic language, however, consumers must be aware, that like mediation, the intervention of an organizational ombuds is informal and behind the scenes. Consumers will need to consider the more formal, quasilegal, or legal channels available to them if their particular ombuds neglects the above ethical principles, advises leadership who does nothing in response to the ombuds recommendation, or otherwise is unable to facilitate a satisfactory or just response to consumer complaints and concerns. Unlike arbitration where the consumer has contracted away their more formal legal recourse in exchange for agreeing to arbitration, the consumer does not give up their rights when engaging an ombuds. If consumers are dissatisfied with the ombuds or organizational response, they are encouraged to consider consulting with a trusted lawyer or that organization's quasilegal or legal offices available for consumer redress.

An organizational ombuds office might be a useful first step to surveying organizational climate and responsiveness to consumer concern. It is encouraging to see that many organizational ombuds describe their most important role as an early warning mechanism providing upward feedback and otherwise catalyzing systemic improvement. If a consumer is satisfied with simply contributing to needed organizational improvement over time, that consumer may be content with simply reporting concerns to the organizational ombuds. Otherwise, the consumer must take responsibility for ensuring that individual concerns are adequately addressed.

If a consumer decides to meet with an organizational ombuds, the consumer should know that according to the ethical language advocated by the International Association of Ombudsman, the ombuds office should be located so that it protects visitors' privacy and honors the confidentiality promised. The office, for example, should not be located within the view of administrators overseeing that particular organization. Ideally, it should not be within the view of anyone in the organization who might be the subject of a consumer complaint.

Consumers need to appreciate the tough challenges organizational and other ombuds face to be realistic in their expectations of what can occur after engaging an ombuds. While organizational ombuds are often warm and welcoming staff who sincerely wish to hear and understand consumer concerns, they have no ethical responsibility or capacity for ensuring that organizational leadership respond to consumer concerns in any way. Newer and lesser experienced organizational ombuds may not yet be fully prepared to skillfully and effectively navigate organizational power and politics. Their power and influence depend on building ethical alliances with those holding institutional power. Personality plays a role. Even when the organizational ombuds are masterful, highly ethical and courageous, courts have not consistently recognized the ombuds' promise of confidentiality.

Yet, despite the challenge and uncertainty, a masterful organizational ombuds may be exactly what a consumer needs when seeking to bring attention to a concern and stimulate organizational change. The best organizational ombuds have critical access to those with decision-making power. They are skilled in conflict resolution tools and prepared to engage in dialogue with leadership when complaints reveal organizational behavior that contradicts the organization's mission and values. Some know the value of doing a reality check with leadership, or reviewing the potential consequences and costs of failing to address a complaint. If a consumer is willing to participate in a mediation, or informal meeting with those involved in a complaint to attempt to discuss and resolve it to everyone's satisfaction, many organizational ombuds are prepared to facilitate.

Nevertheless, consumers must be prepared to assess their ombuds office and the organizational climate, perhaps with ombuds assistance, to discern what is realistic and in their best interests. In one survey, several organizational ombuds reported systemic abuse of power as their greatest challenge, with ombuds' disclosure being met with apathy and even hostility from leadership tolerating this abuse. The best of organizational ombuds cultivate ethical alliances with organizational champions and support those who work with them to confront such wrong. Their moral courage can inspire, but they cannot be expected to perform miracles. They can review and refer to formal channels if needed. Consumers may wish to meet with them to fully explore the costs, risks, and benefits of each avenue available to them. The website of the American Bar Association provides valuable information to help consumers with this decision-making.

Nancy D. Erbe

See also: Arbitration, Mediation; National Consumer Law Center (NCLC)

References and Additional Readings

Erbe, N. D. (2006). Appreciating mediation's global role in promoting good governance. *Harvard Negotiation Law Review, 11,* 355–340.

Erbe, N. D., Guillermo-Newton, J., & Reddy, M. (2007). How ombuds succeed when raising tough issues. *The Journal of the California Caucus of College and University Ombuds, 9,* 15–20.

Erbe, N. D., & Sebok, T. (2008). Shared global interest in skillfully applying IOA standards of practice. *Journal of the International Ombudsman, 1,* 28–44.

Gadlin, H. (2000). The ombudsman: What's in a name? *Negotiation Journal, 16*(1), 37–48.

Riskin, L. L., Westbrook J. E., Guthrie, C., Reuben, R. C., & Robbennolt, J. K. (1987). *Dispute resolution and lawyers*. St. Paul, MN: West Publishing.

Rowe, M. (1995). Options, functions and skills: What an organizational ombudsperson might want to know. *Negotiation Journal, 16*(2), 99–114.

One Hundred Million Guinea Pigs

One Hundred Million Guinea Pigs: Dangers in Everyday Foods, Drugs, and Cosmetics was written by Arthur Kallet and Frederick J. Schlink. Its release in 1933 detailed the authors' perceived wrongdoings perpetrated on the American people (the population was 100 million at that time). In short, they alleged that consumers were unwittingly being used as guinea pigs in a large "human" experiment conducted by producers of foods, drugs, and cosmetics. They believed that the food and drug laws enacted to protect consumers were not effective, largely because of the relationship between government and large corporations.

An excerpt from *One Hundred Million Guinea Pigs*

In the magazines, newspapers, over the radio, a terrific verbal barrage has been laid down on 100 million Americans, first, to set in motion a host of fears about their health, their stomachs, their bowels, their teeth, their throats, their looks; second, to persuade them that only by eating, drinking, gargling, brushing, or smearing with Smith's Whole Vitamin Breakfast Food, Jones' Yeast Cubes, Blue Giant Apples, Prussian Salts, Listroboris Mouthwash, Grandpa's Wonder Toothpaste, and a thousand and one other foods, drinks, gargles, and pastes, can they either postpone the onset of disease, social ostracism, business failure, or recover from ailments, physical or social, already contracted.

If these foods and medicines were—to most of the people who use them—merely worthless; if there were no other charge to be made than that the manufacturers', sales managers', and advertising agents' claims for them were false, this book would not have been written. But many of them, including some of the most widely advertised and sold, are not only worthless, but are actually dangerous. That *All-Bran* you eat every morning—do you know that it may cause serious and perhaps irreparable intestinal trouble? That big juicy apple you have at lunch—do you know that indifferent government officials let it come to your table coated with arsenic, one of the deadliest of poisons? The *Pebeco* toothpaste with which you brush your teeth twice every day—do you know that a tube of it contains enough poison if eaten, to kill three people; that, in fact, a German army officer committed suicide by eating a tube full of this particular toothpaste? The *Bromo-Seltzer* that you take for headaches—do you know that it contains a poisonous drug that has been responsible for many deaths and, the American Medical Association says, at least one case of sexual impotence?

Using the feeble and ineffective pure food and drug laws as a smokescreen, the food and drug industries have been systematically bombarding us with falsehoods about the purity, healthfulness, and safely of their products, while they have been making profits by experimenting on us with poisons, irritants, harmful chemical preservatives, and dangerous drugs.

Just how we consumers are being forced into the role of laboratory guinea pigs through huge loopholes in obviously weak and ineffective laws is described at length in the chapters that follow. A brief glance at a few cases that show our present helplessness will suffice here.

Source: Kallet, Arthur, & Schlink, F. J. (1932). *100,000,000 Guinea pigs, dangers in everyday foods, drugs, and cosmetics.* New York: The Vanguard Press (pp. 3–18).

The book was well received by American consumers, whose senses were heightened since the depression, and became one of the best-selling books of its decade. The authors regaled and disgusted readers with real-life horror stories and scientific data to illustrate the damage done to consumers by dangerous and sometimes deadly food and cosmetic products. They called out, by name, popular products common in consumers' lives. To further illustrate their point, the authors applied economic principles to the damage these items caused to consumers, assigning a dollar value for time lost due to related minor and major illness, as well as, the cost of untimely death. They portrayed food and drug manufacturers, simply, as killers, often leading consumers to a slow death caused by tainted products.

The Authors

Both authors were well known for touting consumer causes and championing consumer safety and protection. Kallet was an engineer who, with Schlink, helped found Consumers' Research in 1928. There, Kallet served as a board member before becoming the Founding Executive Director of Consumers Union in 1936. Due to a bitter strike at Consumers' Research, allegedly related to issues surrounding communism, several strikers, including Kallet, joined together to create Consumers Union. Kallet served at Consumers Union until 1957.

Schlink was a mechanical engineer and physicist, as well as a prolific writer and coauthor, collaborating with others to write books about consumer protection issues including wasteful consumer spending and the consequences of industrialization. Throughout his career, he held top posts at the National Bureau of Standards, The American Standards Association as well as serving on the boards of Underwriter's Laboratories and the American National Standards Institute. With Kallet, he helped create Consumers' Research which later published *Consumers' Research Bulletin*. Schlink worked with Consumers' Research for 54 years.

Both men, and the book, *One Hundred Million Guinea Pigs*, did much to further the crusade on behalf of consumers. Legislation and valuable consumer organizations can be linked to both of these important men and the exposé.

Wendy Reiboldt

See also: Consumers Union; Food and Drug Administration (FDA); Food Safety; Product Labeling; Underwriters Laboratories (UL); Wiley, Harvey

References and Additional Readings

Canadian Medical Association Journal. (1934). One hundred million guinea pigs: And ten million more. *Canadian Medical Association Journal, 30*(3), 310–311.

Kallet, A., & Schlink, F.J. (1932). *100,000,000 guinea pigs: Dangers in everyday foods, drugs and cosmetics.* New York: The Vanguard Press.

Organic Foods

Background

The United States has been practicing organic production since the 1940s. Organic farming began with small, experimental garden plots and has grown to industrial size, with major farms producing all types of agricultural products under a special organic label. In addition to organic agriculture, food manufacturers have also created lines of specialty organic processed foods. This growth is what drove the need for verification that products are produced according to specific standards.

In 1990, Congress passed the Organic Food Production Act (OFPA). This required that the Secretary of Agriculture establish a National List of Allowed and Prohibited Substances to identify synthetic and nonsynthetic substances that can and cannot be used in organic production and handling operations in addition to developing national standards for organically produced agricultural products. The National Organic Program (NOP, a subdivision of the U.S. Department of Agriculture (USDA)) went into effect on December 21, 2000, assuring consumers that the organic agricultural products they purchase are produced, processed, and certified to consistent national organic standards. The NOP has stringent labeling standards that farmers and food manufacturers must meet in order to claim that their products are organic. Standards differ by food category; the two major categories are raw, fresh products and processed food products. It is important to note that the organic label does not guarantee that a food product is safe or meets any particular nutritional standard.

What Is in the NOP Regulations?

In order to use the label "organic," food producers must meet a variety of requirements at several different stages of the food production process. Organic livestock managers, for example, must ensure that their animals are fed with organic feed and that have access to the outdoors. Organically raised livestock cannot be administered antibiotics or growth hormones. Organic crops must be raised without using conventional pesticides, petroleum-based fertilizers, or sewage sludge-based fertilizers. Food companies that sell organic processed foods must meet further requirements. Prohibited methods of food production include genetic engineering, radiation, and any use of sewage sludge.

The full Code of Federal Regulations that governs organic food production can be found online at www.ecfr.gov. The code contains the specific requirements that were put in place by the National Standards on Organic Agricultural Production and Handling rule (the NOP rule). The Environmental Protection Agency (2012) highlights the following provisions of the NOP rule:

- Production and handling requirements, which address organic crop production, wild crop harvesting, organic livestock management, and processing and handling of organic agricultural products;
- The National List of Allowed Synthetic and Prohibited Non-Synthetic Substances (7 CFR 205.600–205.606);
- Labeling requirements for organic products;
- Compliance, testing, fee, and state program approval requirements;
- Certification and record-keeping requirements;
- Accreditation requirements for receiving and maintaining accreditation, as well as requirements for foreign accreditation; and
- Other administrative functions of the NOP, which include evaluation of foreign organic certification programs.

Labeling Standards

Standards for labeling are based on the percentage of organic ingredients in a product. To have the label "100 percent organic," the food must contain only organically produced ingredients. The label "organic" means that a product has at least 95 percent organically produced ingredients. Both may use the United States Department of Agriculture (USDA) Organic seal. If a processed product contains at least 70 percent organic ingredients, then the label can list up to three of the organic ingredients in the principal display area, and it claim that it is "made with organic ingredients." This claim may not use the USDA organic seal. If a person knowingly sells or labels as organic a product that is not produced and handled in accordance with the NOP, they can be fined up to $11,000 for each offense.

Certification Standards

In order to use the organic label, food producers must first become certified by submitting to a certifying agent an organic system plan. This plan details all the substances and methods that will be used in the production process. It must include exhaustive details, up to and including a systematic plan for record keeping and for ensuring that there is no commingling of organic and nonorganic products. The certification process also requires an on-site inspection by a certifying agent.

The certification process was designed for large producers of organic goods; small producers that sell less than $5,000 a year in organic agricultural products are not required to complete the certification process. Small producers must nevertheless follow the NOP regulations, and while they can label their products "organic," they cannot use the USDA organic seal.

Grocery stores and other retail operations do not have to be certified unless they want to. However, they are responsible for appropriate pest management and the prevention of commingling.

Accreditation Standards

The purpose of accreditation is to establish uniformity, consistency, and impartiality. The same standards apply to international food producers as to domestic producers; imported products must be certified by USDA-accredited certifying agents in order to be sold under the organic label.

Crop Production Standards

The EPA highlights the following general standards for organic crop production (2012):

- Land will have no prohibited substances applied to it for at least three years before the harvest of an organic crop.
- The use of genetic engineering (included in excluded methods), ionizing radiation, and sewage sludge is prohibited.
- Soil fertility and crop nutrients will be managed through tillage and cultivation practices, crop rotations, and cover crops, supplemented with animal and crop waste materials and allowed synthetic materials.
- Preference will be given to the use of organic seeds and other planting stock, but a farmer may use nonorganic seeds and planting stock under specified conditions.
- Crop pests, weeds, and diseases will be controlled primarily through management practices including physical, mechanical, and biological controls.
- When these practices are not sufficient, a biological, botanical, or synthetic substance approved for use on the National List may be used.

Livestock Production Standards

Different standards apply to the production of animals used for meat, milk, eggs, and products that will be represented as organically produced. The EPA highlights the following aspects of the NOP rule for livestock production (2012):

- Animals for slaughter must be raised under organic management from the last third of gestation, or no later than the second day of life for poultry.
- Producers are required to feed livestock agricultural feed products that are 100 percent organic, but may also provide allowed vitamin and mineral supplements.
- Producers may convert an entire, distinct dairy herd to organic production by providing 80 percent organically produced feed for 9 months, followed by 3 months of 100 percent organically produced feed.
- Organically raised animals may not be given hormones to promote growth, or antibiotics for any reason.

- Preventive management practices, including the use of vaccines, will be used to keep animals healthy.

- Producers are prohibited from withholding treatment from a sick or injured animal; however, animals treated with a prohibited medication may not be sold as organic.

- All organically raised animals must have access to the outdoors, including access to pasture for ruminants. They may be temporarily confined only for reasons of health, safety, the animal's stage of production, or to protect soil or water quality.

The organic foods market continues to grow strong. Available numbers indicate that organic sales brought in over 23 billion dollars in 2010, which is over 8 percent growth from 2009. It is anticipated that the increasing trend in sales will continue to increase. Also, according to the Rodale Institute's Farming Systems Trial, the longest running academic comparison of organic versus conventional modes of agricultural farming, organic farmers can earn more than farmers that use chemicals, and on less land. This discrepancy is anticipated to continue as the organic foods market becomes more popular among consumers.

Diane E. Carson

See also: Department of Agriculture (USDA); Environmental Protection Agency (EPA); Food Labeling; Food Safety

References and Additional Readings

Agricultural Marketing Service. (2012). National Organic Program. Retrieved from http://www.ams.usda.gov/AMSv1.0/nop

Environmental Protection Agency. (2012). Organic farming. Retrieved from http://www.epa.gov/oecaagct/torg.html

Food and Agricultural Organization of the United Nations. (2001). Codex Alimentarius—Organically Produced Foods. Retrieved from http://www.fao.org/DOCREP/005/Y2772E/Y2772E00.htm

Gold, M. V. (1999). Sustainable agriculture: Definitions and terms. Retrieved from http://www.nal.usda.gov/afsic/pubs/terms/srb9902.shtml

Gold, M. V. (2008). Organic agricultural products: Marketing and trade resources. Retrieved from http://www.nal.usda.gov/afsic/AFSIC_pubs/OAP/srb0301.htm

International Federation of Organic Agriculture Movements. (2005). The principles of organic agriculture. Retrieved from http://www.ifoam.org/about_ifoam/principles/index.html

Kuepper, G., & Gegner, L. (2004). Organic crop production overview. Retrieved from http://attra.ncat.org/attra-pub/organiccrop.html

The National Agricultural Law Center. (n.d.). National organic program. Retrieved from http://www.nationalaglawcenter.org/readingrooms/organic program/

OSHA (Occupational Safety & Health Administration).

See Department of Labor (DOL)

P

Patent and Trademark Office

The U.S. constitution established the right of Congress to issue patents by stating that "congress shall have the power . . . to promote the progress of . . . [the] useful arts, by securing for limited times to . . . inventors the exclusive rights to their . . . discoveries" (Article 1, Section 8). Congress enacts laws to implement the constitutional mandate of the patents, and the U.S. Patent and Trademark Office (USPTO) grants and the patents according to those laws and regulations. The USPTO is an agency of the U.S. Department of Commerce. A patent is a property right that is granted by the government to an inventor. A patent does not give an inventor the right to use the invention, rather it grants the inventor the right to exclude all others from making, using, or selling the invention.

In exchange for creating a new, useful, and nonobvious invention, and explaining the invention to the public so that industry and technology may advance, the government gives inventors "the right to exclude others from making, using, offering for sale, or selling" the invention in the United States, or "importing" the invention into the United States. The inventor is granted a number of years of exclusive use of the invention to make money from the invention, the patent itself is published thereby sharing knowledge and encouraging further inventions, and, at the end of the patent term, the public is given the benefit of the invention for free so that it may further advance science and technology. In addition, since the patent is a property right, the inventor may sell or license the patent and thereby also receive money for the invention.

There are three types of patents: (1) utility patents are granted for any new and useful process, machine, article of manufacture, or composition of matter, or any new and useful improvement thereof; (2) design patents are granted for a new, original, and ornamental design for an article of manufacture; and, (3) plant patents are for the invention or discovery and asexually reproduction of any new and distinct variety of plant. Generally, a utility or plant patent is either 17 years from when it is granted or 20 years from its earliest effective U.S. filing date, whichever is longer. A design patent is granted for 14 years. However, patent terms are also subject to adjustments for delays and other considerations that may affect when it expires.

Any inventor, whether a U.S. or foreign citizen, can apply for a U.S. patent by filing the required documents and paying the required fees to the director of the USPTO. An application must include a written document containing the specification, which is a description of how to make and use the invention, and one or more "claims" that specifically set out the claimed invention. In addition, drawings of the invention should be filed, if necessary, to explain it. The inventor must swear an oath or declaration that he or she is the inventor. And, there are filing, search, and examination fees that must be paid. Current fees are published by the USPTO and posted on its website.

A patent attorney or agent is not required in order to file an application for a patent, but the patent application and review process are complicated with very specific laws and rules, and a patent attorney or agent may be desired to make sure that the invention is fully protected by the patent. The USPTO has information to assist independent inventors pursue patent on their own inventions.

A U.S. patent is valid only in the United States and its territories. Most countries grant patents, but an inventor must apply for and obtain a patent in each country in which protection for the invention is sought. However, under U.S. law an inventor who desires to file a patent application in a foreign country within the first six months of filing the U.S. patent application, must first obtain a license from the director of the USPTO for the foreign filing. After the first six months, a foreign filing license is not required unless the invention has been ordered to be kept secret.

Once a patent is issued, protection of the patent rights is up to the inventor. When someone interferes with an inventor's rights under a patent, the rights are enforced by a suit in a federal district court, and a decision of the district court may be appealed as a matter of right to the Court of Appeals for the Federal Circuit (CAFC). The U.S. Supreme Court is not required to accept appeals from the CAFC, but may hear an appeal if it thinks the issues involved are important to decide. Although not required, patent litigation is complex and an inventor should consider hiring an attorney to represent his or her interests in court.

In general, a patent is a governmental grant of a significant property right to an inventor. A patent is often compared to a deed for land. However, holding a patent does not automatically mean that the inventor will make money from the invention. Patents give an inventor a period of years to manufacture and sell the invention, or license the patent to others to make and sell the invention in return for money. A patent holder should consider licensing the patent in return for cash or royalties as well as making, marketing, and selling the invention.

Michael K. Botts

See also: Counterfeiting; Fair Trade; Small Claims Court; Supreme Court

References and Additional Readings

U.S. Constitution. Article 1, Section 8.

USPTO. (2013a). 2701 Patent term [R-2]. Retrieved from http://www.uspto.gov/web/offices/pac/mpep/s2701.html

USPTO. (2013b). What is a patent? Retrieved from http://www.uspto.gov/patents/index.jsp

USPTO. (2013c). Retrieved from http://www.uspto.gov

USPTO. (2013d). General information concerning patents. Retrieved from http://www.uspto.gov/patents/resources/general_info_concerning_patents.jsp

USPTO. (2013e). Inventors resources. Retrieved from http://www.uspto.gov/inventors/index.jsp

World Intellectual Property Organization. (2013a). The Paris convention for the protection of industrial property. Retrieved from http://www.wipo.int/treaties/en/ip/paris/

World Intellectual Property Organization. (2013b). The international patent system. Retrieved from http://www.wipo.int/pct/en/

Patient Protection and Affordable Care Act (PPACA)

In 2010, Congress created the Patient Protection and Affordable Care Act (PPACA) to begin the process of transforming health care. Instead of using an incremental model to change the healthcare policy, a rational-comprehensive approach was used. The intension of the PPACA is to ensure all Americans have access to quality, affordable health care. Responsibility for implementation of the act will be shared by the healthcare system and the insurance market. Although many of components of the act more directly impact the healthcare system rather than the insurance market. Following are the essential components of the act, identified as Titles ("The Patient Protection and Affordable Care Act: Detailed Summary," 1):

Title 1: Quality, affordable health care for all Americans

Title 2: The role of public programs

Title 3: Improving the quality and efficiency of health care

Title 4: Prevention of chronic disease and improving public health

Title 5: Health care workforce

Title 6: Transparency and program integrity

Title 7: Improving access to innovative medical therapies

Title 8: Community living assistance services and supports

Title 9: Revenue provisions

Providing affordable health care for everyone is the notable component of the act and the issue most influential in shaping public opinion. The American Medical Association estimates the act will "expand health insurance coverage to 32 million more Americans." The other eight components are integral in ensuring quality health care.

Eliminating insurance restrictions for individuals with preexisting conditions, providing tax credits and no increase in premiums, which is possible because of an increase in the insurance pool, are the initial provisions in providing affordable health care for all Americans ("The Patient Protection and Affordable Care Act: Detailed Summary," 1). Immediate improvements are intended to provide insurance coverage for young adults who may not be in established careers and cannot afford health insurance, early retirees who need temporary insurance to fill a gap between Medicare and insurance previously provided through the workplace, and individuals with preexisting conditions. The goal of affordable coverage will be achieved through changes in medical underwriting and preexisting conditions, capping out-of-pocket limits and deductibles, establishment of an exchange within states to help individuals and small employers and refundable tax credits for American with incomes between 100 and 400 percent of the federal poverty line. By 2014, individuals will be required to maintain a minimum essential coverage or pay a tax penalty.

The role of public assistance programs, Medicaid and Children's Health Insurance Programs, is expended through the PPACA ("The Patient Protection and Affordable Care Act: Detailed Summary," 3). A significant change is the expansion of eligibility to families with incomes up to 133 percent of the federal poverty limit. Federal funding will be available for states to fund the increase in number of participants.

Title III of the PPACA focuses on improving the quality and efficiency of health care, specifically medical care services and Medicare and Medicaid enrollment ("The Patient Protection and Affordable Care Act: Detailed Summary," 4). The Health and Human Services Secretary will be responsible for establishing a strategy to implement changes to improve delivery of healthcare services, outcomes for patients, and overall health of the population. This component involves making major changes to a system that has historically experienced incremental policy changes.

To address the prevention of chronic disease and improvement of public health, Title IV of the act implements a set of initiatives to provide an infrastructure that will be carried out by the Prevention and Public Health Investment Fund ("The Patient Protection and Affordable Care Act: Detailed Summary," 6). These initiatives will address modernizing disease prevention and public health systems, increase access to clinical preventive services, create healthier communities, and provide support for prevention and public health innovations. Grants funded by the Health and Human Services Secretary will provide financial support to carry out the initiatives.

As of March 23, 2010, the Elder Justice Act, enacted as part of the Patient Protection and Affordable Care Act (PPACA), sets forth provisions to address federal and state efforts related to the prevention and response of abuse, neglect, and exploitation of older adults. Part of the act is the authorization of assigned funding sources for Adult Protective Services, long-term care ombudsman services, development of forensic centers for prevention of elder abuse, improvement of Medicare-based long-term care facilities, and several other necessary activities.

The increase in number of Americans who are insured will create a need to increase the supply of healthcare workers. To continue providing quality care, a demand for training and education will need to be met, which is addressed by Title V of the act. Competitive grants will be established to enable states to conduct needs assessments and create strategies to develop the healthcare workforce ("The Patient Protection and Affordable Care Act: Detailed Summary," 7). Key areas of education and training will be targeted and the federal student loan program will be modified to further financially support individuals entering the field of health care. Quality of care will be addressed by expanding the funding to improve emergency medical services for children and specialty care mental and behavioral health settings.

Title VI creates new requirements to ensure transparency and program integrity to reduce the incidence of fraud and abuse in public and private programs ("The Patient Protection and Affordable Care Act: Detailed Summary," 9). Physician-owned hospitals will need to complete a provider agreement to participate in Medicare. Transfers or gifts from supply manufacturers will need to be reported. Patient referrals will need to inform patients in writing of all exams and procedures needed and other physicians who can provide those services. Nursing home ownership will need to be disclosed. Improved staff training, background checks for employees who provide a direct-patient service, patient-centered outcomes research, and state entitlement program qualifications will have additional requirements to ensure transparency and integrity. Titles VII, VIII, and IX address improvement of access to innovative medical therapies, community living assistance services and supports, and revenue provision, respectively ("The Patient Protection and Affordable Care Act: Detailed Summary," 12).

A criticism of the PPACA is the expenses that will contribute to a larger national budget deficit. While many of the titles described do relate to grant and funding provisions, the overall effect of the act will be to stream line the process of American getting access to health care. Access does not only mean everyone having insurance, it also means everyone being able to go to a healthcare facility and receive the care that is needed. The act is a momentous change to the healthcare system and will take some getting used to by care providers and consumers.

Lorna Saboe-Wounded Head

See also: Administration on Aging (AoA); Confidentiality; Department of Health and Human Services (HHS); Health and Healthcare; Long-Term Care; Medicare; Older Americans Act (OAA)

References and Additional Readings

American Medical Association. (2013). Patient Protection and Affordable Care Act (PPACA). Retrieved from http://search0.ama-assn.org/main/jsp/templates/primaryJSP/fullview.jsp?keyword=ppac&FilterList=&advancedSearch=&sort=&pagination=

Dye, T.R. (2013). *Understanding public policy* (14th ed.). Boston, MA: Pearson Education, Inc.

U.S. Senate. (2012). *The Patient Protection and Affordable Care Act: Detailed summary.* Retrieved from http://dpc.senate.gov/healthreformbill/healthbill04.pdf

Pawn Shops

The pawn process involves consumers pledging personal property as collateral in exchange for receipt of a cash loan, lower than the amount the product is worth. Basically, anything of value can be pawned, including jewelry, cars, collectibles, antiques, and electronics, to name a few. The borrower will be required to sign a contract and consumers should always require that the transaction be in writing. The borrower may also be required to give a fingerprint. The typical pawn loan lasts about one month but may vary based on the contract and uses the borrower's item(s) as a guarantee against the loan. If the borrower decides to collect the property, payment of the original loan amount and fee are required. Redeeming the property is optional on the part of the buyer, and this option is available until the contract expires. If the borrower decides not to reclaim his or her property, the items are sold by the pawn shop and there is no credit consequence to the borrower.

The pawn industry is governed by the major federal laws that apply to entities designated as financial institutions including Patriot Act, Truth in Lending Act, Equal Credit Opportunity Act, as well as data privacy and safeguard of consumer information as part of the Federal Trade Commission rules. Pawn shops are required to disclose shop-specific rules regarding collateral and time periods for repaying pawn loans. Under the Truth in Lending Act, pawn shops are required to disclose all credit terms including interest and fees.

Pawn shops that deal in firearms are regulated federally by the Bureau of Alcohol, Tobacco, Firearms and Explosives, and they may also be Federal Firearms License holders. The pawn shop industry has been federally regulated for decades, and there are local licensing and regulation

Pawn shops have become popular in recent years due to their prevalence in reality television shows. However, consumers should be aware of contractual obligations, including high fees. (Luckydoor/Dreamstime.com)

efforts as well. For example, pawn transactions are the only type of consumer credit that requires reporting to local law enforcement agencies. Reporting is required daily in many states and must include thorough consumer information (i.e., ethnicity, gender, date of birth, address, and hair color).

Interest Rates and Service Fees

Interest rates and service fees, such as storage fees, on loans are limited or capped in most states. Generally, a borrower can expect to pay anywhere from 5 to 25 percent in interest on his or her loan. In addition to the interest fee, most states allow pawn shops to charge a service fee in money (i.e., $10) or additional interest (i.e., 20 percent) each month. For example, in Florida the maximum interest rate and service fee charged per month is capped at a combined 25 percent compared to Indiana where the interest rate is capped at 3 percent per month and the service fee is capped at 20 percent per month making the total allowable finance charge 23 percent per month.

Increase in the Number of Consumers Who Use Pawn Shops

While the concept of "pawning" items dates back thousands of years the United States has witnessed an increase in the number of individuals who pawn items as well as an increase the loan value. The United States recently went through its longest (December 2007 through June 2009), and by most measures worst economic recession, labeled the "Great Recession," since the Great Depression. Since that recession, consumers have increasingly turned to pawn shops to make ends meet. According to the National Pawnbrokers Association's 2010 survey, the average pawn loan nearly doubled in value from $80 in 2008 to $150 in 2010 where over 7 percent of consumers took out a pawn shop loan and 80 percent of those took a loan twice that year. Unbanked and under banked consumers represent about 40 percent of the pawn borrower's. The most common reason given by consumers who patronize pawn shops is because they find it easier or more convenient to obtain money from a pawn shop as opposed to qualifying for a bank loan (FDIC, 2012). In addition, reality television such as *Pawn Stars* that appeared in 2009 has likely made pawn shops more intriguing to consumers, often portraying pawn shops in a positive light.

Consumer Safety and Protection
Regarding Pawn Shops

For many consumers obtaining a pawn shop loan may be a costly mistake. Pawn shops have increasingly come under scrutiny for predatory lending practices. The annual percentage rates (APR) for pawn shop loans typically vary between 120 and 300 percent, much higher than the APR charged on credit cards. Supporters of pawn shops argue that the APR is not predatory because the loans are meant to be short-term and they assume the liability and risk (of selling) for the property. However, even in the short term, the interest rates are generally higher than the typical monthly interest rate for credit cards and bank loans. Consumers must become aware of predatory lending by reading contracts and being familiar with interest rates. While pawn shops may be advertised as a way to solve financial troubles, obtaining these loans may lead to higher and more expensive debt or loss of a personal item that may have sentimental value.

Martie Gillen

See also: Banking; Debt Management; Federal Deposit Insurance Corporation (FDIC); Title Pawn; Usury

References and Additional Readings

Federal Deposit Insurance Corporation (FDIC). (2012). 2011 FDIC national survey of unbanked and under banked households. Retrieved from http://www.fdic.gov/householdsurvey/2012_unbankedreport.pdf

National Pawnbrokers Association. (2012). Pawn industry overview. Retrieved from http://assets.nationalpawnbrokers.org/2010/10/NPA-IO-Interim.pdf

Urban Institute. (2010). Research on financial behaviors and use of small-dollar loans and financial services. Retrieved from http://www.treasury.gov/resource-center/financial-education/Documents/Research%20on%20Financial%20Behaviors%20and%20Use%20of%20Small-Dollar%20Loans%20and%20Financial%20Services%20-%20Literature%20Review.pdf

Payday Lending

Payday lending, also known as check advance or payday anticipation loans, involves small dollar amount loans made for short periods of time to low- and moderate-income consumers. They typically are for $100 to $500 but can be up to $1,000 in some jurisdictions and generally have a two- to four-week duration. The borrower instigates the loan by writing a postdated check for the loan amount plus fees of $15 to $20 per $100 of principal. At the due date—possibly the consumer's next payday—the customer may redeem his/her check with cash or allow it to be deposited to pay off the loan. Due to the small loan size this is necessarily a high-volume business. For efficiency, the underwriting process is very streamlined—essentially verifying identity, income, and the existence of a bank account. In states that regulate the transaction, the firm may additionally have to verify loan eligibility by checking a central data base.

The annual percentage rate (APR) on one of these loans can easily exceed 400 percent. Such APRs would normally be considered usurious thus making this business illegal; however, a commonly offered justification is that the existence of such loans provides consumers a cheaper alternative—allowing them to avoid overdrawing their bank checking accounts and incurring the associated overdraft fees. In addition to the cost issue, consumer advocates are also concerned about a potential "credit trap" due to a borrower's need to "roll over" these loans. This occurs because of the appeal of such lending to financially constrained borrowers whereby the payment of the relatively high fees serves to exacerbate their financial situation leading to additional or continuing loan demand and so ever higher effective APRs on the borrowings.

Should the consumer fail to turn up at maturity, the presence of the postdated check provides an easy collection mechanism. Its existence does not, of course, guarantee that there will be sufficient funds in the account. However, the fact that bouncing the check will generate bank overdraft fees, further increasing the cost of the loan, does provide an incentive to the borrower. At the same time, from a business standpoint, making such loans is risky. For example, loan loss rates are often between 8 and 14 percent of gross revenue.

The industry from its start in the early 1990s has seen significant growth. According to the industry trade group, Community Financial Services Association of America (CFSAA), there are currently 20,600 payday advance locations in the United States providing $38.5 billion in short-term credit to some 19 million households. Six large companies control about 20 percent of the payday industry. The largest firm is Advance America with over 2,500 locations; it, along with Cash America, with over 800 locations, are both New York Stock Exchange-listed companies. The other majors are ACE Cash Express Inc., Check 'n Go, Dollar Financial, and Check Into Cash; all four of these companies are also publicly traded. The rest of the U.S. industry is composed of smaller local and regional firms. Internationally, a similar payday loan model is employed in Australia, Canada, and the United Kingdom. While the industry is composed of nondepository institutions, a few banks—including U.S. Bank and Wells Fargo &

Co.—offer a comparable product, a direct-deposit advance, whereby the consumer gets his or her loan then at payday, following receipt of the direct deposit, the loan plus fees is automatically withdrawn from his or her account. While there is still the risk that the consumer could have lost his or her job in the interim, this product clearly has a lower default risk than a payday loan.

Regarding regulation, there are no federal statues in place but most states have laws governing payday lending (a total of 40 states plus the District of Columbia). Generally speaking the laws limit permissible fees, maximum loan amounts (most expressed in dollar terms, a few as a percent of gross monthly income), and possibly the number of such loans a consumer can have outstanding at any point. Two states, Arizona and North Carolina, have allowed their payday legislation to sunset. The remaining eight states—Connecticut, Maryland, Massachusetts, New Jersey, New York, Pennsylvania, Vermont, and West Virginia—either have no explicit regulations or require payday lending to comply with consumer loan caps (thereby effectively prohibiting payday lending). The regulatory experience in Florida is currently being explored.

Michael H. Anderson

See also: Banking; Pawn Shops; Rent-To-Own

References and Additional Readings

Anderson, M. H., & Jackson, R. (2010). Perspectives on payday loans: The evidence from Florida. *Review of Business Research, 10*(5), 154–161.

Lawrence, E. C., & Elliehausen, G. (2008). A comparative analysis of payday loan customers. *Contemporary Economic Policy, 26*(2), 299–316.

Stegman, M. A. (2007). Payday lending. *Journal of Economic Perspectives, 21*(1), 169–190.

Penny Stocks. *See* Investing Regulations

Peterson, Esther

This entry discusses the life and legacy of Esther Peterson, a remarkably resourceful and effective individual, who, over the course of the 20th century, made many landmark contributions to the welfare of American consumers as well as consumers in other nations. In addition, Peterson is remembered for a multitude of major pioneering accomplishments in the fields of labor and women's rights. Indeed, she was a leading activist in the consumer, labor, and women's movements.

The fifth of six children of Danish immigrants, Peterson was born on December 9, 1906, in Provo, Utah. She was raised in a Mormon household where her father ran the family farm while serving as superintendent of schools for Utah.

Peterson graduated from Brigham Young University in 1927 with a bachelor's degree in physical education. Three years later she earned a master's degree from Columbia Teacher's College. While at Columbia, she met her husband-to-be, Oliver Peterson, a man attracted to radical political ideas who introduced her to issues of class struggle as well as the rights of the working class. The couple married in 1932.

For the next five years Peterson taught at an elite girl's school in Boston while also teaching night classes as a volunteer at the local YWCA where her students were nonelites, such as domestic workers. She spent summers as recreation director for a college program to help unschooled women workers gain access to training and education. These were consciousness-raising experiences for Peterson and they led to her interest and involvement in the women's labor movement.

This new chapter in Peterson's life began with her position as a union organizer for the American Federation of Teachers in 1938. A year later she moved to New York where she held a series of positions with the Amalgamated Clothing Workers of America (ACWA) culminating in 1944 as ACWA's first legislative representative, working for a higher minimum wage while campaigning for Franklin Roosevelt and Harry Truman. Then in 1948, Peterson's husband was named labor attaché to the American embassy in Sweden. She and the family's three children joined him in Stockholm for 10 years, and these years gave her an opportunity to attend many international meetings and to work with European women who were trade union leaders. Then, upon returning to the United States, she assumed a new position as lobbyist for the Industrial Union Department of the American Federation of Labor and Congress of Industrial Organizations (AFL/CIO).

It was just a few years later that Peterson's career in government began in 1961 when President Kennedy appointed her to two high-level posts: assistant secretary of Labor and director of the Women's Bureau. Among her many accomplishments in these positions were leading a successful campaign for federal legislation to assure equal pay for equal work, and assuming responsibility for the direction of the first President's Commission on the Status of Women.

Peterson's major achievements as a consumer leader soon followed when she was appointed to a new position, special assistant for Consumer

Affairs, first to President Johnson and later to President Carter. In these two positions she helped pass new laws to aid American consumers including legislation on truth in packaging, truth in lending, truth in advertising, open dating, unit pricing, and meat and poultry inspection. She also took steps that led in 1967 to the establishment of the Consumer Federation of America. After serving as the top consumer aide under two presidents, Peterson decided to remain in Washington to serve as vice president for consumer affairs at Giant Food Corporation and as president of the National Consumers League.

In 1981, President Carter honored Peterson by presenting her with the Presidential Medal of Freedom, the nation's highest civilian award. And 12 years later President Clinton named her, at the age of 87, as a delegate to the United Nations General Assembly, where she served as a representative to UNESCO. While serving at the United Nations, Peterson lobbied the body successfully to adopt in 1986 the United Nations Guidelines for Consumer Protection, a breakthrough document that has stimulated passage of new consumer laws on three continents. Four years after she was named to the UN post, Peterson died on December 20, 1997, just 11 days past her 91st birthday.

Admired and respected by many who knew her, Peterson was an inspirational figure who will be remembered for her pioneering 20th-century accomplishments advancing the consumer, labor, and women's movements. Noted consumer activist Ralph Nader, who knew her well, had this to say about Peterson in appreciation of a life well spent: "She had a remarkable mix of personality and character traits which, I believe, made possible so many productive careers and accomplishments. She was not seized with ambition or intrigue or chronic temper. Never self-righteous in her fight for social justice, she was unfailingly cordial and gentle, but always pressing for results." And later, Nader concludes, "This complete public servant and public citizen did it all, raising four children, taking loving care of her husband who was stricken by cancer for years, and elevating the standards of living and justice by her work, her inspiring example and the institutions that survive her."

In addition to these personal observations by Nader praising Peterson in 1997 is the memorable statement by President Carter accompanying his presentation of the Presidential Medal of Freedom to her in 1981:

Once government's highest ranking woman, Esther Peterson still ranks highest among consumer advocates. She has advised Presidents and the public, and has worked for labor and business alike, always keeping the rights of all Americans to know and to be treated fairly as her highest priority. Even her staunchest foes respect her integrity and are warmed by her grace and sincere concern.

To end this essay on a personal note, this writer felt privileged to work for and with Esther Peterson for 24 years, first as a consultant during her time in the White House and with Giant Food, and later as a friend and colleague.

Monroe Friedman

See also: Kennedy, John F.; Nader, Ralph; United Nations (UN); Warne, Colston

References and Additional Readings

Brobeck, S. (1997). Esther Petereson. *Encyclopedia of the consumer movement* (pp. 426–442). Santa Barbara, CA: ABC-CLIO.

Nader, R. (1997). In appreciation of Esther Peterson, restless activist. *The Multinational Monitor, 18*(12).

Peterson, E., & Conkling, W. (1995). *Restless: The memoirs of labor and consumer activist Esther Peterson.* Washington, DC: Caring Publishing.

Phishing. *See* Frauds and Scams; Privacy: Online

PIRGs. *See* Public Interest Research Groups (PIRGs)

Plain Writing Act

In 2010, President Obama signed into effect the Plain Writing Act, a federal law requiring federal agencies to use "clear government communication that the public can understand and use." The act is an important movement to increase accessibility of the federal government to the consumer. Use of plain language is important for American adult consumers who read between 8th and 9th grade levels.

The law unveils the Plain Language Action and Information Network (PLAIN), a document developed by a group of federal employees in the 1990s to provide advice on communicating clearly. Five guidelines that teach writers to write in plain language are as follows: (1) think about the audience (who they are and how they will use the information), (2) organize (outline and plan), (3) write the document (the bulk of the work), (4) write for the web (how will it be accessed and utilized), and (5) test the technique (test for usability). The group offers free half-day training in Washington, D.C., for federal agency employees.

An Example of "Before" and "After" Texts for an Army Information Security Program Handbook

The rewritten version of an Army Information Security manual makes good use of subsections and white space and eliminates irrelevant information.

Before

Methods of Transmission or Transportation: 7-301. Secret Information

Administrative procedures shall be established by each DOD component for controlling secret information and material originated or received by an activity; distributed or routed to a subelement of such activity; and disposed of by the activity by transfer of custody or destruction. The control system for secret information must be determined by a practical balance of security and operating efficiency and must meet the following minimum requirements:

a. It must provide a means to ensure that secret material sent outside a major subordinate element (the activity) of the DoD component concerned has been delivered to the intended recipient . . .

b. It must provide a record of receipt and dispatch of secret material by each major subordinate element. The dispatch record requirement may be satisfied when the distribution of secret material is evident and addressees or distribution lists for classified documentation . . .

c. Records of receipt and dispatch for secret material shall be retained for a minimum of 2 years . . .

After

Transmission, Methods: 4–102. Secret

A. You may send secret information by U.S. Registered Postal Service mail within and between the United States and its territories.

B. You may use Federal Express and U.S. Post Service express mail for transmitting secret mail within the United States and between the United States and its territories under the following STRICT condition security:

1. Mail should meet the weight and size limits of the carrier used.

2. You should follow the inner wrappings and receipt requirements in this handbook.

3. You should ensure delivery by Friday so that the carrier is not in possession of the package over the weekend.

Source: O'Flahavan, L. (January 21, 2011). Write plainly. Retrieved from http://www.howto .gov/sites/default/files/write-plainly-an-update-on-plain-writing-slides.pdf

The law not only refers to federal websites, but also the regulations themselves. Under the Plain Writing Act, "legalese," or typical legislative language is discouraged. The use of plain language is equally, if not more important in health and financial communications from the federal government. The Plain Language "movement," according to the website, is also pushing for greater use of plain English in the sciences and legal professions. The law is a positive step in the right direction for American consumers.

Wendy Reiboldt

References and Additional Readings

The Plain Language Action and Information Network. (2013). Retrieved from http://www.plainlanguage.gov

Ponzi Schemes

A Ponzi scheme can be simply defined as ". . . an illegal business practice in which new investor's money is used to make payments to earlier investors" (Wells, 2012, 1). Government regulators familiar with this type of fraud often refer to it as "robbing Peter to pay Paul." A typical Ponzi scheme is an investment scam where the money invested downstream pays dividends and any withdrawals on the part of early investors thus giving the allusion that the investment is solid and lucrative. Although a Ponzi is a type of pyramid scheme, it differs from multilevel marketing whereas direct selling plans typically involve a product and are legal when regulatory guidelines are followed. Ponzi schemes usually do not involve products other than financial instruments and are never legal. These schemes came to the forefront in the 1990s and early 21st centuries with government agencies filing charges against dozens of entities whose frauds run into millions and sometimes billions of dollars.

Ponzi schemes probability existed before its namesake became notorious with a multimillion dollar scam perpetrated on poor immigrants in Boston in the 1920s. Charles Ponzi's scheme was to promise 50 percent returns in 90 days for an investment in postal reply coupons using later investor's money to pay off early investors. Although he was sent to jail, this fraud was so lucrative and infamous that it later bore his name.

Sometimes Ponzi schemes are a fraud from the onset. A perpetrator may develop what he or she claims as a unique and profitable financial plan, give it a glamorous and authentic sounding name, while promising safe and much higher than market returns. Usually these are private unregistered securities sold by unlicensed agents. He or she then sets out to find investors among friends, relatives, and members of his or her social circles or church. To establish credence for the investment, the scammer proceeds to pay dividends to the initial investors with money contributed by later investors. Word-of-mouth tales of fantastic returns spread to enlarge the investor network. Often the early subscribers roll over their dividends when they see on paper the high returns they are receiving. However, not all Ponzi schemes begin as frauds. For many, they begin as legitimate investment opportunities. However, when the principles find they cannot meet the expected returns they use new investor money to pay dividends hoping that

Exconvict Charles Ponzi, surrounded by Boston police and immigration officers, waves good-bye as he is deported to Italy in 1934. (Library of Congress)

future profits will make up any shortfalls and all investors will eventually be made whole. In most cases, this becomes a slippery slope leading to a full-blown Ponzi scheme. In the former, there is never a real business and in the latter, there may be an actual investment but one that is unable to cover the promised returns. In both cases, principles skim most of the investor's money for their own personal use.

There are many reasons why a person may become a victim of a Ponzi scheme. One of the more common is that he or she often knows and trusts the principles or they are acquainted with, or hear of, initial investors who tell of great returns with little risk. Sometimes the testimonial is not given by a real investor but a shill planted by the Ponzi perpetrators. Today's social media, such as Facebook, facilitates these communications both in advertising the scheme and as a means of one investor telling others of his or her good fortune. Also Ponzi schemes offer investment returns that are far in excess of legitimate investments playing on the greed of some of the victims. Another reason why people invest in such schemes is that investment instruments, even legitimate ones, have become so complicated that many cannot understand them leaving the victims to trust the explanations of the perpetrator without further investigation. Those familiar with Ponzi schemes say that even sophisticated investors are conned into Ponzi schemes and that a successful scheme often involve investors who think they are smarter than they really are and that they are given a special opportunity that no one else has.

When does a Ponzi scheme finally collapse and the victims become aware they have been scammed? One of the primary causes occurs when additional investors are difficult to recruit thus limiting an infusing of new money. Another cause is the perpetrators may become suspicious that regulators are on to them and decide to jump ship before being prosecuted. Often, however, one or more of the investors becomes suspicious of legitimacy of the investment plan and when rumors of this suspicion spread, there is a run on the plan resulting in insufficient funds to pay the claims. This is more likely to happen in an economic downturn especially for Ponzi schemes that may have been initially legitimate financial investments. Ironically, when a Ponzi scheme collapses due to an open investigation, some Ponzi scheme principles blame regulators for the failure saying if the agency had not caused a run on the plan, investors would have been able to recouped their investment.

The federal agencies primarily responsible for action against Ponzi schemes are the Securities and Exchange Commission (SEC), Federal Trade Commission (FTC), Commodities Futures Trading Commission (CFTC), and the Federal Bureau of Investigation (FBI). State agencies may also take action on localized Ponzi schemes. In the past, federal agencies were slow to act as in the most famous of all Ponzi schemes, the Madoff case, but in recent years, partly due to this case, they have sped up the investigation and prosecution of such frauds. Web searches of government regulatory agencies reveal the multitude of actions that have been taken. No matter what the results of prosecution, the probability of recovery of lost investments is minimal, if any. Usually, the principles have either spent the victim's money for their own personal use and/or have sequestered their ill-gotten gains in an offshore bank. However, in some cases the later investors have standing in court to get restitution from the early investors who profited from a Ponzi scheme.

What are the red flags of a Ponzi type of investment fraud? The SEC and the CFTC lists several that are compiled and amplified here:

- Claiming high investment returns with little or no risk.
- Paying overly consistent returns whereas typical investments fluctuate over time.

- Offering unregistered securities by unlicensed brokers.
- Unwilling to provide sufficient and proper paperwork.
- Creating difficulty in receiving payment and encouraging the rollover of promised payments.
- Making details of the securities secretive and offering investment strategies that are overly complex to foster the illusion that the security is original and special.
- Stating that the investor has been given a unique opportunity to be invited into an investment plan because he or she is a member of some designated group.
- Pressuring the investor to make the purchase decision immediately while discouraging the investor from seeking professional advice.
- Offering testimonials that cannot be verified.

Ponzi schemes will continue to be part of the investment fraud landscape as long as there are clever schemers, expanding means of communication, ignorant and susceptible victims, and government regulators without the will or resources to investigate and prosecute the offenders.

John R. Burton

See also: Affinity Fraud; Commodities Futures Trading Commission (CFTC); Federal Bureau of Investigation (FBI); Federal Trade Commission (FTC); Madoff, Bernie; Multilevel Marketing and Pyramid Plans; Securities and Exchange Commission (SEC)

References and Additional Readings

Chilton, B. (2011). *Ponzimonium.* Washington, DC: Commodity Futures Trading Commission, 73 pages.

Securities and Exchange Commission. (2012). Ponzi schemes: Frequently asked questions. Retrieved from http://www.sec.gov/answers/ponzi.htm

Touryalai, H. (2012). Zeek rewards and why Ponzi schemes will never go away. Forbes.com. Retrieved from http://www.forbes.com/sites/halahtouryalai/2012/08/20/zeekrewards-and-why-ponzi-schemes-will-never-go-away/

Valentine, D. A. (1998). Pyramid schemes. Federal Trade Commission. Retrieved from http://www.ftc.gov/speeches/other/dvimf16.shtm

Walsh, J. (1998). *You can't cheat an honest man: How Ponzi schemes and pyramid fraud work . . . and why they're more common than ever.* Aberdeen, WA: Silver Lake Publishing.

Wells, J. T. (2013). What is a Ponzi scheme? Association of Certified Fraud Examiners. Retrieved from http://www.acfe.com/ponzi-schemes.aspx

Post Office (USPS, U.S. Postal Service)

As the U.S. Postal Service confronts ever-increasing deficits and faces an uncertain future with a badly broken business model, it is reasonable for Americans to be concerned about what the future of the provision of their mail service will look like. But that is not the only area where their big-picture concerns merit consideration. Can the Postal Service's consumers of monopoly products and services be confident they are getting what they pay for? Or are they being required to pay more than their fair share, in terms of dollars and reduced quality of service, with the proceeds going to subsidize other Postal Service functions or activities? Whatever solutions are deliberated by policymakers in the months and years to come, American consumers have a major stake in whether any proposed outcome will improve their position in this regard.

To understand these questions, one first must appreciate that the U.S. Postal Service of today differs greatly in scope and mission from the role envisioned at any other point in its history. This largely reflects the major changes in the marketplace for postal services, not just in the United States but worldwide. In fact, meeting the needs of household consumers has become a secondary consideration in the decision-making of senior Postal Service executives, as it has for the leaders of national posts around the world.

On September 28, 2012, the U.S. Postal Service reached its debt limit of $15 billion. This means that the Post Office can no longer borrow money, because the U.S. Treasury is its only lender and Congress has barred additional borrowing and lending. The Postal Service lost $5.1 billion in 2011, a majority of which was charged to workers' compensation costs. The Postal Service must now decide whether to raise prices, cut services, or close more offices; all of which negatively affect consumers.

Source: Liberto, J. (October 17, 2012). Postal Service barred from borrowing more. Retrieved from http://money.cnn.com/

Of tantamount concern to those household consumers are the extent to which the Postal Service business model requires them to subsidize their other businesses that involve other customers. A major factor is the model's inability to control its own costs due to a variety of factors, including inflexible collective bargaining agreements with employees and congressional interference. As mail volume and the revenue it generates have declined precipitously in recent years, a trend most experts expect will continue, the danger that they will be expected to fund even steeper subsidies makes current reform deliberations concerning these questions crucial.

The U.S. Postal Service was created by decree of the Continental Congress in 1775, mainly to deliver mail between Congress and the armies. Helping to achieve the national goal of maintaining a well-informed electorate was a fundamental purpose. Today, still wholly owned by the government, it delivers 168 billion pieces of mail each year to more than 151 million addresses. The average household receives 21 pieces of mail per week. Of this now-declining total, the Postal Service estimates that 64 percent is advertising mail, 12 percent is bills, 5 percent is financial statements, 5 percent is periodicals, and only 4 percent is personal correspondence. To accomplish this, the Postal Service has 546,000 career employees, down from 623,128 in 2009. If it were a private company, it would rank 35th on the Fortune 500. And, as Postmaster General Patrick Donahoe is fond of stating, there are more post offices in the United States than McDonalds, Walmarts, and Starbucks' combined. Contrary to what most people may think, the modern Postal Service is not funded by appropriating taxpayer dollars. It generates its revenue from shippers and mailers. To make this work, the Postal Service presides over two statutory government monopolies, one for first-class mail and the other granting it exclusive use of postal mailboxes. In exchange for its monopoly privileges, Congress requires the Postal Service to provide Americans with universal postal service. The exact meaning of the term and the obligation it carries is difficult to nail down. In fact, as noted postal historian James I. Campbell Jr. observes in his 2008 study on the subject commissioned by the Postal Regulatory Commission, that Title 39 of the United States Code, which contains the foundations within U.S. law for the modern U.S. Postal Service, does not use the term universal service even once. None of the major pieces of federal legislation detailing postal reforms, in fact, address central questions to defining the terms of the obligation. The Postal Reorganization Act of 1970, however, does state in Section 101 that "Postal rates shall be established to apportion the costs of all postal operations to all users of the mail on a fair and equitable basis." This requirement still stands as a principle governing the provision of postal services in the United States, and serves to frame a pertinent discussion about whether today's costs meet this standard for all postal consumers.

U.S. Postal Service Today

The price of mailing a first-class letter anywhere in the United States, as of January 2013, is 46 cents—surely by most standards that must constitute a bargain. It is, after all, among the lowest rates among industrialized countries. But a more thorough understanding of the context of this pricing within the context of postal economics makes the extent of this bargain less clear. It also raises fundamental questions about whether consumers of the Postal Service's monopoly products and services are in fact receiving pricing on the "fair and equitable basis" required in law. This would appear to make a strong case that first-class mail, the mail most household consumer's use for correspondence and bill paying, effectively subsidizes the delivery of the competitive and other, less lucrative products.

The Postal Accountability and Enhancement Act of 2006 charged the Postal Regulatory Commission with ensuring that the Postal Service does not abuse its monopoly privileges by overcharging its monopoly consumers to subsidize its products that compete directly with the private sector. But this is easier said than done, especially because the Postal Service has consistently maintained 40–45 percent of its operating costs unattributed to specific products and services as institutional overhead. In 2004, Secretary of the Treasury John W. Snow criticized "this large, unallocated portion [as] a sort of 'elephant in the room' that forces stakeholders, employees, competitors, the regulator, Board of Governor, USPS management, and others to invest substantial time, energy and expense calculating, debating or contemplating a myriad of important issues." Secretary Snow went on to argue that serving the public interest and trust "demands" improved transparency in cost allocation and outweigh any confidentiality concerns the Postal Service management would employ to defend this nontransparent accounting. first-class mail, and particularly the single-piece first-class mail that consumers generally use, is contributing half of the revenue it generates to institutional overhead. Standard Mail, a business bulk-mailing product used mostly for advertising mail that is also defined as a market-dominant category, contributes about a third. But Priority Mail, the Postal Service's flagship competitive product, contributes only one-fourth of its revenue to institutional overhead. Periodicals operate at a deficit according to this same calculation. See Figure 7.

Cost coverage, the official method of demonstrating the contribution each product makes to unattributed, general overhead, shows a very similar pattern: first-class mail contributes the greatest percentage of its revenue toward institutional overhead. See Figure 8.

That's precisely why the postmaster general commented last year that, "Even with growth in our package business, we cannot replace the profit contribution of First-Class Mail that has been lost over the past few years and will continue to decline in the future." The risks that the Postal Service

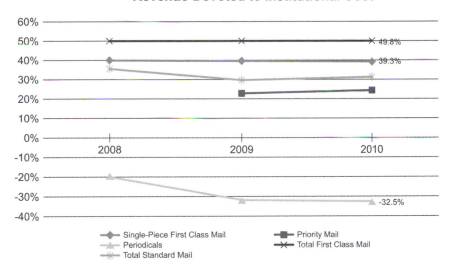

Figure 7. Pulling Their Weight: Percentage of Post Office Revenue Devoted to Instutional Cost. (*Source:* U.S. Postal Regulatory Commission Annual Compliance Determination Report, Fiscal Years 2008–2010.)

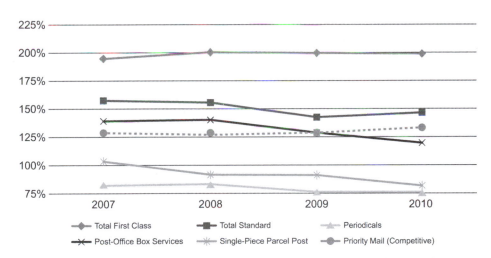

Figure 8. Cost Coverage in Each Category Over Time. (*Source:* USPS Cost and Revenue Analysis.)

expects such subsidies to increase appear to only escalate as the Postal Service's financial condition continues to decline. In March 2010, the Postal Service projected $115 billion in cumulative losses by 2020 if it achieved all cost savings that it asserted were under its control. USPS projected $238 billion in cumulative losses according to current trajectories without new reform strategies. Ever mindful of trends in mail usage, the Postal Service has generally targeted the business mailing community as the customer base to generate new revenue to sustain its present business model. Its business strategy has relied heavily on generating increased mail volume through aggressive work-sharing discounts, enhancing the program of services it offers domestic business mailers, and even a widely advertised 2009 "summer sale" for bulk mailers.

Postal Service management has repeatedly used targeted discounts to generate new business from corporate mailers. In January 2011, the service reached a special "Negotiated Service Agreement" with Discover Financial Services, serving as a model for such agreements with other large, corporate mailers. Such agreements are generally priced based on either volume or work-sharing discounts. But officials including some Postal Regulatory commissioners have questioned with the Postal Service is negotiating such deals poorly, resulting in some cases in offering discounts that exceed the savings achieved. In such cases, it is once again the Postal Service's monopoly consumers who are left subsidizing any such shortfalls. In concurring with the landmark 2007 Negotiated Service Agreement with major corporate mailer Bank of America, Chairman Ruth Goldway raised such concerns. In arguing that the agreement would result in losing $25–45 million for the Postal Service's (a shortfall for which monopoly consumers must subsidize), she noted "the Postal Service is not yet capable of negotiating a good bargain. . . . [T]he complex bureaucracy of the Postal Service has not yet been capable of identifying, analyzing, and distributing the appropriate data needed to make accurate cost-benefit decisions." Postal management also frequently discusses looking to the potential other new product offerings hold for generating additional revenue. But as noted in the August Senate hearing by Chairman Goldway, a longtime advocate for the Postal Service's monopoly consumers, its past forays into nonpostal services have generally proven unsuccessful. The Government Accountability Office (GAO) noted that in the second half of the 1990s, USPS had publicly introduced 19 new product offerings. Three of these involved strategic alliances with private sector companies, such as a deal with SmartTalk Teleservices, Inc to sell First Class Phone Card in post offices. But GAO noted that 5 of the 19 had been discontinued before 1998. More telling was its analysis that total revenues for the 19 offerings through 1997 was $148.8 billion, while total expenses totaled $233.5 million. What makes this critical to consumers is that when the Postal Service loses money on new products or services, it is monopoly consumers who must pay for them.

Service Reductions Targeted at Consumers

Another potential type of abuse of the terms of the first-class mail monopoly is whether its consumers are forced to accept more than their fair share of reductions in service quality. Postal cost-cutting strategies have been focused largely on monopoly consumers. The widespread removal of collection boxes, and the elimination of afternoon collection times from those boxes that remain, is another cause for similar concerns that often gets overlooked. Whenever newspaper clips documenting these disappearing boxes appear around the country, nearly every article cites community concern over the loss and resulting inconvenience.

Postal Regulatory Commission Chairman Ruth Goldway has noted that over 100,000 have already been removed from American neighborhoods. Besides the disappearing blue boxes, we often find that those that remain have fewer, and earlier collection times. If these trends are in fact part of a systematic strategy, it is a major concern that this strategy did not come at the disproportionate expense of the monopoly consumer. Two cost-cutting strategies that have received much discussion in recent months are eliminating Saturday delivery and closing some 700 post offices, would have significant and arguably disproportionate impacts on household and small business consumers. Both have proven highly controversial amid strong resistance from postal labor unions and political leaders. In December 2011, Postmaster General Patrick Donahoe proposed a reduction in service standards that would reportedly save the service $3 billion annually, or less than 5 percent of annual expenditures. This reduction is part of a larger plan to reduce operating costs by $20 billion by 2015. Under the proposed new standards, no longer would a consumer be able to mail a card or letter and expect it to arrive the next day. Next, as Postal Service management seeks to address its badly broken business model and dire financial forecasts, ideas for new products and services with potential to generate new revenue are frequently being suggested. Some prominent examples have included offering the public e-mail boxes, financial services, and even leveraging data collected from these and other postal services as a way for the Postal Service to create new income. Each of these areas would represent a serious challenge to the present regulatory infrastructure. It is also very likely that for some of these, privacy concerns, or simply the dangers of creating a money-losing and ill-conceived business debacle too far off the Postal Service's core competencies, would ultimately prove too much to overcome. But for each new product that does emerge, it will be crucial that the same standards for consumer protections be applied from the beginning.

The Mailbox Monopoly—Benefit or Detriment to Consumers?

The second major Postal Service monopoly, on the use of consumers' mailboxes, also can be observed as infringing on consumers' rights and best interests. After all, consumers are themselves responsible for purchasing and maintaining mailboxes. But only mail for which postage has been paid through the U.S. Postal Service may be placed in mailboxes. Community notices, coupons delivered by hand from the local pizzeria or birthday party invitations to neighborhood children are barred from being placed in mailboxes. Currently, the United States is the only country with such restrictions on mailbox access.

A 2003 Presidential Commission on the U.S. Postal Service proposed that consumers choose whether to allow private individuals or delivery companies to access their mailboxes, "so long as it does not impair the universal service or open homeowners' mailboxes against their will." A 2007 report by the Federal Trade Commission agreed. Congress enacted the restriction on mailbox access in 1934 in response to concerns about private companies, circumventing the postal service and placing circulars and account statements into mailboxes. Specifically, the statute states: Whoever knowingly and willfully deposits any mail-able matter such as statements of accounts, circulars, sale bills, or other like matter, on which no postage has been paid, in any letter box established, approved, or accepted by the Postal Service for the receipt or delivery of mail matter on any mail route with intent to avoid payment of lawful postage thereon, shall for each such offense be fined under this title. The postal service's monopoly on mailbox use "limits consumer choice and artificially increases the costs of private carriers," it concluded. The mailbox monopoly is particularly inconvenient to those who live in urban apartment buildings without a front desk or in rural areas. If consumers are unable to sign for delivery, their only choice is the post office. Increasingly, post office hours in many jurisdictions are limited, especially on weekends, and often require patrons to stand on long lines for service.

Conclusion

Americans have consistently told pollsters and interviewers that they not only like their mailman, but that they attribute value to daily mail delivery beyond simple transactional benefits, and they would like to see the U.S. Postal Service continues as a lasting entity in the future. But the arguments and examples described earlier raise serious questions about the extent to which the U.S. Postal Service is serving the needs of the consumers of its government monopoly at prices and with quality both fair and equitable, and if the protections provided to these consumers are adequate and consistent with federal law.

In official proceedings that determine the rates and service levels that define postal customers' interactions with the nation's post offices, its household and small business consumers of monopoly products and services seldom receive the professional representation that regularly benefit other, large and generally corporate customers or other interested parties. In order to ensure that their protections are adequate and compliant with existing legal frameworks, it will be crucial that postal decision-makers ensure that the best interests of monopoly postal consumers be adequately represented in future deliberations, and considered in the decisions that will determine future directions for the provision of postal services in the United States.

Don Soifer

See also: Congress; Federal Trade Commission (FTC); Frauds and Scams; Government Accountability Office (GAO); Privacy: Offline

References and Additional Readings

Campbell, J. I. Jr. (n.d.). Universal service obligation: History and development of laws relating to the provision of universal postal services. Retrieved from http://www.prc.gov/PRC-DOCS/library/USO%20Appendices/Appendix%20B.pdf

Consumer Postal Council. (2012). Index of postal freedom: 2012 Edition. Arlington, VA. Retrieved from http://www.postalconsumers.org/postal_freedom_index/images/2012_CPC_IPF_WEB.pdf

Federal Trade Commission. (2007). Accounting for laws that apply differently to the United States Postal Service and its private competitors (pp. 6–18). Retrieved from http://www.ftc.gov/os/2008/01/080116postal.pdf.

Government Printing Office. (n.d.). Activities of the committee on governmental affairs. United States Treasury Secretary John W. Snow, Testimony before Joint Session of the Committee on Government Reform United States House of Representatives and Government Affairs United States Senate, March 23, 2004. Retrieved from http://www.gpo.gov/fdsys/pkg/CRPT-109srpt368/html/CRPT-109srpt368.htm

Lexington Institute. (2011). A quick reference on the U.S. Postal Service. Retrieved from http://www.lexingtoninstitute.org/library/resources/documents/post alreform/postalprimer2011lex.pdf

Lexington Institute. (2012). Postal TrendwatchQ1 FY 2012: Monopoly Service to Worsen, competitive service to improve? Retrieved from http://www.lexing toninstitute.org/postal-trendwatch-q1-fy-2012-monopoly-service-to-worsen-competitive-service-to-improve

Postal Regulatory Commission. (2007). Opinion and recommended decision. Retrieved from http://www.apwu.org/news/webart/2007/webart-0799-boansa-071029.pdf

Postal Service. (2010). Household diary study FY 2010, Table A1-3. Retrieved from http://about.usps.com/studying-americans-mail-use/household-diary/2010/fullreport-pdf/usps-hds-fy10.pdf

Postal Service. (2011). Postmaster general/CEO Patrick R. Donahoe testimony before the U.S. Senate Committee on Homeland Security and Governmental Affairs. Retrieved from http://about.usps.com/news/speeches/2011/pr11_pmg0906.htm

Postal Service. (2012). Postal facts. Retrieved from http://about.usps.com/who-we-are/postal-facts/welcome.htm#H1

Soifer, D. (2008). Consumers can 'police' their own mailbox. *South Florida Sun Sentinel.* Retrieved from http://articles.sun-sentinel.com/2008-04-04/news/0804030208_1_postal-service-monopoly-mailbox

Soifer, D. (2010). Revenue reality: In a new commercial reality, posts learn to diversify. *Postal Technology International, 36–37.*

U.S. Senate Committee on Homeland Security and Governmental Affairs. (2008). Statement of Ruth Y. Goldway. Retrieved from http://www.prc.gov/(S(pnd zdl224ina3qzoce1mu3rw))/prc-docs/library/refdesk/speeches/goldway/US%20Senate%20Committee%20on%20Homeland%20Security%20and%20Govern mental%20Affairs.pdf

Poverty Guidelines

Each year during the latter part of January the federal government releases an official income level for poverty called the Poverty Guidelines, often informally referred to as the "federal poverty level." They are issued each year in the *Federal Register* by the Department of Health and Human Services (HHS). The poverty guidelines are one version of the U.S. federal poverty measure, and are used to determine financial eligibility for certain programs. The benefit levels of many low-income assistance programs are based on these poverty guidelines.

Another measure of poverty is the poverty thresholds that are the original version of the of the federal poverty measure. The thresholds, originally developed by Mollie Orshansky of the Social Security Administration, are updated yearly by the Census Bureau. The thresholds are primarily for statistical purposes, including estimating the number of Americans in poverty each year. The poverty thresholds, not the poverty guidelines, are used for official calculation of poverty population data.

Poverty guidelines vary by family size. A chart with the poverty guidelines will list the number of persons in each household and the corresponding amount of income designating poverty status. There is one set of figures for the 48 contiguous states and the District of Columbia. There is a different set of figures for Alaska as well as Hawaii.

Some programs use the guidelines or percentage multiples of the guidelines—for instance, 125 percent or 185 percent of the guidelines to determine eligibility for the program. Some examples of these programs include Head Start; Low-Income Home Energy Assistance Program; Supplemental Nutrition Assistance Program (SNAP)—formerly the Food Stamp Program; National School Lunch Program (for free and reduced priced meals only); Special Supplemental Nutrition Program for Women, Infants, and Children (WIC); Weatherization Assistance for Low Income Persons; and the Children's Health Insurance Program.

Numerous state and local governments use the federal poverty guidelines in their programs and activities, including financial guidelines for child support enforcement and determination of legal indigence for court purposes. Furthermore, some private companies (e.g., telephone, utilities, and pharmaceutical companies) and some charitable agencies use the guidelines to determine service eligibility for low-income clients.

Major means-tested programs that do not use the poverty guidelines in determining eligibility include the following:

- Temporary Assistance for Needy Families (TANF) and its predecessor, Aid to Families with Dependent Children (AFDC) (in most cases)
- Supplemental Security Income (SSI)
- Earned Income Tax Credit (EITC)
- State/local-funded General Assistance (in most cases)
- Large parts of Medicaid (69 percent of eligibles in Fiscal Year 2004)
- Section 8 low-income housing assistance
- Low-rent public housing (U.S. Department of Health and Human Services, 2012).

Overall, poverty guidelines (unlike the poverty thresholds) are designated by the year in which they are issued.

Joanne Bankston

See also: Department of Health and Human Services (HHS); Department of Housing and Urban Development (HUD); Medicaid; Social Services; Social Welfare; Supplemental Nutrition Assistance Program (SNAP)

References and Additional Readings

Department of Health and Human Services. (2013a). 2012 HHS poverty guidelines. Retrieved from http://aspe.hhs.gov/poverty/12poverty.shtml

Department of Health and Human Services. (2013b). Frequently asked questions related to the poverty guidelines and poverty. Retrieved from http://aspe.hhs.gov/poverty/faq.shtml

Prepaid Cards. *See* Credit Cards

Privacy: Offline

Privacy laws vary state by state. A "tort" is a wrongful action causing damage that is recognized by a court and for which an injured party may bring a lawsuit for relief.

Each state is free to create tort causes of action, a claim in a lawsuit for which a court may award damages or other relief. These are designed to protect its citizens, and to create the elements of that tort. The privacy causes of action have their roots in the common law, which are the laws arising from court decisions and are based on long-recognized rights and obligations originating in England and latter applied by the U.S. courts. They are distinguished as not being based on "statutes" or laws written by a legislative body. A person's right to bring a lawsuit under a privacy tort does not depend on whether that particular person is offended, but rather whether the facts of the case would be found offensive to a reasonable person (a theoretical person who represents that average feelings of a person). The reasonable person is embodied in the jury hearing the case, or in the judge who sits as the "fact finder" if there is no jury. The four generally recognized privacy torts are as follows: (1) appropriation; (2) intrusion; (3) public disclosure of embarrassing private facts; and (4) false light. Each tort protects a slightly different personal or privacy interest.

"Appropriation" is the use of a person's name, likeness, or identity for trade or advertising purposes, without that person's consent. The courts recognize that it is fundamentally unfair to permit someone to profit from the personality of someone without permission. The tort occurs when the use of the person's identity is publically used without permission. Appropriation is often the most clear privacy tort to allege and win, because there is usually a person who clearly did not give consent to use of his or her personality, and there is usually a clear advertisement. Defenses to an allegation of appropriation include asserting that the use of the person's likeness was newsworthy, that there was actual consent to the use of the likeness, or that the individual was not actually identified.

Some states distinguish between a private person's right to privacy, and that of a "public person," such as a celebrity. A private person has the obvious interest to be generally left alone to his or her life and business. The protection of a public person is based on that person's right to make a profit from his or her personality or protect him or her from financial loss. Another distinction is that private persons generally don't make a profit from his or her personality and the privacy right of appropriation generally dies with the person, whereas a public person may have publicity-related financial interests that may be inherited or sold, and the public person's appropriation right may not disappear with the person's death.

"Intrusion" is a physical, electrical, or mechanical invasion of someone's private space. This tort protects against the invasion of privacy and it is actionable based on the invasion itself. There is no requirement that any information be obtained or used publically. This tort is actionably from the offense of the invasion itself. A tort of intrusion is very similar to that of trespass, and the claims are often brought together in the same lawsuit.

A lawsuit against the press for intrusion often depends on whether the press instigated or knew about the intrusion. Depending on the facts and the particular court in which the lawsuit is brought, a media, press, defendant may be permitted to publish information obtained by an intrusion, if the press did not participate or otherwise know about the intrusion.

A person in a public place is considered to have little expectation of privacy, because he or she chose to be in a public place. However, courts will generally protect a person from harassment, even in a public place.

Intrusion by prying into someone's private places is a clear intrusion. This would include opening someone else's mail, peeping into doors or windows. Catching an intruder in the act committing these intrusions is usually an easy tort to win, and often exposes the intruder to criminal prosecution as well. Electronic intrusion includes hidden photo and sound-detecting devices. Where there is a hidden device, or bug, it is often an easy case to win and is often a criminal violation. One area of electronic intrusion that is not as clear is when a person can record a telephone conversation. It is clear in all states that a third party recording a telephone conversation, without being a participant to the call, is wiretapping and is a serious crime.

Recording a phone conversation when participating is highly dependent on the state of both parties. State laws vary widely on the legality of recording a phone call. Some states require consent by both parties to the recording, and some states only require that the person making the recording be a party to the conversation. Also, some states will consider it illegal even if recording in a state where it is legal or legal as long as you are on the call, but the other person is located in a state where it is illegal without consent of all parties. As of the time of the writing of this article, about 15 states have laws regulating recording phone conversations. Before recording a phone conversation, it is wise to research the laws in the pertinent states. A best practice is to obtain the express consent of all parties to be recorded.

Defenses to an allegation of intrusion are generally limited to a media defense that it did not commit or know about the intrusion, and the defense that there was actual consent by the person intruded upon.

"Public disclosure of embarrassing private facts" is the non-newsworthy publication of something that is true, but its disclosure to the public is generally considered to be highly offensive to a reasonable person. Legitimately newsworthy facts, such as an arrest for a crime, are not actionable because the public has an interest in such information. This tort recognizes a person's right to have secrets and things he or she does not want made public. A lawsuit under this tort very much depends on the specific facts of what is disclosed, when, and for what purpose. In general, the fact disclosed must be considered outrageous and offensive to an average reasonable person. Public disclosure cases are very fact specific. The lawsuits are most often brought against media defendants, but the defenses to this tort are very strong in favor of the media. The most common defenses are that the fact was newsworthy, that there was consent to publish the fact, that the media had some sort of privilege—such as the fact being made public by another at a public meeting, that the fact is not offensive to a reasonable person, and that the fact was an event that took place in public—therefore not "private."

"False light" is the publication of false and highly offensive facts about a person. The fact must be false, and highly offensive to a reasonable person. A "false light" tort is akin to an action for defamation (generally an unprivileged false statement made about another that causes harm to that person's reputation or stating in the community) and they are often alleged together in the same lawsuit. The difference between a false light tort and a defamation tort is usually a matter of the degree of offensiveness of the fact. Often it will be left to the judge or jury to decide as the "reasonable person" which theory is to be applied to the facts in the case. Defenses include that the fact was true. As in a defense to defamation, truth of an alleged false light fact is a complete defense. Other defenses include that the person was not identified, that the information came from a privileged source, such as a court document, that the fact was not offensive to a reasonable person, that there was consent to the publication, and that the plaintiff did not act with malice or negligently. Specifically, malice in the false light context is a statement of fact made with an intent to cause harm to another without justification or excuse. Negligence in the false light context is the failure to exercise reasonable care in stating a potentially harmful fact about another.

Most privacy torts are based on the general consensus of the community, the "reasonable person." The legal actions are based on what people in general feel are proper of actionably offensive. If personal privacy has been violated, or if contemplating taking some act that may violate the privacy of another, it is wise to first consult with an attorney to consider the facts of the case in light of the statutes and case law in the particular state.

Michael K. Botts

See also: Privacy: Online; Public Safety; Small Claims Courts; Supreme Court

References and Additional Readings

Prosser, W. (1960). *Privacy,* 48 California Law Review, 383, 389–392.

Prosser, W. (1964). *Law of torts* (3rd ed.). St. Paul, MN: West Publishing Co.

Restatement of the Law, Second, Torts, § 652C.

Restatement of the Law, Second, Torts, § 652B.

Restatement of the Law, Second, Torts, § 652D.

Time, Inc. v. Hill (1967). 385 U.S. 374

Privacy: Online

While the Internet has become nearly universal in use around the world, this powerful tool also comes with an entirely new set of challenges and potential danger for consumers of all levels of technological sophistication. All of the historical scams and frauds have been enhanced by the advent of the Internet. The dot com world can quickly turn into a "dot con" nightmare! Compared to frauds and scams that use the mail and telephone, the Internet opens vast new markets for criminals and con artists by greatly multiplying the potential number of victims as well as reducing their costs of doing business. They no longer have large telephone bills or postage fees to contend with and they can remain nearly invisible when creating and launching online scams that can spread rapidly. By the use of anonymous e-mail addresses, disposable websites, and falsified domain name registrations, many of these con artists are able to strike quickly, victimize hundreds if not thousands of victims, and then disappear without a trace.

This is due to several reasons. Consumer's online visits and browsing history can be tracked secretly and oftentimes easily. Also, cookies (a type of message that is given to a Web browser by a Web serve to identify users and possibly prepare customized Web pages for save site login information provided by consumers) in the cyberworld are often distributed to a number of other sites (for a fee of course) that will target the consumer's recent search or purchase history. While most of these cookies are harmless, some websites will be very aggressive when selling personal information. Further, when consumers log into a website, they will notice that most begin with either http:// or https://. That added "s" at the end indicates a secure, encrypted layer for to conduct a transaction but unfortunately, the effectiveness of this layer is often diminished by a browser with poor implementation or the security of the host computer where the data resides. Reports of data breaches indicate that millions of personal security data or other secure data have been exposed, often from large, well-known websites all too often. Not surprising, according to the Internet Crime Complaint Center run by the FBI, more than 300,000 complaints regarding online privacy were filed last year, of which 120,000 were forwarded to various

---

Privacy Online: National Protect Your Identity Week (PYIW)

In 2012, the focus of PYIW focus was "ID Theft Protection on the Go." Specifically, the week suggested ways to protect identity while using mobile phones. Identity theft is the most common complaint reported to the FTC. While the true number is unknown due to underreporting, over 8 million people do report being victimized each year. Sadly, this trend will continue to rise due to the increased use of and widespread access to technology. Consumers must be aware of how to protect themselves from identity theft by utilizing the resources available to them. National PYIW is one step in the right direction, as it is aimed at educating the public and arming consumers with knowledge, information, and resources. The site *ProtectYourIDNow.org* provides excellent tips and information for consumers. Further information and consumer education resources associated with credit cards, identity theft, and mobile banking can be found at Consumer-Action.org or Privacy-Information.org.

law-enforcement agencies around the nation. As far as malicious software attacks, this number is approaching one billion according to Kapersky, Norton, and other cybersecurity firms. Unfortunately, with the rapid growth of technology, many consumers find it difficult to stay current with all of the latest developments. Further, because of the rapidity of these operations, and the fact that many of them originate in overseas operations, law enforcement is often not practical or effective.

Which do you think is the best password: "#$4Gyo89" or "RubaDubDub3meninatub"? Actually it's the second one. The first example has eight characters and can be cracked by special software within four hours. The second, longer password would take hundreds of years to be cracked by the same software simply because of its length and the laws of probability.

To create a good password, consider the following:

- Change your passwords on a regular basis. Rule of thumb is every three months for noncritical sites such as social networking sites, and every month for critical sites such as your bank account logins.
- Using the example above, longer passwords are more difficult to crack even if they are phrases that are in common usage.
- The use of special characters, upper and lower case letters, and numbers also make cracking passwords more difficult for the bad guys.
- Have separate passwords for each account. Using the same password for a number of accounts, while convenient, presents the hacker who cracks one of them with a much larger bounty of information.
- Avoid passwords that contain your name, children's names, birth dates, home towns, and other publically available information.
- Never use numbers such as your passport, driver's license, or social security numbers
- Avoid some of the obvious suspects: ABCDEF, 123456, Password, etc.

After you have created all these passwords, how do you keep track of them? One thing NOT to do is write them all down on paper and keep that paper close to your computer! There are several websites out there now such as Dropbox that allows you to store information (often for free) in cyberspace. That way, you only have to remember one password to get to the rest of them. Google has a program called LastPass which will automatically log you in to any number of websites while logged into your Google account. While nothing is entirely secure, these methods seem to have some good security protocols in place.

Remember if large companies or governmental agencies can be hacked and even shut down, you can always be a target.

Fortunately, more and more states are enacting laws that require online businesses to report these breaches immediately to those affected. Moreover, litigation against these firms who negligently handle personal information is becoming more commonplace. Interestingly, these breaches of security can come not only from outside of the organization, but also from within in the form of careless handling by employees, or malicious intent.

While anyone is susceptible to these scams, those involved in the social media are obviously highly vulnerable. With nearly a billion members, Facebook would qualify as the second or third largest country in the world! They report that nearly 500 million people login to their Facebook accounts daily, providing enormous amounts of potentially damaging information. Millions of users have "friends" that they have never seen, let alone actually met. Many of these so called "friends" have less than honorable intentions unfortunately, and a great deal of care should be taken. There seems to be competition to see who has the most "friends" or "followers" on these sites.

Here are some the biggest privacy concerns that are associated with Facebook:

- Malware attacks from advertisers;
- Third parties can gain access to personal information;
- Scammers can create fake accounts in order to pretend that they are someone else and obtain access to credit card information or child predation;
- Posting pictures on Facebook—pictures become the property of Facebook, and Facebook may use them at their discretion.

Regarding photographs on websites like Facebook, a user should be very careful about what and when images are posted. For example, if a tourist is on vacation in Nepal and posts some vacation pictures while there, the unwanted attention of home robbery experts will likely know that no one is at home and thus have greater success at breaking in. Also, most images contain geographic data that can pinpoint the exact location of the picture. This has obvious implications, especially for vulnerable populations. It is recommended that consumers use privacy settings set to the maximum.

In addition, the older population in general also seems to be a popular target to online frauds and scams. There are a number of reasons for this; they often have their nest egg of retirement funds in a bank, many are homeowners with either small of paid-off mortgages, usually have good credit, and may be under increased medical supervision, often paying significant amounts for prescription drugs and other durable medical equipment. According to the Kaiser Family Foundation, one in three older adults goes online, and depend more on the Internet than books and newspapers as a source for health information.

Common Scams

Chain letters: While chain letters are not new, the online version of them allows for a far greater rate of expansion than ever before. It may show up as something like "Retweet this and $5 will be donated by Warren Buffet to help eliminate famine in Africa!" Odds are that Mr. Buffet would not use this medium to raise the needed funds. The best action in this case is to simply break the chain by not forwarding the letter.

Cash grabs: The main purpose of social networking sites is to socialize. People do this with existing friends as well as making many new friends in the process. In the real world, people get to actually see this new friend and have much more information available to decide about the person. Online, everyone is basically anonymous, and can easily misrepresent themselves on a number of fronts. This often takes the guise of a new friend who may have "lost his wallet" and needs some quick cash to get back home. Be very wary of this ploy, and confirm the facts first before sending any money.

Hidden charges: Many times on social networking sites users will find various surveys asking for identity verification by providing a name and phone number first. With this information, scammers can submit the consumer to service charges without their knowledge. These new charges suddenly show up on the phone bill, and are difficult to remove.

Phishing requests: This often will start with a message on the user's wall that says something like "someone has just tagged you with these photos, check them out here!" When clicking on the link it will ask for a login and password, *Stop at this point!* Once the scammer has this information, they now have control of the account. The best plan of action is to log into the account the normal way and see if any of this material is actually present. Chances are good that these photos never existed.

Hidden URLs: Often the user will see shortened URLs (Web addresses). This is commonly seen on Twitter; but beware because it is unclear where the site is bouncing. It could end up going to the intended site, or one that automatically installs all sorts of malware on the computer. While URL shorteners can be useful, they also harbor hidden dangers. Be sure that the computer has current versions of antispyware and virus protection installed. In addition to the concerns mentioned earlier, Hamiel and Moyer

(2008) have taken the position that data have now become currency, and as such, needs increased protections.

Identity theft: The important thing to remember here is that Google never forgets. Simply searching for a person's name on Google can often turn up a surprising amount of information about that person. In the hands of a skilled scammer, enough information can be unearthed to steal that person's identity totally online. While the financial impact can be substantial (e.g., credit card purchases) there are far more serious possibilities. Horror stories abound of people being detained at airports, supposedly on no-fly lists, simply because of identity theft. Crimes can be committed in the name of the victim of such theft.

Phishing: This is a process whereby the con artist attempts to obtain vital information such as credit card numbers, passwords, birthdates, or social security numbers. Typically they will forge e-mail messages that will appear to come from a bank or other known agency, usually with a threat to close or verify an account that often causes concern for the recipient of the e-mail. Investigators report that these types of e-mail scams will yield a positive return rate of between 1 and 5 percent. While this rate may seem small, it is actually staggering considering the hundreds of thousands of these emails that are sent out in a very short time span. This form of identity theft can cause great damage by fraudulent purchases and even large loans taken out in the victim's name. For example, nearly one-third of older adults are not aware of the dangers of identity theft.

Health insurance: Since Medicare is such a vast and growing enterprise, many scammers don't have to take the time to discover which insurance company the older adult may be enrolled with. They simply have to pose as a Medicare representative in order to gather personal information about the Medicare recipient. Once armed with this information, the scammer can bill Medicare and the older adult may not ever realize that they have been scammed. This took on a political tone in Missouri recently when these scammers visited retirement homes offering the residents an opportunity to participate in *ObamaCare* by paying a fee.

Counterfeit prescription drugs: Individuals on fixed incomes constantly face the pressure of costs regarding medications and often will go to the Internet to find better pricing on their medications. According to the FDA, the scam of providing counterfeit medications at attractive prices through online *Pharmacies* is growing at an alarming rate. This scam has the potential of not only costing money for fake drugs, but also increases the risk on these unsafe substances causing additional medical issues.

Funeral and cemetery: This type of fraud usually takes one of two forms. In the first instance, the relatives of a recently deceased person are contacted with the message that the deceased had an outstanding debt with some fake entity, and money is extorted, or scammers will pose as an online funeral home that offers cut-rate prices on such items as caskets, or cremation upgrades, and suddenly disappear when payments are received.

Fraudulent "antiaging" products: It is hard to watch a TV show, or browse a magazine these days without being bombarded with all sorts of products to keep us looking and feeling younger. Our society's obsession with youth has put a great deal of pressure on many older adults to appear younger. In attempting to apply the phase, *60 is the new 40,* many older adults put themselves at risk of scammers. While there are a number of options out there, the fake Botox seems to be the most popular with scammers. Unfortunately, misuse of the root ingredient, botulism neurotoxin, can have drastic consequences.

Internet: There are a number of traps being set by scammers on the Internet. One of the most common is the pop-up window warning that the computer is infected with a deadly virus, and only the purchase and downloading of a particular program can save the day. Usually, there is no viral threat, and oftentimes the victim downloads an actual virus. Another sad side-effect to this practice is that victim's names and e-mail addresses are sold to other scammers.

Nigerian Prince needing a partner: Beware of any e-mail or other communication that even hints that it is associated with Nigeria. The typical scam is of some poor Nigerian prince who desperately needs a partner to share millions of dollars with. The only catch is that the victim needs to put up some seed money to release the funds. If it sounds too good to be true, it is most likely a scam.

Real estate: At the time of this writing, a number of California homeowners received an official looking message supposedly from the County Assessor's Office offering the homeowner a reassessment of the property's value for a fee. Another closely related scam involves the reverse mortgage scam which has grown exponentially in recent years. In this scam, often originated by online offerings, the scammers will attempt to convince the homeowner to give title to their property in exchange for cash or other property.

Sweepstakes/lottery: In this scam, the victim is advised by an official-looking e-mail that they have won a large prize, and only need to forward a handling fee to unlock the reward. On some occasions the victims are sent a check that will eventually bounce while the scammers quickly collect the handing fee.

Disaster recovery: The period after a disaster is a prime time for scams, frauds, and other consumer protection issues. Charity and home repair scams are common examples; oftentimes, fraudsters target disaster-affected areas in the hopes of cashing in on insurance settlements and governmental financial relief given to those affected by disasters.

Internet auctions: While there are a number of reputable auction sites available (Ebay) there are a number of complaints filed every year about auction sites that either deliver inferior products or don't deliver anything at all. The solution is to carefully check out the seller, and never pay with a money order or use a wired money service.

Internet access services: There are a number of consumers who have been trapped into long-term contracts for Internet access, usually with large cancellation penalties. Often this starts with a check arriving in the mail with the offer. If the consumer cashes the check, the contract becomes valid. Be very careful of this *free money* and read all of the enclosed material before acting.

Credit card fraud: There are a number of websites that will allow the user to view content for free by simply providing them with a credit card to prove adult age (over 18). This often results in scam artists using that credit card information in a fraudulent manner. The good news is that federal law limits liability to $50 if the card is misused.

Free websites: In this scam, victims are offered a free trial website in exchange for some information. Consumers complain that their telephone bills often reflect added charges that were not authorized. This happens whether the consumer has accepted the offer of a free trial or not.

Multilevel marketing/pyramid schemes: This age-old scam has hit the Internet in a big way. As the traditional scam operates, so does the high-tech version. Typically consumers who buy into these schemes find that their customers are not the general public, but other distributors. Buying and selling just between distributors generally does not result in a positive cash flow situation. Schemes that require the consumer to recruit other distributors should be avoided as well as building up an inventory of products.

Travel/vacation Plans: The consumer is offered fantastic deals on luxury trips for bargain-basement prices through online offerings. Many consumers report substandard accommodations and services, or no trip develops at all. Often, there are hidden charges that suddenly appear after payment.

Self-Employment opportunities: "Be your own Boss" is often the lead line in these types of scams. Many consumers have invested in businesses that promise great financial gains only to find that the business opportunity turns out to be a business flop. Carefully check out these offers and find other investors to learn about their experiences.

Investment schemes: Typically, these online scams are focused on the opportunities available as a day trader. They involve the consumer to make an initial investment to be utilized in the purchase of *hot stocks* or other high-yield instruments. These *get rich quick* scams result in only the scam artist getting rich. The ultimate example of this is the recent Bernie Madoff scandal.

Healthcare products/services: In this scam, items that are not traditionally sold through normal channels are offered with claims that they are *proven* to cure serious or even life-threatening health issues. One major negative effect of these scams is that the victims often put off the necessary health care they need in the hope that this "miracle" cure will solve everything.

Online dating scams: This has become a multibillion dollar industry that millions of Americans use on a daily basis. So do the scammers, who prey on victims who are often lonely and vulnerable. Scammers will look for targets that they can convince to send money in the name of love. Some things to look out for are the other person wants to establish communication outside of the dating site, they seem to fall in love very quickly, may claim to be from the United States, but are currently overseas and plans to return once they back up on their feet. Some will claim that they are in the armed forces stationed overseas.

Affinity marketing/fraud: Often, the scammer will attempt to identify with his or her victims by stating that he or she share similar religious beliefs, ethnic backgrounds, language, culture, age, profession, or other common characteristics. One of the dangers in this type of fraud is that once a respected leader in a particular community personally becomes involved with a product, often others in that same community will wish to participate as well. Unfortunately, due to shame or embarrassment, this type of fraud is not always reported to the appropriate authorities.

Viatical/life settlement scams: People who are terminally ill will often sell the death benefit of their life insurance policy at a discount for cash, or they are offered cash to take out a life insurance policy for a cash payment. The brokers in this process then sell shares to investors to receive a proportionate share of the benefit paid out. While many of these investments are *guaranteed* most are extremely risky. A precise time of death is impossible to predict, as well as the fact that most if not all insurance policies are contestable for a period of two years after issuance. If the policy can be shown to have been fraudulently obtained, the policy and all premiums are cancelled.

Personal Privacy Survival Guide

There are many number of ways that personal privacy can be violated. There are large communities of hackers who can gain access to personal information and create serious social and financial concerns. Many employers can also get access to user's Internet activity while using workplace computers. In Internet cafes, unscrupulous owners can also monitor activity while on their wireless network. Fortunately, there are a number of guidelines that can be implemented to reduce the attempts of hackers and increase online protection. The FTC and other consumer agencies offer a number of tips to assist in avoiding getting caught by one of these predators. Perhaps most obviously, be very wary of extravagant claims about performance or earnings potential. Consumers should get all promises in writing and review them carefully before making any payments, signing any contracts, or giving out any personal information. It is also important to read the fine print and look for any links on the website that relate to the offer. Like the fine print found on many traditional contracts, these also exist online. Consumers are wise to check to see if there is a privacy policy. If there is not, or if it is unclear, move on and find a reputable company. Always be skeptical of any company that doesn't identify itself clearly with name, street address, and a telephone number. When in doubt, check with the local Better Business Bureau, or the State Attorney General. In short, *inspect what you accept*.

Consumers should use security software that updates automatically because scammers are constantly finding new creative ways to carry out their scams, software must follow suit. The same is true for not only security software but also for operating system and web browser updates. Not taking these precautions can result in scammers inserting malicious software, called malware into the computer. There are a number of free and paid security software options available. As mentioned earlier, do not respond to pop-up messages that claim to have scanned your computer and found malware, and strongly suggest that the only solution is to buy their software, which often worthless or malware itself.

A good rule-of-thumb is to treat personal information like it was cash. If official-looking messages that ask for verification regarding an account by providing any personal information such as social security numbers, credit card numbers, bank account numbers, or passwords are received, log into the company's website directly rather than respond to the email. All reputable companies do not ask for this information, the scam should be reported to the company and appropriate agency or organization.

If there is doubt about a company's offer, search for that company's name along with the words, review, or scam. This often will provide information from others who have had dealing with this company. Often, these companies will suggest that they are affiliated with known companies, even using their logos as part of their offering.

When giving out personal information on a trusted site, be sure to check that the site is encrypted. To determine if the site is protected in this manner, look for *https* at the beginning of the web address. Be sure that this https shows up on every page of the site for complete protection. Password protection is vital. The longer the password, the more difficult it is to be cracked by scammers. Use at least 10 characters, with 12 or more being ideal. Mix up letters, numbers, and special characters. Avoid using information such as birthdates, social security numbers, or children's or pet's names. Avoid using the same password on multiple accounts because if the password is compromised, a number of sites are likewise compromised. Remember, legitimate companies will *never* ask for a password.

As with any computer files, backing up is vital if the information has personal value. Hard drives crash on occasion so a backup system is important. This could be an external hard drive or a number of cloud-based systems are available for valuable documents and photographs.

As a rule, consumers should find out what is in the credit report at least on an annual basis. A good way to remember this is to do on a birthday. To avoid getting calls from (most) telemarketers, consumers should sign up for the national "do not call" registry. Once on this registry, enrollment is permanent. Consumers can also opt out of preapproved offers of credit. This may be done for a period of five years or permanently. Consumers should tell financial institutions that they may not sell or share any personal customer data with other companies. A yearly privacy notice from financial institutions provides a form or toll-free number to insure privacy.

Moreover, consumers should avoid entering sweepstakes and other contests that will put personal information on lists that attract a great deal of unwanted attention. Wipe out or destroy old computer's hard drive when discarding or selling it. Deleting data alone will not protect personal information. Ascertain whether personal medical history is stored in the insurance industry data base, called the Medical Information Bureau (MIB). Consumers are entitled to a free annual report. More information follows on this. Loyalty clubs that many supermarkets and other businesses operate can be good money-savers, and also excellent data-collection sources on personal purchasing habits. One way to avoid this is to create a generic identity without providing telephone or address information.

Continually evaluate if material on social networking sites really needs to be there. Adjust privacy setting on all social media connections. When on the Internet, do not send sensitive personal information in chat boxes, e-mail, instant messages, forum postings, or your personal online profile. Be extra cautious about giving out social security numbers online. Typically, these numbers are associated with credit reports, bank accounts, and tax returns. If the SSN falls into the hands of the wrong person, victimization is a real possibility.

Additionally, consumers are encouraged to communicate with government agencies that need to be aware of online privacy violations, including credit reporting agencies, the U.S. Social Security Administration, the U.S. Securities and Exchange Commission, the IRS, the U.S. Department of Health and Human Services, Adult Protective Services, and Federal Trade Commission.

Casey Goeller

See also: Credit Reporting Agencies; Department of Health and Human Services (HHS); Federal Trade Commission (FTC); Frauds and Scams; Funeral Protection Rule; Securities and Exchange Commission (SEC); Social Security; Working from Home

References and Additional Readings

Department of Justice. (2011). National center for disaster fraud. Retrieved from http://www.justice.gov/criminal/oilspill/about/ncdf.html

Federal Emergency Management Agency (FEMA). (2013). Retrieved from www.fema.gov

Federal Trade Commission. (n.d.a). Disaster preparedness. Retrieved from http://www.ftc.gov/bcp/edu/microsites/recovery/

Federal Trade Commission. (n.d.b). Disaster recovery. Retrieved from http://www.ftc.gov/bcp/edu/microsites/recovery/consumer_info.html

USAID. (2013). Retrieved from www.usaid.gov

Producer Sovereignty

When a producer has the power and ability to influence consumer decisions, the market is in a state of producer sovereignty. Simply put, producer sovereignty is the producer's ability to control a free market. In its purest form, producer sovereignty rewards efficient manufacturers and encourages others to provide goods consumers will desire. Producer sovereignty is influenced by supply and demand, producer protection of consumer rights, consumer access to resources necessary to ensure those rights, and a shift to a global marketplace.

The economic principle of supply and demand is rooted in the premise of supply and demand; producers make what consumers demand. This puts the power in the hand of the consumer, and if consumption lags behind production it is difficult for producers to plan for this ever-changing marketplace. Therefore, the more producers can influence consumption, the easier it is to plan to meet market demand.

While on the surface this appears to disempower the consumer, caveat venditor (let the seller beware) reminds us that producers take risks simply by operating a business. These risks, or more precisely costs of doing business, include such things as overhead (rent, production costs, utilities) and employees (salaries and benefits), products that do not sell, or delays in transportation that advantage their competition. Therefore, market manipulation is not perceived as unethical if the six basic consumer rights to safety, education, service, free choice, information, and voice are not violated by the producer or by the marketplace. A major assumption of producer sovereignty, which has a positive influence on economic balance and the free market, is that consumer sovereignty works in cohort with it. Power is freely given to the producers by the consumer to encourage timely response to consumer needs. This relationship is effective when the consumer has the knowledge and information to choose products they believe they will benefit from, and the resources to protect themselves from abuse. Resources available to both consumers and producers fall under three primary categories: time, money, and people.

The concept of producer sovereignty assumes producers have "power" over consumers, despite the fact that consumers are responsible for their purchases and will only buy what they really want. At the same time, producers will seek to manipulate consumers through advertising and other persuasive techniques. However, if consumers do not have access to the resources necessary to ensure their six consumer rights, producer sovereignty could inadvertently violate those rights. For example, if a purchaser is being persuaded, and they do not have access to decision-making resources (i.e., time to sift through all the information, money to gain access to that information, and people to refer them and help interpret that information) then their rights as a consumer to make informed decisions may be violated. The economic theory implying that markets are efficient and rational assumes that producers will market only products desired by consumers, and purchasing habits will cause the market to self-regulate. However, a rapidly changing marketplace and persuasive marketing tactics can shift the balance of power away from consumers to producers.

In a balanced marketplace, where supply and demand are equal, producer sovereignty could be effective, but producers may make little to no profit. A producer's primary goal is not to protect consumers, but to protect the producer's own interests. If repeat customers or word-of-mouth advertising are critical parts of an organizational structure, then consumer satisfaction is critical to this primary goal. In a community marketplace, this can be a highly effective means of business self-regulation, but in a global marketplace the producer is often removed several steps from the consumer, making this form of regulation less likely, unless brand competition is strong.

Additionally, consumers may be falsely comforted by the perception of brand competition, which is often less than it seems. For example, grocery stores appear to present consumers with a vast array of product choices. However, firms may be cooperating and collaborating instead of competing, in which case a handful of corporations may control a variety of smaller brands. Therefore, even when several brand choices appear on a shelf, each may be controlled by the same corporate entity and may even be the same product under a different label. This practice limits choices in a way that deceives the consumer. In addition, access to choice may be influenced by income level, regardless of product pricing. Often, proximity to product outlets can dictate consumer choices. For example, a health food store might be located in an upper income neighborhood, while lower income neighborhoods might have numerous fast food outlets. While choice exists, access to these choices is limited by proximity, which can be manipulated by the marketplace based on income level.

Consumers have the right to product education, and producer sovereignty assumes this right will occur naturally within the marketplace. Caveat emptor, or "let the buyer beware," is the principle by which buyers are responsible for making purchases of a desired value, unless the seller is offering a guarantee of quality. Limits on consumer time and other resources make this nearly impossible in a rapidly expanding global marketplace. Producers can use this lack of resources to influence buying habits in a way which helps them better predict purchasing trends, further enhancing producer sovereignty.

This ability to predict trends is essential in a global economy that operates on surplus, because producers will only make as much as they can predictably sell. This model of global production, dominated by producer sovereignty, eventually requires overconsumption to maintain a balance between production and consumption. In a pure supply and demand economy, where consumer sovereignty dictates production, surplus would not occur and the market would remain balanced.

Trena T. Anastasia

See also: Caveat Emptor; Caveat Venditor; Consumer Sovereignty

References and Additional Readings

Evans, R. G. (2012). A new paradigm for health economics? We have three already! *Nordic Journal of Health Economics, 1*(1), 1–16.

Product Labeling

The average U.S. household spends more than $11,000 per year on consumer goods such as clothing, groceries, grooming aids/cosmetics, and other household items. To enable consumers to make informed decisions about their purchases and to protect them from deceptive packaging, federal laws are in place requiring manufacturers to label consumer products with specific information. Under the Fair Packaging and Labeling Act (FPLA), 15 U.S.C. §§1451–1461, most consumer commodities must be labeled to inform consumers of (1) product identity; (2) net contents (weight, measure, or count); and (3) the name and place of business of the manufacturer, packer, or distributer. The U.S. Food and Drug Administration (FDA) enforces the FPLA for food, drugs, medical devices, and cosmetics. The Federal Trade Commission (FTC) enforces the FPLA for other consumer commodities, and the Secretary of the Treasury is authorized to enforce the law with respect to imports coming into the country.

Under FPLA regulations, 16 C.F.R. Pt. 500 et seq., the product identity must be a generally recognized term (e.g., detergent, alarm clock) which is easily readable and placed as a principal feature on the product's primary display panel. The primary panel must also disclose the net quantity (i.e., weight or mass, measure, or numerical count) of the contents near the bottom using both the metric system as well as the customary inch/pound system. Where applicable, the net quantity per serving is also required. The corporate name and principal place of business of the manufacturer, packer, or distributor must be placed conspicuously on the product, as well. Although some products are exempt from the FPLA, other important federal or state labeling

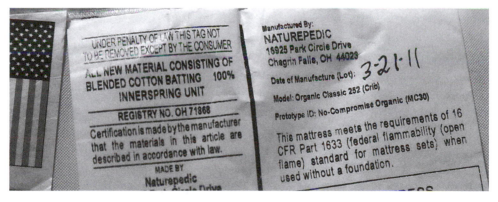

The law requires that all mattresses must carry a label listing the origin and type of materials used. (AP Photo/Elaine Thompson)

rules may apply. Similarly, some products that are covered by the FPLA may be subject to additional federal or state labeling requirements.

Apparel and Textile Products

The Textile Fiber Products Identification Act (TFPIA), 15 U.S.C. §§70 et seq., and its regulations, 16 C.F.R. §§300 et seq., require marketers to affix a label or stamp to textile products (e.g., most apparel, bedding, window treatments, and towels) disclosing in English to the consumer (1) fiber content; (2) country of origin; and (3) the manufacturer's identity. In addition, most garments sold in the United States must include care labels that instruct consumers on appropriate refurbishing. While the TFPIA requires label information to be securely attached to the product only until it is delivered to the consumer, the FTC's Care Labeling Rule, 16 C.F.R. Pt. 423, requires care instructions to be permanently affixed for the anticipated life of a garment. Thus, most manufactures affix permanent labeling for both types of information. The TFPIA makes the importation or sale of misbranded or deceptively marked textile products an unfair method of competition and an unfair and deceptive act under the FTC Act, 15 U.S.C. §41 et seq.

Fiber Content

Meeting the labeling requirement for fiber identification of textile products includes disclosing the generic name and percentages of each fiber present. Both natural (cotton, linen, silk, wool) and man-made fibers must be identified by generic name. Generic names recognized in TFPIA regulations include, among others, acetate, nylon, polyester, rayon (viscose), and spandex (elastane). A trademarked fiber name such as Tencel® may be used on a content label as long as it appears immediately next to its generic fiber name (Lyocell). A newly developed fiber cannot be used on a product label until it has been recognized by the FTC. Fiber weight must be listed on the label by percentages, in descending order. For example, a cotton-blend T-shirt might be marked "60% cotton, 40% polyester". An all-cotton T-shirt could be marked either "100% cotton" or "all cotton." Fibers that make up less than 5 percent of the product's fiber weight may be listed collectively as "other fibers" unless the fiber is wool or unless the fiber makes a significant contribution to the function of the garment, such as spandex, which provides elasticity. Thread, findings, structural linings, cuffs, collars, and trim or ornamentation that covers less than 15 percent of the garment's surface area need not be identified.

Wool and Other Animal Hair Fibers

Most textile products must be labeled to disclose to consumers any amount of wool present. This includes products that may be otherwise exempt from TFPIA (e.g., hats and slippers). The Wool Products Labeling Act of 1939 (WPLA), 15 U.S.C. §68 et seq., covers textile products containing the fleece of the sheep or lamb, hair of the Angora (mohair) or Cashmere goat, camel, alpaca, llama, or vicuna. Though all may be identified simply as "wool," they may instead be identified by their specialty name. Fibers that have not previously been processed in any way may be labeled "new wool" or virgin wool." Any reclaimed or recycled wool fibers must be identified as "recycled wool" unless they are used only in underlining. Animal hair fibers not identified in the WPLA, such as rabbit hair, may be specifically named if they comprise at least 5 percent of the fiber weight.

Fur

The Fur Products Labeling Act (FPLA), 15 U.S.C. §§69, et seq., applies to products made of animal hair that is attached to the skin. Under the FLPA and its regulations, such products must contain a label at least 1.75 × 2.75 inches identifying (1) whether the fur is natural or treated (e.g., pointed, dyed, or bleached); (2) the English-language name of the animal; (3) whether the product composed more than 10 percent of pieces (e.g., paws, waste fur); (4) country of the fur's origin (if not United States); (5) the identity of the manufacturer or dealer; and (6) the wool or textile content (if for warmth) of the product. At the time of this publication, the FTC was considering simplifying fur labeling requirements and updating its Fur Products Name Guide. Because for many years the FPLA exempted from consumer disclosure fur products valued up to $150, the Truth in Fur Labeling Act, Pub. L. 111–313, which became effective in 2011, now requires all textile products containing any genuine fur to be labeled as such. The Dog and Cat Protection Act of 2000, 19 U.S.C. §1308, prohibits importing, exporting, manufacturing, and selling any products made with domestic dog or cat fur. In 2007, an investigation by the Humane Society revealed that coats sold at several U.S. stores were trimmed with fur from domestic dogs. Most of the offending products were imported from China.

Leather

The Guides for Select Leather and Imitation Leather Products (Leather Guides), 16 C.F.R., §24, apply to the manufacture and sale of all types of leather or simulated-leather luggage, accessories, and footwear.

Manufacturers may not label as leather (i.e., hide from an animal that has been put through the tanning process) items that are not composed in all or substantial parts of leather. Manufacturers must clearly disclose if all or part of a product is made of nonleather material that appears to be leather. For example, a vinyl handbag could be labeled "Vinyl," or "Imitation leather" but not "Faux Leather." When a leather product has been embossed or otherwise processed to appear like another type of leather, the actual leather type used must be disclosed to the consumer.

Country of Origin

Products covered by the FPLA, TFPIA, WPLA, and Leather Guides must bear a conspicuous label that shows on its front side the item's country of origin. For consumer products that have been imported, the label must identify the country where the item was processed or manufactured. Items that are made in the United States of materials that have been imported must be labeled accordingly. For example, the label on a blouse might read "Made in the U.S.A. with imported fabric." Because Customs and Border Patrol requires "flat goods" such as sheets, towels, and tablecloths to identify also the country where the fabric was made, those products might be labeled as "Made in the U.S.A. of fabric made in China" (19 C.F.R. Pt. 102.21). Only those items made entirely of U.S. materials and manufactured in the United States may be labeled "Made in the U.S.A." In 2009, a California-based manufacturer of computer and television screen magnifiers (subject to the FPLA) agreed to settle charges brought by the FTC based on country of origin mislabeling. Because several of the company's products contained large portions of foreign-made components, the "Made in the U.S.A." label was found to be deceptive.

Manufacturer's Identity

In addition to identifying fiber content and country of origin, textile labels must disclose either the Registered Identification Number (RN) or the name of the manufacturer, importer, or marketer of the product (16 C.F.R. Pt. 303.19). Upon application, the FTC will issue an RN to any qualified firm in the United States that manufactures, imports, markets, or distributes textile, wool, or fur products. For products that are manufactured outside the United States, the label could bear the name of the foreign manufacturer or the name or RN of the U.S. importer or wholesaler. Retailer names and RNs may be used on labels only with the retailer's express consent. Some retailers, such as bridal shops, may wish to remove original labels so that patrons cannot easily learn the manufacturer's identity. Such a practice would be unlawful unless the retailer substitutes another label containing its own name or RN with all other required information, and keeps record of the original label for at least three years.

Care

Under the Care Labeling Rule, 16 C.F.R. Pt. 423 et seq., manufacturers and importers are required to attach care instructions to garments worn to cover or protect the body (not including shoes, gloves, and hats). Specifically, complete instructions for regular care must be permanently affixed for the useful life of the garment. For piece goods sold to consumers, care information must be clearly and conspicuously placed on the end of each roll or bolt of fabric. Care symbols developed by the American Society for Testing and Materials (ASTM) may appear on labels in place of words, but the symbols must meet the requirements of the Care Labeling Rule. In short, those symbols include (1) washtub/washtub with hand to indicate machine/hand washing; (2) triangle to indicate bleach; (3) square to indicate machine drying; (4) iron to indicate ironing; (5) circle to indicate dry cleaning; and (6) "X" over the symbol warning "do not" (ASTM, 2007). At the time of this publication, the Federal Trade Commission was considering allowing the use of International Organization for Standardization (ISO) care symbols on labels, and also recognizing "professional wet cleaning" as a method of care. Care instructions, if followed, cannot cause substantial harm to the item. The Care Labeling Rule permits more than one method of care, provided there exists a reasonable basis (i.e., reliable evidence of support) for each instruction. In addition, warnings about procedures that are known to harm the garment must be identified. However, a reasonable basis must exist showing that the procedure does, in fact, harm the garment. For example, a manufacturer may not label a jacket "Dry Clean Only" without proof that washing will harm it. In 2002, U.S. fashion conglomerate, Jones Apparel Group, Inc., agreed to an injunction and $300,000 fine by the FTC for failing to have a reasonable basis for its "Dry Clean Only" instructions on both flocked garments that were damaged during dry cleaning and cashmere sweaters that could be safely hand washed.

Food, Drugs, and Cosmetics

The Food, Drug, and Cosmetic act (FDCA), 21 U.S.C. 301 et seq., regulates the testing, manufacture, distribution, and sale of food, drugs, cosmetics, and medicinal devices. The law was enacted in the early 1900s in response to public outcry over unsavory manufacturing practices exposed in Upton Sinclair's fictional account of the U.S. meat packing industry in *The Jungle*. The U.S. Food and Drug Administration (FDA) administers the FDCA and most rules related to packaged food and dietary supplements. Meat, poultry, and egg products are regulated by the U.S. Department of Agriculture (USDA).

Packaged Food

The FDCA prohibits the shipment, distribution, or sale of "adulterated food," disallows false and misleading labeling of food products, and requires list of ingredients on food packages and point-of-purchase materials. Whether produced domestically or imported, packaged retail food items sold in the United States must meet labeling rules under the FDCA, FPLA, and applicable regulations. The Nutrition Labeling & Education Act of 1990 (NLEA), Pub. L. 01–535, amended the FDCA, requiring packaged food labels to disclose the number of calories per serving, fat, dietary fiber, and cholesterol. The NLEA also requires food, beverage, and dietary supplement labels that bear nutrient content claims and certain health messages to comply with specific requirements.

Food labels must disclose on the principle display panel (PDP) (i.e., the part of the label most likely to be displayed or examined) a statement identifying, in common and readable terms of sufficient size, the food product (e.g., tomato soup, sliced pears) and net quantity in terms of weight, measure, numeric count, or fluid measure. Quantities must be expressed in both metric (e.g., grams, liters) and customary measures (e.g., ounces, pounds). The country of origin must be conspicuously placed on the package, as well. If a foreign language is used anywhere on the label, all required label statements must appear both in English and in that language. Only those claims that have been defined in the regulations and are supported by appropriate nutrition labeling may be used on packaged food products. For example, to support a claim that a product is a "reduced calorie" food, it must contain at least 25 percent fewer calories per serving than the ordinary product. New foods, such as processed cheese-like products, which resemble a traditional food but contain less protein, essential vitamin, or mineral content, are considered substitutes for their traditional counterparts and must be labeled as an imitation. Beverages that purport to contain fruit or vegetable juice must declare the percentage of juice present, unless the beverage contains only small amounts for flavoring. Only those beverages made with 100 percent juice may be labeled "juice"; beverages containing diluted juice should be identified with a term such as "juice drink" or "juice cocktail" (FDA, 2011).

On the panel to the immediate right of the PDP, in prominent print, the manufacturer must place an information box disclosing (1) the manufacturer's name and business address (unless indicating "Manufactured for" or "Distributed by"); (2) the ingredient list in descending order of weight predominance (including water and colorants added); (3) nutrition information; and (4) any required allergy warnings. Information that is not required by the FDA, such as a UPC code, may not appear in, or otherwise interrupt the information box. Incidental additives that have no function or technical effect need not be included on the ingredient list. Only approved chemical preservatives may be added to foods, and the ingredient list must include both the common name and its purpose (e.g., "Ascorbic acid to promote color retention"). When added to a processed food, spices, natural flavors, and artificial flavors need not be identified individually, but may be listed as simply "spices," "natural flavor," or "artificial flavor" (21 C.F.R. 101).

The Food Allergen Labeling and Consumer Protection Act of 2004 (FALCPA), Pub. L. 108–282, requires packaged foods regulated by the FDA to disclose the presence of major food allergens in the nutrition information area of the information box. Ninety percent of all food allergies are associated with just eight foods or their protein derivatives, and have been identified by the FDA as "major food allergens." These include milk; eggs; fish; crustacean shellfish (e.g., crab, shrimp); tree nuts (e.g., almonds, pecans); wheat; peanuts; and soybeans. The FALCPA disclosure requirement may be met by either (a) including the specific food source in parentheses after the usual name of the food in the ingredient list or (b) placing the word "Contains" followed by the name of the food source immediately after the ingredient list. While fresh fruits and vegetables are exempt from the FALCPA, it does cover prepackaged foods sold at foodservice outlets.

Nutrition information may appear either on the PDP or with the ingredient list and manufacturer information. Some foods, such as infant formula, baby food, fresh fish and produce are not required to disclose nutrition information. In addition to disclosing percentages of recommended daily allowance (RDA) of FDA-specified nutrients, the number of calories per serving and grams/milligrams of fat, dietary fiber, and cholesterol must also be disclosed. Although a simplified nutrition information label may be used for some foods that provide limited nutritional value (e.g., sugarfree soda) five core disclosures (calories, total fat, cholesterol, sodium, and protein) must appear on all "Nutrition Facts" labels, even if the content level is zero. Note that trans fatty acids must be listed on the label in response to studies demonstrating a link between their consumption and an increased risk of coronary heart disease. For more information on interpreting food labels, see *How to Understand and Use the Nutrition Facts Label,* available at www.fda.gov. With a goal of helping consumers make more informed food purchase decisions, new regulations for many packaged raw meat and poultry products became effective in 2012. Enforced by the USDA's Food Safety and Inspection Service, the rules require some of the most popular meat and poultry products to bear nutrition fact labels providing information such as calories, fat content, and sodium.

Dietary supplements are products taken by mouth that contain ingredients such as vitamins, minerals, herbs, and amino acids that are intended to supplement the diet. They are made available to consumers in various forms, such as tablets, liquids, and powders, and do not require FDA approval before marketing. However, manufacturers must ensure that product label information is truthful and in compliance with the FDA's Current Good Manufacturing Practices for Dietary Supplements (21 C.F.R. Pt. 111). Under those regulations, dietary supplements must be labeled to disclose (1) descriptive name stating that it is a "supplement"; (2) the manufacturer's name and business address (unless indicating "Manufactured for" or "Distributed by"); (3) a complete list of ingredients; and (4) the net quantity of the product. The ingredient list identifying each ingredient contained in the product must appear in a "Supplement Facts" panel along with the nutrition information (21 C.F.R. Pt. 111).

Nutrition Facts

The Food and Drug Administration requires food labels on foods that are prepared (breads, cakes), canned (beans, corn), frozen (pizza, vegetables) as well as, drinks (soda, juice, flavored water). The serving size must be standardized and easy to understand. The calories must be provided and calculated on a per serving basis, including calories from fat. Items also required to be on the label are: total fat-saturated and trans, cholesterol, sodium, carbohydrates, dietary fiber, sugar, and protein. Vitamin A, C, calcium and iron is also a requirement on the label even if they are not present in the item, because many Americans are deficient in these nutrients. The bottom footnote is not required, but helps consumers interpret the products contribution to percent of daily values (based on a 2,000 calorie per day diet).

Drugs, Over-the-Counter (OTC)

The FDCA protects consumers by prohibiting the manufacture, distribution, and sale of adulterated or misbranded drugs and requiring important disclosures about the use and potential side-effects of drugs. The FDA oversees all drugs and ensures that they are properly labeled. Over-the-counter (OTC) drugs are those that are available to consumers without a prescription. The Drug Facts labeling regulation, 21 C.F.R. Pt. 201, provides standardized labeling requirements for all OTC drug and drug-cosmetic products (i.e., products with both drug and cosmetic attributes). Specifically, OTC drugs must bear a label entitled "Drug Facts" on the outside package (or the actual container if not enclosed in packaging). On it, the manufacturer must provide the following information to consumers: (1) active ingredient(s) (i.e., any component intended to furnish affect on treatment or prevention of disease); (2) purpose(s) of active ingredient(s); (3) approved use of the drugs; (4) warning(s) in the order of importance or impact; (5) dosage directions; (6) other information, as required or permitted for the particular drug; and (7) inactive ingredients, listed in alphabetical order. "Keep out of reach of children" and accidental overdose/ ingestion warnings are required on most OTC drugs. Following these disclosures, the manufacturer may opt to provide contact information for consumer questions or comments. Trade/company names or any graphical image (e.g., UPC code, seal, or certification mark) may not appear in, or otherwise interrupt, the Drug Facts box.

Topical sunscreens, an OTC drug, are widely used to prevent sunburn and other skin damage. While sunburn is primarily caused by ultraviolet B radiation (UVB), both UVB and ultraviolet A radiation (UVA) are known to cause sunburn, skin cancer, and premature skin aging. Those risks can be substantially reduced by applying to exposed skin a topical sunscreen that protects against both types of radiation (broad spectrum) with a Sun Protection Factor (SPF) of 15 or greater. Under FDA regulations effective in June 2012, over-the-counter sunscreens may be labeled "broad spectrum" only if they pass a pass test that demonstrates protection against both UVB and UVA. Sunscreen products that both meet the test and also have a SPF of 15 or higher may be labeled "broad spectrum" and "SPF 15" (or higher) on the product's front. Because it suggests complete protection from the damaging effects of the sun, the term "sunblock" may not be used, regardless of SPF. Manufacturers must inform consumers on the back of the product that sunscreens labeled both "broad spectrum" and "SPF 15" (or higher) protect against sunburn, and when used as directed, can reduce the risk of skin cancer and premature aging. A sunscreen that is not broad spectrum or that has an SPF value below 15 must contain a warning that exposure to the sun increases the risk of skin cancer and premature aging, and that the product has been shown only to help prevent sunburn. Substantiated claims of water resistance may be placed on the front of the product, advising the consumer how long (either 40 or 80 minutes) the full SPF value will last while swimming or perspiring. Manufacturers may not claim that a sunscreen is either water- or sweat-proof.

Cosmetics

The term "cosmetics" covers those consumer products intended to be applied to the body for cleansing, beautifying, or altering the appearance without affecting the structure or function of the body. This includes items such as skin cream and lotion, perfume, make-up and lipstick, nail polish, hair shampoo and color, toothpaste, and deodorant. Most soap that makes no additional claim on the label will not considered a cosmetics product. The FDA ensures that cosmetics are properly labeled for consumers. All cosmetics produced or distributed for retail sale in the United States must meet the labeling requirements of the FDCA, FPLA, and federal regulations found at 21 C.F.R. Pt. 700–740. First, cosmetic packaging must disclose in common English on the PDP a statement or illustration identifying the nature and use of the product and the net quantity of contents. In addition, the following basic information should be prominently displayed on a conspicuous panel of the product or package: (1) manufacturer's name and business address (unless indicating "Manufactured for" or "Distributed by"); (2) material facts, such as directions for safe use; (3) warnings or cautionary statements, such as flammability statements; (3) ingredients, in descending order of predominance. Because cosmetics that are also OTC drugs (e.g., lipstick with sunscreen, antidandruff shampoo) must meet labeling requirements for both OTC drug and cosmetic ingredient labeling, the active drug ingredient(s) will be declared before the cosmetic ingredients. For cosmetics distributed via mail order or online channels, instructions for locating or obtaining the ingredient declaration may be enclosed with the package in lieu of an information panel of the product. Specific warning statements are required for some cosmetics, including aerosol sprays, feminine deodorant sprays, and children's bubble bath. A cosmetic is considered misbranded under the FDCA if it does not bear the required labeling information. No cosmetic may be labeled with statements suggesting that FDA has approved the product (21 C.F.R. Pt. 701).

Perfumes and other fragranced cosmetic products are subject to the cosmetics labeling requirements. However, the regulations provide that a manufacturer may be exempt from disclosure of certain ingredients because fragrance formulas are considered "trade secrets" worthy of protection against disclosure to competitors and other third parties. Consequently the FDA, upon application from a cosmetics company, may waive that portion of the ingredient disclosure. Rather than revealing the specific ingredients in the fragrance formula, the phrase "and other ingredients" may be used instead (21 C.F.R. Pt. 701.3(a)). In addition, where an insignificant level of fragrance is added to a cosmetic product to mask the odor of other ingredients, it need not be disclosed on the label. Thus, there is some concern that phthalates (chemical plasticizers suspected of posing health risks to humans) may be present in cosmetics products without knowledge of the consumer.

Appliances

Under the FTC's Appliance Labeling Rule, 16 C.F.R. Pt. 305 et seq., most new household appliances, such as refrigerators, dishwashers, clothes washers, water heaters, and room air conditioners must be labeled with energy efficiency information. These yellow and black "Energy Guide" labels enable consumers to comparison shop for energy-efficient household appliances, plumbing, and lighting products. The label, which may be removable adhesive or hang-tag style, must disclose to consumers (1) the name of the manufacturer; (2) model number; (3) capacity; (4) estimated annual energy cost to operate; and (5) the cost range of operating similar models. For new televisions, the label must disclose the cost range of operating other televisions with the same screen size (16 C.F.R. Pt. 305.17). A manufacturer's energy use data must be based on testing procedures developed by the U.S. Environmental Protection Agency. For products generally using 20–30 percent less energy than required by federal standards, an "Energy Star" logo or label may be placed on the product.

The Appliance Labeling Rule also requires energy disclosures for certain lighting products and water use labeling for some plumbing products. Recent amendments to the Appliance Labeling Rule require manufacturers of light bulbs to disclose on the front of the package both brightness and energy-cost information. A detailed "Lighting Facts" label must appear on the reverse, advising consumers about brightness in lumens, energy cost, bulb life, light appearance, and watts.

Jewelry and Precious Metals

The FTC's Guides for the Jewelry, Precious Metals, and Pewter Industries (Jewelry Guides) describe how to accurately mark and advertise fine jewelry products. Such items include, but are not limited to, gemstones, pearls, and metallic items such as flatware that are fabricated from gold, silver, platinum, pewter, and their imitations. It is unlawful to misrepresent the type, quality, size/weight, color, or other key aspect of any fine jewelry product. Where a representation is made about an item, it must be accurate and in accordance with the Jewelry Guides. For example, a jewelry item labeled or advertised as "Platinum" must be composed of at least 95 percent pure platinum. For diamonds, when weight is described in decimal parts of a carat, the figure should be accurate to the last decimal place. Thus, ".50 carat" could represent a diamond that weighs anywhere from .495 to .504 carat. When weight is described in fractions, the variance may be slightly greater, and the retailer should disclose that the weight is not exact. Retailers must disclose to the customer whether pearls are cultured (cultivated) or imitation (artificial). The term "pearl" without either qualifier indicates that the pearl is natural.

Mattress Products

Often the subject matter of both consumer confusion and comedians' jokes, labels attached to mattresses, pillows, and other filled products are known as "law labels." Intended to inform consumers regarding the contents of bedding and furniture products, these state laws require disclosure of filling contents in descending order of prominence. Not all states require law labels on filled bedding products, and among states that have enacted such laws, requirements vary. However, despite warnings to distributors and retailers that they may not remove a law label under penalty of law, the consumer, upon purchasing the product, may do so as desired.

Karen E. Edwards

See also: Department of Agriculture (USDA); Environmental Protection Agency (EPA); Fair Trade; Federal Trade Commission (FTC); Food and Drug Administration (FDA); Food, Drug and Cosmetic Act (FD&C Act); *The Jungle*; Made in USA; Underwriters Laboratories; Warnings

References and Additional Readings

Associated Press. (2013). Retailers pull fur-trimmed coats after dog hair is found. *LA Times.* Retrieved from http://articles.latimes.com/2007/feb/24/business/fi-dogfur24

ASTM D5489-07. (2007). Standard guide for care symbols for care instructions on textile products. *ASTM.* (n.p.).

Bureau of Labor Statistics. (2011). Consumer expenditure survey, 2010. *Focus on Prices and Spending*, 2(12), 1–5.

Consumer Expenditure Survey, 2010. (2011). U.S. Bureau of Labor Statistics. *Focus on Prices and Spending*, 2(12), 1–5.

Department of Agriculture. (2012). Key nutrition information for most popular meat and poultry products coming to a store near you. Retrieved from: http://www.usda.gov/wps/portal/usda/usdamediafb?contentid=2012/03/0073.xml&printable=true&contentidonly=true

Food and Drug Administration. (2001). Cosmetic labeling guide: Fragrances and flavors. *Cosmetic Labeling Manual*. (n.p.).

Food and Drug Administration. (2004). How to understand and use the nutrition facts label. Retrieved from: http://www.unh.edu/dining/nutrition/pdf/food-label.pdf

Food and Drug Administration. (2009a). Guidance for industry: Labeling OTC human drug products, small entity compliance guide. Center for Drug Evaluation and Research.

Food and Drug Administration. (2009b). Guidance for industry: A food labeling guide. Office of Nutrition, Labeling and Dietary Supplements.

Food and Drug Administration. (2011). FDA sheds light on sunscreens. *Consumer Health Information*. Retrieved from: http://www.fda.gov/forconsumers/consumerupdates/ucm258416.htm

Federal Trade Commission. (1999). Wedding gown labels: Unveiling the requirements. *Facts for Business.*

Federal Trade Commission. (2001a). Clothes captioning—Complying with the care labeling rule. *For the Consumer.*

Federal Trade Commission. (2001b). In the loupe: Advertising diamonds, gemstones, and earls. *Facts for Business.*

Federal Trade Commission. (2002). Jones apparel group agrees to pay $300,000 civil penalty to settle FTC charges of violating the care labeling rule. Press Release, 2 April 2002.

Federal Trade Commission. (2005). Threading your way through the labeling requirements under the textile and wool acts. *Bureau of Consumer Protection*, May 2005.

Federal Trade Commission. (2009). Manufacturer settles with FTC for making misleading made-in-USA claims. Press Release, 20 July, 2009.

Singer, N. (2005). Labels can hide the presence of phthalates. *New York Times.*

Public Citizen

Public Citizen is an influential Washington, D.C.-based organization founded in 1971 by well-known consumer advocate Ralph Nader. While headquartered in Washington, D.C., the organization also has an office in

Austin, Texas (founded in 1984). They are funded by foundation grants, publication sales, and support from their members and supporters, 300,000 strong. They accept no funding from corporations or government. Two separate entities exist under the name Public Citizen, Public Citizen, Inc. and Public Citizen Foundation. The main difference between the two entities surrounds lobbying. Public Citizen, Inc. lobbies congress to further their mission of protecting public health and safety, as well as, advancing government transparency, and urging corporate accountability. Public Citizen Foundation focuses mainly on education and litigation, serving as the public interest lobby. Because the foundation arm is a 501 (c)(3), and operates as a nonprofit, all donations are tax deductible; Public Citizen, Inc. is not a designated nonprofit and therefore donations are not tax deductible.

Public Citizen, prides itself for being the people's voice in Washington, D.C. They focus on citizen interests and have championed these interests before Congress, the executive branch agencies and the courts. They have focused on abuses in the areas of pharmaceuticals and the automobile industry, among others. They also focus on fairness in trade agreements, specifically those that focus on the best interests of large corporations at the cost of citizens throughout the world.

The organization consists of five policy groups: Congress Watch division, the Energy Program, Global Trade Watch, the Health Research Group, and their Litigation Group. The Congress Watch Division grew out of Public Citizen, publishing its first publication, *Who Runs Congress?* in 1972. Stemming from over 14,000 pages of material about congressional members and key committees, it sold more copies than any other book about Congress at that time. Today, the Congress Watch Division works to promote consumer interests in Congress and also, stemming from its original goals, serves as a government watchdog. The division also serves the role of advocate and public educator. There are several focuses that drive the group. They seek to strengthen safety, health, and financial protections including consumer financial protections, as well as the safety of patients, automobiles, and employees. They also aim to ensure access to courts by citizens including holding corporations accountable for harms perpetrated. They have addressed forced arbitration, protections for whistleblowers, medical liability, and maintaining state consumer laws. And, finally, they want to strengthen democracy through exposure of the harmful impact of money in the political arena. To this end, they have focused on money in politics, ethics in government, and lobbying reform efforts.

Since its humble beginnings, the division has been both active and successful. The Congress Watch Division helped usher through the Freedom of Information Act Amendments in the mid-1970s, promoting one of their cornerstones, transparency in government. The division also had a hand in the Magnuson–Moss Warranty Act, auto safety, pesticide and food safety, toxic waste management, and many more.

The Energy Program under Public Citizen focuses on combating climate change through promotion of energy that is affordable, safe, and sustainable. They work to protect Americans from nuclear power dangers, as well as, championing market transparency and protection of consumers from market manipulation. They also serve as activists around the United States toward their goal of sustainable energy. According to the website, their focuses are on affordable energy, lean energy (boosting fuel economy, low carbon fuels, watchdogging big oil), clean, affordable transportation, nuclear relapse (fatal flaws of nuclear power, new reactor proposals), and dirty energy (dirty coal, hydraulic fracturing, tar sands).

One of their recent petitions surrounds the BP Oil spill in the Gulf Region in 2010 where nearly 5 million barrels of oil leaked into the Gulf of Mexico over an 87-day period. The Department of Justice is seeking $25 billion in settlement costs. Public Citizen's Energy Program has a petition on the website asking that government hold BP accountable, seeking a fair settlement, for the tragedy. Other current areas of interest include the Japanese nuclear power catastrophe, California's Hydrogen Highway Initiative, and a clean energy movement at the Texas office of Public Citizen.

The Global Trade Watch arm of Public Citizen purports the following mission, according to the website:

> to ensure that in this era of globalization, a majority have the opportunity to enjoy America's promises, economic security, a clean environment, safe food, medicines and products, access to quality affordable services such as health care and the exercise of democratic decision-making about the matters that affect their lives. (Public Citizen, 2012, About our Global Trade Watch)

This group is a member of Our World is Not for Sale (OWINFS), which is a group of activities organizations fighting corporate globalization in trade, but supporting sustainability and democracy in trade. Not aligned with the World Trade Organization (WTO), the Global Trade Watch Division seeks to fight the corporate globalization they feel the WTO promotes. Their book, *Whose Trade Organization?* expands on these and other ideas.

Other current issues the Global Trade Watch Division is focusing on include:

- Alternatives to corporate globalization (fast track replacement, TRADE Act, trade in elections, WTO turnaround)
- Democracy, sovereignty, and federalism (congressional voting records, dispute resolution and trade tribunals, effects of state and local government, standardization/harmonization)
- Deregulation and access to services (energy and climate change, environment and zoning, financial services, health and education, land use policy and zoning)
- Import safety, environment and health (environmental sustainability, food and product safety)
- Jobs, wages, and economic outcomes (agriculture and development, immigration, jobs, offshoring, U.S. trade deficit)
- NAFTA, WTO, other trade pacts (CAFTA, Columbia, and Panama, Korea)

The Health Research Group is focused on promoting research-based, system-wide changes in healthcare policy and drug safety. They attempt to ban or relabel drugs and medical devices that are either unsafe or ineffective in an effort to make the work environment safer for workers by reducing exposures to hazardous chemicals. The group also has an education arm, educating the public about drug and drug interaction dangers via newsletters and their website, WorstPills.org. Their education efforts also seek to push medical boards to do a better job in their disciplining doctors. They also promote a "single-payer, Medicare-for-all system." Some of their recent accomplishments have involved the testing of the Anthrax vaccine, over the counter drug availability, Alzheimer's remedy Aricept; NIH's involvement in a superbug outbreak, FTC involvement in bed handles, among other diverse topics. Recent points of interest for the group, are listed as follows: drugs, devices, and supplements (drug projects, drug policy, device projects, device policy, dietary supplement projects, dietary supplement policy), physician accountability, consumer product safety, worker safety, health care delivery, auto and truck safety (bigger, heavier trucks, pedestrian and cyclist safety, rollovers, truck driver safety, vehicle-to-vehicle compatibility), global access to medicines, and infant formula marketing.

The website provides an impressive timeline of activities and accomplishments since the group's inception in 1971 by Ralph Nader and Sidney

Wolfe, MD. Perhaps one of the most famous and earliest cases (1971) involved their petition to the Food and Drug Administration to ban Red Dye No. 2, a potential cancer-causing substance. The dye was banned, after much research and legal challenges, five years later.

One of the most influential sides of Public Citizen is its Litigation Group. Touted as a public interest law practice, it was founded in 1972 by Ralph Nader and Alan B. Morrison. Attorneys from this group litigate cases at both the federal and state levels, specializing in

> health and safety regulation, access to courts, consumer rights, open government, and the First Amendment, including Internet free speech. These efforts are pursued through litigation and through programs such as the Supreme Court Assistance Project (SCAP) and the Freedom of Information Clinic (FOIC). We also provide legal advice and assistance to Public Citizen researchers and lobbyists, to congressional staffers, and to staff at other public interest organizations. (Public Citizen, 2012, "About Our Litigation Group")

Their current features include work on government transparency, consumer justice, the first amendment, and healthy, safety and the environment. The website provides a list of litigation and arbitration by the group. Large corporations such as John Hancock Life Insurance, The Coffee Beanery, T-Mobile, AT&T Mobility LLC, Rent-a-Center West, Inc., and many others are listed. Their priorities, as stated on the Public Citizen website, include access to courts and court remedies. campaign finance and election laws, constitutional rights and requirements, health, safety, and the environment, open government and open courts (Freedom of Information Act, Open Court Proceedings), representing consumers (Class Actions, Consumer Justice), and workers' rights.

The Public Citizen Litigation Group is focusing on access to the court system, arguing four cases before the Supreme Court in Fall of 2012. The website has a Supreme Court Assistance Project page that provides the Public Citizen docket, as well as listing active Supreme Court cases in which they are involved.

The website highlights accomplishments achieved by Public Citizen since its inception in 1971. These highlights are largely due to the dedicated and powerful leadership Public Citizen has enjoyed from consumer champions like Joan Claybrook, auto safety advocate, Sidney Wolfe, M.D., drug safety and health policy expert, Andrew Friedman, attorney and class action expert, Jim Hightower, radio commentator and champion against corporate power, and others. Some of the more recent accomplishments include success in the courts and legislative activities surrounding the following topics: auto-dialed calls, anti-protesting ordinances, antibiotics in animal feed, the Freedom of Information Act, and many others. The agency has served the consumer well as its watchdog.

Wendy Reiboldt

See also: Activism; Department of Justice (DOJ); Federal Trade Commission (FCC); Freedom of Information Act (FOIA); Magnuson–Moss Warranty Act; Nader, Ralph; World Trade Organization (WTO)

References and Additional Readings

Bollier, D. (1997). *Public Citizen.* In S. Brobeck (Ed.), *Encyclopedia of the consumer movement.* (pp. 460–465). Santa Barbara, CA: ABC-CLIO.

Public Citizen. (2013a). About our litigation group. Retrieved from http://www.citizen.org/Page.aspx?pid=2326#litgroup

Public Citizen (2013b). About our global trade watch group. Retrieved from http://www.citizen.org/Page.aspx?pid=1328

Public Interest Research Groups (PIRGs)

Public Interest Research Groups (PIRGs) are nonprofit groups that work at the grass roots level for the greater good on behalf of consumers. Historically, PIRGs involved groups of college students interested in consumer-related issues at both the local and national levels. The movements to start PIRGs began in the 1970s, largely spawned by Ralph Nader's call to action in his coauthored book *Action for a Change.* PIRG funding largely comes from student fees (a controversial source of funding for college PIRGs) and donations. State PIRGS operate independently and are citizen funded. State PIRGs celebrated their 40th year in 2012.

In line with its roots, STUDENT PIRGs are still active and have a website detailing activities and issues on their agenda. According to the website, their mission is "together we can make change happen." They offer help in getting a PIRG started, as well as internship opportunities. There are over 100 PIRGs on college campuses. Recent topics of interest include healthy foods, zero waste, textbook prices, student debt, national parks, among other things.

The most notable PIRG is the Consumer Federation of America's U.S. Public Interest Research Group (U.S. PIRG). Their website notes the following: "U.S. PIRG, the federation of state Public Interest Research Groups (PIRGs), stands up to powerful special interests on behalf of the American public, working to win concrete results for our health and well-being." Their mission statement is as follows: "U.S. PIRG is an advocate for the public interest. When consumers are cheated, or the voices of ordinary citizens are drowned out by special interest lobbyists, U.S. PIRG speaks up and takes action. We uncover threats to public health and well-being and fight to end them, using the time-tested tools of investigative research, media exposés, grassroots organizing, advocacy and litigation. U.S. PIRG's mission is to deliver persistent, result-oriented public interest activism that protects our health, encourages a fair, sustainable economy, and fosters responsive, democratic government." Recent issues on their agenda include contractor loopholes, rail travel, credit card protections, affordable health care, promoting ethical standards for elected officials, medication safety, among others.

Wendy Reiboldt

See also: Consumer Federation of America (CFA); Nader, Ralph

References and Additional Readings

Plunkett, T., & Mierzwinski, E. (2009). Consumer federation of America: U.S. public interest research group (U.S. PIRG). *Congressional Digest, 88*, 176–190.

Student PIRGs. (n.d.). Student action for the future. Retrieved from http://www.studentpirgs.org

U.S. PIRG. (n.d.). Standing up to powerful interests. Retrieved from http://www.uspirg.org

Public Safety

Public safety concerns the entire nation and directly impacts the well-being of individuals and communities at large. Issues of public safety are addressed through efforts aimed at protecting the public with prevention and intervention strategies, correctional methods, and educating consumers on proper responses and resources. Public safety issues such as crime, social disorder, and fear of crime are an everyday concern for the citizens of the United States. A variety of services offer support for individuals and communities to increase their safety at home, work, school, and other public settings. Preventative efforts aimed at protecting the safety of the public are the responsibility of administrative offices and organizations at both the state and federal levels.

Public safety goals can be met through community support, information exchange, and collaboration. All of these efforts aim to protect the

Among the 50 plus agencies within the Department of Justice, several exist to ensure the public safety of citizens. For example, the Bureau of Alcohol, Tobacco, Firearms and Explosives is designed to protect the public by reducing violent crime and assisting other law enforcement agencies. Another example is the Community Relations Service which is the only federal service mandated to assist, among other arenas, community groups to resolve and prevent racial conflicts.

public from threats to persons and property. Recently, the advances in technology have generated new and innovative approaches to disseminating information about emergencies, crimes, and other threats to public safety. With these technological developments, the rise of new and improved communication strategies has introduced more efficient and effective ways to prepare for and respond to crimes, emergencies, and other forms of danger to the public. In addition, these technological advancements have allowed for quicker response and alert systems that change the way emergency responders communicate and operate (Public Safety Communications Evolution).

Advances in Public Safety

Communication and Technology

Information about threats to public safety reaches the public through a variety of channels. Multichannel communication strategies are one of the most notable advances in public safety, allowing for quicker and more effective emergency response and alert systems. The evolution of communication networks has improved the capability of emergency responders to reach public safety agencies in the state, local, and tribal jurisdictions Nationwide. Emergency communications and response effectiveness will be improved by increases in mobile access to necessary applications and access to real-time information (Public Safety Communications Evolution). Wireless broadband networks provide a means for public safety entities to perform operations such as digital dispatch, text messaging, and transmission of images (Public Safety Communications Evolution).

Communication and collaboration is critical for governance operating at multilevels of government across the nation. It is critical that public safety stakeholders form partnerships and engage in nationwide, statewide, regional, and tactful planning (Public Safety Communications Evolution).

Statistics provided by the Bureau of Justice provide records indicating that in 2005 there were more than 160,000 inmates convicted of sexual assault and rape crimes in state prisons (http://www.ojp.usdoj.gov/smart/sexoffendermgmt.htm). The vast majority of these offenders have been released, as well as continued expected releases schedules at some point in the near future. The management of the concerns raised by the release of sex offenders is in the hands of justice authorities and other public safety officials who are charged with the task of confronting this threat to the public safety. Authorities must come up with solutions to this potential problem, and recently the methods used to manage sex offenders have undergone changes. Changes in the management of sex offenders have been brought about by the technological evolution of communication and collaboration methods. Criminal justice professionals supervise and treat sex offenders much differently than they used to in the past. The comprehensive approach to sex offender management includes ways to reduce recidivism. The comprehensive management framework promotes the importance of collaboration and use of strategic management strategies (http://www.csom.org/pubs/csom_bro.pdf). The framework provides some suggestions that different public safety jurisdictions should consider when planning their response and prevention initiatives. Informed and integrative practices and policies share the common goal of ensuring the safety of communities and ensuring support and protections for victims of sexual assault (http://www.csom.org/pubs/csom_bro.pdf).

Technology and the use of Internet-based databases have proven to be instrumental in the efforts to inform the public of threats to their safety. The Dru Sjodoin National Sex Offender Website (NSOPW) hosts sex offender registries that are available to the public free of charge. The website allows visitors to use an advanced search tool that gives users the opportunity to submit a request to obtain information about sex offenders. This tool is very useful as a preventative measure in keeping the public informed about offenders in their neighborhood.

Governmental Agencies

The federal government is committed to providing financial resources needed to ensure that public safety can be supported in various community settings.

Department of Justice

The U.S. Department of Justice (DOJ) is the department in charge of law enforcement at the federal level. The DOJ receives their leadership from the attorney general and within the department there are multiple offices relevant to efforts to ensure public safety. The following offices are included within the DOJ: the Office of Justice Programs (OJP); Office of Sex Offender Sentencing, Monitoring, Apprehending, Registering and Tracking; Office for Victims of Crime; and the Office on Violence Against Women (http://www2 .ohchr.org/english/bodies/crc/docs/AdvanceVersions/CRC-C-OPSC-USA-2.doc). The DOJ remains the leading authority for federal programs and activities related to the prevention and reduction of juvenile delinquency as well as missing and exploited children (www.justice.gov).

Office of Juvenile Justice and Delinquency Prevention (OJJDP): From serious, violent, and chronic offenders to victims of abuse and neglect, the OJJDP collaborates with professionals from diverse disciplines to improve juvenile justice policies and practices. The duties of the OJJDP include the following; "sponsoring research, programs, and training initiatives; develop priorities and goals and sets policies to guide federal juvenile justice issues; disseminating information about juvenile justice issues; and awarding funds to states to support local initiatives that protect the public" (http://www.ojjdp.gov/about/DivList.asp).

The OJJDP is a constituent of the Office of Justice Programs, and as provided on their website, it is stated that the OJJDP accomplishes its mission "by supporting states, local communities, and tribal jurisdictions in their efforts to develop and implement effective programs for juveniles" (http://www.ojjdp.gov/about/DivList.asp). The office serves the juvenile justice system by supporting efforts to protect public safety, holding offenders accountable for crimes, and providing services that focus on the needs of youth and their families (http://www.ojjdp.gov/about/about.html).

Other DOJ offices include the Office for Victims of Crime (OVC), which provides programming and research support for outreach to crime victims, victims of sexual violence, and the victim's families. The National Center for Victims of Crime is also included in the OVC.

National Center for Victims of Crime (NCVC)

The mission of the National Center for Victims of Crime (NCVC), as stated on their website, is "to forge a national commitment to help victims of crime rebuild their lives. They are dedicated to serving individuals, families, and communities harmed by crime" (http://www.ncvc.org/ncvc/main). The NCVC works in cooperation with local, state, and federal partners, advocating for policies and regulations that ensure the rights, as well as provide protections for victims of crime. NCVC supplies informational resources relevant to the needs of crime victims. The center also offers services to enhance awareness, outreach, and policies for supporting crime victims in a variety of ways. They are the nation's leading source of up-to-date information on victims' issues and play a central role in shaping the national discussion on victims' rights, protections, and services. The NCVS gathers information on reported and unreported nonfatal crimes and provides statistics on national levels of victimization to person and property, organizes information on the characteristics of crimes and victims, and the resulting consequences of victimization on victims (http://www.ncvc.org/ncvc/main).

Children—Crimes against

Unfortunately, every day children are reported missing, abducted, abused, or exploited. These offenses must be met with prompt, orderly, and effective responses in order to be successful in the prevention and intervention of these offenses. Cooperative federal activities are an instrumental force in the effort to fight crimes related to abducted and exploited children. (Federal Agency Task Force, 2007). The Federal Agency Task Force for Missing and Exploited Children's mission, as written on their website, is "to coordinate federal resources and services to meet the needs of missing, abducted, and exploited children and their families. In doing so, it plays an important role in responding to the offended" (www.justice.gov/opa/pr/2003/April/03_ag_266.htm).

The Prosecutorial Remedies and Other Tools to End the Exploitation of Children Today (PROTECT) Act passed in 2003 (www.ncjrs.gov/pdf files1/ojjdp/231619.pdf) provided the task force an additional instrument in addressing crimes against children. The passage the PROTECT Act has since enhanced the ability of law enforcement to investigate, arraign, and punish those convicted of violent crimes. This law also acted as the catalyst for formally establishing the federal government's role in the America's Missing: Broadcast Emergency Response (AMBER) Alert System (http://www.scribd.com/doc/48989184/Federal-Resources-on-Missing-and-Exploited-Children).

The National Center for Missing & Exploited Children: After Congress passed the Missing Children's Assistance Act in 1984, the National Center for Missing & Exploited Children (NCMEC) was established and designated to act as the national resource center and informational clearinghouse for missing and exploited children. As part of the congressional mandate, NCMEC works with the U.S. Department of Justice to disseminate information relating to national programs, services, and policies that assist missing and exploited children (http://www.scribd.com/doc/48989184/

Federal-Resources-on-Missing-and-Exploited-Children). The mission of the organization, as stated on their website, is "to serve as the nation's resource on the issues of missing and sexually exploited children. The organization provides information and resources to law enforcement, parents, children; including child victims as well as other professionals" (www .missingkids.com).

Code ADAM Alert Program: On April 23, 2003, the Code Adam Act of 2003 (www.ojp.usdoj.gov/smart/pdfs/sorna_faqs.pdf) became law, mandating that designated authorities for public buildings establish procedures for a child missing in a federal facility. In other words, the Code ADAM Alert Program established the procedure for locating a child in public locations.

AMBER Alert Program: AMBER stands for America's Missing: Broadcast Emergency Response and its name pays homage to nine-year-old Amber Hagerman, who was kidnapped in Arlington, Texas, and then brutally murdered. The AMBER Alert's mission, as written on their website, is "to safely recover missing, endangered, or abducted children through the coordinated efforts of law enforcement, media, transportation, and other partners by using training and technology to enhance response capacities and capabilities and increase public participation" (http://www.amber-net.org/index.htm). AMBER Alerts activate an urgent bulletin in serious child-abduction cases, with the intention of immediately precipitating the entire community to assist in the search and the safe recovery of the child (http://www.amberalert.gov/). The National AMBER Alert works in collaboration the U.S. Department of Justice (DOJ) to increase the likelihood that abducted children will be recovered as quickly and safely as possible.

Schools—Safe Schools

Safe Schools/Healthy Students Initiative (SS/HS): The SS/HS Initiative aims to develop and implement best practices that provide positive school environments that are supportive of children's learning and development (http:// www.sshs.samhsa.gov/initiative/about.aspx). Acting as a comprehensive approach to youth violence prevention, it is stated on their website, "The SS/HS Initiative is a unique Federal grant-making program designed to prevent violence and substance abuse among our Nation's youth, schools, and communities" (http://www.sshs.samhsa.gov/initiative/about.aspx). The SS/HS program is supported by the collaboration of the following three federal agencies: the U.S. Departments of Education, Health and Human Services, and the Department of Justice.

Community Policing

Community Oriented Policing: (COPS): Community Policing defined, as stated on their website, is "a philosophy that promotes organizational strategies that support the systematic use of partnerships and problem solving techniques, to proactively address the immediate conditions that give rise to public safety issues such as crime, social disorder, and fear of crime (http://www.cops.usdoj.gov/RIC/ResourceDetail.aspx?RID=513)." Community policing works in partnership with the U.S. Department of Justice, and is charged with the responsibility of crime prevention and elimination of public fear created by crime. The philosophy emphasizes the importance of the role of the public in prioritizing public safety problems.

Nicole Kelly

See also: Bullying; Department of Education (ED); Department of Health and Human Services (HHS); Department of Justice (DOJ); Good Samaritan Law; Social Services; Social Welfare

References and Additional Readings

Department of Education. (2012a). Office of Safe and Drug Free Schools. Retrieved from http://www2.ed.gov/about/offices/list/osdfs/index.html?src=oc

Department of Education. (2012b). Safe schools healthy students (SS/HS) initiative. Retrieved from http://www.sshs.samhsa.gov/initiative/default.aspx

Department of Health and Human Services. (2013). Retrieved from www.mental health.samhsa.gov

Department of Homeland Security. (2011). Public safety communications evolution. Retrieved from http://www.ojp.usdoj.gov/smart/sexoffendermgmt.htm

Department of Justice. (n.d.a). Amber alert. Retrieved from http://www.am beralert.gov/

Department of Justice. (n.d.b). Amber alert. Mission statement. Retrieved from http://www.amber-net.org/index.htm

Department of Justice. (2002). Center for Sex Offender Management, A project of the Office of Justice Programs. An overview of sex offender management. Retrieved from http://www.csom.org/pubs/csom_bro.pdf

Department of Justice. (2006). Office of Justice Programs. *Strategic Plan FY 2007–2012.* Retrieved from http://www.cops.usdoj.gov/RIC/ResourceDetail.aspx?RID=513

Department of Justice. (2007). Federal agency task force on missing and exploited children: *Office of Juvenile Justice and Delinquency Prevention* (5th ed.). Retrieved from https://www.ncjrs.gov/pdffiles1/ojjdp/216857.pdf

Department of Justice. (2013). COPS. Community Oriented Policing Services. Retrieved from http://www.cops.usdoj.gov/

Small Business Administration. (2013). U.S. Department of Health and Human Services. Retrieved from http://www.sba.gov/content/us-department-health-and-human-services-hhs

The National Center for Missing and Exploited Children. (2013). Retrieved from http://www.missingkids.com/missingkids/servlet/PageServlet?Language Country=en_US&PageId=4362

Public Utilities Commission

In the U.S. economy, the competitive market sets prices and conditions for service when there are multiple ways for consumers to obtain items. Because of the high expense of the infrastructure required, utilities were traditionally considered natural monopolies. It was believed that it was not reasonable expect competition and not economically reasonable to support multiple providers. Thus, regulation replaces competition. Unbiased regulators are charged with balancing the interests of utility companies and their customers. Their goal is to determine the public interest, assuring that the businesses have the opportunity to obtain reasonable return and the businesses and residential customers who use their services pay reasonable rates and get reasonable service. The agencies that make these decisions at the state level are known as Public Utilities Commissions (PUCs). The decision-makers are called commissioners. In some states they are selected by citizens in a popular election; others are appointed by a governor or the state legislature. They are responsible for regulating telecommunications, electricity, gas, water, and transportation. Legally, they are charged with assuring reliable utility service at fair, just, and reasonable rates. They also make decisions concerning placement of infrastructure such as electric transmission lines and determining when a landline telephone territory has sufficient competition to deregulate, removing the PUC's authority to set rates and conditions of service. They must follow state law as they make these decisions and utilities expend much effort and money to influence those laws; utilities are among the top contributors to legislative campaigns. The National Association of Regulatory Utility Commissioners (NARUC) was created in 1889 and most state utility regulators and key staff members are involved. It provides three membership-wide meetings each year and now includes regulators in other countries. The push to deregulate the marketplace that began with President Reagan's term has made regulators' responsibilities evolve. Wireless telephone businesses are not regulated by any level of government. In many cases, government agencies are not even allowed to compile customer complaints concerning wireless service. Wireless providers contend that the service would not have been created if telecommunications had not been deregulated in the 1970s and deregulation makes it easier for the industry to innovate to meet consumer needs. Consumers often find themselves in "take it or leave it" situations with wireless providers. Cable providers only have to negotiate with local governments about service and service areas. However, consumers who have access to cable may also have access to similar entertainment service via satellite and some traditional telephone companies also offer access to the internet and entertainment. Since telephone service may be provided by traditional landlines, wireless service, or over the Internet, it has become deregulated in many states. Even fact that the wireless service that competes with wireline service is a branch of the wireline company has not slowed deregulation. The infrastructure required to provide these services is expensive and in the current marketplace, utilities are rarely even required to assure that all consumers have access. In New Hampshire, the traditional telephone company sold the rural part of its service territory. Because rural areas are more expensive to serve and there are fewer customers per mile, the company has been able to increase its income and lower the rates and offerings in more populated areas so it can more easily compete with cable and wireless providers. However, rural consumers have many challenges to obtain service.

State regulatory commissions became stronger after the Great Depression to counter the power of railroads. Legislators were highly pressured by railroad representatives so giving PUC's responsibility for making highly technical decisions with the support of expert professional staff made the decisions more balanced and less political. They addressed fair pricing and other marketplace issues to make access and prices reasonable so that all businesses, communities, and consumers could prosper and no party received unfair benefit. After the energy crisis of the 1970s many states created or designated agencies to act as independent ratepayer advocates before state and federal agencies and in the courts. In 1979, 16 of these state advocates created the National Association of State Utility Advocates so that those appointed by states could work together. Today 41 states and the District of Columbia are involved. Governors appoint utility advocates (SUAs) in 29 states and state attorneys general appoint them in 12 states. A few states have Citizens Utility Boards (CUBs) to represent consumers. However, funding issues have reduced and limited them recently. Proceedings before PUC's, called cases, are conducted with rules similar to those used in courtrooms. Typically cases are established by proclamation of the PUC that is prompted by utilities, their customers, or schedule established by the rules. They are announced in multiple ways including publication in newspapers across the state. Parties interested in the case may petition to participate. Those who represent the participants in the proceedings are required to have law degrees and follow the rules established by the PUCs.

This requirement means that it is very costly for consumer representatives to participate in cases. They must often depend upon the official SUA who is significantly outnumbered and out resourced (for retention of expert witnesses, etc.) by business representatives. Political pressure and state goals greatly influence the robustness of this representation. Generally parties to cases are required to submit their witnesses' testimony in advance of the hearing where each presents their position to the commissioners. PUC rules dictate, but the written documents are often in question and answer form, beginning with a series of questions that establish the witness' expertise and justification of selection as the best person to explain the position. These documents, minus any information deemed proprietary or sensitive which will be redacted, are typically made public. Participants were generally required to send paper copies to the PUC and all other participants until the internet made it easy to distribute copies electronically.

When a case involves an issue of widespread public interest, the PUC may hold a hearing or a series of hearings in the affected communities, often in the evening and allowing anyone to speak. Often a Hearing Examiner will conduct these hearings and report the results to the commissioners but sometimes commissioners conduct the hearings themselves. These are opportunities that consumers should take. Generally, all that is required is arriving prior to the start of the hearing to sign up to speak. It is possible that there will be a bailiff who will get speakers to swear that what they say will be the truth. Some speakers bring a written form of their comments that they submit but it is not required. There are typically limits for speakers—possibly three to five minutes so more information can be provided in writing. The most effective speakers are those who make their points succinctly and quickly. Occasionally, the Hearing Examiner or Commissioner will ask a question of a speaker, but they should be taken as friendly. They seek to create an environment where citizens feel comfortable sharing their information and concerns. Sometimes parties involved in the case will bring are many supporters of their position. They may even have their supporters wear the same button or shirt. Often few of these people speak but someone who does may ask all who agree with the presented perspective to stand. PUC's may also accept written comments about a case via the Internet or traditional mail. Even a few sentences explaining a consumer's position or concerns are valuable contributions. Sometimes groups organize large campaigns to send many postcards or identical letters to the PUC. While these demonstrate widespread concern, often even a handful of individual statements will make a similar impact. Contributors should be sure to include the case number in the correspondence. Finally, the day that the hearing for the case begins at the PUC, there is typically an opportunity for consumers to speak as a "public witness." It is a good idea to prepare a written statement to submit, to contact the staff to confirm the expectations, and even sign up in advance. Most of those at the hearing will be dressed in suits and ties and although it is generally not required that public witnesses adhere to this standard, it is a good idea to follow it. Speakers should arrive 15–30 minutes before the hearing to begin and check in with staff. When invited to come forward, expect to make a brief verbal presentation after being sworn in by the bailiff. Questions may be asked by the commissioners or by any of the attorneys representing the participating parties. However, this should not discourage consumers from speaking; generally few questions are asked and those asked are things the speaker should be able to easily answer. The PUC may have rules that encourage consumers to take advantage of one of these opportunities to participate, not all of them. In addition to making information used in PUC cases more readily available, technology also makes it more possible for consumers to follow the actual hearing without being in the court room. Virginia's PUC, for example, streams the audio portion of key hearings over the Internet. Typically, it is possible to listen live and for about 24 hours later. Written transcripts can be obtained, but are expensive and not immediately available. Streaming allows interested consumers to keep up with what is happening without having to take time off from work or travel to the PUC. Sometime after the hearing ends, often weeks later, the PUC issues a decision in written form. A nontechnical press release may also be provided to the media. State rules apply, but in Virginia, PUC decisions can only be appealed to the State Supreme Court. Appeals are rare, but in the 1970s the Virginia Citizens Consumer Council, a grassroots statewide volunteer organization of consumers, successfully appealed an electric rate case, forcing the utility to return millions of dollars to rate payers.

Although states have been the focal point for most utility regulation, today some federal agencies have jurisdiction over some aspects of some utilities. The Federal Energy Regulatory Commission (FERC) has a much greater role in provision of electricity today. Most electric utilities are members of regional independent system operators (ISOs) that are charged with maintaining reliable service as electricity is transmitted from generators to utilities. When ISOs were created, PUCs became less involved in transmission and instead of making most of the decisions around transmission, today primarily retain only responsibility for siting new transmission lines. This means that when consumers seek to influence decisions, they must get involved in the ISO processes. Most ISOs have boards that make key decisions after extensive committee work that involves stakeholders.

Companies that build and operate the electric system are heavily involved in these efforts and typically have extensive staff dedicated to them. States often have the opportunity for a state consumer utility advocate to be involved, but they must fund that participation. Since this is a relatively new expense, involvement of many states is limited by the current challenging economic environment. Consumers find these proceedings difficult to participate in due to location, frequency, and cost of travel. Other stakeholders are unwilling to assist with funding even limited consumer representatives; they believe consumers should find a way to do so themselves and several ISOs have denied requests to fund greater consumer representation. In October 2012, FERC approved a settlement for unfair market practices in three ISOs and at least one will use part of it for consumer participation.

Numerous changes have been made in how electricity is regulated by states over the last decade and PUC responsibilities continue to evolve. In some regions of the country, electric rates are no longer regulated by a PUC but are ruled by the competitive market. There are many variations in state laws concerning utility regulation and there is no sign that the changes will stop soon. Negotiated agreements among parties to cases that are approved by a PUC more frequently replace PUC rulings. The frequency and intensity of these processes make it increasingly difficult for volunteer consumer advocates to participate.

Irene Leech

See also: Activism; Department of Energy (DOE); Federal Communications Commission (FCC); Volunteer Protection Act (VPA)

References and Additional Readings

Cameron, J. D. (1977). Place for judicial activism on the part of a state's highest court. *The Hastings Constitutional Law Quarterly, 4, 279*.

Federal Communications Commission. (n.d.a). Retrieved from www.fcc.gov

Federal Energy Regulatory Commission. (n.d.b). Retrieved from www.ferc.gov

Lewis, T. G. (2006). *Critical infrastructure protection in Homeland Security: Defending a networked nation*, Hoboken, NJ:Wiley-Interscience.

National Association of Regulatory Utility Commissioners. (2013). Retrieved from www.naruc.org

National Association of State Utility Consumer Advocates. (2013). Retrieved from www.nasuca.org

Pyramid Plans. *See* Multilevel Marketing and Pyramid Plans

Q

Quackery

The word "quack" originated during the Renaissance when quicksilver (mercury) was a popular remedy for syphilis. Wandering peddlers known as "quacksalvers" promised that their mercury ointment would cure everything. The term was later shortened to "quacks," which became a symbol of evil medical practice.

Quackery can be defined as the promotion of health products and services that are unsubstantiated and lack a scientifically plausible rationale. Quackery's victims seldom realize how often or how skillfully they are cheated. Most people think that quackery is easy to spot. Often it is not. Many of its promoters use scientific terms and quote (or misquote) scientific references. Talk show hosts may refer to promoters as experts or as "scientists ahead of their time." The very word "quack" helps their camouflage by making us think of an outlandish character selling snake oil from the back of a covered wagon—and, of course, no intelligent people would buy snake oil nowadays, would they?

Snake oil may not be selling so well, but business is still booming for health quacks. Their annual take is in the billions! Hair analysis, the latest diet book, megavitamins, "stress formulas", homeopathic "remedies," magnets, phony cancer cures, chelation therapy, products that "cleanse and detoxify your system," spot reducers, "immune boosters," water purifiers, "ergogenic aids," systems to "balance body chemistry," and special diets for arthritis. Their product list is endless. Medical historian James Harvey Young, PhD, deftly noted that "quacks never sleep."

To those in pain, quacks promise relief. To the incurable, they offer hope. To the nutrition conscious, they say, "make sure you have enough." To a public worried about pollution, they say, "buy natural" and get detoxified. To one and all, they promise better health and a longer life.

Most victims merely waste money on things that don't work. But those who rely on worthless methods instead of effective treatment can suffer serious physical harm.

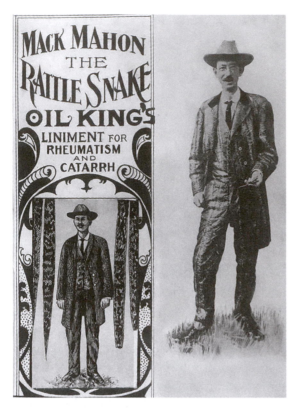

In the late 19th century, entrepreneurs, such as Mack Mahon, duped the public with wild claims about the healing powers of their patent medicines. (Food and Drug Administration)

Problematic Practices

The phrase "complementary and alternative medicine" (CAM) is a widely used marketing term. The National Institutes of Health Center for Complementary and Alternative Medicine defines it as:

A group of diverse medical and health care systems, practices, and products that are not presently considered to be part of conventional medicine.

Complementary medicine is used together with conventional medicine, and alternative medicine is used in place of conventional medicine.

Unfortunately, the CAM marketplace is dominated by products and services that neither complement nor serve as alternatives to standard methods of care. They include:

- Acupuncture is a system of treatment purported to balance the body's qi (life force) by inserting needles (or using other procedures) at points on alleged channels called "meridians." Its theory and practice are not based upon the body of knowledge related to health and disease that has been widely accepted by the scientific community. Acupuncture may have ability to relieve pain but has no demonstrated effect on the course of any major illness.

- Chelation therapy involves the administration of drugs that increase the excretion of heavy metals. It is claimed to be effective against kidney and heart disease, arthritis, autism, Parkinson's disease, emphysema, multiple sclerosis, gangrene, psoriasis, and many other serious conditions. However, no controlled trial has shown that it can help any of them.

- Chiropractic is a conglomeration of practices, most of which are based on the faulty notion that spinal problems are the cause, or an underlying cause, of most health problems. For example, parents may be told that spinal "adjustments" can be effective against their child's asthma and earaches. Unfortunately, while spinal manipulation can help some people with legitimate back and neck pain, many chiropractors promote unnecessary services, oppose vaccination, and sell useless products.

- Dietary supplements include vitamins, minerals, amino acids, antioxidants, and many other substances found naturally in foods. Many people can benefit from taking supplements of vitamin D, calcium, folic acid, and a few other essential nutrients. But the vast majority of supplement products are a waste of money and some are harmful.

- Herbal products are often marketed with unsubstantiated claims that they are effective against the gamut of disease. Although a few products can be useful, many have adverse effects and the vast majority has no practical use.

- Homeopathy is a pseudoscience based on notions that (a) a substance that produces symptoms in a healthy person can cure ill people with similar symptoms and (b) that infinitesimal doses can be highly potent. Many products do not contain a single molecule of the supposed active ingredient. Homeopathic products have no rational use.

- Naturopathy is a pseudoscientific approach to health care based on beliefs that the disease is the result of violation of nature's laws. Most naturopaths advocate "detoxification" and other regimens that have no proven value.

- Reiki and therapeutic touch are methods in which the hands are said to be used to correct "energy imbalances" by lightly stroking the body or placing the hands above the afflicted part. Unlike therapeutic massage, which has proven benefits, these methods supposedly work by transferring "energy" from healer to patient. Neither the forces involved nor the alleged therapeutic benefits have been demonstrated by scientific testing.

CAM proponents typically include standard dietary strategies and exercise as within their scope in order to assert that many of the things they advocate have been proven. This propaganda trick is rarely challenged in the popular media.

Protecting Yourself

In the United States, government attempts to control quackery began in response to the huge number of patent remedies marketed during the 19th century. During the 20th century, powerful laws were passed. The Food, Drug, and Cosmetic Act and the Federal Trade Commission Act were developed to form a powerful fabric of protection. However, quack products and services vastly exceed the resources available to control them.

Consumers who wish to protect themselves should not assume that health claims must be true or else they "would not be allowed." Claims should be evaluated by asking, "what is the evidence?" Reliable information comes mainly through use of the scientific method, a procedure for exposing hypotheses (assumptions) to critical examination and testing. The scientific method does not rely on testimonials as evidence of fact. Rather, it provides an objective way to collect and evaluate data. The fact that a person recovers after doing something is rarely sufficient to demonstrate that the recovery was caused by the action taken and is not simply due to the natural course of the ailment. The gold standard for evaluating treatment is controlled experimentation that compares many people who do something with similar people who do not.

Medical "facts" are determined through a process in which hundreds of thousands of scientists share their observations and beliefs. Editors and editorial boards of scientific journals play an important role by screening out invalid findings and enabling significant ones to be published. Expert panels convened by government agencies, professional groups, voluntary health agencies, and other organizations also contribute to this effort. When controversies arise, further research can be devised to settle them. Gradually, a shared set of beliefs is developed that is considered scientifically accurate.

Many people think that the best way to evaluate claims is to search with Google for information about their concerns. But because many sites (particularly commercial ones) are untrustworthy, it is far more prudent to stick with sites that experts have identified as scientifically valid. Government agencies, major professional organizations, and major voluntary groups tend to provide high-quality information. Internet Health Pilot (www.ihealthpilot.org) links to more than 500 trustworthy websites. Sites that market dietary supplements and herbs or promote CAM methods should never be used for educational purposes.

Stephen Barrett

See also: Federal Trade Commission (FTC); Food and Drug Administration (FDA); Frauds and Scams; Health and Healthcare; Public Safety

References and Additional Readings

Barrett, S. (2006). How to spot a 'quacky' web site. Retrieved from http://www.quackwatch.com/01QuackeryRelatedTopics/quackweb.html

Barrett S. (2008). Why TCM diagnosis is worthless. Retrieved from http://www.acuwatch.org/reports/diagnosis.shtml.

Barrett S. (2010). Dietary supplements: Appropriate use. Retrieved from http://www.quackwatch.com/03HealthPromotion/supplements.html

Barrett S., & Herbert, V. (2008). Twenty-five ways to spot quacks and vitamin pushers. Retrieved from http://www.quackwatch.com/01QuackeryRelatedTopics/spotquack.html

Barrett, S., London, W., Kroger, M., Hall, H., & Baratz, R. (2012). *Consumer health: A guide to intelligent decisions* (9th ed.). New York: McGraw-Hill.

Singh, S., & Ernst, E. (2008). *Trick or treatment: The undeniable facts about alternative medicine.* New York: W.W. Norton.

R

Recalls

Product recalls occur when a manufacturer deems the risks involved with a product exceed what is acceptable or when a government agency requires a manufacturer to take a product off the market and/or to "call in" a product that may already be on store shelves, in the virtual marketplace, or in the hands of consumers. Most often this occurs because the product is unsafe for normal use or consumption because of product design, contamination, mislabeling, or failure to meet standards. The standards for safety vary by product and for intended user groups. A product an adult can safely use may pose undue risks to children.

Recalls may be related to one of three types of defects. The seriousness may not be directly related to the type of defect—design, manufacturing, or insufficient or no warnings. A design defect is inherent to a given product and is present in each item produced until the design is changed. Recent examples include window blind cords and hooded sweatshirts or jackets with drawstrings, with the potential for strangulation; vehicle recalls due to the design of gas tanks; and folding chairs that are prone to collapse. Announcements of these recalls often include large number of the product over several months. The hazard often is not identified until a number of consumers have purchased and used the product. In contrast, manufacturing (processing) defects occur when an irregularity or problem develops in the production process of a limited number of items. Examples include metal shavings in boxes of cereal and canned fruits or vegetables containing pesticide levels above agency standards.

Deficiencies in warnings involve the product labeling and packaging. Labeling may include those that are embossed or printed directly on the product, not removable (e.g., on appliances—do not remove or modify this plug, on clothing—do not bleach or dry clean only). In foods warnings may indicate that processing is not 100 percent effective, as shelled walnuts "may include shells" or pitted prunes "may include pits."

The Food and Drug Administration (FDA) has responsibility for most food products, cosmetics, prescription and over the counter drugs, vaccines, blood and blood products, transplantable human tissues, medical devices (artificial hips, thermometers), radiation-emitting products (microwave ovens), and animal food and drugs. Three categories of recall include Class I—products or foods that are dangerous or defective such that they cause serious health problems (malfunctioning pacemakers) or possible death (pathogens in food); Class II—products where temporary reversible consequences may result (drug lacks potency; food label excludes an ingredient); and Class III—least severe, use or exposure unlikely to cause adverse consequences (added water exceeds standard). Alerts may also be issued for medical safety devices often referring users to consult with medical personnel.

Meat and poultry products including eggs come under the jurisdiction of the U.S. Department of Agriculture and recalls are similar to those of the FDA. Food products are most frequently recalled because of suspected or actual pathogen contamination (*Escherichia coli*), inclusion of allergens (peanuts), and mislabeling (ingredient label did not include eggs).

The Consumer Product Safety Commission (CPSC) addresses most products used in daily living including products intended for children (equipment, furniture, toys, clothing) and household products (appliances, tools, recreational equipment, whether used indoors or outdoors). Although the products recalled change over time, frequent recalls are children's products: nursery products, clothing, and toys manufactured overseas, which account for most of the recalls. Potential hazards are injury, choking, or exposure to levels of lead or other heavy metals (cadmium) that exceed allowable limits. Potential hazards may also result from toys being mislabeled as to age appropriateness, for example, exposing young children to toys with small parts.

There is an expectation, though no specific guidelines, that a manufacturer is to recall a product when deficiencies are identified or injuries reported to the company. Thus, a manufacturer exercises judgment as to when and if a recall is issued. When CPSC notes a pattern of injuries and/or deaths resulting from use of a product, a ban must be issued preventing its importation and sale. Healthcare facilities submit data related to injuries and illnesses that may be product related. This may require that a product be discontinued or redesigned. Examples include the redesign of cribs to prevent strangulation. Whether recalled or banned, high-risk products often have a long life as many consumers do not become aware of the recalls, and the product may be used by subsequent generations or resold/shared in the used market without awareness of the hazard (infant cribs are one example).

The National Highway Traffic Safety Administration (NHTSA) works with vehicle safety (autos and school buses) and products/accessories (tires, infant and child seats, and restraints). When a vehicle recall is identified the auto manufacturer notifies the purchaser (leasee) as to the nature of the recall and the corrective action needed by the owner and the dealership. Large scale recalls needing new parts for repair may take some time for the parts to become available. Consumers can enter the make and model of a particular vehicle, tire, or child restraint device and learn its recall history (www-odi.nhtsa.dot.gov/recalls/recallsearch.cfm). This can be valuable information when selling or purchasing a previously owned vehicle or product.

The U.S. Coast Guard has jurisdiction over water craft and related products (personal flotation devices) including standards that enable consumers to match personal flotation devices to body size.

The Environmental Protection Agency (EPA) has responsibility for pesticides, rodenticides, and fungicides in commercial and household products. They also are involved with motor vehicles' emission standard violations, which involves vehicle parts and software that may compromise emission control systems.

The recall of food, drug, and household products are listed on the agencies' websites and may be announced in the media when large scale or the risk for illness or injury is great. Major retailers may post notices of recalls and in high risk cases (contaminated food) track purchases. Tracking systems have become more sophisticated especially for food and drugs and often involve state health departments attempting to pinpoint the source of the problem (plant where food was processed), outlets where it may have been sold, brand names under which product was sold, and consumers who may have purchased it. In addition healthcare providers and laboratories are reporting outbreaks and test results with the objectives to find the source and eradicate the causative factor and to gain knowledge to prevent future outbreaks.

Consumers have the responsibility to follow-up on recalls for products they own or intend to purchase to assure the safety and health of themselves, their families, and their communities. Recall notices include sufficient information to identify the product by name of manufacturer/distributor/retailer, dates of production and sales, brand, color, size/dimensions, approximate number recalled, and often photos of the product (online). Recalls include the information relevant to handling of the product: return for repair (vehicle, appliance), exchange/replace (computer, lawn mower), or refund (food). Other recalls may suggest cautions (product may contain gluten). The manufacturers or sellers have received guidance from the appropriate agency on handling of the recalled product to prevent continued availability or to ensure safe disposal if a serious problem.

Consumers need to be aware that for most recalled products (toys, appliances, recreational equipment), only a small portion of the products are returned or disposed of as instructed by the recall. Therefore, it is recommended that the consumer seeks recall information before making purchases at flea markets, online, garage sales, at other places. This is another example of "caveat emptor" (consumer beware!). In addition to being aware, consumers should report illness or injury caused by a product, as consumer are a crucial link in monitoring product safety and quality. The information provided by consumer and healthcare facilities (when consumers seek care) serves as the eyes and ears for the responsible agencies and retailers. It must be recognized that every product has not been tested to determine if it has defects or does not meet standards.

Carole J. Makela

See also: Caveat Emptor; Consumer Product Safety Commission (CPSC); Department of Agriculture (USDA); Environmental Protection Agency (EPA); Food and Drug Administration (FDA); National Highway Traffic Safety Administration (NHTSA); Warnings

References and Additional Readings
Rustad, M. L. (2007). *Everyday law for consumers*. Boulder, CO: Paradigm Publishers.

Recycling

The expanded Consumer Bill of Rights includes the right to a healthy environment. One of the ways individuals can help ensure everyone has access to this right is through recycling. Recycling is defined as *to adapt to a new use or bring back*. Alter and reuse are synonyms. Throughout the United States there are many programs encouraging the practices of reduce, reuse, and recycle.

If individuals focus on buying only what is needed and reusing items already owned, effectively the amount of waste needed to be dealt with would drop dramatically, as it was never produced to begin with. Unfortunately, the amount of waste produced per person in the United States has been increasing rather than decreasing. According to the Environmental Protection Agency (EPA) between 1960 and 2010 the amount of waste each person created increased from 2.7 to 4.4 pounds per day. EPA also estimates that recycling one ton of paper saves 17 trees and 700 gallons of water.

There are many benefits of recycling. The first and most important is the benefit to the environment. Recycling has been proven to reduce the emission of greenhouse gases, which are linked to global warming. It requires less energy to recycle products into new uses rather than use virgin materials. Recycling helps us to conserve our natural resources and save energy. Recycling has also been shown to have economic benefits. In some states recycling fees are charged as deposits for aluminum cans and bottles.

Consumers not only help the environment but also receive monetary compensation for their recycling efforts. (Shutterstock.com)

Returning the cans and bottles allows for recouping the deposit fees. Recycling has an economic impact throughout the United States. The U.S. Recycling Economic Information Study showed more than 56,000 recycling establishments, employing 1.1 million people in 2001. Despite the many positives of recycling and the existence of a federal agency focused on the environment, the United States does not have a federal recycling law. Many states and cities have passed their own laws regarding recycling. One example is bottle bills, which exist in nine states.

Steps to recycling include collecting appropriate materials, sorting these materials, and connecting them to recycling centers where they can be prepared to be changed into marketable commodities. There are four primary ways recyclable materials can be collected: curbside pick-up, drop-off facilities, buyback centers, and deposit/refund programs. The more convenient recycling programs are for consumers, the more likely they are to participate in them. Another factor impacting the willingness of individuals to participate in recycling efforts is the direct economic impact. Some communities have had success with significant reduction of waste products when they charge by weight or piece for garbage collection, rather than having one flat fee or community garbage pickup.

Determining appropriate materials to recycle begins by checking with local recycling

Recycling

The "chasing arrows" symbol does not have a universal meaning. It can mean the product or package is made of recycled materials or that the product or package is recyclable.

centers as to what they will recycle. Plastics are labeled using a number system. The numbers from one through seven denote the type of plastic the bottle has been made from. Some communities will allow recycling of all plastics while others may specify only number one and two bottles are able to be recycled. Some recycling programs provide consumers with color-coded bins to separate their materials into. Individuals may be instructed to separate aluminum, paper, plastics, and glass. Other guidelines allow all recyclables to be combined in one bin. One key factor to participating in recycling is to make it a habit for each individual in the household. Setting up practices and guidelines that make it convenient for recyclable trash to end up in an appropriate spot will ensure recycling becomes a way of life for families.

One recent issue related to recycling is the usage of plastic bags as receptacles for carrying groceries. Some states have banned the distribution of single use plastic bags, requiring they be replaced with compostable, paper, or reusable bags. Another variation to encourage individuals to reuse bags for grocery shopping is to charge a fee for each plastic or paper bag used.

Composting is another way consumers can join in the recycling movement. Compost is a material that enriches our soil and adds nutrients to the earth. Compost materials include yard waste and food residuals that compose almost 27 percent of our solid waste. There are regional and state composting programs in many areas of the United States. Composting can be started easily in the backyard or indoors.

In addition to recycling, buying recycled products is another way consumers can participate in positive environmental practices. It is important to be able to decipher the information related to recycling listed on product labels. Determine if the recycling claim relates to a product itself, or the package itself. If a product is labeled as recycled, it must be 100 percent recycled or include a statement of what percent of the product or package comes from recycled material. Don't confuse the terms recycled and recyclable. Recyclable means the item itself can be recycled.

Susan Reichelt

See also: Consumer Bill of Rights; Environmental Protection Agency (EPA); Federal Trade Commission (FTC)

References and Additional Readings

Environmental Protection Agency. (n.d.). Reduce, reuse, recycle. Retrieved from http://epa.gov/recycle/index.html

Federal Trade Commission. (n.d.). Saving starts at home. Retrieved from http://www.ftc.gov/bcp/edu/microsites/energysavings/index.html

Renter's Rights

Basics

State laws govern the rights and responsibilities of renters (tenants) and landlords. The laws for each state can be found online, usually under the state's Department of Consumer Affairs of Attorney General's Office website. Despite the fact that each state law is unique, there are some basic principles that apply to tenant rights, responsibilities, and remedies. Renters have the right to a clean, safe, and functioning dwelling which will be maintained. Landlords have the right to have their property returned in the same condition it was provided, with only normal wear and tear. Landlords also have the responsibility to address issues of safety and usability.

Rental Property Types

Apartments: Apartments are typically covered under state renter's laws. Duplexes are usually covered as well because they, like apartments, typically share common areas like hallways, stairs, foyers, heating facilities, hot water equipment, or any other essential facility or service.

Motels/hotels/manufactured homes: Motels and boarding houses are typically covered under state renter's laws if the tenant lives in such residence for a specified number of days, depending on the state law.

Public housing and housing choice vouchers (Section 8): Landlord–renter relations in public housing, housing choice vouchers or Section 8 housing, and other federally subsidized housing are managed by the United States Department of Housing and Urban Development (HUD). Renters in subsidized housing may have certain rights from the state and HUD. HUD policies and rights may be found at the local housing authority, housing agency, or through HUD.

Single family housing: Laws may also apply to single-family housing, but may vary depending on the state requirements of landlord ownership.

Rights of Renters

Renters, as well as landlords, have rights and responsibilities. Depending on specific state law provisions, there are numerous rights provided to renters. Renters have the right to a fair application review. Landlords cannot decline to rent to a person based on race, religion, gender, family status, national origin, or a person's disability status. These rights are covered under the Fair Housing Act, overseen by HUD. Renters have the right to a fair application fee. Landlords may require an application

An Example of Renter's Rights in Action

Dwelling Condition Checklist

Tenant: Address:

CODE: G = good   F = fair U = unsatisfactory

In = condition at Move-In   Out = condition at Move-Out

INTERIOR

	Kitch.		Bath 1		Bath 2		Liv. Rm.		Hall		Fam. Rm.		BR 1		BR 2	
	In	Out	In	Out	In	Out	In	Out	In	Out	In	Out	In	Out	In	Out
Ceiling																
Walls																
Floors																
Windows																
Doors																
Cabinets																
Electrical																
Ventilation																
Plumbing																
Refrigerator																
Stove																
Oven																
Table																
Chairs																
Furniture																

DETAIL UNSATISFACTORY CONDITIONS:_____

_____

_____

_____

EXTERIOR

Walls		Doors		Roof		Yard	
In	Out	In	Out	In	Out	In	Out

Landlord and Tenant to sign and date agreement at move in and move out.

fee with a rental application. Some states allow for refunds of the application fee if the refund is rejected; specific day limits may also exist. Renters have the right to privacy, including information provided on the rental application. The exceptions to this are usually as follows: if written permission is given; if the information is a matter of public record; if the information is requested by law enforcement or public safety personnel; states may specify other conditions under which personal information may be shared; the right to refuse unlawful or unreasonable entry into the dwelling; landlords are not allowed to abuse the right to enter the property. Unless an emergency situation exists, the landlord may not enter the property. If proper advanced notice is given however, the landlord must be allowed to enter. In situations where a tenant feels harassed by a landlord's repeated requests for entry, the lease may be terminated in some states. Renters have the right to be informed when there is a change in management, ownership, or change of property use. The landlord must, within a specified period of time, notify the tenant of plans to evict if the property is going to be rehabilitated, demolished, or when a change in ownership or management is occurring. Renters have the right to a decent and safe place to live. This is broadly defined in most states, but typically includes adhering to local building and health codes in the dwelling and in common areas, including electrical, plumbing, ventilation, air conditioning, heating, trash, appliances, elevators. If a landlord does not maintain a safe and decent property, the tenant has rights and recourses specified in state laws. Renters have the right to a certain level of security. Depending on the state law, certain lock types may be required. If additional security measures are installed by the tenant, state law may provide for legal requirements governing any damage these security measures (usually locks) may cause to the property as well as repairs that may be required. Renters have the right to proper notice before pesticides are applied to the dwelling. Typically, depending on the state, 48 hours notice is provided for pest control procedures' type and location. Renters have the right to proper notice of a rent increase or decrease in services provided. Under most circumstances, lease increases can only occur when the lease expires. For month to month or week to week rentals, the period is allowably shorter. Renters have the right to a lawful eviction notice. Without a lease, landlords may evict without notice, and for any reason in most states; with 30-day written notice. In most states, a 5-day pay or quit notice will be issued when rent is not paid. This allows 5 days for rent to be paid, or the landlord may go to court to continue the eviction process. Each state has specific rules regarding eviction procedures. Renters have the right to a fair security deposit. Each state prescribes legal limits of security deposit amounts. Typically, security deposits may not be withheld for normal wear and tear on the property. Further, each state governs the number of days a security deposit can be held after the property is vacated. Deductions taken from the security deposit must be provided to the tenant by the landlord with a list of specific charges and damages.

Renters' Responsibilities

With rights come responsibilities. In general, there are several things that renters must do. Renters must pay rent on time without the landlord's reminder. Renters must also sign and keep a copy of the lease. Renters must be given a copy of the lease (aka rental agreement) within one month of the move in date. However, despite having a copy of the agreement, the terms are still binding if the renter pays rent and subsequently occupies the dwelling. No changes may be made to the lease terms by either party unless both consent in writing and the changes are allowed by the lease and the states' governing laws. Renters must follow the terms of the lease; both parties must follow the terms of the lease. Eviction is only a legal option when the lease expires or if the terms of the agreement are not followed. It is suggested a renter writes down damages to the dwelling upon moving in. The tenant and landlord are typically both responsible for reporting and noting any damage present in the dwelling. Most laws provide a number of days for damages to be reported to the landlord if the landlord does not report the damage to the tenant. Also, upon moving out, the list of damages should be revisited. Any damage not listed on the agreed upon move-in sheet is typically damage caused by the tenant. Repairs made to fix damages caused by the tenant may be taken out of the security deposit or charged to the tenant, in most states. Renters should obey the rules and regulations of the dwelling and surrounding community and agree to reasonable entry into the dwelling if required by the landlord. The landlord has a right to enter the property with required notice (see state law for requirements). The following are appropriate reasons for the landlord entering the property: inspect the property; make repairs; make alterations or improvements, supply necessary or agreed services; or show the apartment to prospective or actual purchasers, mortgagees, tenants, workmen, or contractors. The landlord may enter the dwelling without tenant consent in an emergency situation; however, the landlord may not abuse the right of entrance or use it to harass the tenant. The landlord may only enter at reasonable times and days, with the exception of emergency situations.

The landlord must provide notice of plans to enter the dwelling, except in emergency situations.

The renter should keep the dwelling in good condition, typically including: obeying building and housing codes affecting health and safety; keeping the apartment as clean and safe as the conditions permit; removing garbage, ashes, and waste in a clean and safe manner into the appropriate containers; keeping all plumbing fixtures in the dwelling as clean as their condition permits; notifying the landlord of any repairs that need to be done to the apartment as soon as possible. The notice should be in writing and dated; using all utilities and all electrical, plumbing, heating, ventilation, air-conditioning, and other facilities and appliances including elevators in the property in a correct manner; being responsible for personal conduct and the conduct of other persons on the property; and abide by all reasonable rules and regulations imposed by the landlord. Renters should also give proper notice before moving. Written notice is required in most cases before moving out; the amount of time is usually specified in the lease agreement. Typically, a 30-day notice is provided, before the next month's rent is due. If a week-to-week agreement exists, typically 10 days notice is sufficient. Renters must provide accurate information on the rental application. If false information is provided on the application, in many states, the landlord has the right to terminate the lease.

There are also several things renters must not do, including deliberately or carelessly destroy, deface, damage, impair, or remove any of the property or permit any other person to do so. Renters must also not tamper with or remove a properly working smoke detector.

Tenant Solutions

Regardless of whether the landlord is doing their part, tenants should continue to pay rent on time and in full. If a landlord will not make required repairs to the dwelling, there are provisions in the state law that can help tenants address these issues. In some cases, if a court is involved, the tenant may pay rent directly to the court or an escrow account through the court if this is an acceptable provision in the state law. A few other issues and provisions may be covered in the state laws with solutions and procedures. If the landlord breaks the rules and does not stick to the terms of the rental agreement or meet the requirements of the state law that affect the health or safety of the tenant, a written notice to the landlord may be served. The written notice must specify the problem and say that the lease will end in a specified number of days after the landlord receives this letter if the problem is not dealt within a specified number of days (depending on the allowances in the state law). Furthermore, military personnel may require early lease termination in areas where they are deployed or relocated. Members of the armed forces of the United States or the State's National Guard serving on full-time duty or as a Civil Service Technician may be allowed to terminate the rental agreement early without being charged with early termination fees or for damages by the landlord. And finally, if the landlord does not supply essential services required for safe and healthy living and if a landlord willfully or negligently fails to supply heat, running water, hot water, electricity, gas, or other essential service, a lawyer or the court may be notified to give a written notice to the landlord stating the violation. Most state laws stipulate steps that must be followed to correct situations of this nature, including the possibility of recovering attorney fees and damages.

As noted earlier, state laws govern rental property rights and responsibilities of owners and tenants. Basics have been covered here; however, consumers should consult with their own state's laws via their Department of Consumer Affairs for specific stipulations and allowances that may apply.

Celia Ray Hayhoe and Wendy Reiboldt

Note: Sadly, Dr. Celia Ray Hayhoe passed away in March 2012. She was an Associate Professor and Family Resource Management Extension Specialist at Virginia Tech. Her research and service centered around the personal finance habits of consumers, with particular interest in savings, credit, and bankruptcy. Celia received numerous professional awards including the 2007 Distinguished Fellow Award from the Association for Financial Counseling and Planning Education and the College of Liberal Arts and Human Sciences Outreach Award in 2006.

See also: Departments of Consumer Affairs (DCA); Department of Housing and Urban Development (HUD); Small Claims Court

References and Additional Readings
Department of Housing and Urban Development. (2013). Retrieved from http://www.hud.gov

eHOW. (2013).

Information on renter's rights. Retrieved from http://www.ehow.com/about_6576861_information-renters-rights.html#ixzz271rsUdXS

Portman, J., & Stewart, M. (2012a). *Every Tenant's Legal Guide.* Berkeley, CA: Nolo Press.

Portman, J., & Stewart, M. (2012b). *Renters Rights: The Basics.* Berkeley, CA: Nolo Press.

Schoshinski, R. S. (1980). *American law of landlord and tenant.* Eagan, MN: Lawyers Co-operative Publishing Company.

Rent-To-Own (RTO)

Rent-To-Own (RTO) is a mechanism allowing consumers immediate access to merchandise—most commonly appliances, electronics, or furniture—with neither credit check nor down payment in exchange for a series of payments due either weekly, biweekly, or monthly. The agreement is for a fixed time period, usually 12 to 24 months; at the same time, the customer maintains the ability to terminate the arrangement at any point either by returning the item—making it into a rental transaction—or by making a final lump sum payment. Should all payments be made, or the early purchase option utilized, the customer takes ownership of the merchandise. However, no adverse credit action occurs if the consumer decides to terminate after only one payment or after just a few. Adding to the value of the transaction, merchandise delivery, set-up, and service (as well as pick-up, if required) are all included. Because RTO customers are predominately lower income and/or financial constrained, RTO is generally viewed as part of the subprime financial industry along with businesses like check-cashing firms, payday lenders, and pawn shops.

The merchandise under RTO agreement can typically be categorized as either appliances, computers, electronics, or furniture. Four categories represented some 93 percent of transactions with furniture being the largest followed by appliances and then electronics. Appliances, in order of importance, contained washers and dryers, air conditioners, refrigerators, freezers, stoves, microwaves, and vacuums. Computers consisted mainly of desktops along with computer desks and printers. Electronics included televisions, stereos, and video games along with VCRs, DVD players, and camcorders. Furniture broke down into pieces for the living room, bedroom, general (e.g., lamps, rugs, and wall units), and dining rooms. Finally, there are various miscellaneous items, most notably jewelry.

Interestingly, because of the nature of the RTO business, merchandise may be new or used. Due to the ability of customers to return items at any point, the store inevitably ends up in possession of used goods. Typically such returned items are re-rented and, while the customer can request to rent a brand new item, the benefit of getting used merchandise is that the contract terms are relaxed to reflect the good's condition. As the age of the item increases or the condition deteriorates, the total amount required for ownership is reduced—this is achieved by reducing the periodic payment and/or by shortening the contract's duration. Consequently, renting used merchandise is generally more economical for the consumer.

The RTO industry had its beginnings in the 1960s. Ernie Talley is generally credited as the creator of the RTO concept. Talley first experimented with the idea in a Wichita, Kansas, appliance store that he owned, eventually opening the first RTO store—Mr. T's TV Rental—in Tulsa, Oklahoma. By the end of the 1960s, there were approximately 300 stores offering RTO. Starting in the mid-1970s and continuing well into the 1980s, the combination of high interest rates and state usury ceilings greatly impaired the ability of banks and other financial intermediaries to offer consumer credit. This provided a major opportunity to the RTO business model. In less than five years, the industry expanded from hundreds of stores to 3,000 and became established as a viable alternative for subprime consumers.

The industry has grown to over 8,600 stores in the United States, annually serving over four million customers, and generating over $7.6 billion in revenue. The industry consists of two publicly traded companies—Rent-A-Center (RAC) and Aaron's—and a number of privately owned businesses. RAC is largest with 39 percent of the stores in the United States; Aaron's is second with 13 percent, and the remaining 48 percent of stores are run by independent operators although some of these are franchisees of either RAC or Aaron's. The big two firms taken together generate 60 percent of the industry's revenue. The basic RTO business model is also employed in Australia, Canada, and the U.K. In the U.K., BrightHouse Rent-to-Own is the major company with 240 stores; in Canada, Easyhome Ltd. has over 240 stores (some are in the United States); and, in Australia, Radio Rentals operates 75 appliance rental stores. Further, Rent-A-Center entered the Mexican market in 2010 opening five stores and plans further expansion in there and into Canada as well.

One distinguishing feature of RTO is the presence of multiple embedded options. First, the contract contains a "put option" on the merchandise— the consumer retains the right to return the item at any point. This is clearly valuable for dealing with uncertainty faced by the consumer. Thus, while this is useful if one knows that the need for an item is only short term, it is arguably even more useful if there is uncertainty over duration of need, that is, one believes that they have only a limited need but recognize there is a nontrivial chance the need will be longer or even permanent. It is also useful in allowing a consumer the ability to resolve uncertainty over a good's utility without suffering "buyer's remorse." In fact, many goods are returned in order to exchange them for a similar item, such as a customer renting a TV then returning it and, nearly simultaneously, renting a different TV, possibly repeating such an exchange several times. However, given the constrained financial status of the typical customer, this option is possibly most useful for dealing with basic uncertainty over the ability to pay. The fundamental structure of RTO provides a mechanism for a consumer to deal with an income shock, for example, a cut-back of work hours or outright layoff, as well as an expense shock, for example, an unexpected medical procedure or an automobile breakdown. The ability to back out of a transaction without adverse consequence is clearly of value to someone concerned with the affordability or utility of an item and is not a feature offered by retailers in general.

Second, the agreement contains a "call option" on the item—if, at any point, a consumer wants to obtain immediate ownership the consumer can exercise an early purchase option by paying a prespecified proportion of the remaining payments—typically about one-half. While generally more expensive than a straight purchase would have been, this can result in substantial savings over continuing to make the periodic payments up to the contractual maturity (paying to term). The consumer may well feel that the premium paid, over the cost of an outright purchase, will be justified in that it allows her to dictate the contract's ultimate outcome and actual duration in response to how financial circumstance or perceived need evolve over time. Related to this, many RTO stores offer "90 days same as cash" programs where if a prespecified amount is paid within the set period, the transaction is considered a straight sale; should the customer fail to fully pay that amount, it continues on as if it was always a rental agreement. The associated "cash price" is typically higher than straight retail but can be reasonably competitive, especially on used merchandise.

Third, reinstatement is another commonly offered option. To understand this feature, suppose that due to some financial setback a customer has to return an item she was hoping to purchase, reinstatement would allow that customer once "back on her feet" to resume the contract with credit given for the payments already made (possibly full credit given). This option would clearly be valued by, say, a consumer with little financial slack who is concerned with the possibility of an adverse financial shock. The option also speaks about the ability of the RTO business model to respond to the unique needs and challenges faced by their core customer base.

A fourth contract option, relatively unique to RTO, is that consumers can choose their payment periodicity—monthly, semimonthly, biweekly, or weekly. Thus, consumers can choose to have a payment frequency that is in sync with their paydays. Alternatively, one could choose on the basis of his or her perceived contract usage. For example, a renter may prefer weekly payments as this allows for increased flexibility; other renters may prefer monthly payments to increase convenience of payment. In practice, RAC encourages weekly schedules, while Aaron's prefers monthly, and the independents generally offer a blend of payment frequencies. Interestingly, a very high proportion of payments are made physically in the store and in cash. For instance, over 90 percent of all payments were made in the store and, and of those, 96 percent were in cash. Many low-income consumers are served by this industry. As such, consumer advocates argue this opens the door to predatory practices whereby low-income consumers, who cannot afford to pay high prices, will be taken advantage of. In the case of RTO, it is argued that RTO agreements are really attempts to exploit consumers who are unaware of masqueraded installment loans with usurious interest rates. Others, however, argue that RTO contracts contain many option-like features that are valuable for such consumers but are costly to provide. They further argue that most investigators have assumed ownership as the primary motive and did not factor in the value of the various options. Consequently, for a financially constrained customer, RTO may indeed be rational and utility maximizing. The issue of whether RTOs are "good" for consumers is a strong consideration for public policy makers. For instance, both advocates and critics of the RTO model have sought federal legislation to uniformly define the transaction. To date, no federal act has passed despite ongoing attempts. As of the time of writing, a bill, H.R. 1588, defining the RTO transaction as a lease, has been placed on hold.

Interestingly, 47 states have passed laws regulating RTO transactions (North Carolina, New Jersey, and Wisconsin are the three exceptions). The FTC provides a good regulatory overview. One reason federal legislation may be desirable is to rationalize the patchwork of differing rules that the states have created. State regulations can generally be organized into rules that require various disclosures and rules that place controls on permissible fees and prices. Eighteen states have mandated in-store price tag disclosures. This typically requires the tag hanging on the merchandise on the store floor to disclose the cash price, the rental payment, number of payments, and total dollar amount required for ownership. Note that this disclosure assumes payment to term although the majority of purchasers exercise the early purchase option and so pay a lesser amount. All states that have passed legislation mandate agreement disclosures—very much akin to requirements for consumer loan disclosures. Generally speaking, the contract must speak to whether the merchandise is new or used, the cost of ownership, the customer's rights, the terms of the options, if a manufacturer's warranty will apply after ownership, and other related information. These states also have advertising disclosures wherein, whatever media is employed, the business must disclose, in general, that it is a RTO transaction, that the customer has no equity in the item until ownership occurs, and the number and size of the payments required to get ownership (paying to term).

Most states also have limits on fees, for example, whether the store can charge a late fee, a delivery fee, or an in-home collection fee (this is interesting commentary on the nature of the business: if a customer is late in paying, a store employee may be dispatched to their residence to collect). The fee restrictions also address what grace period for late payments must be given and whether a reinstatement fee may be assessed if a transaction is resumed after having been temporarily suspended. Finally, five states (California, Hawaii, Maine, New York, and West Virginia) have placed caps on cash prices and total payment-to-term RTO prices—said caps expressed as multiples of the store's wholesale cost.

Rent-to-own customers tend to be lower income, younger, and predominately female. According to the Association of Progressive Rental Organizations (APRO), the industry trade group, demographics as of 2009 are as follows. Notably, 68 percent of customers are females. This may reflect women traditionally having a greater role in purchase decisions or may be driven by "single moms." In terms of education, 3 percent failed to graduate high school, 58 percent are high school graduates, 23 percent report some college, and 16 percent are college graduates. Table 32 shows this by age and income.

As the U.S. Median Income level in 2009 was $50,221 (U.S. Census Bureau), 97 percent of customers are in the bottom half of the income distribution. Further, as the 2009 Poverty Line was $14,570 ($22,050) for a family of two (four) (U.S. Department of Health and Human Services), 13 (41) percent of the customer base can be classified as poor under the former (latter) standard. Additionally, repeat customers seem common in this industry, for example, many report repeat rates around 40 percent; the latter also reports a referral rate above 15 percent. These repeat and referral rates seem

Table 32 Age and income breakdown of RTO consumers

Age	(%)	Income ($1000s)	(%)
<25	5	<15	13
25–34	20	15–24	28
35–44	33	24–36	31
45–54	28	36–50	24
55–64	11	50–75	3
65+	3		

to suggest customer satisfaction and/or prolonged periods of continuing financial hardship.

Consumer advocates have frequently focused on annual percentage rates (APRs). If ownership occurs after making all required payments to term, the transaction's APR can exceed 250 percent. Such rates can be partly rationalized by considering the value of the embedded options as well as the associated business risk of dealing with such a customer base. Namely, in a nontrivial proportion of deals the customer stops paying yet the store does not recover the merchandise—in industry parlance, this is referred to as skip/stolen. Further, it is not uncommon for the merchandise to have to be picked up due to collection problems. Late payments are also quite common. At the same time, such APRs are clearly usurious if the intent is always to purchase merchandise. Consequently, attention is paid to the "keep rate," that is, the proportion of deals that end in ownership. Using survey data, FTC (2000) found a keep rate of 64 percent; by contrast, others have calculated a 27 percent rate and, by calculating the proportion of customers who had made at least one purchase using RTO, reported an upper bound of 43 percent on the keep rate in their sample.

Michael H. Anderson

See also: Banking; Pawn Shops; Payday Lending; Usury

References and Additional Readings

Anderson, M. H., & Jackson, R. (2001). A reconsideration of rent-to-own. *The Journal of Consumer Affairs*, 35(2), 295–306.

Anderson, M. H., & Jackson, R. (2004). Rent-to-own agreements: Purchases or rentals? *The Journal of Applied Business Research*, 20(1), 13–22.

Anderson, M. H., & Jaggia, S. (2009). Rent-to-own agreements: Customer characteristics and contract outcomes. *Journal of Economics and Business, 61*(1), 51–69.

Anderson, M. H., & Jaggia, S. (2012). Return, purchase or skip? Outcome, duration and consumer behavior in the rent-to-own market. *Empirical Economics, 43*(1), 313–334.

Association of Progressive Rental Organizations (APRO). (2011). 2011 APRO industry data survey. Austin, TX: Association of Progressive Rental Organizations.

Federal Trade Commission (FTC). (2000). Survey of rent-to-own customers. Bureau of Economics Staff Report, Washington, D.C.

Roosevelt, Franklin D.

At the 1932 Democratic National Convention, Franklin D. Roosevelt set forth his pledge to make a "new deal" for Americans. The current policy agenda can be attributed to the policies implemented during Roosevelt's tenure as president. Income tax, unemployment compensation, public works, Social Security, wage legislation, bank deposit insurance, and food stamps were all created in response to the Great Depression. Social and economic programs implement as a result of these policies were intended to reestablish American's faith in the government and to help families regain economic control of their lives.

In an attempt to provide relief for the unemployed and the poor, jobs were created that not only provided income but also made available resources farm and rural families were not able to access (Franklin D. Roosevelt American Heritage Center, 1). The Federal Emergency Relief Administration revitalized relief programs by distributing funds to the local agencies. The issue of unemployment was addressed with the Civil Works Administration (CWA), Civilian Conservation Corps (CCC), Tennessee Valley Authority (TVA), and Works Progress Administration (WPA). Each of these policies created jobs for unemployed Americans, the work improved the infrastructure of communities by building, repairing, or maintenance of roads, parks, airports, and schools (Franklin D. Roosevelt American Heritage Center, 1–2). The Food Stamp program was also created to provide relief to families who did not have access to healthy food. Programs that provided relief are known as entitlement programs, which are government benefits in which the eligibility criteria are age, income, retirement, disability, unemployment "entitle" individuals to receive the benefits (Dye, 2013, 141).

Economic recovery need to occur to stimulate the economy back to normal levels. Providing opportunities for the unemployed to work was a step in the right direction. Fair labor practices, production issues, and business practices needed to be addressed so Americans were not taken advantage of during a time of need (Franklin D. Roosevelt American Heritage Center, 2). The National Industry Recovery Act (NIRA) was created to help boost prices to help businesses and workers. Codes were written to regulate wages, working conditions, production, and prices. An unfortunate outcome of this act was the cycle of rising prices that caused a decrease in consumer purchases. Home owners were able to refinance mortgages through the Home Owners Loan Corporation (HOLC). The Farm Security Administration (FSA) provided loans to farmers and established migrant worker camps. Unfair labor practices were regulated through the National Labor Relations Act (NLRA), creation of unions, and the Fair Labor Standards Act (FLSA), banned child labor, and a minimum wage. Minimum hourly wage and a standard 40-hour work week were established through the FLSA of 1937 (Dye, 2013, 156).

The financial system needed reform to prevent a repeat depression (Franklin D. Roosevelt American Heritage Center, 1). Congress passed the Emergency Banking Act in order to inspect the health of all the banks and then established Federal Deposit Insurance Corporation to ensure deposits up to $5,000. To provide financial security for individuals, the Social Security Act was created. This system, which provided income to old-aged pension workers, survivors of victims of industrial accidents, unemployment insurance, and aid for dependent mothers and children and the disabled, helped to prevent families from experiencing the extreme conditions of poverty (Shlaes, 2008, 229). Social Security was intended to be a preventative strategy by requiring all individuals to purchase the insurance to reduce the risk of experiencing loss of income when a situation occurred in which they had to control (death of family income provider, loss of job, old age, or disability) (Dye, 2013, 148).

Roosevelt's New Deal was not openly welcomed by everyone; Republicans questioned the cost and effectiveness. There was disagreement about whether these policies created a change in values that focused on providing a commitment to welfare or if the policies were just a response to the depression and the need for economic recovery. During the Great Depression most of the policies were successful in providing income and resources for families. The success of many of the policies is apparent in the continuation of the policies today.

Lorna Saboe-Wounded Head

See also: Congress; Minimum Wage; Social Security

References and Additional Readings

Dye, T.R. (2013). *Understanding Public Policy* (14th ed.). Boston, MA: Pearson Education, Inc.

Franklin D. Roosevelt American Heritage Center, Inc. (2013). Retrieved from http://www.fdrheritage.org/welcome.htm

Shlaes, A. (2008). *The forgotten man: A new history of the Great Depression.* New York: HarperCollins Publisher.

S

Safety Data Sheets (SDS). See Material Safety Data Sheets (MSDS)

SBA (Small Business Administration). *See* Small Business Administration (SBA)

Schlink, Frederick. *See One Hundred Million Guinea Pigs*

SEC. *See* Securities and Exchange Commission (SEC)

Section 8 Housing. *See* Department of Housing and Urban Development (HUD)

Securities and Exchange Commission (SEC)

Introduction

The Securities and Exchange Commission (SEC) is a U.S. federal agency created with the Securities Exchange Act of 1934 and charged with a mission, as written on its website, "to protect investors, maintain fair, orderly, and efficient markets, and facilitate capital formation." The main role of the SEC is the oversight and enforcement of legislation related to U.S. security markets. The SEC is the investor's advocate. As written on their website:

> As more and more first-time investors turn to the markets to help secure their futures, pay for homes, and send children to college, our investor protection mission is more compelling than ever. As our nation's securities exchanges mature into global for-profit competitors, there is even greater need for sound market regulation. And the common interest of all Americans in a growing economy that produces jobs, improves our standard of living, and protects the value of our savings means that all of the SEC's actions must be taken with an eye toward promoting the capital formation that is necessary to sustain economic growth. (SEC, 2012, Investor's Advocate)

History

The stock market crash of 1929 precipitated a number of federal reforms, the creation of the SEC is one among them. Prior to the crash, securities had been regulated only loosely by state-level laws, commonly referred to as "Blue Sky laws," requiring the registration of securities transactions. The losses experienced by consumers in the 1929 crash, combined with banking and brokerage abuses uncovered in a 1932 inquiry (the Pecora Commission) resulted in congressional attention. Two pieces of legislation were passed: the Securities Act of 1933, which principally regulates the primary securities market (initial offerings), and the Securities Exchange Act of 1934, which regulated the secondary securities market and created the SEC. Joseph P. Kennedy was appointed by President Franklin D. Roosevelt as the first chairman of the SEC.

Organizational structure

The SEC leadership is comprised of five commissioners who are appointed by the president. Of these, one commissioner is appointed to be the SEC chairman. The chairman is the chief executive of the agency, and, among other duties, is responsible for appointing office chiefs. The commission is nonpartisan; therefore, the five-year commissioner terms are staggered, and no more than two of the five commissioners may be from the same political party. To ensure the independent nature of the commission, a commissioner's appointment may not be terminated by a president. Responsibilities of the commission, include interpreting federal securities laws, issuing and amending new and existing rules, overseeing securities firms, brokers, accounting and auditing businesses, investment advisers and ratings agencies and the inspection of these entities. The commission also coordinates U.S. securities regulations in accordance with state, federal, and international authorities.

To assist in accomplishing its mission, the SEC is organized into five divisions and 18 offices. Each division and office has a unique responsibility and function.

Divisions of the Securities and Exchange Commission

Division of Corporation Finance: This division is primarily responsible for reviewing disclosure documentation required of corporations and operating the EDGAR (see later). This documentation is filed with the SEC in order to provide information to investing shareholders. Additionally, the Division of Corporate Finance oversees accounting standards used to formulate generally accepted accounting principles (GAAP) and U.S. registrants of International Financial Reporting Standards. Finally, the Corporate Finance Division provides guidance or interpretation of legislation for companies seeking clarification on an action not directly addressed (e.g., a new marketing technique).

Division of Trading and Markets: This division is tasked with the oversight of the exchanges, self-regulatory agencies, credit rating agencies and all broker-dealer firms, and investment houses. In addition, the Trading and Markets Division reviews proposals for new or changes to existing rules related to securities markets. Finally, this division regulates a nonprofit organization that insures consumer brokerage accounts called the Securities Investor Protection Corporation (SIPC).

Division of Investment Management: Investor protection is the primary focus of the Division of Investment Management. This includes the oversight of financial advisors and mutual fund managers, and the review of investment company/advisor disclosure documentation. The division also ensures retail investors are treated fairly by making sure disclosure information is appropriate and consumer costs are not excessive. Finally, the Division of Investment Management provides interpretation on securities-related legislation, specifically related to inquiries related to investors or investment management.

Division of Enforcement: This division has the substantial responsibility of enforcing the securities-related legislation through the investigation of possible violations and prosecution of suspected misconduct. The division works closely with law enforcement when criminal charges are appropriate.

Division of Risk, Strategy, and Financial Innovation: Established in 2009, this division primarily provides analysis, research, and training related to three broad areas: risk and economic analysis, strategic research, and financial innovation. The division is also responsible for conducting research into new and developing trends in the financial markets, and advising the commission on how these trends may influence future regulation.

Offices of the Securities and Exchange Commission

Office of the General Counsel: The general counsel is appointed by the chairman and is the chief legal officer of the SEC. The general counsel represents the SEC in all legal proceedings related to enforcement.

Office of the Chief Accountant: The chief accountant is responsible for SEC matters related to accounting principles and auditing. This office assists in enforcement actions due to its expertise in financial records.

Office of Compliance Inspections and Examinations: This office conducts inspections of organizations requiring compliance with SEC regulations. The office may address deficiencies directly or refer them to the Division of Enforcement.

Office International Affairs: International affairs represents the SEC in international arenas. In addition, this office assists developing countries in establishing securities markets.

Office of Investor Education and Advocacy: This office is comprised of three subsections: the Office of Investor Assistance, which responds to consumer communication directly; the Office of Investor Education, responsible for educating investors through material, training events, and seminars; and the Office of Policy, responsible for advocating for consumer focused input on agency action and disclosure material.

Office of the Chief Operating Officer: The SEC chief operating officer is responsible for the management policies of the SEC, including budget, resources, technology, and staffing.

Office of Administrative Services: Administrative Services is responsible for the SEC's Washington, D.C., headquarter and 11 regional offices. This office oversees facilities, property management, printing and publication, and equipment management.

Office of Financial Management: Financial Management oversees the budgetary functions of the SEC.

Office of FOIA, Records Management and Security (OFRMS): The OFRMS is responsible for processing information under the Freedom of Information Act.

Office of Human Resources: This office is responsible for the staffing and human resource management of the SEC.

Office of Information Technology: Information Technology operates the EDGAR (see later) system and supports all IT programs.

Office of Legislative Affairs and Intergovernmental Relations: This office is the SEC's formal liaison with the U.S. Congress and state and local governments.

Office of Public Affairs: The Office of Public Affairs works with SEC groups and the media to inform the general public of commission-related issues in an appropriate manner.

Office of the Secretary: This office is responsible for the administration and record-keeping of SEC meetings, the maintenance of SEC administrative records, and the publication of SEC official publications such as releases in the Federal Registrar and the SEC Docket.

Office of Equal Employment Opportunity: The mission of the EEO office, according to their website, is to prevent employment discrimination, including discriminatory harassment.

Office of the Inspector General: The inspector general is responsible for conducting internal audits of SEC to further operational efficiency and ensure SEC program effectiveness.

Office of Administrative Law Judges: The Administrative Law Judges (ALJ) hear administrative cases brought by the commission for violations. After hearing these cases, the ALJ prepares a publicly available initial decision, which can be appealed to a U.S. Court of Appeals.

Scope of Responsibilities

Information Dissemination (EDGAR Database)

EDGAR, the electronic data gathering, analysis, and retrieval system was established over a three-year period between 1994 and 1996. This system is for both the submission of required documents and the access to desired documentation by potential investors. In 1998, a Public Dissemination Service (PDS) was created that allows paid subscribers to receive documentation electronically in real-time. The SEC provides a tutorial for using the EDGAR system.

Regulation and Oversight

Another of the SEC's major responsibilities is to interpret the major pieces of legislation related to securities. This is done through the rulemaking process. As new rules are required, the SEC issues a rule proposal for public comment. After 30–60 days of posting, the commission will agree and vote on a final version of the rule. If passed, the rule will become part of the governance of the securities industry.

Unfortunately, violations of securities legislation occur. The SEC reports violations that often lead to an investigation by the SEC. Some examples of these violations are security misrepresentation or omission of information, manipulation securities' market price, theft of securities funds from consumers, unfair treatment of customers, insider trading, or selling unregistered securities.

When a violation is suspected, the SEC may open an investigation. Investigations are conducted privately, and information may be gathered through a number of sources including whistleblowers, disclosure documentation filed with other Divisions of the SEC, self-regulatory agencies, and the interview of witnesses. If a violation is evident, the commission may choose to settle with the violating organization/individual, or file either an internal administrative action (potentially resulting in sanctions) or a legal civil action (potentially resulting in legal action including monetary penalties). In addition, SEC investigators may work with law enforcement to file criminal charges.

Major Legislation

As part of the New Deal legislation, the original Securities Act of 1933 focused on the registration of securities, with the end goal of information disclose to investors. This disclosure was intended to curb investor fraud and provide a federal system for ensuring compliance. However, the Securities Act primarily covered securities in the primary market (original issues of securities).

Shortly after the Securities Act, Congress passed the Securities Exchange Act of 1934, creating the Securities and Exchange Commission. This act covered the secondary market, and sought to regulate stock exchanges, self-regulatory agencies, and brokerage houses. The act further detailed disclosure and reporting requirements, and required the registration of additional market participants, including self-regulatory agencies, exchanges, and brokers and dealers.

Although there were additional pieces of legislation in the intervening years, the Sarbanes–Oxley Act of 2002 instituted major reforms in the securities industry. This act included a number of items related to financial auditors and controls for audits, the responsibilities of securities analysts and senior executives in financial reporting accuracy, and strengthens the (criminal) penalties for fraud. Major adoptions also include the establishment of the Public Company Accounting Oversight Board (PCAOB), an independent body to oversee firms providing financial auditing services, and a requirement that corporate officers certify the integrity of their company's financial reports.

Finally, the Dodd–Frank Wall Street Reform and Consumer Protection Act as signed into law in 2010 provided additional regulatory changes, specifically related to consumer protection and advocacy in securities markets.

Angela Fontes

See also: Commodity Futures Trading Commission (CFTC); Dodd–Frank Wall Street Reform and Consumer Protection Act; Federal Reserve; Investing Regulations

References and Additional Readings

Dodd–Frank Wall Street Reform and Consumer Protection Act. Pub.L. 111–203, H.R. 4173.

Federal Reserve Bank of St. Louis. (2013). Retrieved from http://fraser.stlouisfed.org/publication/?pid=87

Sarbanes–Oxley Act of 2002. (2013). Public Law 107–204. Retrieved from http://www.sec.gov/about/laws/soa2002.pdf

Securities Exchange Act of 1934. (2013). Securities Exchange Act of 1934. Retrieved from http://www.sec.gov/about/laws/sea34.pdf

Securities Act of 1933. (2013). Retrieved from http://www.sec.gov/about/laws/sa33.pdf

Securities and Exchange Commission. (2013a). Retrieved from http://www.sec.gov/about/whatwedo.shtml

Securities and Exchange Commission. (2013b). The investor's advocate. Retrieved from http://www.sec.gov/about/whatwedo.shtml

Securities and Exchange Commission. (2013c). SEC proposed rules. Retrieved from http://www.sec.gov/rules/proposed.shtml

Securities and Exchange Commission. (2013d). How do I use EDGAR? Retrieved from http://www.sec.gov/edgar/quickedgar.htm

Securities and Exchange Commission. (2013e). Blue sky laws. Retrieved from http://www.sec.gov/answers/bluesky.htm

Sexual Harassment

The U.S. Equal Employment Opportunity Commission (EEOC) enforces federal laws that make it illegal to discriminate against an employee or potential employee based on that person's race, color, religion, sex, ethnicity, age, and functional ability. These laws also apply to work situations, including sexual harassment, a form of sex discrimination that violates Title VII of the Civil Rights Acts of 1964. According to the EEOC website, "It is unlawful to harass a person . . . because of that person's sex. Harassment can include 'sexual harassment' or unwelcome sexual advances, requests for sexual favors, and other verbal or physical harassment of a sexual nature. Harassment does not have to be of a sexual nature, however, and can include offensive remarks about a person's sex. For example, it is illegal to harass a woman by making offensive comments about women in general" (U.S. Equal Employment Opportunity Commission, 2013a). Additionally, harassment is illegal when it is frequent in nature or severe leading to a hostile or offensive work place environment. Examples of sexual harassment are:

- "The victim as well as the harasser may be a woman or a man. The victim does not have to be of the opposite sex."
- "The harasser can be the victim's supervisor, an agent of the employer, a supervisor in another area, a co-worker, or a non-employee."
- "The victim does not have to be the person harassed but could be anyone affected by the offensive conduct."

Professor Anita Hill was active in sexual harassment and related policy making efforts in the 1990s. Since then, sexual harassment advocacy groups have become essential to protect consumers in the workplace. (Center for the American Woman and Politics)

- "Unlawful sexual harassment may occur without economic injury to or discharge of the victim."
- "The harasser's conduct must be unwelcome" (U.S. Equal Employment Opportunity Commission, 2013b).

Contemporary guidance on defining sexual harassment and establishing employer liability is guided by *Meritor Savings Bank v. Vinson* (477 U.S. 57) a 1986 case that marked the U.S. Supreme Court's recognition that sexual harassment is a violation of the Civil Rights Act. This case also set precedent for establishing standards and guidelines for how to determine if work-place conduct is unlawful and if an employer should be held legally responsible. In this case, Mechelle Vinson, a bank employee, sued Sidney Taylor, the vice president of the bank, with the charge that Taylor forced Vinson to have sexual relations with him and that he demanded sexual favors while at work. The primary outcome of the case was the establishment that sexual harassment leading to noneconomic injury is also a form of sexual harassment.

Sexual Harassment

In August 1999, the EEOC settled its first male-on-male sexual harassment class action law suit. The settlement set a precedent that the EEOC has a "zero tolerance" policy for all harassment, including men against men and disability-based harassment. The Supreme Court held that same-sex harassment by men against men violates Title VII of the Civil Rights Act of 1964.

During 2011, the EEOC received and filed over 11,000 charges of sexual harassment; nearly 84 percent of cases filed were by females. With the increase in women's labor force participation, the incidence of sexual harassment cases by women is also likely to increase. Additionally, with the increase of migrant workers, the EEOC has engaged in lawsuits surrounding sexual harassment and abuse of farmworkers, both of men and women. According to a EEOC press release, this is "a group which is particularly vulnerable due to isolated working conditions and lack of familiarity with the protections of the law" (U.S. Equal Employment Opportunity Commission, 2012) These three cases join earlier farmworker cases, all in ongoing attempt to protect workers in agricultural industries. As explained by current EEOC General Counsel David Lopez, "All workers are entitled to a workplace that is free of harassment and discrimination, and employers should think twice before assuming that vulnerable workers will not exercise their rights due to fear or the lack of understanding" (U.S. Equal Employment Opportunity Commission, 2012).

Melanie Horn Mallers

See also: Activism; Commission on Civil Rights; Department of Labor (DOL); Discrimination; Equal Employment Opportunity Commission (EEOC)

References and Additional Readings

Cochran, A. B. (2004). Sexual harassment and the law: The Mechelle Vinson Case. Lawrence, KS: *Kansas University Press,* 256.

U.S. Equal Employment Opportunity Commission. (2012). EEOC sues to redress sexual harassment of vulnerable farmworkers. Retrieved from http://www1.eeoc.gov/eeoc/newsroom/release/10–5-12.cfm

U.S. Equal Employment Opportunity Commission. (2013a). Sexual harassment. Retrieved from http://www.eeoc.gov/laws/types/sexual_harassment.cfm

U.S. Equal Employment Opportunity Commission. (2013b). Facts about sexual harassment. Retrieved from http://www.eeoc.gov/eeoc/publications/fs-sex.cfm

Vinciguerra, M. (1989). The aftermath of Meritor: A search for standards in the law of sexual harassment. *Yale Law Journal, 98*(8), 1717–1738.

Sherman Antitrust Act

The Sherman Antitrust Act, principally written by John Sherman, a Republican from Ohio, was passed and signed into law by President Benjamin Harrison in 1890. The act served as the first federal measure to prohibit business activities that reduce marketplace competition such as trusts. Furthermore, it required federal investigation of business activities that appear to act as cartels or monopolies. International commerce is also regulated by the act, with cooperation being of high priority. Before its passage, several states had enacted similar restrictions, but that legislation was limited to intrastate commerce.

The Clayton Act of 1914 furthered the jurisdiction of the Sherman Antitrust Act by addressing anticompetitive problems such as mergers and acquisitions of stocks or assets "where in any line of commerce or in any activity affecting commerce in any section of the country, the effect of such acquisition may be substantially to lessen competition, or tend to create a monopoly," according to the Department of Justice website. The Clayton Act may also perform investigations to stop mergers before they occur through a cease and desist order or via an injunction.

The Sherman Antitrust Act is enforced by the Department of Justice and the Federal Trade Commission, allowing for civil and criminal suits. Typically, the act enforces allegations of such things as price fixing (agreeing to set a price amongst a group of competitors, thus controlling supply and demand and pushing a high price and reaping high profits), bid rigging (promise of a contract or bid to one bidder but accepting other bids as well; a form of collusion), or collusion (collaboration or agreement between a group of competitors to create an unfair advantage; e.g., wage fixing and kickbacks). Corporations found guilty of violations may face fines up to $10 million, others may receive fines up to $350,000 and up to three years imprisonment.

The act was put to the test early in high-profile cases involving Standard Oil and the American Sugar Refining Company in the 19th century, with more recent cases involving Microsoft and AT&T in the 20th century. To this day, the act serves as the primary foundation for antitrust litigation, also known as competition law.

For additional information, refer to the Primary Source Appendix: The Sherman Anti-Trust Act.

Wendy Reiboldt

See also: Department of Justice (DOJ); Federal Trade Commission (FTC)

References and Additional Readings

Anderson, W. L., Block, W. E., DiLorenzo, T., & Westley, C. (2001). The Microsoft Corporation in collision with antitrust law. *Journal of Social, Political, and Economic Studies, 26*(1), 287–302.

Department of Justice. (2013). Retrieved from www.justice.gov

Federal Trade Commission. (2013). Retrieved from www.ftc.gov

Lande, R. H. (1997). Consumer sovereignty: A unified theory of antitrust and consumer protection law. *Antitrust Law Journal 66*, 713–746.

Our Documents. (2013). Retrieved from www.ourdocuments.gov

Short Sales. *See* Foreclosures

Silent Spring

Silent Spring is a book by Rachel Carson (1907–1964), published in 1962 by Houghton Mifflin. In *Silent Spring* Carson critically examines the (then prevailing) use of synthetic herbicides and pesticides like dichlorodiphenyltrichloroethane (DDT) and other chlorinated hydrocarbons and organophosphates. She strongly argues that pesticides have many adverse effects on animals, plants, and the human health that massively outweigh their benefits. Important adverse effects include the low selectiveness of the chemicals and most notably the property of DDT and other pesticides to accumulate through the food chain.

Silent Spring provoked a controversial public debate, and its arguments were severely attacked by the chemical industry. Criticism of the book included one-sidedness, lack of scientific rigor, ecological fanaticism, and lack of support for Carson's theses by scientific and experimental evidences. The debate also included verbal attacks on Carson's style of writing, her person, and her gender. Experts have marveled at the inappropriate use of

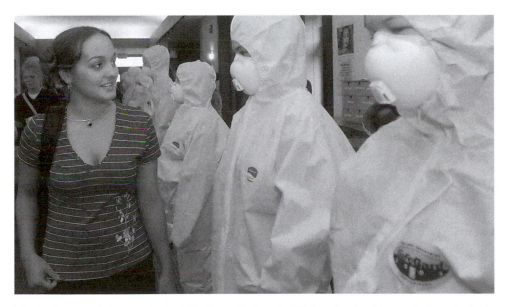

Nicole Persson, left, a student at Chatham College in Pittsburgh, checking out other students who were part of a silent protest on the school's campus Friday, September 27, 2002. The protest was part of a program commemorating the 40th anniversary of the publication of *Silent Spring*, written by environmentalist and school alumna Rachel Carson. (AP Photo/John Heller)

gendered language oftentimes used to discredit Carson. At the same time, Carson and *Silent Spring* achieved tremendous support by the public as well as scientists. As a consequence of the long debate induced by *Silent Spring* the majority of the pesticides criticized in the book have eventually been banned in the United States. In 2001, the Stockholm Convention banned the *dirty dozen* of the worst persistent organic pollutants from use internationally; the vast majority the toxins covered by the Stockholm Convention had been criticized by Rachel Carson in 1962.

The book has 17 chapters. It starts with a vivid description of possible long-term effects of pesticide use, the proverbial silent spring without birds and birdsong. The following chapters 2 and 3 lay a foundation for the general argument developed in the book. Carson frames the use of pesticides as a deliberate act, based on a decision with alternatives and briefly discusses chemical and toxicological characteristics of synthetic pesticides and herbicides. Chapters 4 through 6 extensively cover the spread of biocides via water, its accumulation through the food chain, the storage of residues in soil and plants. In chapters 7 through 9 Carson describes the low selectiveness of pesticides and herbicides and details their impact on birds, fish, and aquatic fauna in general. Following an excursus on the application of biocides by means of aerial spraying, individual use in households, contaminated food, and safety limits three chapters cover adverse effects of pesticides on humans. Chapter 12 discusses harms to the nervous system, Chapter 13, effects on fertility and mutagenic properties of the chemicals, and Chapter 14 covers carcinogenic properties. In the last three chapters Carson first cautions against to the development of resistances against biocides and the increased occurrence invasive species under conditions of pesticide use, and then points to alternative, biological means of pest control.

Parts of the book were prepublished in *The New Yorker* magazine in June 1962. The full book was published in late September 1962 and was immediately chosen as a "Book of the Month Club Selection." The publication gained even further prominence when the CBS's report "The Silent Spring of Rachel Carson" was broadcasted on April 13, 1963, at prime time by CBS.

In addition to leading to these tangible consequences, the books is widely considered as one of the most influential books of the 20th century and is frequently cited as one of the fundamental works of the American ecology movement. When Carson was posthumously awarded the Presidential Medal of Freedom in 1980, President Jimmy Carter concluded about Rachel Carson:

Never silent herself in the face of destructive trends, Rachel Carson fed a spring of awareness across America and beyond. She welcomed her audiences to her love of the sea, while with an equally clear voice she warned Americans of the danger human beings themselves pose for their own environment. Always concerned, always eloquent, she created a tide of environmental consciousness that has not ebbed.

Henning Best

See also: Activism; Carson, Rachel; Environmental Protection Agency (EPA); Public Safety

References and Additional Readings

Carson, R. (1962). *Silent spring*. Boston, MA: Houghton Mifflin.

Children's Literature Network. (2013). Rachel Carson. Retrieved from http://www.childrensliteraturenetwork.org/birthbios/brthpage/05may/5–27cars.html

Dunn, R. (2012). In retrospect: Silent spring. *Nature, 485*, 578–579.

Lear, L. (2009). *Rachel Carson: Witness for nature*. Boston, MA: Mariner.

Lytle, M. H. (2001). *The Gentle subversive. Rachel Carson, silent spring, and the rise of the environmental movement*. Oxford: Oxford University Press.

Smith, M. B. (2001). Silence, Miss Carson! Science, gender, and the reception of "Silent Spring." *Feminist Studies, 27*(3), 733–752.

Small Business Administration (SBA)

The Small Business Administration (SBA) is an advocate for small businesses in Washington, D.C., serving as the collective voice of the nation's small businesses. The office was created in 1953 and evolved into the entity it is today with the mission to provide services to small business owners across the United States and protect free economic trade. The office provides help to small business owners through services such as financing and education as well as outreach to special populations such as women, minorities, and veterans. Additionally, the SBA provides counsel for international trade and assistance to victims of natural disasters. The four main functions of the SBA are to provide the American people with access to business financing; education and technical assistance for entrepreneurial development; federal procurement for government contracting; and advocacy.

While the office of the SBA was founded in 1953, it was created in the spirited of earlier initiatives set forth by the government to address the volatile economic climate of the Great Depression and World War II. Support for small businesses at the federal level began with the Hoover administration in 1932, which began a program entitled the Resolution Finance Corporation (RFC). The RFC was created to alleviate the financial crisis of the Great Depression and provided loans for businesses, both large and small. In 1942, Congress created the Smaller War Plants Corporation (SWPC) to help small businesses compete against the new large corporations that had formed in response to the war efforts. As the first office to focus on the needs of the small business owner, the SWPC advocated to make credit available for private entrepreneurs. The SWPC dissolved after the war, and was replaced by the Small Defense Plants Administration (SDPA) during the Korean War. The new office had similar practices but maintained closer ties to the RFC, which retained lending authority. In 1952, Eisenhower abolished the RFC in order to propose a new office to focus on protecting the small businesses. The decision was finalized in 1953. Congress created the new office of the SBA to "aid, counsel, assist and protect, insofar as is possible, the interests of small business concerns." The other role of the SBA was to allot a "fair proportion" of government contracts and sales of surplus property. Section 15(g) of the Small Business Act mandates that the SBA's Office of Government Contracting reaches the goal of 23 percent contract dollars to small businesses.

The organization of the SBA includes several offices and services within the administration. The administration is overseen by an administrator, appointed by the president and confirmed by the U.S. Senate. The administrator serves on the president's economic team, representing the interests of small businesses and entrepreneurs and their contribution to economic growth in America. The office also employs a deputy administrator who is similarly appointed by the president and confirmed by the U.S. Senate. The third administrator is an inspector general, serving in the U.S. SBA's Office of Inspector General. The inspector general is responsible for providing oversight and accountability for the SBA programs.

An important office within the administration is the ombudsman office that investigates unfair enforcement by federal agencies, including excessive fines and penalties. The National Ombudsman and Assistant Administrator for Regulatory Enforcement Fairness has the following mission statement, according to the website: "The National Ombudsman's mission is to assist small business when they experience excessive or unfair federal regulatory enforcement actions, such as repetitive audits or investigations, excessive fines, penalties, threats, retaliation or other unfair enforcement action by a federal agency." The office is working with each federal agency to develop a policy on nonretaliation by its employees against a small business seeking assistance. The SBA currently has a policy in place for its employees.

The services of the SBA are rendered to the American public at offices located throughout the country. Headquarters is located in Washington, D.C., and there are offices in each state that provide walk-in access to education and information on SBA programs to the public. Regional offices provide support to larger geographic areas. Additionally, there are smaller branches open throughout the United States located on university campuses, and throughout major cities in metropolitan areas.

Marie Botkin

See also: Congress; Department of Labor (DOL); Inspector General; Ombuds Offices

References and Additional Readings

Bean, J.J. (2001). *Big government and affirmative action: The scandalous history of the small business administration.* Lexington: University Press of Kentucky.

Parris, A. (1968). *The small business administration.* New York: F.A. Praeger.

Small Business Administration. (2013). Retrieved from http://www.sba.gov

Small Claims Courts

Small claims courts afford the opportunity for those who have cases involving small monetary amounts to have them resolved expediently and inexpensively. Sometimes called "conciliation courts," these are solely state courts; no federal analog exists, and the details of these courts among the states differ. However, they exist to provide a venue for civil cases between private individuals or companies. Often litigants will represent themselves in small claims cases, and the rules and procedures are simplified from those in regular civil trials to enable them to do so.

Every state has a small claims court system. Hundreds of thousands of small claims cases are filed every day all over the country (one estimate puts the number of small claims cases filed in Los Angeles county alone each day at over 4,000). Individuals can use small claims courts to sue companies for bad work, and companies often use them to sue consumers for unpaid bills. Examples of small claims cases might include attempts to receive a rental security deposit refund, to receive merchandise that was paid for but not delivered, or to get money back for repairs that were ineffective.

Early courts that could be labeled small claims courts existed in England as early as the 1600s, in the form of debtor's courts. In the United States, these courts developed in the 1900s out of a judicial reform movement that focused on the slow speed and high cost of adjudicating civil cases with small monetary outcomes. The first such court in the United States was established in 1913 in Cleveland, Ohio, called the Conciliation Branch of the Municipal Court. Other states followed suit, with a renewal of interest and reforms in the 1960s.

Small claims courts are a form of alternative dispute resolution, or ADR. The concept behind these courts was that the average person should be able to represent him/herself in court, rather than having to engage a costly attorney and deal with cumbersome court procedures. For example, there are rarely juries in small claims courts (in fact, it is typically written into the state statute establishing the small claims system that no juries are permitted), and the remedies in these courts tend to be limited to monetary awards.

Most small claims courts have a monetary limit on the claims that can be awarded. If a claim is above that dollar amount, the case cannot be brought in small claims. Jurisdictions vary on the amount. In many states the original upper limit was $1,000, but in most states that number has gone up over the years. Both New York and California have a limit of $5,000 (although "natural people" rather than companies can claim up to $7,500 in California), while in Texas and Illinois the limit is $10,000. These courts usually charge filing fees as well from $15 to 150 is average. Some states, such as Maine, require that litigants meet with an arbitrator and engage in good-faith arbitration before going to court to see if the issue can be resolved.

One of the most significant complaints about small claims courts is that while it can be easy to win a case, it can be difficult to collect the judgment. Winners may have to spend additional money to enforce their award—thus, reducing their potential financial gain. Because successful litigants have to follow regular civil court procedures to collect, they sometimes do not bother to do so, or they must hire an attorney to help them collect. Some studies suggest that the judgment collection rate can be as low as 25 percent. A 1993 empirical study of the Denver small claims courts system found that 85 percent of plaintiffs who filed claims and appeared in court won their cases, but of these winning plaintiffs, 55 percent never collected any part of the judgments they won. Calls for reform in this area include suggestions that courts be more supportive and involved in collection actions, including providing more information on how to go about collecting a judgment.

Moreover, the rules on representation by an attorney vary by state. Some states ban attorneys altogether, while some permit limited assistance from counsel and others allow full participation. While allowing attorney representation in small claims court dilutes the "everyone as his/her own counsel" foundation behind these courts and adds cost and formality to the process, some suggest that having attorneys present can reduce any experience disparity between litigants and help those litigants assert and protect their rights. In recent years there has been a shift from the traditional adversarial system of resolving small claims toward mediation and arbitration; some commentators suggest that these forms of ADR better serve the needs of small claims litigants.

Television has enhanced the visibility, if not the reputation, of these courts. At the height of *The People's Court* show's popularity, more Americans could recall the name of the judge of that court, Judge Joseph Wapner, than any actual Supreme Court justice. Reality shows such as *Judge Judy* and *The People's Court* portray themselves as small claims courts, although they are really forms of binding arbitration, not actual small claims cases (although the parties have usually filed small claims actions, the records of which are combed for possible show appearances). Litigants are often paid a stipend to appear.

Several other countries have small claims courts. For example, in Canada there are two different models: in most provinces, the courts are separate from the superior courts that hear most other claims. But in others, the small claims courts are a branch of the regular superior court. And in Europe, there is a European small claims procedure that deals with cases involving litigants from different countries in the European Union. Claims are limited to €2,000.

Genelle I. Belmas

See also: Arbitration; Mediation; Supreme Court

References and Additional Readings

Bestf, A., Zalesne, D., Bridges, K., & Chenoweth, K. (1993). Peace, wealth, happiness, and small claim courts: A case study. *Fordham Urban Law Journal, 21*(2), 343–379.

Elwell, S.E., & Carlson, C.D. (1990). The Iowa small claims court: An empirical analysis. *Iowa Law Review, 75,* 433–538.

Steele, E.H. (1981). The historical context of small claims ccourts. *American Bar Foundation Research Journal, 6*(2), 293–376.

Zucker, B., & Herr, M. (2003). The people's court examined: A legal and empirical analysis of the Small Claims Court System. *University of San Francisco Law Review, 37,* 315–350.

SNAP (Supplemental Nutrition Assistance Program. *See* Supplemental Nutrition Assistance Program (SNAP)

Social Networking. *See* Privacy: Online

Social Security

History of Social Security

President Roosevelt announced his intention to provide a program for social security on June 8, 1934. The original purpose of social security retirement benefits was to alleviate hardship and provide economic security. The Social Security Act was signed in 1935. It is generally viewed as one of the legislative accomplishments in the history of the United States. The Social Security Act has been amended many times but the overall purpose remains the same.

The first social security card was issued in November, 1936. Workers' began accumulating credits toward social security benefits in 1937. The first check was issued in 1937 as a one-time payment, only paying benefits to the primary worker. Ernest Hackman received the first one-time payment of 17 cents. In 1939, a spouse of a retired worker was first paid dependent benefits; and survivor benefits were paid to the family in the event of the premature death of a covered worker. The first increase in benefits occurred during 1939. In 1940, monthly social security payments were initiated for aged retired workers and their aged wives or widows, their children under age 18, and their surviving aged parents. Ida May Fuller received the first month check in the amount of $22.54. The second increase in benefits occurred during 1952. In 1956, women were given the option of receiving actuarially reduced benefits beginning at age 62 and men were provided this option in 1961. Also, in 1956 disability benefits were added. Medicare was established in 1965. Automatic annual cost of living adjustments (COLAs) to benefit amounts began in 1972.

Social Security Administration (SSA)

The Social Security Administration's strategic plan, which goes through 2013, is to concentrate on four goals: (1) eliminate backlog of hearings and prevent recurrence; (2) improve the speed and quality of disability process; (3) improve retiree and other core services; and (4) preserve the public's trust in social security programs.

For more information, see http://www.socialsecurity.gov

A 1977 amendment provided an increase in benefits for individuals who delayed electing benefits beyond age 65; 1983 brought an increase in the age of eligibility for unreduced benefits and increase in the delayed retirement credit in gradual steps. The annual mailing of social security statements to all workers age 25 and over was initiated in 1999. The Social Security Administration ceased mailing annual statements to workers in 2011 citing budget constraints. The retirement earnings test for workers at or above their normal retirement age was eliminated in 2000 and the claim and suspend option was added at that time. Under the Senior Citizens' Freedom to Work Act of 2000, individuals who are over their normal retirement age can choose to elect and suspend benefits. This allows the individual to suspend their social security retirement benefit. If an individual decides to suspend his or her social security benefits, then current benefit amounts are replaced by increased future monthly benefit amounts.

New York City postal workers waving social security applications as they begin to deliver the forms in November 1936. More than 3 million forms were distributed in New York City alone. (Library of Congress)

The normal social security benefit retirement age has gradually increased. An amendment enacted in 1983 increased the age of eligibility for unreduced benefit amounts in two stages to age 67 by the year 2027. Workers born in 1938 were the first group affected by the increase in the normal retirement age. Benefits remain available at age 62, but with a greater reduction. A 1977 amendment provided an increase in benefit amounts for individuals who delayed electing benefits beyond age 65 or their normal retirement age. Additionally, in 1983, an amendment was enacted that increased the delayed retirement benefit amount in gradual steps from 3 percent for workers reaching normal retirement age (age 65) before 1990, to 8 percent for workers reaching normal retirement age after 2008.

Social Security Today

Social Security provides three types of benefits: (1) retirement benefits, (2) disability benefits, and (3) survivor benefits. Qualification requirements exist in order to receive social security benefits. Social Security is funded by tax dollars. Consumers pay social security taxes on earnings up to a certain amount ($110,100 in 2012). However, the money paid in taxes is not held in a personal account to use when benefits are paid out. Rather, taxes are being used right now to pay people who now are receiving benefits and to pay for the cost of managing the program. Currently, the tax rate is 4.2 percent for workers and employers pay an additional 6.2 percent for workers. Prior to 2011, the tax rate was 6.2 percent for both workers and employers. The tax rate reduction is temporary (2011 and 2012) and will revert back to the higher rate (6.2 percent) unless extended by Congress.

Social Security Numbers

To date, 453.7 million different numbers have been issued. Consumers should guard their social security numbers. Anybody can ask for a social security number, but that doesn't mean it has to be given out. According to the Social Security Administration (2012a), "specific laws require a person to provide their Social Security number for certain purposes." For example, a social security number is required by:

Internal Revenue Service for tax returns and federal loans, employers for wage and tax reporting purposes, states for the school lunch program, banks for monetary transactions, Veterans Administration as a hospital admission number, Department of Labor for workers' compensation, Department of Education for student loans, states to administer any tax, general public assistance, motor vehicle or driver's license law within its jurisdiction, states for child support enforcement, states for commercial driver's licenses, states for food stamps, states for Medicaid, states for unemployment compensation, states for Temporary Assistance to Needy Families (welfare), and U.S. Treasury for U.S. Savings Bonds. (U.S. Social Security Administration, 2012a)

According to the Social Security Administration (2012a), "utility companies and other services ask for a social security number, but do not need it; they can do a credit check or identify the person in their records by alternative means." For example, when trying to obtain TV services such as cable or satellite and the company representative asks for a social security number, Consumer Action (2012) recommends asking them the following questions before giving out the number:

(1) Why do you need my SSN?
(2) How is my number going to be used?
(3) What laws require me to give you my SSN?
(4) What are the consequences if I refuse to provide you with my SSN?
(5) Are there any alternative numbers I can use to obtain this service?

Remember that you can ask the company if you can create an individual password or PIN instead of your social security number in the future.

Also, consumers should be very careful when using social networking sites. For example, never provide or post a social security number or other personal information that could be used by criminals. In determining appropriate information to post to a social networking site, it may be beneficial to picture the site as a billboard. For example, don't disclose anything personal that cannot be made public, including personal and financial information.

Social Security Benefits

According to the Social Security Administration (2012b), "when people apply for Social Security benefits, they state that all information they provide on the forms are true and correct to the best of their knowledge. If an individual reports something they know is not true, it may be a crime.

It may also be considered fraud if a person makes a false statement on an application. It may also be considered fraud if a person makes a false statement on an application". The Social Security Administration (2012b) provides the following examples, "it may be considered fraud if a person fails to report that they are working, have returned to work or are in jail or if they fail to notify the Social Security Administration of the death of a beneficiary and continues to receive and cash the checks of the deceased person."

The Social Security Administration also makes accommodations for people who are not able to handle their own financial affairs. For example, the elderly can have a friend or relative appointed to handle their social security benefits. It is a crime for that person to misuse the recipient's benefits. Responsibilities of the designated assistant include:

(1) determining the beneficiary's total needs and using the benefits received in the best interests of the beneficiary;

(2) maintaining a continuing awareness of the beneficiary's needs and condition, if the beneficiary does not live with the representative payee, by contact such as visiting the beneficiary and consultations with custodians;

(3) applying the benefit payments only for the beneficiary's use and benefit;

(4) notifying the Social Security Administration of any change in his or her circumstances that would affect performance of the payee's responsibilities; and

(5) reporting any event that may affect the amount of benefits the beneficiary receives and to provide written reports accounting for the use of the benefits.

The Office of Inspector General is responsible for investigating suspected fraudulent activities. Consumers can report suspected fraudulent activities online or by phone.

Social Security Retirement Benefits Options

An important retirement decision pivots on the age at which to elect receipt of social security retirement benefits. This decision has several options: (1) begin receiving actuarially reduced social security benefits at 62, or sometime between 62 and the normal retirement age; (2) wait to receive social security benefits until the normal retirement age, which currently ranges from ages 65 to 67 depending on date of birth; or (3) delay receipt of benefits even longer to increase monthly social security retirement benefit payments until after the normal retirement age up to the age of 70. In addition, widows may be eligible to elect actuarially reduced social security benefits beginning as early as age 60.

Social Security was never intended to be a retiree's sole source of retirement income. If older adults elect receipt of social security retirement benefits early, they may be jeopardizing their future economic security because early recipients receive actuarially reduced benefits. Benefit reductions for electing early receipt of benefits range from 20 to 25 percent depending on the date of birth. Workers can receive an 8 percent increase for each year they delay receipt of their social security benefits past their normal retirement age. Additionally, employment may reduce the social security retirement benefit amounts for individuals who opt to receive social security benefits before reaching normal retirement age.

Social Security Survivors Benefits

Social Security often provides survivor's benefits to a certain family member of the deceased insured worker including widows, widowers (and divorced widows and widowers), children and dependent parents. According to the Social Security Administration 98 children out of every 100 children are eligible to receive survivor's benefits if a working parent dies. Furthermore, Social Security pays more benefits to children than any other federal program.

Unmarried children under the age of 18 (19 if attending an elementary or secondary school) may qualify to receive social security survivor's benefits based on their deceased parent's work history. According to the Social Security Administration, children are eligible to receive benefits, provided they are the natural child, adopted child, stepchild, or dependent grandchild of the deceased insured worker. Children of divorced parents are eligible for benefits regardless of whether they lived with the deceased parent or if the living parent remarries.

Social Security Disability Benefits

"Disability" under Social Security is based on a worker's inability to work and adheres to a strict definition. The Social Security Administration considers a person disabled under social security rules if that person cannot resume work for medical reasons and if the disability is expected to last for at least one year or to result in death.

Qualifying for Social Security Benefits

When working and paying social security taxes, credits are earned toward final social security benefits. The maximum years of work needed to be eligible for any social security benefit is 10 years. However, depending on the benefits fewer years may still result in benefits depending on the specific situation. For example, the number of work years needed for a family to be eligible for social security survivor benefits depends on age at death. The younger the age at death, the fewer years needed to work to qualify. Additionally, under a special rule, if a person has worked for only one and one-half years in the three years just before death, benefits can be paid to children and spouse caring for the children.

This holds true for social security disability benefits as well. Generally, 10 years of work or 40 credits is needed 20 of which were earned in the last 10 years ending with the year the disability occurs. However, younger workers may qualify with fewer credits. In addition to meeting the work credits consumers must have a medical condition that meets Social Security's definition of disability.

Martie Gillen

See also: Administration on Aging (AoA); Department of Justice (DOJ); Department of Labor (DOL); Department of Veterans Affairs (VA), Frauds and Scams; Privacy: Offline; Privacy: Online

References and Additional Readings

Consumer Action. (2012). Should I give my social security number to a cable provider or the utility company? Retrieved from http://www.consumer-action .org/helpdesk/articles/social_security_number_safety/

Social Security Administration. (2007). Retirement benefits. Retrieved from http:// www.ssa.gov/pubs/10035.html

Social Security Administration. (2009a). Historical background and development of social security. Retrieved from http://www.ssa.gov/history/briefhistory3.html

Social Security Administration. (2009b). How work affects your benefits. Retrieved from http://www.socialsecurity.gov/pubs/10069.html

Social Security Administration. (2009c). Delayed retirement credits. Retrieved from http://www.ssa.gov/retire2/delayret.htm

Social Security Administration. (2011). Survivors benefits. Retrieved from http:// www.ssa.gov/pubs/10084.pdf

Social Security Administration. (2012a). Legal requirement to provide your SSN. Retrieved from http://ssa-custhelp.ssa.gov/app/answers/detail/a_id/78/~/legal-requirements-to-provide-your-ssn

Social Security Administration. (2012b). What is fraud, waste, or abuse? Retrieved from http://oig.ssa.gov/what-abuse-fraud-and-waste

Social Services

While all consumers are entitled to certain rights and protections, vulnerable or disadvantaged populations have been given additional attention and willingness from individuals and the government to provide necessary, comprehensive services. This oftentimes includes prevention and intervention programs for several groups of people including those living in poverty and the underemployed; children; persons who are physically and/or mentally disabled; older adults; and victims of abuse or criminal behavior. Support for these groups oftentimes comes in the form of services and programs designed to meet their specific individual needs, as well as the needs of their family and community. Professionals in the field often work as counselors or therapists, welfare specialists, advocates, and policy makers.

Though states vary by how and what services are offered to human services-related populations, four types of agencies typically exist. These are social welfare, mental health, corrections, and education.

Social Welfare Agencies

These include nonprofit agencies and government funding such as for shelters for homeless persons and battered persons, hospice support for terminally ill, and rehabilitation facilities for persons addicted to substances. Social welfare has its origins in the work done by President Franklin D. Roosevelt who essentially developed the United States first federal system of social welfare. In response to the 1929 stock market depression that led the United States into an historic Depression, FDR created the New Deal. In response to the Social Security Act of 1935, this created financial assistance for older adults, unemployment compensation, aid to dependent mothers and children, and aid to the blind and disabled. The Federal Deposit Insurance Corporation (FDIC) and the Securities Exchange Commission (SEC) were developed years later to ensure that the crash of 1929 did not happen again. More recently, President Obama and Congress passed the American Recovery and Reinvestment Act of 2009, which among other things, provides economic support to social welfare provisions and to

Americans suffering financially. In addition, the federal government, as run by individual states and local agencies, offers the Supplemental Nutrition Assistance Program (SNAP), which is designed to help low-income persons buy food.

Social Services Programs

Behavioral health is a component of service systems that improve health status and contain health care and other costs to society. Yet, people with mental and substance use disorders, because of their illness, have largely been excluded from the current healthcare system and rely on public "safety net" programs. Last year alone approximately 20 million people who needed substance abuse treatment did not receive it and an estimated 10.6 million adults reported an unmet need for mental health care. As a result the health and wellness of the individual is jeopardized and the unnecessary costs to society ripple across America's communities, schools, businesses, prisons and jails, and healthcare delivery systems.

Source: SAMHSA. (2012). About the agency. Retrieved from http://www.samhsa.gov/

Mental Health Agencies

These include nonprofit agencies, as well as government funding, such as for child protective services (CPS) and adult protective services (APS). Care for the mentally ill began in 400 BC when Greek physician Hippocrates treated mental illness as a function of impaired physiology (e.g., bodily fluids referred to as humours), and not due to demonic gods or spirits, as was previously viewed. During early Christianity and the Middle Ages, prayer and faith healing, as well as compassion and charity became noteworthy. Mental health and social services continued to evolve during the Renaissance. For example, in 1601 Queen Elizabeth of England, in response to the practice of inhumane treatment of the poor and sick, established the Elizabethan Poor Laws, which authorized the British government to provide care and support to the less fortunate. By the late 1700s Phillipe Pinel, a physician, reformed insane asylums by forbidding the use of chains and shackles, as well as dungeons, which was common treatment of the mentally ill. In colonial America, public health and human services for children, the sick, and poor were formally developed. During the 1800s Dorothea Dix and Jane Hull worked to develop better conditions for the mentally ill via improved living conditions and access to services. Twentieth-century developments in mental health include work by Sigmund Freud, who set the stage for modern-day counseling with psychoanalytic approach to treating emotionally ill people. By the 1940s Gerald Caplan and Eric Lindemann developed crisis intervention counseling. In 1946, President Harry Truman signed the National Mental Health Act, which called for a National Institute of Mental Health (NIMH) to conduct research and reduce mental illness. As a result of this, the NIMH was formally established in 1949. In 1963, the Mental Retardation Facilities and Community Mental Health Centers Construction Act, also known as the Community Mental Health Act, was passed. The act provided the first federal funding for developing a network of community-based mental health centers required to provide crisis management and suicide prevention to formerly hospitalized patients. In 1979, the National Alliance for the Mentally Ill (NAMI) was founded to provide support, education, and advocacy for people with mental illness. Today NAMI is the largest grassroots mental health organization. In 1996, the Mental Health Parity Act was passed; and it hinders employee-sponsored group health insurance plans from limiting coverage for mental health benefits on a greater basis than other benefits. In 2008, the Paul Wellstone and Pete Domenici Mental Health Parity and Addiction Equity Act was signed into law; and it requires group health plans (those with 50 or more insured employees) that offer coverage for mental illness and substance use disorders to provide these benefits at the same levels as medical benefits. The federal parity law today is primarily enforced in part by the Department of Labor and the Department of Health and Human Services. This program is administered under the Bureau of Justice Assistance within the Department of Justice (DOJ) to address the issues to incarceration among those who are mentally ill including provision of case management and relapse-based prevention services. Acts like these assist in reducing the practice of unequal health treatment and improving access to equitable coverage for those that are in need of these services.

More recent mental health-related efforts include state lottery monies used to fund community-based mental health centers and the implementation of the federal Mental Health Courts Programs in 2000. This program is administered under the Bureau of Justice Assistance within the DOJ to address the issues to incarceration among those who are mentally ill including provision of case management and relapse-based prevention services. Other federal legislation includes the New Freedom Act, established by President George W. Bush, designed to identify and remove barriers to community living for individuals with mental disabilities and long-term mental illness. Other developments include Health

Maintenance Organizations (HMOs) to provide mental health services that cost less.

In addition, the Department of Health and Human Services (DHHS) houses programs that are designed to protect and intervene when citizen's mental well-being, due to physical abuse or neglect, are threatened. For example, within the DHHS is the Administration for Children and Families, which is designed to promote the well-being of children, individuals, and communities. One program they oversee is the Children's Bureau. Among its focus areas are child abuse and neglect. The Child Abuse and Prevention Treatment Act, signed into law in 1974 and reauthorized most recently in 2003, was designed to provide federal funding to U.S. states in support of prevention, assessment, investigation, prosecution, and treatment of children who have been abused or neglected. This act is based on the concept of parens patriae, a legal terms that holds that government has a role in protecting children and in intervening when parents fail to provide safety and proper care. States and localities are also principally responsible for protecting seniors and vulnerable adults from abuse and providing victims with protective services and treatment. They commonly do so through APS agencies. The National Adult Protective Services Association (NAPSA) is a national nonprofit organization formed in 1989 to provide state and local APS programs. It currently includes members in all 50 states, as well as the U.S. Virgin Islands and Guam. As noted on the NAPSA website, its mission is "to improve the quality and availability of protective services for adults with disabilities and older persons who are abused, neglected, or exploited and are unable to protect their own interests. NAPSA is the national voice of APS programs, professionals and clients, and advocates on their behalf with national policy makers" (National Adult Protective Services Association, n.d.). As of 2011, NAPSA began operations of the first national adult protective resource center designed to serve as the main knowledge base for the fight against elder abuse. This resource center was funded through a grant provided by the Administration on Aging (AoA) and several other partners, such as the National Association of States United for Aging and Disabilities (NASUAD), the National Committee for the Prevention of Elder Abuse (NCPEA), and the National Council on Crime and Delinquency (NCCD).

One other example of how government supports individual's well-being is via the Substance Abuse and Mental Health Services Administration (SAMHSA), created in 1992, to improve behavioral health services and specifically reduce the impact of substance abuse and mental illness. As noted on the SAMHSA website, "The rise of the consumer and recovery movements has made it possible for individuals to be active participants in their own care and recovery. The development of community coalitions, trauma-informed care, treatment drug courts, and offender re-entry programs has helped communities and families build resilience and helped people get the assistance they need" (Clay, 2012). With the Paul Wellstone and Pete Domenici Mental Health Parity and Addiction Equity Act, discussed earlier, equity is also in place to protect those with substance use disorders. Interestingly, in 1995, SAMHSA hired its first consumer affairs staff person to develop and implement consumer information activities, consumer-operated networks, and antistigma efforts related to Community Mental Health Services (CMHS).

Correctional Facilities

Early colonial criminal law responded to deviant behavior in very aggressive ways. Punishments were typically public and involved either quick, corporal torture, or sustained disgrace. Whipping posts, branding, and water torture were commonly used. As the social welfare system was developing in the United States, headway was also being made in the criminal justice system. By the late 1800s, the 19th-century view of punishment was rejected; in 1876, one of the nation's first prisons, the Elmira Reformatory, was opened. Elmira reformed the prison system to include rewards, individualized treatment, and parole procedures. It set the foundation for today that even prisoners have rights. Today, federal and state laws govern the establishment and administration of prisons, as well as certain rights that prisoners. For example, inmates are entitled to a minimum standard of living and are protected under the eighth amendment of the constitution from cruel and unusual punishment. Under the 14th amendment, inmates are also entitled to due process and equal protection, that is, they are protected against unequal treatment due to race, religion, sex, or ethnicity. Additionally, in response to a growing body of literature linking poverty and criminal behavior, the prison system has evolved to include focus on more humanistic approaches to rehabilitation, including the development of probation and parole programs oftentimes with provisions of mental health intervention programs. For example, housed in

> Interestingly, while violent crime in the United States has steadily declined since the early 1990s, the prison and jail populations have increased. In fact, the United States has the highest prison population as compared to other countries worldwide.

the DOJ, the U.S. Parole Commission was designed to "promote Public Safety and strive for justice and fairness in the exercise of its authority to release, revoke and supervise offenders under its jurisdiction" (U.S. Department of Justice, 2013). Their vision is to do this while providing ". . .fair and equal treatment with dignity and respect for offenders, staff, and the community . . ." (U.S. Department of Justice, 2013). Also within the DOJ is the Department of Corrections. Among its goals are to effectively manage prisons, jails, and correction programs, as well as maximize safety of the public and increase law-abiding behavior among offenders. The DOJ also oversees the Office of Juvenile Justice and Delinquency Prevention (OJJDP) which supports states' and communities' efforts to develop programs for the needs of juvenile offenders and their families. Today, in addition to counseling offenders, there exists a restorative justice program, a community program that brings together offenders, victims, and families for conflict resolution. These programs are designed to not only assist the victims and their families in the healing process, but also to support the offenders in their rehabilitation. Correctional counselors today are encouraged to have multicultural competence training in order to effectively work with people of various socioeconomic and cultural backgrounds.

Specialized Education Programs

Efforts throughout history to improve education are noteworthy. In early U.S. history, Horace Mann, known as the "great equalizer" worked with Thomas Jefferson to create systematic education programs for everyone, marking the beginning of government-funded school systems. Education efforts progressed during the 1950s and 1960s when Martin Luther King Jr., and other civil rights leaders, campaigned for equal educational rights for minorities and for the end of desegregation. In time, state governments also began passing legislation for funding for programs for learning-disabled and developmentally challenged children. The Education for All Handicapped Children Act of 1975 requires, among other things, that children with special needs receive all support services necessary to achieve their academic success. Additionally, the current McKinney–Vento Education for the Homeless Children and Youth Program aids children in managing their academic challenges due to being homeless. The act ensures, for example, the inclusion of homeless children into mainstream classrooms, provision of transportation, and designation of a liaison to identify and support homeless children.

Some facts about black history:

Four college students from North Carolina Agricultural and Technical College sat down at an all-white Woolworth lunch counter in Greensboro, North Carolina, and politely refused to leave until they were served. Although they were not served lunch, their sit-in was a landmark moment in the Civil Rights Movement that sparked a wave of sit-ins and economic boycotts of Woolworth stores nationwide. Six months later, the students were served lunch.

1968. The first Black Studies Department in the United States is established at San Francisco State University.

1998. The University of California Berkeley establishes the first U.S. doctoral program called African Diaspora Studies.

Source: Gladen-Rockler, Naomi. (2006). Black history of College Education. Retrieved from http://suite101.com

---

Melanie Horn Mallers

See also: Activism; Administration on Aging (AoA); Community Mental Health Centers (CMHC) Act; Department of Health and Human Services (HHS); Department of Justice (DOJ); Department of Labor (DOL); Dix, Dorothea; Federal Deposit Insurance Corporation (FDIC); King, Martin Luther Jr.; Mann, Horace; McKinney–Vento Homeless Assistance Act; Ombuds Offices; Public Safety; Roosevelt, Franklin D.; Securities Exchange Commission (SEC); Social Security; Social Welfare; Supplemental Nutrition Assistance Program (SNAP)

References and Additional Readings

Clay, R. (2012). Celebrating two decades of progress in the behavioral health field. *SAMHSA News, 20*(2). Retrieved from http://www.samhsa.gov/samhsa newsletter/Volume_20_Number_2/twentieth-anniversary.aspx

Correction History. (n.d.). Elmira. Retrieved from http://www.correctionhistory .org/html/chronicl/docs2day/elmira.html

Department of Health and Human Services. (2003). The Child Abuse Prevention and Treatment Act. Retrieved from http://www.acf.hhs.gov/sites/default/ files/cb/capta2003.pdf

Department of Justice. (2013a). About the commission. Retrieved from http:// www.justice.gov/uspc/about-comm.html

Department of Justice. (2013b). Agencies. Retrieved from http://www.justice .gov/agencies/

Kanel, K. (2008). *An overview of human services.* Boston, MA: Houghton Mifflin.

Legal Information Institute. (2012). Prisoner's rights. Retrieved from http://www .law.cornell.edu/wex/prisoners_rights

Martin, M. E. (2011). *Introduction to human services. Through the eyes of practice settings* (2nd ed.). Boston, MA: Allyn and Bacon.

National Adult Protective Services Association. (n.d.). About NAPSA. Retrieved from http://www.apsnetwork.org/About/about.htm

Social Welfare

Any governmental program designed to insulate citizens from economic hardships may be referred to as a social welfare program. The most common types of programs provide benefits to the elderly, ill, or disabled persons, dependent survivors, mothers, the unemployed, the work-injured, and to lower-wealth families.

In 2010, the number of Americans living in poverty has increased to 46 million. There are currently 46,681,833 people in the United States on food stamps. Food stamp spending is at a record high of $75.7 billion in the last fiscal year. This number has doubled in the last 4 years. Medicaid enrollment has reached 50 million people as unemployment rates have skyrocketed.

Dating back as far as Greek and Roman societies, financial assistance was given to those who met certain requirements and had a need. The earliest forms of social welfare were religiously affiliated, churches being the main provider through the Middle Ages. As industrialism gained momentum, national and local governments, and many private agencies began to take over the charitable duties that churches had begun.

The German government, in 1883, first introduced a modern government-supported social welfare program providing health insurance for all workers (not just the poor), and later accident insurance and retirement pensions. In the next 50 years, the interplay between socialist theory and organized labor groups created some social welfare system in most of the world's countries. Methods of financing and management and the depth and breadth of types of assistance vary among countries. Britain and the Scandinavian countries over time developed the broadest range of social welfare programs, including, but not limited to, free medical care. A broad and diverse reach of programs in these areas of the world has earned them the moniker "welfare states."

Terms and their relative meaning are not consistent across countries. Each country's needs and the ability to address them determine each society's range of welfare services. In some countries a distinction is made between "social services" (health care and education servingthe general population) and "welfare services"(aid directed to specific vulnerable people and groups).

County- and state-administered programs backed by U.S. federal government funding dominate the American Social Welfare landscape. Local governments directly administer some programs while private agencies, contracted by public entities deliver other services. The Department of Health and Human Services is the federal agency from which most federal funds flow. Each state has a counterpart that further disseminates funds regionally and locally.

In the United States, a series of economic programs introduced in the first term of Franklin D. Roosevelt's presidency implemented between 1933 and 1936 focused on restabilizing and recovering America after the Great Depression. An important piece was the Social Security Act of 1935 that provided federally funded financial assistance to the elderly, the blind, and dependent children during the Great Depression in order to give assistance to those who had little or no income. The Social Security Act also provided funds for states to administer Unemployment Insurance Programs. The national elderly pension system that is now known as "Social Security" began building its pool of funds through taxation in 1938 and the first pension payments were made in 1940. A small piece of the Social Security Act also provided Aid to Dependent Children (ADC).

The next great expansion came during the Johnson administration in the 1960s, when Medicare, Medicaid, public housing, and other programs were established by way of Social Security Act amendments. Medicare is one of the better-known provisions, providing medical insurance to older citizens. Medicaid, a medical coverage program for lower-income families, is also well recognized. Between 1967 and 1977 some programs were shifted under the control of other agencies and a philosophical shift was made toward improving quality of life rather than to the traditional focus on poverty abatement. Problems of child abuse, alcohol, and drug dependence, and mental health services have garnered increasing support in recent decades.

For over 100 years, until 1996, when a Republican Congress passed, and Democratic President Bill Clinton signed, a sweeping welfare reform law that dramatically reduced the number of participants receiving support in various federal welfare programs, the social welfare system in America has increased in scope, depth, and volume of service provision. The reform ushered in changes in many states' systems, including introducing time limits for how long a person or family can receive benefits, work requirements known as "workfare," and more stringent standards for qualifying for disability payments known as supplemental security income.

The Clinton administration's efforts to curb long-term dependence on welfare programs was perceived as a response to the criticism of individuals potentially abusing the system designed to recover them by purposefully not applying for jobs, having more children just to get more aid, and staying unmarried to qualify for benefits in larger amounts or for longer periods of time. While the Clinton reforms cut the population on welfare significantly, the reforms remain open to criticism that they did little long term to improve independence since poverty rates have not changed. The "workfare" or "welfare to work" program requirements have become increasingly rigorous through 2005.

Federally linked programs, employer-, and state-sponsored welfare programs and hybrid approaches that dovetail public, voluntary, and private resources in addressing social problems have grown to fill service gaps and to provide a mix of service options. Most states offer basic aid such as health care, food stamps, child care assistance, unemployment, cash aid, and housing assistance. In general, eligibility for a welfare program is determined based on income, size of the family, and any crisis situation such as medical emergencies, pregnancy, homelessness, or unemployment.

Megan J. O'Neil

See also: Americans with Disabilities Act (ADA); Community Mental Health Centers (CMHC) Act; Health and Healthcare; Medicaid; Medicare; Poverty Guidelines; Public Safety; Social Security; Social Services; Roosevelt, Franklin D.

References and Additional Readings

Almanac of Policy Issues. (2012). Social welfare. Retrieved from http://www.policyalmanac.org/social_welfare/

Encyclopædia Britannica Online. (2012a). Social welfare program. Retrieved from http://www.britannica.com/EBchecked/topic/551539/social-welfare-program

Encyclopædia Britannica Online. (2012b). Social service. Retrieved from http://www.britannica.com/EBchecked/topic/551426/social-service

InfoPlease. (2012). Social welfare: Modern welfare programs. Retrieved from http://www.infoplease.com/ce6/society/A0861156.html#ixzz208t86Vpd

New Deal 2: Analysis online. (2012). Impact of New Deal Programs on welfare. Retrieved from http://www.analysisonline.org/site/aoarticle_display.asp?issue_id=8&sec_id=140002434&news_id=140003198

Welfare Information. (2012). Retrieved from http://www.welfareinfo.org/

Society of Consumer Affairs Professionals (SOCAP)

The changing needs and expectations of consumers back in 1973 helped to create the Society of Consumer Affairs Professionals in Business (SOCAP). The Council of Better Business Bureaus (CBBB) in Anaheim, California, assisted in the initial formation by authorizing various resources to help establish the SOCAP. At the foundation meeting on May 24, 1973, Jack

Scarcliff, director of consumer affairs for Firestone Tire and Rubber Company, was elected SOCAP's first president. To celebrate the establishment of the organization, an unsolicited letter was sent to Chairman pro tempore Scarcliff from Lewis A. Engman, chairman, Federal Trade Commission, on April 27, 1973, stating, "I am looking forward to the Society's contributions . . . to insure fair market practices and to encourage free and open communications among consumers, business and government."

Society of Consumer Affairs Professionals (SOCAP)

Purpose:

- Founded in 1973, the Society of Consumer Affairs Professionals in Business (SOCAP International) represents a thriving global profession of best-in-class customer care experts across all industries. SOCAP is a member-driven organization committed to promoting customer care and customer engagement as a competitive advantage in business. The association's members include vice presidents, directors, managers, and supervisors of customer care and consumer affairs from top Fortune/Forbes 1000 companies as well as hundreds of business partner organizations. SOCAP provides the educational tools and professional resources to help its members drive business transformation within their companies. Additionally, SOCAP's exclusive network gives members access to thousands of customer care experts across the globe.

SOCAP International Mission:

- Develop experts who drive successful business strategy through customer engagement.

SOCAP International Vision:

- SOCAP International promotes an integrated approach to customer care that drives successful business strategy and elevates its global community of customer relationship experts.

SOCAP International Core Values:

- Customer care must be integral to the execution of successful business strategy.
- Education and networking are fundamental to developing effective customer relationship experts.
- Member involvement is essential to the success of the association.
- Collaboration and partnerships play an important role in SOCAP's strategy.
- Fiscal responsibility is vital to long-term success.
- Strategic diversity and inclusion build connected, diverse, and integrated networks of customer relationship experts.

Source: Society of Consumer Affairs Professionals. (n.d.) Purpose & mission. Retrieved from http://www.socap.org

Prior to the establishment of SOCAP, the early 1970s was full of unrest and change was occurring at all levels in the United States. Computer technology was emerging as an important business tool, and plastic credit cards were becoming popular with consumers; both were moving businesses further and further from direct consumer contact. Quality Control or Customer Relations departments did not exist and were also not a top priority item for most corporate owners.

Consumers, on the other hand at this time, were dissatisfied with businesses that ignored their rights and interests. They believed their voices were not being heard at any level of government. After much frustration, dissatisfied consumers began targeting business owners about defective products and unfair business practices. There were many product recalls during this time.

Despite all of the disruptions and challenges that existed between the various business and consumer groups, there were considerable opportunities and a desire to learn and share information at all levels. Networking began to develop between individuals and groups. There was a need to foster the integrity of business in its dealings with consumers, promote harmonious relationships between business and government and consumers, and advance the consumer affairs profession. So, in 1973, with the establishment of SOCAP, businesses became more receptive to consumer demands and encouraged exciting business transformations within their companies.

Corporate executives soon realized that the "new consumerism" movement was here to stay. SOCAP was renamed to the Society of Consumer Affairs Professionals—International and was comprised of professionals who had the skills to put themselves "in the customer's shoes." These new consumer affairs professionals came from home economics, quality assurance, marketing, advertising, public relations, customer relations, and public affairs disciplines. Many businesses liked the idea of a "consumer affairs" person and many offices of consumer affairs were created throughout the United States.

Purpose

According to SOCAP, the association is a member-driven organization committed to promoting customer care and customer engagement as a competitive advantage in business. The membership is comprised of numerous business organizations from top executives to managers and supervisors of customer care and consumer affairs. SOCAP provides the educational tools, networking, and professional development resources to help its members succeed in this global economy.

A new vision and mission were adopted at the 2007 Annual Business Meeting in Palm Springs, California. The SOCAP International mission, vision, and core value, as written on their website, are as follows: "Develop experts who drive successful business strategy through customer engagement"; "SOCAP International promotes an integrated approach to customer care that drives successful business strategy and elevates its global community of customer relationship experts"; and "Customer care must be integral to the execution of successful business strategy. Education and networking are fundamental to developing effective customer relationship experts. Member involvement is essential to the success of the association. Collaboration and partnerships play an important role in SOCAPs Strategy."

Over time, SOCAP has built a large membership of consumer affairs officials, presidents, and vice presidents of Fortune 500 companies, and many international business partner relationships providing expertise to all members. A professional research journal titled *Consumer Relationship Management* provides current topics in globalization, sourcing strategies, and technological developments. This journal also highlights retail and direct issues.

Sandra L. Poirier

See also: Activism; Better Business Bureau (BBB)

References and Additional Readings

Society of Consumer Affairs Professionals. (2013a). History of SOCAP & profession. Retrieved from http://www.socap.org/LinkClick.aspx?fileticket=6E8xMX4SAnw%3d&tabid=92

Society of Consumer Affairs Professionals. (2013b). SOCAP International: Customer relationship experts. Retrieved from http://www.socap.org/

Society of Consumer Affairs Professionals. (2013c). History. Retrieved from http://www.socap.org/CustomerCareProfession/HistoryOfSOCAPProfession.aspx

Supplemental Nutrition Assistance Program (SNAP)

History

The first *Food Stamp Program* was established May 16, 1939, and is the brain-child of Secretary of Agriculture Henry Wallace and the program's first Administrator, Milo Perkins. The purpose was to help needy families during the Depression era. The program allowed people on relief to buy orange stamps in an amount equivalent to their normal daily food expenditures. For each dollar's worth of orange stamps purchased, 50 cents worth of blue stamps was received. In turn, the blue stamps were used to purchase department-approved surplus food; the orange stamps could buy any food. In spring of 1943, the program ended. The program known today started in 1961 as a pilot program; receiving permanent authorization in 1964.

The Food Research and Action Center (FRAC):

- conducts research to document the extent of hunger, its impact, and effective solutions;
- seeks improved federal, state, and local public policies that will reduce hunger and malnutrition;
- monitors the implementation of laws and serves as a watchdog of programs;
- provides coordination, training, technical assistance, and support on nutrition and antipoverty issues to a nationwide network of advocates, service providers, food banks, program administrators and participants, and policy makers; and
- conducts public information campaigns to help promote changes in attitude and policies.

FRAC also leads efforts to "identify and communicate the connections among poverty, hunger, inadequate resources for healthy diets, and obesity among low-income people. FRAC also is working to broaden the reach of and improve the quality of public nutrition programs as a strategy to reduce obesity."

Source: FRAC. (n.d.) About FRAC. Retrieved from http://frac.org/about/

SNAP is the name chosen for the Federal Food Stamp Program as of October 1, 2009, the acronym for Supplemental Nutrition Assistance Program. The program reflects changes that serve to better meet the needs of clients with a focus on nutrition and increase in the amount of benefits. In 2010, SNAP was provided to 40.2 million low-income people via electronic benefits similar to a debit card. Recipients may purchase food at businesses authorized by the USDA. The USDA administers SNAP via the Food and Nutrition Services (FNS) at the federal level while state agencies administer the program at state and local levels, determining eligibility and distribution of benefits.

According to the USDA website, SNAP households must meet eligibility requirements and provide information and verification about the household; U.S. citizens and some permanent aliens may qualify. The Welfare Reform Act of 1996 ended eligibility for many legal immigrants, but, Congress restored some benefits to select children and elderly immigrants. The Welfare Reform Act also placed time limits on benefits for those individuals who are able bodied, childless, and/or unemployed. Other details described on the website include participation, deductions, rules, and more, as given next.

Who Can Participate in SNAP?

There are several considerations to determine SNAP eligibility. Consumers are eligible if they meet several conditions. Households can have no more than $2,000 in countable resources. Countable resources include bank accounts, for example. If one person in the household is age 60 or older, then $3,000 is allowed. Houses are not counted; automobiles are determined at the state level. Currently, 39 states exclude the value of the vehicle entirely while 11 states totally exclude the value of at least one vehicle per household. Gross monthly income of the household must be 130 percent or less of the federal poverty guidelines which is equivalent to $2,389 per month for a family of four in most locations; gross income includes cash payments. Net monthly income must be 100 percent or less

Table 33 Income descriptions

Households have to meet income tests unless all members are receiving TANF, SSI, or in some places general assistance. Most households must meet both the gross and net income tests, but a household with an elderly person or a person who is receiving certain types of disability payments only has to meet the net income test. Households, except those noted, that have income over the amounts listed below cannot get SNAP benefits.
(October 1, 2012, through September 30, 2013)

Household size	Gross monthly income(130% of poverty)	Net monthly income (100% of poverty)
1	$1,211	$ 931
2	1,640	1,261
3	2,069	1,591
4	2,498	1,921
5	2,927	2,251
6	3,356	2,581
7	3,785	2,911
8	4,214	3,241
Each additional member	+429	+330

Gross income means a household's total, nonexcluded income, before any deductions have been made. Net income means gross income minus allowable deductions.

• SNAP gross and net income limits are higher in Alaska and Hawaii.

Source: Supplemental Nutrition Assistance Program. (2012). Eligibility. Retrieved from http://www.fns.usda.gov/snap/applicant_recipients/eligibility.htm

of federal poverty guidelines which is equivalent to $1,838 per month for a household of four in most places. Net income is calculated by adding the household's gross income and then taking a number of approved deductions for child care, shelter costs, and other expenses. If an elderly or disabled person is part of the household, they are required to pass the net income test. Adults who are able bodied must meet stated work requirements, and all members of a household must provide a social security number. One exception of note is in California where SSI recipients are ineligible for SNAP benefits due to the fact that they receive state benefits in SSI benefits in place of SNAP benefits (Table 33).

What Deductions Are Allowed?

Standard deductions exists for all households including (1) a 20 percent earned income deduction, (2) dependent care costs (when required for work, training, or education), (3) legally owed child support payments, (4) medical costs for elderly and disabled people, and (5) an excess shelter cost deduction.

Medical deductions more than $35/month may be deducted for elderly and disabled members except when an insurance company or other party pays them. Special diet costs are not allowable medical costs. Proof is required.

Shelter deductions equaling more than half of the households' income (following other deductions) constitute the shelter deduction. Allowable costs include payments for rent or mortgage, taxes, interest, and utilities.

Benefits, Allotments, Allowances, and Restrictions

To request benefits, consumers may fill out an application at a local SNAP office, and may do so on the same day. Applications are not mailed, but some states allow applicants to apply online. Benefits are based on the Thrifty Food Plan, a low-cost diet plan based on the National Academy of Sciences' Recommended Dietary Allowances and food choices of low-income households. The average monthly benefit of SNAP is $101 per person and $227 per household (Wolkwitz and Trippe, 2009).

SNAP benefits can be used to purchase foods to eat, such as breads and cereals, fruits and vegetables, meats, fish, and poultry, dairy products and seeds and plants SNAP benefits do not cover items such as beer, wine, liquor, cigarettes, or tobacco, as well as nonfood items such as pet food, soap, paper products, vitamins, medicines, food consumed in the store, and hot foods.

Special Rules for Elderly and Disabled

According to the USDA (2012), a person is elderly if he or she is 60 or older and a person is considered to be disabled for SNAP benefits if he/she:

- Receives federal disability or blindness payments under the Social Security Act including SSI;
- Receives sate disability or blindness payments based on SSI rules;
- Receives a disability retirement benefit from a governmental agency because of a disability consider permanent;
- Receives an annuity under the Railroad Retirement Act and is eligible for Medicare or is considered to be disabled based on SSI rules;
- Is a veteran who is 100 percent disabled, permanently housebound, or in need of regular aid and attendance; or
- Is a surviving spouse or child of a veteran who is receiving VA benefits and is considered to be permanently disabled.

National SNAP participation as of 2012 was 46,681,833 people, which was 1,336,360 people higher than the previous year. Economists explain that this increase is obviously in part due to high unemployment and underemployment rates in the country. Luckily, SNAP has made a difference for several struggling families and their children. Reports from the U.S. Census Bureau and the Department of Agriculture (USDA) indicate that SNAP benefits, if counted as income, would have brought 3.9 million Americans (including 1.7 million children) above the 2011 poverty guidelines. More work needs to be done, especially given that many people who qualify for SNAP, unfortunately underutilize their benefits.

Diane E. Carson

See also: Department of Agriculture (USDA); Department of Veterans Affairs (VA); Medicaid; Poverty Guidelines; Social Security; Social Welfare

References and Additional Readings

American Journal of Agricultural Economics. (2013). The new normal: The supplemental nutrition assistance program (SNAP). *American Journal of Agricultural Economics, 95*(2), 325–331.

Brownell, K. D., & Ludwig, D. S. (2011). The supplemental nutrition assistance program, soda, and USDA policy. Who benefits? *The Journal of the American Medical Association, 306*(12), 1370–1371.

Department of Agriculture. (2012). Supplemental nutrition assistance program: Special rules for the elderly and disabled. Retrieved from http://www.fns.usda.gov/snap/applicant_recipients/eligibility.htm#special

Leftin, J., & Wolkwitz, K. (2009). *Trends in supplemental nutrition assistance program participation rates: 2000 to 2007.* Washington, DC: Mathematica Policy Research.

Wolkwitz, K., & Trippe, C. (2009). Characteristics of supplemental nutrition assistance program households: Fiscal year 2008. Retrieved from http://www.fns.usda.gov/fns/research.htm

Supreme Court

The U.S. Supreme Court is the highest court in the United States. It has both appellate jurisdiction over the various lower federal courts, as well as original jurisdiction over a certain subset of cases. Article III, Section 2 of the constitution allows for the Supreme Court to have original jurisdiction over cases between states, cases involving ambassadors and other public ministers, as well as cases of admiralty and maritime law. Further appellate jurisdiction is provided to the Supreme Court under various statutes passed by Congress, including 28 U.S.C. § 1251 et seq. As to the creation of the Supreme Court, Article III, Section 1 of the constitution decreed that creation, along with "inferior Courts as Congress may" create from over time. Congress created the Supreme Court in the Judiciary Act of September 24, 1787, and the court was organized approximately three years later on February 2, 1790.

The court's makeup consists of nine justices, whose number can be set by the U.S. Congress. It consists of a chief justice of the United States, and eight associate justices (as currently set by Congress, at 28 U.S.C. § 1). The president of the United States possesses the power to nominate justices to the Supreme Court. The president makes these appointments with the "advice and consent" of the U.S. Senate. Supreme Court justices have life tenure and may resign at their pleasure; justices may only be removed by the impeachment process outlined in the constitution. Additionally, Congress provided the Supreme Court with the power to prescribe rules of procedure to be followed by the lower federal courts.

The court receives more than 10,000 petitions per year, which are known as "petitions for certiorari" or "cert. petitions." These cert. petitions generally explain to the Supreme Court why it should take the case on its merits and why the lower court's decision is in conflict with Supreme Court jurisprudence or other lower courts' jurisprudence. The

Justices of the U.S. Supreme Court in 2009. Seated (left to right) are Clarence Thomas, Antonin Scalia, John G. Roberts, Anthony Kennedy, and Ruth Bader Ginsburg. Standing (left to right) are Sonia Sotomayor, Stephen Breyer, Samuel Alito, and Elena Kagan. (Steve Petteway, Collection of the Supreme Court of the United States)

justices of the Supreme Court discuss these cert. petitions on a periodic basis and may vote to grant or deny review of the case. The Supreme Court will grant certiorari if it decides to review the merits of the case as discussed in the cert. petition. Given that the Supreme Court receives many cert. petitions each year, only about one in each 100 cert. petitions is granted. If the Supreme Court denies the granting of certiorari in a case, the decision of the lower court will stand. After the Supreme Court grants certiorari, the parties are required to provide a merits brief to the court. These merits brief explain to the court the reason why the party should win its case on the merits. Nonparties may file an "amicus curiae" brief, also known as a "Friend of the Court" brief. Such a brief may be filed by an entity, person, or group that desires to provide the Supreme Court with its own perspective on the issue facing the court.

The Supreme Court's term is generally divided into "sittings," wherein the justices hear cases and deliver opinions, and "recesses," wherein the justices write opinions and consider other business of the court. These sittings

The Federal Judicial Center is the second part of the Judicial arm of government. Created in 1967 by Congress, it is an education and research agency aimed at improving the judicial administration of the federal courts.

Their duties are broadly defined as follows:

- Conducting and promoting orientation and continuing education and training for federal judges, court employees, and others;
- Developing recommendations about the operation and study of the federal courts;
- Conducting and promoting research on federal judicial procedures, court operations, and history.

Oversight of the Federal Justice Center's Board is provided by the chief justice of the United States. Other members of the board include the director of the administrative office of the U.S. courts, and seven judges elected by the judicial conference. The board appoints the center's director and deputy director. The director appoints center staff.

In addition to maintaining a judicial administration library, the education division creates and distributes educational programs and services for judges and court personnel while the research division empirically investigates the courts' management and processes. The center also houses a Federal Judicial History Office and an International Judicial Relations Office. According to the 2011 annual report, the center produced 17 new videos, broadcasted 51 programs, published or updated 18 documents, completed 15 major research projects, provided 290 in-person programs for court employees, developed 2 e-learning programs, distributed over 34,000 publications, conducted an institute for history teachers, and coordinated 555 briefings in the last year, among other regular duties.

For more information, see http://www.fjc.gov/

and recesses generally alternate in two-week intervals. By law, the term of the Supreme Court begins on the first Monday in October and lasts until the first Monday in October of the next year.

The Supreme Court has heard numerous cases involving certain aspects of consumer protection. Some of these are listed in Table 34.

Once the Supreme Court has ruled, the ruling becomes the "law of the land." The lower federal courts (and generally, the state courts) are required to follow the precedent provided by the Supreme Court. The Supreme

Table 34 Examples of cases involving consumer protection

- Interpretation of provisions of the Credit Repair Organization Act (Compucredit Corporation v. Greenwood, 2012)

- Concurrent federal and state court jurisdiction for violations of Telephone Consumer Protection Act, 2012

- Violations of the Fair Debt Collection Practices Act (*Jerman v. Carlisle, McNellie, Rini, Kramer & Ulrich LPA*, 2010)

- The Bankruptcy Abuse Prevention and Consumer Protection Act (*Milavetz, Gallop & Milavetz v. United States*, 2010)

- Preemption of state law by Federal Aviation Administration Authorization Act (*Rowe v. New Hampshire Motor Transport Association*, 2008)

- Preemption of farmer's claims by Federal Insecticide, Fungicide and Rodenticide Act (*Bate v. Dow Agrosciences LLC*, 2005)

- Preemption of state law cigarette advertising laws by the Federal Cigarette Labeling and Advertising Act (*Lorillard Tobacco Company v. Reilly*, 2001)

- Indecent and obscene programming and the Cable Television Consumer Protection and Competition Act (*Denver Area Educational Telecommunications Consortium v. Federal Communications Commission*, 1996)

- Carrying of local broadcasting television stations on cable television systems, in accordance with the Cable Television Consumer Protection and Competition Act (*Turner Broadcasting System v. Federal Communications Commission*, 1997; *Turner Broadcasting System v. Federal Communications Commission*, 1994; *Turner Broadcasting System v. Federal Communications Commission*, 1993)

- Fair Debt Collection Practices Act application to attorneys (*Heintz v. Jenkins*, 1995)

- Control of hydroelectric power project water flow rates (*California v. Federal Energy Regulatory Commission*, 1990)

- Unreasonable restraint of trade (*Federal Trade Commission v. Indiana Federation of Dentists*, 1986)

- Enforcement of cease and desist orders by the Federal Trade Commission (*Federal Trade Commission v. Universal-Rundle Corporation*, 1967; *St. Regis Paper Company v. United States*, 1961; *Federal Trade Commission v. National Casualty Company*, 1958; *Jacob Siegel Company v. Federal Trade Commission*, 1946; *Federal Trade Commission v. Raladam Company*, 1942; *Federal Trade Commission v. Bunte Brothers*, 1941; *Federal Trade Commission v. Royal Milling Company*, 1933; *Federal Trade Commission v. Eastman Kodak Company*, 1927)

- Violations of Federal Trade Commission Act (*Atlantic Refining Company v. Federal Trade Commission*, 1965)

- General review of orders made by the Federal Trade Commission (based on material deceptive advertising practices) (*Federal Trade Com mission v. Colgate-Palmolive Company*, 1965)

- Violations of the Fur Products Labeling Act (*Federal Trade Commission v. Mandel Brothers*, 1959)

(Continued)

Table 34 *(Continued)*

- Violations of price fixing and price discrimination (*Federal Trade Commission v. Ruberoid Company*, 1952)

- Violations of the Food, Drug and Cosmetic Act (*United States v. Urbuteit*, 1948)

- Environmental Impact Statements (*Flint Ridge Development Company v. Scenic Rivers Association of Oklahoma*, 1976)

- Unfair methods of competition (*Federal Trade Commission v. Motion Picture Advertising Service Company*, 1953; *Federal Trade Commission v. Standard Education Society*, 1937; *Federal Trade Commission v. Algoma Lumber Company*, 1934; *Federal Trade Commission v. R.F. Keppel*, 1934)

- Improper advertising by businesses (*Federal Trade Commission v. Klesner*, 1929)

Court generally reviews administrative agency decisions with deference, in accordance with current case law. Accordingly, given the small number of merits cases that actually reach the Supreme Court, most consumer protection laws are not reviewed by the Supreme Court.

Stewart M. Young

See also: Arbitration; Congress; Mediation; Small Claims Court

References and Additional Readings

Abraham, H.J. (2008). *Justices, presidents, and senators: A history of the US Supreme Court appointments from Washington to Bush II*. Lanham, MD: Rowman & Littlefield Publishers.

Fairman, C. (2009). History of the Supreme Court of the United States. *Reconstruction and Reunion, 6*, 1864–88.

McCloskey, R.G. (2010). *The American Supreme Court*. University of Chicago Press.

Supreme Court Official. (2013). Retrieved from http://www.supremecourt.gov/

Toobin, J. (2008). *The nine: Inside the secret world of the Supreme Court*. Anchor.

Surgeon General

The surgeon general's office started in 1798 when Congress established the precursor to the current U.S. Public Health Service. The U.S. Marine Hospital Service provided health care to merchant seamen; it was later reorganized as a national hospital with centralized administration from the supervising surgeon. The title of supervising surgeon later morphed into the current title of surgeon general. In 1871, the first surgeon general was appointed, Dr. John Woodworth. In 1889, Congress formally acknowledged the system by deeming them the Commissioned Corps, following military protocol. The Public Health Service now employs not only doctors, but a cadre of other health professionals.

Under President Johnson, reporting of the Public Health Service was moved from the secretary of Health, Education, and Welfare to the assistant secretary for Health, becoming a principal deputy to that Assistant Secretary. Later, in 1977, the two positions were combined into one, but were separated again just four years later. The Office of the Surgeon General was reestablished under the Office of the Assistant Secretary of Health in 1987 when C. Everett Koop was the surgeon general. He was an

---

The Surgeon General Announces Winners Of Healthy App Challenge:

Four mobile phone applications have been chosen as winners of the Healthy App Challenge launched by Surgeon General Regina Benjamin, MD, to promote her vision for a healthy and fit nation.

Descriptions of the Winning Applications

Lose It! helps individuals achieve their nutrition and physical activity goals by setting daily calorie budgets that require users to record their food intake and physical activity. It also has a feature that allows users to invite their friends to view their logs on Facebook.

GoodGuide makes it easy for individuals to get the information they need about their food, personal care, and household products to help make healthy choices. It has a bar code scanner that allows users to scan products while they shop to get this information.

Fooducate helps you make healthy food choices. When shopping you can scan the product bar code for a quick read on the nutritional values and additional information such as nutrients and additives; the app can offer healthier alternatives and compare two products side-by-side.

Healthy Habits recognizes that good health is not just about staying active and eating well, but is also reliant on other factors, such as sleeping well and mental health. This application addresses health issues such as smoking, wearing sunscreen, and reducing stress by tracking the user's success and goals.

All the winning and recommended apps are available for free download.

Sources: http://sghealthyapps.challenge.gov, http://www.surgeongeneral.gov/, and http://www.surgeongeneral.gov/news/2012/02/pr20120217.html

active and public surgeon general, seeking to enhance all aspects of the office, including, most notably, recruitment of women and minorities. The surgeon general still reports to the assistant secretary for Health under the Department of Health and Human Services.

The duties of the surgeon general, as cited on the website include:

Some quick facts about the Surgeon General History:

Of the 18 past doctors serving as the United States' Surgeon General, Dr. Regina Benjamin is the third woman, the first was Dr. Antonio Novella in 1990; the second was Dr. Jocelyn Elders in 1993.

- Protect and advance the health of the nation through educating the public, advocating for effective disease prevention and health promotion programs and activities, and, providing a highly recognized symbol of national commitment to protecting and improving the public's health;

- Articulate scientifically based health policy analysis and advice to the president and the Secretary of Health and Human Services (HHS) on the full range of critical public health, medical, and health system issues facing the nation;

- Provide leadership in promoting special departmental health initiatives, for example, tobacco and HIV prevention efforts, with other governmental and nongovernmental entities, both domestically and internationally;

- Administer the U.S. Public Health Service (PHS) Commissioned Corps, which is a uniquely expert, diverse, flexible, and committed career force of public health professionals who can respond to both current and long-term health needs of the nation;

- Provide leadership and management oversight for PHS Commissioned Corps involvement in Departmental emergency preparedness and response activities;

- Elevate the quality of public health practice in the professional disciplines through the advancement of appropriate standards and research priorities; and

- Fulfill statutory and customary departmental representational functions on a wide variety of federal boards and governing bodies of non-federal health organizations, including the Board of Regents of the Uniformed Services University of the Health Sciences, the National Library of Medicine, the Armed Forces Institute of Pathology, the

Association of Military Surgeons of the United States, and the American Medical Association.

Today, "America's Doctor" oversees more than 6,500 offices active in the military and allotted to the various agencies inside and outside the Public Health Service. The current initiatives, according to the website are tobacco: preventing use; healthy and fit nation: eating properly and exercising; prevention: better health; support breast feeding: removing obstacles; family Health History: learn the family background. These and other activities on behalf of the nation serve to keep America in good health.

Wendy Reiboldt

See also: Centers for Disease Control and Prevention (CDC); Department of Health and Human Services (HHS); Health and Healthcare; Social Services; Social Welfare

References and Additional Readings

Benjamin, R. M. (2010). The surgeon general's vision for a healthy and fit nation. *Public Health Report, 125*(4), 514–515.

Jackson, Y., et al. (2002). Summary of the 2000 surgeon general's listening session: Toward a national action plan on overweight and obesity. *Obesity Research, 10,* 1299–1305.

Surgeon General. (2013). Retrieved from http://www.surgeongeneral.gov

T

Telemarketing Laws

Complaint statistics are proof that telemarketing—unsolicited calls to consumers to sell a product or service—is hugely unpopular among American households. Consistently bad timing, excessive persistence, aggressive sales tactics and sometimes-unethical business practices—in some cases, fraud—have resulted in an outcry from beleaguered consumers and have made the telemarketing industry a target for consumer advocates, lawmakers, and regulators. The outcome has been the enactment of state and federal legislations designed to protect consumers from unwanted sales calls, and an ongoing effort to curb and control the telemarketing industry.

The first law aimed at moderating the U.S. telemarketing industry was the Telephone Consumer Protection Act of 1991 (TCPA). Among other things, the TCPA severely restricted use of the technology—automated dialing systems, prerecorded messages, or artificial voice systems, and facsimile—that enables telemarketers to reach thousands of consumers per minute with minimal cost. It also required telemarketers to comply with a consumer's do-not-call (DNC) request made during the call by maintaining an internal DNC list.

In 1994, President Clinton signed the Telemarketing and Consumer Fraud and Abuse Prevention Act (Telemarketing Act), aimed chiefly at combating abusive and deceptive telemarketing practices and fraud. Under the Telemarketing Act, the Federal Trade Commission (FTC) adopted the Telemarketing Sales Rule, which went into effect December 31,1995. Among other things, the rule required telemarketers to make specific disclosures of material information such as the name of the seller and the purpose of the call, the total charge, and any refund policy; set payment restrictions for the sale of certain goods and services; prohibited misrepresentations; and limited telemarketing calls to certain hours of the day.

The FTC amended the rule in 2003, 2008, and 2010. The amendment made in 2003 called for the establishment of the National Do Not Call Registry a centralized "opt out" list of consumer numbers managed and maintained by the FTC. Telemarketers are required to access the registry and remove any of the registered numbers from their internal call lists. All telemarketers calling American consumers are bound by registry rules, even if they are calling from outside the United States or across state lines. As of 2011, the list held more than 200 million phone numbers.

Originally, consumers had to renew their listing on the National Do Not Call Registry if they wanted it to remain in effect beyond five years. But the Do-Not-Call Improvement Act of 2007 made registration permanent unless the consumer cancels. Since the TCPA prohibits calls to cell phones made with artificial voices or recordings, it is not necessary for consumers to register their wireless phone numbers, though they are allowed to. Similarly, fax numbers do not need to be registered since the Junk Fax Prevention Act of 2005 prohibits the sending of unsolicited faxes.

In August 2008, the FTC again amended the rule, this time barring prerecorded telemarketing messages unless a consumer has previously agreed in writing to accept such calls from the seller. In other words, having an existing business relationship no longer would suffice as consent to receive automated messages. It also required companies to begin transmitting caller ID information (call-back number and name) and to connect all calls to live representatives within two seconds of the consumer's greeting. And it sets limits on the number of "abandoned" calls allowed—calls that go unanswered by a sales representative and result in "dead air"—and imposed a fine for exceeding the limit.

In August 2010, the FTC further amended the rule to address deceptive and abusive practices associated with debt relief services. Most notably, debt settlement companies were now prohibited from misrepresenting the quality or success of their services to consumers or from charging any upfront fees.

States have passed their own telemarketing laws as well, which often are stricter or more far reaching than federal laws. Some states also require telemarketers to register or obtain a license before making sales calls to residents of the state. In some cases, there may be laws that apply to callers selling specific products or services. For example, California requires that certain financial services firms be registered with the state before doing any telemarketing. As of 2011, some states still maintained their own individual (statewide) do-not-call lists, while most others had discontinued their lists and merged them with the federal list.

The Federal Trade Commission (FTC), the Federal Communications Commission (FCC), and state attorneys general are empowered to enforce compliance with federal telemarketing laws. In many cases, there is more than one route to enforcement. First, the consumer who is called in violation of the law may have the right to sue in a local court and collect damages. Also, states may initiate civil action against violators on behalf of state residents. In addition, the FTC and FCC, acting on complaints filed with the agencies, can assess significant penalties against violators. Cases may also be brought in federal courts. Despite the fact that the crimes can be difficult to investigate and prosecute, the FTC and the U.S. Department of Justice have prevailed in hundreds of cases, resulting in significant fines, restitution to victims and orders to cease telemarketing operations. Several major undercover operations during the 1990s, including Operation Disconnect and Operation Senior Sentinel, resulted in federal criminal charges and had a lasting impact on the fight against telemarketing fraud.

While many legitimate telemarketing firms comply with the ever-increasing legal restrictions on telemarketing, the industry has not always accepted regulations without a fight. For example, telemarketers challenged the TCPA's constitutionality soon after it was enacted. Two cases, *Moser v. FCC* and *Destination Ventures Ltd. v. FCC* effectively settled the issue in 1995, finding in favor of the FCC. Challenges to the National Do Not Call Registry threatened to delay its implementation, but again the court upheld the constitutionality of the law.

When unsuccessful in having telemarketing laws overturned, some telemarketers have attempted to skirt the rules. One tactic is to cloak the call as a survey, when the real intention is to get the consumer to agree to a follow-up call, during which the sales pitch is made. This can work because the DNC registry does not prohibit calls from, among other sources, businesses with which the consumer has an existing relationship (unless the consumer specifically asks the company not to call again); surveyors or pollsters; nonprofit organizations; and political organizations. In another challenge to the established rules, the Mobile Informational Call Act, introduced to Congress in September 2011, proposed federal legislation that would have allowed companies to place "robo calls" (automated calls) to wireless phones without consumers' permission—currently illegal under the TCPA. Passage of the act would have changed the definition of "prior express consent" to include anytime a person provides a telephone number as a means of contact. Consumer advocates argued that such a change would make cell phones fair game to debt collectors as well as cost consumers wireless minutes. Facing overwhelming opposition, the cosponsors of the bill withdrew it from further consideration in December 2011.

The public plays a central role in the enforcement of telemarketing laws, the apprehension of telemarketing fraudsters, and the shaping of new legislation. Consumers are urged to report telemarketing fraud and violations of the law to the FTC, their state attorney general and, in cases where the call was prohibited because the consumer's number was on the National DNC list, the Do Not Call Registry. Consumer complaints are entered into the

Consumer Sentinel Network, a secure database managed by the FTC and made available to hundreds of civil and criminal law enforcement agencies in the United States and abroad.

Future telemarketing legislation is likely to be aimed at closing loopholes, broadening restrictions in response to new technology, and responding to new challenges to consumer privacy. For example, one group, Citizens for Civil Discourse, has attempted to establish a National Political Do Not Contact Registry to help reduce election campaign calls, which do not have to comply with National Do Not Call Registry rules.

Monica Steinisch

See also: Federal Communications Commission (FCC); Federal Trade Commission (FTC); Frauds and Scams; National Do Not Call Registry; Privacy: Offline

References and Additional Readings

Electronic Privacy Information Center. (n.d.).Telemarketing and the telephone consumer protection act (TCPA). Privacy. Retrieved from http://epic.org/privacy/telemarketing/

Federal Trade Commission Bureau of Consumer Protection. (2011). Complying with the telemarketing sales rule. Retrieved from http://business.ftc.gov/documents/bus27-complying-telemarketing-sales-rule

Federal Bureau of Investigation. (2010). A byte out of history: Turning the tables on telemarketing fraud. Retrieved from http://www.fbi.gov/news/stories/2010/december/telemarketing_120810/telemarketing_120810

Federal Trade Commission. (2011). *National do not call registry data book FY 2011.* Washington, DC: FTC.

Federal Trade Commission. (2007). Facts for consumers: Straight talk about telemarketing. Retrieved from http://www.ftc.gov/bcp/edu/pubs/consumer/telemarketing/tel15.shtm

Privacy Rights Clearinghouse. (2011). Telemarketing: how to have a quiet evening at home. Retrieved from https://www.privacyrights.org/fs/fs5-tmkt.htm

Telephone Assistance Programs

Telephone service is crucial for all consumers, not only those with financial means. It provides access to emergency services, allows employees and job seekers to be contacted for work, makes government services and resources more accessible, and provides a lifeline to friends and family. For many low-income households, however, full-price telephone service is an unaffordable luxury—something that is financially out of reach after paying for necessities such as housing, food, and electricity.

In an effort to level the playing field, the U.S. government passed the Communications Act of 1934, which established the policy of providing access to a baseline level of telecommunications service for all American consumers. The Telecommunications Act of 1996 (1996 Telecom Act) expanded the scope of universal service to include reasonable pricing—in other words, access to service not only in the sense of availability, but affordability as well.

To meet the mandates of the 1996 Telecom Act, the U.S. Federal Communications Commission (FCC) created the Universal Service Fund (USF), a "pool" that collects mandatory contributions from all telecommunication companies (a percentage of the company's revenues) to be used to preserve and advance universal service (i.e., pay for a federal subsidy program that reduces the cost of establishing and maintaining phone service for low-income Americans). The FCC administers the USF with the help of the Universal Service Administrative Company (USAC), an independent nonprofit corporation created in 1997 by the FCC to manage the distribution of USF money in a way that is impartial and that is most likely to achieve the universal service goals set by the Telecom Act.

Lifeline Assistance (Lifeline) is the federal/state subsidy program, paid for with money collected by the USF, that offers discounted basic (local) monthly telephone service. Link-Up America (Link-Up) is the other half of the same subsidy program, providing discounts on service connection (or activation, in the case of wireless service) for customers who don't already have service, and giving them the option to pay the remaining connection or activation fee not waived under Link-Up on a deferred schedule, interest free. The actual out-of-pocket initial and monthly costs to the consumer vary by carrier, with established minimum and maximum discounts.

Lifeline and Link-Up are available to consumers in every state, territory, commonwealth, and on tribal lands. It's up to each state's public utilities commission to decide whether to adopt the federal Lifeline/Link-Up program or institute its own program. In some cases, state programs may offer additional benefits for consumers, such as the waiver of certain fees and taxes or a second Lifeline connection for the deaf or hearing impaired.

Regardless of whether the program is federal or state, applicants must qualify under either annual household income guidelines (these vary by state, but generally income must be at or below 135 percent of the federal poverty guidelines) or under program participation guidelines. Qualifying low-income assistance programs include, for example, Medicaid, Food Stamps, and SSI. Broader eligibility criteria and greater discounts exist for Enhanced Lifeline/Link-Up, which is the program for subscribers who live on Tribal Lands.

All eligible telecommunications carriers (ETCs), as designated by the FCC, are required to advertise the availability of the Lifeline and Link-Up programs in ways that are most likely to reach eligible households within their designated service areas. Specific FCC recommendations include public service announcements, information booths, and notices posted at locations most likely to be trafficked by eligible populations. In its 2010 National Broadband Plan, the FCC recommended that state social service agencies take a more active role in consumer outreach and in qualifying eligible consumers.

Subscribership data for 2010 reveals that approximately two-thirds (19.1 million) of 29.3 eligible households were *not* participating in Lifeline/Link-Up. Despite the relatively low participation rate, 26 states and Washington, D.C., had increases in subscribership in 2010. That growth is attributed to the relatively recent addition of prepaid wireless companies in the subsidy programs. Such a conclusion is warranted given findings that almost three out of five Americans (58 percent) would choose a cell phone over a landline phone, and that the cell phone is particularly important to blue collar, minority, less educated, and low-income segments of the population. Perceived delays in certifying wireless service providers may be stalling growth in Lifeline subscribership numbers. As of 2011, some states were still not offering a prepaid wireless Lifeline option. It can be expected that Lifeline participation will increase as more eligible households have, and are aware of, the option to use their subsidies for wireless service.

In its 2010 National Broadband Plan, the FCC recommended increasing broadband (Internet service) adoption among low-income Americans through reforms of the Lifeline and Link-Up programs. In an open letter to the FCC in April 2011, a coalition of 12 consumer advocacy organizations urged the FCC to hasten the expansion of Lifeline and Link-Up to support broadband services. As of late 2011, Lifeline/Link-Up subsidies were not yet available for broadband service.

Monica Steinisch

See also: Activism; Federal Communications Commission (FCC); Poverty Guidelines; Social Services; Social Welfare

References and Additional Readings

Federal Communications Commission. (2010). Broadband action agenda. Retrieved from http://www.broadband.gov/plan/broadband-action-agenda.html

Gallant, P. (2011). *Discounted telephone service for low income consumers.* Washington, DC: Universal Service Administrative Company.

Sullivan, N.P. (2008). *Cell phones provide significant economic gains for low-income American households.* Washington, DC: New Millennium Research Council.

73rd Congress of the U.S. 1934. (n.d.). Communications act of 1934. 61 Statute at large 101. Retrieved from http://www.criminalgovernment.com/docs/61StatL101/ComAct34.html

104th Congress of the U.S. 1996. (n.d.). Telecommunications act of 1996 (1996 telecom act). Reports. Retrieved from http://transition.fcc.gov/Reports/tcom1996.txt

Title Pawn Loans

A Title Pawn Loan, or title loan, is simply borrowing against the equity in one's vehicle. The lender is a specialized firm not affiliated with a depository institution or other conventional lender. The loans can range from small amounts borrowed for short periods of time, for example, $300 for 30 days, to much larger and longer term loans, for example, $5,000 for a year or more. Also, like some other types of subprime lending, the borrower may want or need to roll the loan over at maturity. These loans do not require a credit check nor much documentation as they are, in essence, collateralized by the title to the borrower's vehicle. Consequently, one large appeal of these loans is that the loan amount can be obtained very quickly, typically in a day or two—much faster than, say, a conventional bank loan. Basically, all that is needed for the loan to proceed is for the lender to examine the vehicle to verify that it is worth enough more than the desired loan amount and to determine if the borrower has a clear title to the vehicle.

As the primary focus is "emergency loans" for financially constrained consumers this activity is related to payday lending and, of course, traditional pawnshop borrowing. The target market for this product is low- and moderate-income consumers and, especially, those with bad credit or no credit. As a practical matter, the borrowing amount may be limited by state statute—to date there is no federal regulation, although the Consumer Financial Protection Bureau is considering the matter. In the absence of a regulation, the loan ceiling is determined by the expected wholesale value of the vehicle adjusted for asset recovery costs such as repossession costs and auto auction fees. Adding another wrinkle, some firms will lend even if there is an outstanding bank loan on the vehicle as long as it is "close" to payoff—potentially adding another interested party in the event of default.

For the consumer, the biggest appeal of the loan is also possibly its biggest downside. The ability to offer this product is due in large part to the existence of a very liquid, well-defined secondary market for used vehicles nationally, even for old, high mileage, or damaged vehicles. Further, for many financially constrained consumers their vehicle may be their only or their best asset available to secure a loan of any significance. Thus, this gives them a mechanism to quickly obtain a meaningful amount of funds. At the same time, the possibility of losing one's vehicle is at best problematic as it puts at risk the consumer's access to employment, health care, and other essentials—and the consequences are especially serious for borrowers living in rural areas.

Although some lenders ask for proof of income, one selling point of the loan is that it is not specifically tied to employment or ability to repay. For example, it is marketed to those who are self-employed and so may be unable to verify their income. Arguably, as the lender does not consider such lending basics as the debt-to-income ratio or employment stability, this arrangement creates a potential consumer discipline problem as the customer attempts to service the debt—which threatens to place a consumer already in a bad financial situation in an even worse one.

State regulations vary widely. Some states, for example, Connecticut, Maryland, and Maine, have banned title loans outright, while others have capped either the maximum interest that can be charged or the loan size. For instance, in Illinois the maximum loan amount is $4,000 while in Mississippi and Tennessee it is $2,500. As a practical matter, structuring the transaction as a "pawn" allows the lender to exploit a looser usury ceiling than would apply if it was classified as a consumer loan. For instance, in Georgia, the maximum permissible interest rate on a title pawn loan is 25 percent per month for the first three months of the loan after which it is capped at 12.5 percent per month—thus, loans up to three months can legally carry a 300 percent annual percentage interest rate. By contrast, Georgia has a consumer loan usury ceiling of 16 percent on loans under $3,000 and 5 percent per month for larger loans.

The ability to charge high rates on reasonably well-collateralized loans has fueled dramatic growth in this industry. A significant portion of the loan providers are independent operators and, of those, a fair number are offering title loans as an offshoot of being engaged in a related subprime financing business, be that payday lending, pawn brokerage, or something else. At the same time, there are several companies putting a national face on the industry. For instance, Title Max (www.titlemax.biz) is a privately owned company based in Savannah, Georgia, which started with one store in 1998 and currently has over 700 stores in 12 states—primarily in the southeastern United States. They will lend up to $5,000 requiring only to see the car, a clear title, official ID, and proof of income; they claim the process takes less than thirty minutes. Another operation is Max Cash Title Loans (www.maxcashtitleloans.com) headquartered in Wood Dale, Illinois, which is a referral network established in 2008 in California. Working with multiple lenders, they represent over 400 locations in 22 states and claim to offer loans up to $30,000. A third is Auto Cash USA (www.auto cashusa.com) in Tucson, Arizona, which represents a network of lenders at over 500 locations.

Michael H. Anderson

See also: Consumer Financial Protection Bureau (CFPB); Pawn Shops; Payday Lending; Usury

References and Additional Readings

Bouman, F. J., & Houtman, R. (1988). Pawnbroking as an instrument of rural banking in the Third World. *Economic Development and Cultural Change, 37*(1), 69–89.

Martin, N., & Adams, O. (2012). Grand theft auto loans: Repossession and demographic realities in title lending. *Missouri Law Review, 77*, 41.

TransUnion. *See* Credit Reporting Agencies

Truth in Lending Act

The Truth in Lending Act was passed in 1968, effective July 1969. The purpose of the act was and is to promote the informed use of consumer credit for both open and closed end accounts. By requiring lenders to use a consistent format when disclosing terms and costs, giving consumers the right to cancel certain transactions, imposing limitations on certain home equity plans and prohibiting certain acts or practices, consumers are able to compare products to make an informed decision. In addition to requiring uniform disclosure of information, the act also guards consumers against inaccurate and unfair credit billing and credit card practices, provides consumers with rescission rights, provides a rate cap on certain secured loans for dwellings, imposes limitations on home equity lines of credit and certain closed-end home mortgages, and delineates and prohibits unfair or deceptive mortgage-lending practices

Since 1969, numerous amendments have been made to the act intending to simplify and further protect consumers. Regulation of the act was initially authorized by the Federal Reserve Board but was transferred to the Consumer Finance Protection Bureau in July 2011.

The Truth in Lending Act is implemented by Regulation Z, which is organized into seven subparts. Subpart A provides a general explanation of the coverage terms. Coverage applies to individuals or businesses who extend credit and meet the following conditions: (1) credit is offered or extended to consumers, (2) extension of the credit is practiced on a regular basis, (3) the credit is subject to a finance charge or payable by a written agreement, and (4) the credit will be used primarily for personal, family, or household purposes.

Rules for disclosure on open-ended lines of credit, which include credit card accounts and home equity lines of credit, are described in subpart B. Additionally, rules for resolving billing errors, calculating annual percentage rates, method used to determine fees and credit balances, and advertising open-ended credit are addressed. Specifically, subpart B requires creditors to make clear and conspicuous disclosure in a form the consumer is able to keep (in writing). The disclosure needs to identify the grace period and no finance charges are to be incurred during that time. If a creditor imposes a rate or fee change, a 45-day notice of the changes in terms is required. A reduction in finance charges, change in rates effective on a previously disclosed date (i.e., promotional offer), and changes due to court agreements or terms related to hardship agreements do not require a 45-day notice. For significant changes, consumers have the right to reject within 60 days.

Closed-end accounts, fixed-term loans, and disclosures are addressed in subpart C. Similar to open-ended accounts, disclosures need to include information about treatment of credit balances, interest rate calculations, right of rescission, nonrequirements, and advertising. Calculation of loan balances and annual percentage rates for closed-ended accounts are not as straight forward as for open-ended accounts. Factors that complicate the process are accuracy in regard to regular and irregular transactions, construction loans in which disbursement of the loan is made in more than one transaction, calculation using a 360-day or 365-day year, and variable rate loans.

Subpart D addresses the creditor's role in maintaining records of compliance for the rules and regulations on open and closed-end credit accounts and requires creditors to set caps on variable rate transactions secured by a consumer's dwelling. Subpart E contains special rules for high-cost mortgages, reverse mortgages, and higher priced mortgage loans. Required disclosures include identifying limitations for loans that have rules and fees above specified amounts and total loan cost rate for reverse mortgage transactions.

Subparts F and G address special rules that apply to private education loans and credit card accounts offered to college students. Disclosures need to include information about interest rates, fees, and default or late payment costs, repayment terms, cost estimate, eligibility, alternatives to private education loans, and the rights of consumers.

Table 35 Truth in Lending Act: Amendments made since implementation

- Fair Credit Billing Act of 1974: This act established procedures to protect consumer from billing errors on credit card transactions on open-end credit accounts and limited consumer liability for unauthorized use of credit card.

- Consumer Leasing Act of 1976: Leasers are required to provide the terms and cost for any product consumers can acquire through a lease.

- Truth in Lending Simplification and Reform Act of 1980: Creditors were required to make restitution and adjustments to accounts if the annual percentage rate or finance charges were inaccurately disclosed.

- Fair Credit and Charge Card Disclosure Act of 1988: To help consumer comparison shop, credit card issuers are required to provide information about the APR, method for calculating rates and monthly balance, all fees, and grace period. Annual disclosure of this information is also required if the account has an annual fee.

- Home Equity Loan Consumer Protection Act of 1988: Lenders of home equity loans are prohibited from changing the terms of a loan after a contract has been signed, calling loans before the due date. Long-term interest rates need to be identified in promotional material and variable rates need to be linked to an index. To keep the consumer informed, all information is to be disclosed before any fees are paid.

- Home Ownership and Equity Protection Act of 1994: Protects consumers from predatory lending in the subprime market. Imposes new disclosure requirement and substantive limitation on close-end mortgage loans with fee rates that are above a certain percentage or amount and includes requirements to assist consumers in comparing costs and other considerations for reverse mortgages.

- Economic Growth and Regulation Paperwork Reduction Act of 1996: Requires financial institutions to review their regulations at least once every 10 years in order to simplify and improve disclosures related to credit transactions.

- Electronic Signatures in Global and National Commerce Act of 2000: Facilitate the use of electronic signatures and records as legal contracts and provides guidelines for delivery of electronic disclosures.

- Mortgage Disclosure Improvement Act of 2008: Amended the Home Ownership and Equity Protection Act of 1994 and were prompted by the crash in the subprime mortgage lending market. Requires lenders to give consumers transaction-specific costs after application and before payment of any fees.

- Credit Card Accountability, Responsibility and Disclosure (CARD) Act of 2009: Designed to protect consumers from credit card company practices. The act addresses more advanced notice of rate hikes, statements must be sent 21 days in advance of the due date, disclosure of rate increases, fee restrictions, restrictions for consumers under the age of 21, end of double-cycle billing, fairer payment allocation, gift card protection, and retroactive rate increases. This act is intended to help consumers reduce credit card debt and better manage their credit expenses.

The act also addresses the right of rescission for consumer, which allows time (three days) to review the credit agreement and cost disclosure and to reconsider using their home as security for the credit. The right of rescission also extends the right to rescind for up to three years if the creditor fails to provide certain disclosures. This provision protects the consumer from high-rate predatory home equity mortgages.

The Truth in Lending Act, when it was originally written and implemented, was easily misinterpreted because the meaning of the disclosures was not uniformly understood. In 1977, the act received an over-haul of the closed-end credit and recommended changes to open-end credit provision. Table 35 provides a list of the amendments that have been made to the act since implementation.

The purpose of the Truth in Lending Act is to require creditors to provide disclosures to consumers about open- and closed-end credit account so decisions are made with accurate information. Credit terms are to be disclosed in a manner that is understandable for the consumer. Consistent terms and explanation of rates are required. This will protect the consumer from unfair and inaccurate credit billing and credit practices. As the credit industry evolves, the need for continual amendments to the Truth in Lending Act will be necessary.

Lorna Saboe-Wounded Head

See also: Banking; CARD Act; Consumer Financial Protection Bureau (CFPB); Federal Reserve; FDIC (Federal Deposit Insurance Commission); Home Ownership and Equity Protection Act (HOEPA); Mortgages

References and Additional Readings

Abbott, B. A. (1980). More battles ahead to simplify truth in lending. *Banking Journal*, 72(5), 100.

Anonymous. (1998). The truth in lending act means what it says: You only have 3 years to rescind. *The Army Lawyer*, DA PAM 27-50-309, 28–30.Brandel, R. E.,

Bureau of Consumer Protection. (2001). Electronic signatures in global and national commerce act. Washington, DC: Federal Trade Commission.

Federal Deposit Insurance Corporation. (2012a). FDIC laws, regulations, related acts: consumer protection.

Federal Deposit Insurance Corporation. (2012b). FDIC law, regulations, relate acts: administrative enforcement of the truth in lending act—restitution.

Federal Financial Institutions Examination Council. (2005). Economic growth and regulatory paperwork reduction act or 1996 (EGRPRA). Federal Financial Institutions Examination Council.

Federal Reserve. (2009). Regulation Z Truth in Lending. Retrieved from http://www.federalreserve.gov/boarddocs/supmanual/cch/til.pdf

Federal Reserve System. (2009). Rules and regulations: Truth in lending. *Federal Register*, 74(95).

Garman, T. E. (2006). *Consumer economic issues in America* (9th ed.). Mason, OH: Thomson Publishing.

Moore, T., & Asay, S. (2008). *Family resource management.* Thousand Oaks, CA: Sage Publications.

Whitehouse.gov. (2009). *Fact sheet: Reforms to protect American credit card holders.* Office of Press Secretary, Washington, DC.

U

Underwriters Laboratories

Underwriters Laboratories (UL) has been testing products and materials since 1894 to ensure the safety and security of the products that ultimately improves people's lives and their environment. This is an independent, nonprofit product organization that is accredited by the U.S. Occupational Safety and Health Administration (OSHA) (under the U.S. Department of Labor), the American National Standards Institute (ANSI), and the Standards Council of Canada (SCC). Through its testing procedures UL has become the world's leading safety certification organization, producing "21 billion UL Marks . . . on 72,000 manufacturers' products each year" and ensuring the safety of "customers in 98 counties (Underwriters Laboratories, 2012, n.p.).

Utilizing safety engineering methodologies UL targets five major business areas: product safety, environment, life and health, knowledge services, and verification services. The UL standards ensure product safety by testing components, system performance, assessment of environmental sustainability, and evaluation of innovative technologies, which include renewable energies, food and water products, and recycling systems. These standards provide a benchmark so that businesses and consumers alike can be informed about the safety of these products.

These UL standards are important because technological developments and research create a dynamic environment for goods, products, and materials, which require new standards to be constantly developed and existing standards to be modified. The revising process implements scientific methodologies in conjunction with the expertise of stakeholders to establish a consensus for these standards.

History

In 1894, UL was founded as the Underwriters' Electrical Bureau, and published its first Standard for safety in 1903, "Tin Clad Fire Doors," and continued to focus on fire safety. In 1920s and 1930s, UL certified the first refrigerator, automatic dishwasher, and washing machine. Following the

World War II, UL focused on testing of radio, television, and personal computers. During the 1980s and 1990s, the scope of UL included certification of alternative energy technologies, sanitation of products used in the food industry, and anticounterfeiting operations. By now UL has become the worldwide-known testing organization with 97 UL inspection centers and 63 UL-specialized technology resources satellite locations.

Services of UL

There are many ways by which UL provides services to individual organizations, industries, and ultimately to the general public. The UL certification process begins when a manufacturer submits samples of a product for testing and evaluation in order to obtain the distinct UL Mark. If the product passes its standards and requirements, the product becomes UL-certified and UL authorizes the company to place the UL Mark on the product. Follow-up services that include periodic product audits and occasional retesting at UL laboratories, must be scheduled before the product can be released with the UL Mark. This way the safety of certified products is continuingly monitored and tested, and the certification of products is up-to-date.

The UL Mark is unique and recognized worldwide for its stamp of approval. Only after passing rigorous testing and evaluation procedures can a product carry the UL Mark. Most certified products carry the UL Mark on the product itself, but for some products the mark is placed on the packaging material or the box.

The UL uses different marks and labels in Asia, Europe, Latin American, North America, and the UL family of companies. Smaller parts that can be used on larger products or systems are marked with different set of UL marks. In addition, UL prevents counterfeiting and the resulting danger to customers by collecting counterfeit occurrences and alerting the law enforcement agencies. UL takes counterfeiting operations very seriously because it creates safety hazards for customers and diminishes the integrity of the UL reputation. The ultimate goal here is to protect the lives of customers throughout the world.

Aside from certification, testing, and evaluation processes, UL also serves a global education source and an informer of hazardous products. UL often publishes warnings and alerts of unauthorized UL Marks that could be unsafe or hazardous to customers. For example, UL recently issued warnings regarding "counterfeit UL Marks on electronic ballast for computers, potentially hazardous portable cabinet light in household products, and unauthorized UL Marks on triangular LED lights sold as electrical components."

The UL's educational activities also include research and development, which often involves consumer and manufacturer surveys on attitudes and views of product safety. A recent UL study found that global perceptions with food safety were generally negative and dissatisfied. Seventy-six percent of consumers worldwide have difficulty finding product safety information and 69 percent of these consumers indicated that the country of origin is more important that a product's ingredients. The same study confirmed that consumers fear contracting food-borne illnesses from fresh foods and blamed the performance of food manufacturers. While this may be the case, only 2 percent of these companies believe they are not meeting food safety expectations. Evidently, there is a disjunction in the perceptions of food safety performance for the manufacturers and the consumers. Thus, UL plays a major role in ensuring product safety so that consumers and businesses can be confident in the products they use or produce.

Industries

UL provides testing and certification for a variety of industries. These include appliances and HVAC/R, building materials, chemicals, energy, food, health sciences, high tech, life safety and security, lighting, power and controls, drinking water, and water and cable industries.

Household appliances such as heating, air-conditioning, and refrigeration were discovered in the 1920s and 1930s, and UL tests and evaluates the potential hazards of these products to ensure safety. The UL collaborates with architects, regulatory authorities, manufacturers, insurers, building owners, and retailers to test and analyze building materials to ensure safety, and minimize fire danger from building materials. Also, UL investigates the safety of several chemical and energy products such as alternative fuels, energy verification, gas and oil, large batteries, power generation, renewable energies, motor and generator, and semiconductor manufacturing.

In recent years, UL increased its efforts to service the technology industry working together with installers and manufacturers to safeguard new product safety for its consumers. High-tech product categories include batteries, components, and devices, computing and peripherals, consumer electronics, lasers, power supplies, printed wiring boards (PWB), and telecom products. UL offers certification, validation, testing, and advisory and training for lighting products, power and control industry products, to promote product safety. Power and control product categories include electric/electronic control equipment, electric vehicles and infrastructure, functional safety, industrial control equipment, robots and robotic equipment, semiconductor manufacturing, smart grid, and smart meters. In addition, the UL's 30 Standards for Safety is used to validate wire and cable products in more than 70 different product categories that includes safety protocol, performance, quality assurance, unannounced factory follow-up inspections, and follow-up testing services. Product categories in this group include appliance wiring materials, local area network (LAN) cable, lead and cadmium, and optical fiber cable.

Health and Healthcare-Related Services

The UL has a variety of functions in the healthcare industry. Specifically, the UL's involvement in health care includes research and development, diagnostic testing, therapy and treatment applications, and maintenance service of healthcare products. Some of the products that undergo stringent testing and certification include medical and in-vitro diagnostic devices, laboratory, and test and measurement equipment, and emergency call systems.

The UL has a major role in testing the effectiveness and safety of medical equipment in the United States even though the Federal Drug Administration (FDA) has the authority to approve or disapprove these requests. Most medical equipment manufacturers obtain the fire and safety reports from UL in order to receive FDA approval. The healthcare providers also heavily rely on UL services and products, based on their long reputable history, ensuring the safety of patients and providers who utilize the equipment. For instance the emergency call systems in hospitals, long-term care facilities, and patient homes must be effective and dependable, ultimately assisting in the well-being of patients and efficiency in the healthcare system. The system needs to function each time when there is an emergency.

The global market is continuing to grow and prosper. UL has expanded to about 100 other countries, and established local representatives in the various countries to assess the quality of equipment, and ensure the integrity of the UL certification. By providing local representatives, more medical device manufacturers will seek the reliability and consistency of UL certifications in order to enter the European Union market. According to the UL, the European market is a major avenue for medical device research and development.

Another important line of business for UL is to ensure food safety and to safeguard the global food supply chain through food safety efforts and education, which include food handling, processing, and associated food products to promote health and well-being worldwide. Recent UL efforts have focused on food safety culture and training that ensures the functionality of the different levels of the food workforce collaborate effectively. The food safety product standards are discussed in the entry "Food, Drug, and Cosmetic Act (FD&C Act)."

Tony Sinay

See also: Centers for Disease Control and Prevention (CDC); Consumer Product Safety Commission (CPSC); Department of Labor (DOL); Food and Drug Administration (FDA); Health and Healthcare

References and Additional Readings

Flynn, D. (2012). World consumers doubtful about food safety, UL study finds. *Food Safety News.* Retrieved from http://www.foodsafetynews.com/2012/02/consumers-doubtful-about-food-safety-ul-study-finds/

Underwriters Laboratories. (2012). What we do. Retrieved from www.ul.com.

Unemployment Insurance

Unemployment insurance (UI) was established by the Social Security Act of 1935 in response to the Great Depression, which caused millions of people to lose their jobs. The UI program was developed to accomplish two main goals: (1) to provide temporary and partial wage replacement to workers who lose their job due to no fault of their own and (2) to assist in stabilizing the economy during recessions.

"UI is a $156 billion (2010) federal–state program that temporarily and partially replaces the lost earnings of workers who become unemployed through no fault of their own and who are ready, willing, and able to work" (U.S. Government Accountability Office, 2012, 1). Typically, regular state UI programs provide benefits to unemployed workers for up to 26 weeks. However, in response to the economic recession that began in December 2007, Congress and the states have temporarily extended the period of time that unemployed workers are eligible to receive UI benefits to up to 73 weeks, though the maximum number of weeks is determined by each state.

One important function of UI is to help stabilize the economy during recessions. When the economy thrives, revenue directed to state unemployment insurance programs rises as a result of increased tax revenues.

Program spending typically falls during this time as fewer workers are un-employed and rely on benefits. This creates a surplus of funds available to use for benefit payments in the event of an economic downturn. In contrast, income from tax revenue falls while benefit spending rises during economic downturns as more workers lose their jobs and file for UI benefits.

UI benefits paid to unemployed workers offset a worker's lost earnings by allowing them to buy necessary good and services. This injects money back into the economy. Studies indicate that during periods of high unem-ployment every $1 paid out in UI benefits helps expand the nation's output by about $2 worth of goods and services.

Unemployment insurance is financed by federal taxes under the Federal Unemployment Tax Act (FUTA) and state payroll taxes under the State Unemployment Tax Act (SUTA).

While the U.S. Department of Labor oversees the program, each of the 53 states and territories (the 50 states plus the District of Columbia, Puerto Rico, and the Virgin Islands) administer their own version of the unemploy-ment insurance program within the general rules of federal law, which re-sults in 53 different programs.

Employers pay taxes into the unemployment insurance system on their employees' behalf and those funds provide partial wage replacement to eligible workers if they lose their jobs. According to the FUTA, covered employers must pay a 6.2 percent gross federal tax on the first $7,000 paid annually to each of its employees. However, employers in states with UI programs that comply with certain federal regulations and with no out-standing federal loans may receive a federal credit of up to 5.6 percentage points, or 90 percent of the FUTA rate, which can bring the effective federal unemployment tax rate down to just 0.6 percent. If a state does not comply with federal regulations, employers operating within that state may lose a portion or all of their federal unemployment tax credit, resulting in a higher tax rate.

For those workers who earn more than the $7,000 taxable wage ceiling, the FUTA tax is $42 per worker per year ($7,000 × 0.6 percent), or 2 cents per hour for a full-time worker. Federal revenue finances the administra-tion of the system, half the federal–state Extended Benefits (EB) program, and a federal trust fund account for state loans.

The State Unemployment Tax is predominately placed on employers to finance regular unemployment insurance benefits and the state share of the EB program. States must adopt a taxable wage base at least as high as the federal level, $7,000, or are at risk of losing the 5.6 percentage point tax credit offered by the federal government. In 2012, state ceilings on taxable earnings range from the $7,000 FUTA ceiling (three states and Puerto Rico) to $38,200 (Washington). If a state's trust fund account becomes insolvent and is unable to make UI benefit payments, it may borrow from the federal trust fund. States are charged interest on loans that are not repaid by the end of the year in which they were obtained.

All states levy an "experience rated" tax on their employers based on the amount of unemployment insurance benefits paid to its former employees. Generally, the more unemployment insurance benefits paid to its former employees, the higher the employer's tax rate, up to some maximum determined by each state. The experience rating is intended to ensure an equitable distribution of taxes among employers in their relationship to their use of unemployment insurance as well as to encourage a stable workforce.

In order to qualify for unemployment insurance benefits, workers must have lost a job through no fault of their own and be ready, willing, and able to work. Eligibility requirements for unemployment insurance differ from state to state. Generally, eligibility is linked to work history; an unemployed person usually must have worked recently for a covered employer, earned a minimum amount of wages, and worked for a specified period of time, referred to as the "base period."

Unemployment insurance covers approximately 126.7 million jobs in the United States; 97 percent of all workers on nonfarm payrolls were in jobs covered by unemployment insurance. Working for a covered employer for a period prior to unemployment is called the "base period." Most states require a worker to have worked the first four of the last five quarters prior to filing an unemployment insurance claim.

The regular state unemployment insurance program provides unemployment workers with benefits for up to 26 weeks. States set benefit amounts as a fraction of an individual's average weekly wage up to some weekly maximum. All states disregard some earnings during unemployment spells as an incentive for workers to engage in short-term or part-time work while searching for a permanent job. The national average UI benefit in 2011 was $296 per week. Nationwide, UI benefit payments replaced, on average, 46 percent of a worker's wages prior to becoming unemployed.

The permanent EB program was enacted to provide unemployment insurance benefits to workers who had exhausted their regular benefits during periods of high unemployment. Once regular program benefits have been exhausted, the EB program may provide an additional 13 or 20 weeks of unemployment insurance benefits, depending on worker eligibility, state law, and the economic conditions within a particular state. The EB program is funded 50 percent by the federal government and 50 percent by the states.

In 2008, Congress made additional weeks available through the Emergency Unemployment Compensation (EUC08) program. EUC08 has four tiers of benefits, the first two of which are available in every state and allow eligible workers to receive benefits for up to 34 additional weeks. The second two tiers are only available in states with high unemployment rates and offer up to 19 weeks of additional benefits. Congress has enacted similar legislation to create a federal temporary UI program that has extended unemployment insurance benefits during economic downturns seven other times in history.

The American Economy Recovery and Reinvestment Act, or ARRA, was passed in 2009 and authorized 100 percent federal financing of the EB program. Congress has extended this authorization several times. Under current law, the EUC08 program and full federal financing of the EB program are schedule to expire at the end of 2012.

ARRA also made available $7 billion as an incentive for states to make changes to their unemployment insurance programs. One-third of this funding was contingent on states allowing the use of an alternative base period. The remaining funding was contingent on the state qualifying for the first one-third and containing two of four additional provisions, many of which would benefit low-wage workers. As of September 2011, 39 states have been approved for ARRA incentive payments totaling $4.4 billion.

Jasmine V. Tucker

See also: Department of Labor (DOL); Insurance; Workers' Compensation

References and Additional Readings

Department of Labor, Bureau of Labor Statistics. (2013). Employment and wages online annual averages, 2010. Retrieved from http://www.bls.gov/cew/cewbultn10.htm

Department of Labor Employment and Training Administration. (2013a). Comparison of state unemployment laws. Retrieved from http://workforcesecurity.doleta.gov/unemploy/comparison2011.asp

Department of Labor, Employment and Training Administration. (2013b). Monthly program and financial data. Retrieved from http://ows.doleta.gov/unemploy/claimssum.asp

Department of Labor, Employment and Training Administration. (2013c). Significant provisions of state unemployment insurance laws. Retrieved from http://oui.doleta.gov/unemploy/content/sigpros/2010–2019/January2012.pdf

Government Accountability Office. (2013). Report to the chairman, committee on finance, U.S. senate, unemployment insurance: Economic circumstances of individuals who exhausted benefits, GAO-12-408. Retrieved from http://www.gao.gov/assets/590/588680.pdf

Isaacs, K.P., & Whittaker, J.M. (2011). Unemployment insurance: Programs and benefits. Congressional Research Service.

Vroman, W. (2013). The role of unemployment insurance as an automatic stabilizer during a recession. Retrieved from http://wdr.doleta.gov/research/FullText_Documents/ETAOP2010–10.pdf

United Nations (UN)

The United Nations (UN) was created in 1945 after World War II, with an initial membership of 51 countries. The name was conceived by U.S. President Franklin D. Roosevelt in 1942 when he released the "Declaration by United Nations," a move to unite 26 countries against the "Axis Powers."

While other efforts to work on an international level were evident in telecommunications and postal divisions, the forerunner to the UN was the League of Nations, created in 1919 under the Treaty of Versailles "to promote international cooperation and to achieve peace and security." The League of Nations disbanded after its failure to prevent World War II.

Perhaps one of the most important roles of the UN is protecting human rights. To this end, the UN professes the Universal Declaration of Human Rights. Beyond protection of human rights, the UN announces four main priorities:

The flag of the United Nations (UN) and the famous blue helmet of the UN peacekeeping forces. (Corel)

- To keep peace throughout the world;
- To develop friendly relationships among nations;
- To help nations work together to improve the lives of poor people, to conquer hunger, disease and illiteracy, and to encourage respect for each other's rights to freedoms; and
- To be a centre for harmonizing the actions of nations to achieve these goals.

United Nations (UN) day is celebrated on October 24th each year, the month and day the charter was ratified and the UN came into effect in 1945.

Today, the UN has 193 member states. There are six main bodies in the UN, including General Assembly (all members), Security Council (maintains peace and security worldwide; five permanent members: China, the United Kingdom, Russia, France, and the United States), Economic and Social Council (coordinates economic and social work of UN), Trusteeship Council (oversight of 11 Trust Territories), International Court of Justice (settles legal disputes), and Secretariat (day-to-day work). The main bodies also have subcommittees, commissions, tribunals, and organizations that report to them.

At the helm of the UN is a secretary-general, as of this writing, Ban Ki-moon (Korea) who is entering his second term; he began his first five-year term in 2007. The deputy secretary-general is Jan Eliasson who was appointed by the secretary-general in 2012. The secretary-general is appointed by the general assembly with a recommendation from the Security Council. There is no rule governing the number of terms served by a secretary-general; however, none of the past seven have served more than two terms.

Table 36 Millennium Development Goals 8

Goal 1: Eradicate extreme poverty and hunger	• Target 1a: Reduce by half the proportion of people living on less than a dollar a day • Target 1b: Achieve full and productive employment and decent work for all, including women and young people • Target 1c: Reduce by half the proportion of people who suffer from hunger
Goal 2: Achieve universal primary education	• Target 2a: Ensure that all boys and girls complete a full course or primary schooling
Goal 3: Promote gender equality and empower women	• Target 3a: Eliminate gender disparity in primary and secondary education preferably by 2005, and at all levels by 2015
Goal 4: Reduce child mortality	• Target 4a: Reduce by two-thirds the mortality rate among children under five
Goal 5: Improve maternal health	• Target 5a: Reduce by three quarters the maternal mortality ratio • Target 5b: Achieve, by 2015, universal access to reproductive health

(Continued)

Table 36   *(Continued)*

Goal 6: Combat HIV/AIDS, malaria, and other diseases	• Target 6a: Halt and begin to reverse the spread of HIV/AIDS • Target 6b: Achieve, by 2010, universal access to treatment for HIV/AIDS for all those who need it • Target 6c: Halt and begin to reverse the incidence of malaria and other major diseases
Goal 7: Ensure environmental sustainability	• Target 7a: Integrate the principles of sustainable development into country policies and programs; reverse loss of environmental resources • Target 7b: Reduce biodiversity loss, achieving, by 2010, a significant reduction in the rate of loss • Target 7c: Reduce by half the proportion of people without sustainable access to safe drinking water and basic sanitation • Target 7d: Achieve significant improvement in lives of at least 100 million slum dwellers, by 2020
Goal 8: Develop a global partnership for development	• Target 8a: Develop further an open, rule-based, predictable, nondiscriminatory trading and financial system • Target 8b: Address the special needs of the least developed countries • Target 8c: Address the special needs of landlocked developing countries and small island developing states • Target 8d: Deal comprehensively with the debt problems of developing countries • Target 8e: In cooperation with pharmaceutical companies, provide access to affordable essential drugs in developing countries • Target 8f: In cooperation with the private sector, make available the benefits of new technologies, especially information and communications

Source: United Nations Development Programme. (n.d.). Eight Goals for 2015. Retrieved from http://www.undp.org/content/undp/en/home/mdgoverview/

Recent priorities undertaken by the UN include sustainable development, a safer and more secure world, the importance of prevention, helping countries in transition, and doing more for the world's women and young people. In addition, by 2015, the UN hopes to also meet eight Millennium Developmental Goals (MGDs) in an effort to end poverty worldwide. Shown in Table 36 are the specific goals and related targets.

For additional information, refer to the Primary Source Appendix: The Universal Declaration of Human Rights.

Wendy Reiboldt

See also: Roosevelt, Franklin D.; World Health Organization (WHO); World Trade Organization (WTO)

References and Additional Readings

Hurd, I. (2007). *After anarchy: Legitimacy and power in the United Nations Security Council.* Princeton, NJ: Princeton University Press.

Mertus, J. A. (2009). *The United Nations and human rights: A guide for a new era.* New York, NY: Routledge.

Usury

Usury is a term that describes the practice of lending money to consumers at an interest rate that is unreasonable and illegal (based on each state's level of usury that can range from 2 to 25 percent per month). Usury laws for each state can be viewed at usurylaw.com. Loans made at these very high rates make it virtually impossible for consumers to pay back. Examples include payday loans, loan sharks, pawn shops, title lenders, and other subprime lending. In fact, some interest rates on pay day loans can read equivalent annual interest rates of 1,000 percent or more. These loans are traditionally referred to as usurious, or having a usurious rate.

Historically, usury, as discussed in the bible, was viewed as a means to oppress the poor and in Medieval Latin, "interesse" (interest) was used to mean penalty of death for being late on a payment of a loan. Jewish scholars and law sought to stop usury and make fair and equitable transactions.

Limits on interest rates have existed since borrowing and lending has existed. The poor and underemployed have historically been the users of these high-interest loans. This type of "fringe banking" opportunity is often the only kind of loan available to the poor. The argument for use of these types of lending opportunities is that there is more risk assumed by the lender due to default and flight risk. Despite legislation and state statutes, usury in many forms still exists.

Wendy Reiboldt

See also: Banking; Pawn Shops; Payday Lending; Rent-To-Own (RTO); Title Pawn

References and Additional Readings

Lewinson, M. (1999). Conflicts of interest? The ethics of usury. *Journal of Business Ethics, 22,* 327–339.

Meeks, D. M. (2011). The peril of usury in the Christian tradition: Interpretation. *A Journal of Bible & Theology, 65,* 128–140.

Peterson, R. L. (2012). Usury laws and consumer credit: A note. *The Journal of Finance, 38*(4), 1299–1304.

Persky, J. (2007) Retrospectives: From usury to interest. *Journal of Economic Perspectives, 21,* 227–236.

Stegman, M., & Faris, R. (2003). Payday lending: A business model that encourages chronic borrowing. *Economic Development Quarterly, 17,* 8–32.

Usury Law. (n.d.). Usury law. Retrieved from http://usurylaw.com

V

Volunteer Protection Act (VPA)

Similar to the Good Samaritan Law, the Volunteer Protection Act (VPA) of 1997 (42 U.S.C. § 14503(a)), as signed in by President Clinton, describes the laws that protect people from claims, lawsuits, and allegations of wrongdoing. Congress created it to encourage people to volunteer without fear of volunteer liability [42 U.S.C. § 14503(a)]. When the VPA was adopted, each state had a law limiting the liability of certain volunteers. In its broad context, it is for both people and organizations in the nonprofit sector. "Although numerous researchers, legal authorities and other interested persons have written about these subjects during the past 20 years, a tremendous degree of confusion remains about whether volunteers and nonprofits can be sued and held liable for negligent acts" (Non Profit Risk Management Center, 2001). Given that over 26.7 percent of adults in the United States said they volunteered through an organization, and that there are over 1.4 million nonprofits registered with the IRS, it is reasonable for a volunteer to wonder what his or her personal liability and related protections are.

While every state has a law that relates to the legal liability of volunteers, the laws do differ to a great extent. For example, some states only protect nonprofit directors, while other states extend their protections to emergency service personnel. On the other hand, the act provides the following common state-wide exceptions:

- The exception eliminating the protection for volunteer conduct found to be willful or wanton.
- The exception for gross negligence on the part of the volunteer.
- The exception for wrongful acts committed while operating a motor vehicle.

Additional, yet less common exceptions featured in the state laws include:

- The exception for fraud or fiduciary misconduct;
- The exception for actions brought by an attorney general or other state official;

- The exception for the delivery of certain professional services; and
- The exception for knowing violation of the law (Non Profit Risk Management Center. 2001, 5)

Additionally, there are recurring requirements for the limitation on liability to apply. Examples of the conditions that attach to various volunteer protection laws include the requirement that:

- The nonprofit retaining the volunteer carry liability insurance at a specified level.
- The nonprofit amend its articles of incorporation or bylaws to specifically indemnify volunteers.
- Certain volunteers receive training from the nonprofit.
- Volunteers receive prior written authorization in order to act (Non Profit Risk Management Center, 2001, 6).

However, volunteers working at small nonprofits with few financial resources may not be able to receive protection if their agency cannot afford liability insurance. Other states have adopted unique provisions, such as for athletic volunteers. Interestingly, given recent tragedies in the United States (e.g., 9\11, Hurricane Katrina), nurses and public health workers have particular concern about their liability when volunteering. In general, the VPA indemnifies volunteers for nonprofit organizations and government entities in the following cases:

- *the volunteer was acting within the scope of his or her responsibilities at the time of the alleged act or omission.* Unfortunately, in many cases the scope of a volunteer's responsibility isn't defined. In some cases a volunteer will take it upon him or herself to undertake service for the organization.
- *appropriate or required, the volunteer was properly licensed, certified or authorized to act.* Whether it was appropriate for a volunteer to be authorized to act will not be readily apparent in all instances.
- *the harm was not caused by willful, criminal or reckless misconduct, gross negligence or a conscious, flagrant indifference to the rights or safety of the individual harm.* This condition provides guidance to plaintiff's counsel in terms of wording a complaint so that it will avoid the protection of the VPA. A plaintiff need only state that a volunteer's action was willful or in flagrant indifference to the rights and safety of the individual harm for the matter to require a factual

determination by a court. Therefore, the volunteer is unable to avoid being sued and must defend him or herself.

- *the harm was not caused by the volunteer operating a motor vehicle, vessel, or aircraft where the State requires an operator's license and insurance* (Non Profit Risk Management Center, 2001, 10).

With this law, it is the hope that more people will become volunteers, volunteers across the states will be treated equally, and frivolous lawsuits against caring and proactive community members will decrease. It is critical though that volunteers understand the conditions under which they are and are not protected.

Melanie Horn Mallers

See also: Department of Homeland Security (DHS); Federal Emergency Management Agency (FEMA); Good Samaritan Law

References and Additional Readings

Hodge, J. G., Mount, J. K., Reed, J. F, & Couig, M. (2005). Scope of practice for public health professionals and volunteers. *Journal of Law, Medicine, and Ethics, 33*(4), 53–54.

Non Profit Risk Management Center. (2001). State liability laws for charitable organizations and volunteers. Retrieved from http://sfcard.org/GoodSamaritan Laws.pdf

W

Warne, Colston

Colston E. Warne, one of the leaders of the consumer movement in the 20th century, was born in 1901 in Romulus, New York. He was raised in the Ithaca, New York area and received his bachelor's degree in 1920, and a master's degree in 1921, in economics from Cornell University. He taught from 1921 to 1922 as an instructor at the University of Pittsburg. He continued on to a PhD program from the University of Chicago, graduating in 1925. His doctoral dissertation, published by the University of Chicago Press in 1926, was entitled, *The Consumer Co-operative Movement in Illinois.* He worked as an assistant professor in economics at the University of Denver from 1925 to 1926 and as an assistant professor of economics at the University of Pittsburgh from 1926 to 1930, and then he took a position at Amherst College where he worked in the area of family economics from 1930 until 1969, retiring as a full professor. Warne passed away on May 20, 1987. His wife, Margaret, died in 1982, and he was survived by three children and their families.

Warne played a pivotal role in the consumer movement in the 20th century. His initial interest was in the labor movement, but he became more interested in the consumer aspect of the labor movement, inspired by the book, *Your Money's Worth,* by Stuart Chase and Frederick J. Schlink, published in 1927. Schlink promoted the idea of product testing as a worthwhile source of consumer information. Schlink formed the Consumers' Research consumer testing organization and magazine in 1933, but in 1935, the organization was faced with a labor organizing effort, which resulted in Schlink firing all the workers. Warne was on the advisory board of Consumers' Research but when Schlink fired the workers, Warne supported the workers. Efforts to resolve the strike failed, although the Consumers' Research organization continued to operate for a number of years. Warne left the organization in 1935 when the strike negotiations failed and in 1936, he was instrumental in establishing Consumers Union. He served as the first president of Consumers Union and continued his presidency until 1980.

> *If Colston Warne didn't exist,*
> *We wouldn't have the imagination to invent him,*
> *so we're glad that he did.*
>
> Esther Peterson

Warne's career in academics and advocacy centered on the idea that consumers needed information about products and services in the marketplace so the consumer could make rational decisions about purchases. His work involved providing full information to consumers through scientific testing of the products and then disseminating that research to the average consumer. He felt that this information would provide power to the individual consumer, since the individual consumer had little power in the face of businesses with their workforce of experts who produced and advertised the products. Consumers Union was the organization that put Warne's ideas into action.

Consumers Union started with a shoestring budget. The first issue was published in May 1936 with 10 staffers and distributed to 3,000 subscribers. One major operating principle of Consumers Union was that no private business contributions or advertising would be accepted in order to avoid the influence and pressures that accepting such money would present. An associated principle was that all products tested would be purchased in the marketplace in a manner similar to the everyday purchases made by consumers. A second principle was that scientific methods would be used to test products. Over the years, Consumers Union hired many product testing staff members with the ability to create and conduct valid and reproducible tests of products. The methodology would be transparent and would be communicated in clear terms to consumers. Finally, no business would be allowed to use Consumers Union test results in their own advertising, since any business support could be construed as a potential bias from Consumers Union in favor of a particular business' products. Warne was instrumental in establishing the operating principles of Consumers Union in its formation and the organization adhered to these principles for the decades following, under Warne's leadership. The organization continues to operate successfully and is considered one of the few organizations that unequivocally operates on behalf of the consumer.

Warne's advocacy was not universally viewed as a benefit to the country. The period of time from the late 1930s through the mid-1950s was an era where the United States experienced great concern over the expansion of communism in Russia, Eastern Europe, and other parts of the world. Representative Martin Dies was named the chairman of the newly created House

Committee on Un-American Activities in 1938 and the committee began a campaign to identify communistic groups in America. In 1939, Consumers Union was identified as an organization fronting for communism and placed on the House of Representatives Un-American Activities Committee's list. Warne worked to get the organization off the list, only succeeding in 1954. Additionally, in 1947, President Truman required a loyalty oath on the part of federal employees. Warne was serving on the Consumer Advisory Committee of President Truman's Council of Economic Advisers at the time, and was asked to sign the oath. Warne refused, stating that the oath was in such opposition to the principles of democracy that he could not comply with the request or the oath itself.

Despite these serious allegations and the difficulties presented under the political climate at the time, Warne continued to provide leadership to the consumer movement. In 1953, Warne met with a number of academics at the University of Minnesota to establish the Council on Consumer Information. The council eventually changed its name to the American Council on Consumer Interests in 1969, and it still exists as the leading academic research organization supporting high-quality research on consumer issues. In 1967, the organization began publishing the *Journal of Consumer Affairs*, which currently operates as a respected academic research journal.

As the 1950s progressed, the postwar economic expansion brought a new level of consumption to American households. Political leaders at the state and federal levels became aware of consumer problems in areas such as consumer credit and product safety. Warne was appointed to many political offices to represent the consumer point of view. For example, in 1955–1959, Warne was appointed by Governor Averell Harriman to the Consumer Counsel in the Office of the Governor of New York State. Then in 1959–1964, Warne served on the Consumer Advisory Committee of the Commonwealth of Massachusetts. During that time, President Kennedy delivered his historic consumer message to Congress on March 15, 1962. As part of his historic speech outlining the four rights of the consumer, President Kennedy also directed the Council of Economic Advisers to set up the Consumer Advisory Council, and Warne became a member of this council. After Kennedy's assassination, President Johnson appointed the Consumer Advisory Council and the President's Committee on Consumer Interests. Colston Warne was a member of both the groups, working with Esther Peterson, who was the special assistant to the president for consumer affairs for several years. Later, in 1973–1974, Warne was appointed as a member of the National Consumer Energy Committee of the Federal Energy Office.

During the time period of Colston Warne's, he and other consumer advocates such as Ralph Nader, Ether Peterson, and others served steadfastly on behalf of American consumers. Important policy was established due to the general focus on consumer concerns, such as the Truth in Packaging Act, the Truth in Lending Act, Kennedy's consumer rights, and many other federal and state initiatives. Nonprofit organizations, such as the Consumer Federation of America, the American Home Economics Association, and consumer cooperatives used the momentum of the consumer movement to advance programs on behalf of consumers and households. Even businesses absorbed the messages of fairness, safety, and transparency of information in their ability to woo and retain consumers as customers. Warne was an indefatigable and highly respected scholar and advocate who served American consumers with integrity and an unwavering sense of purpose.

Deborah C. Haynes

See also: American Council on Consumer Interests (ACCI); Consumer Federation of American (CFA); Consumers Union; Kennedy, John F.; Nader, Ralph; Petersen, Esther

References and Additional Readings

Brooks, T. (1987). *Biographical sketch of Colston E. Warne.* Thomas Brooks Collection. Kansas State Libraries, Kansas State University, Manhattan, KS. Retrieved from www.lib.k-state.edu/depts/spe c/findaids/pc1988-44.html

Hudson, E. (1987). CE. Warne dies; consumer leader. *The New York Times.* Retrieved from http://www.nytimes.com/1987/05/21/obituaries/ce-warne-dies-consumer-leader.html.

Morse, R.L.D. (1993). *The consumer movement: Lectures by Colston E. Warne.* Manhattan, KS: Family Economics Trust.

Warnings

The universal warning "caveat emptor" (buyer beware) applies to products and services whether in the commercial or public marketplace, suggesting that consumers need to be knowledgeable about the consumption choices they make. In the marketplace, safety warnings are manufacturers' or providers' disclosures, in the form of alerts or messages that action and care need to be taken to limit or prevent loss, injury, or death. Disclosures including warnings may be required by law or regulation. "For external use only" indicates the product is not to be ingested. "No swimming" indicates a risk related to undertow, contamination, or attack. "Wash in cold water" suggests a loss of quality characteristics may occur if the label instruction is not followed. Fine print in a contract or advertisement often includes warnings of consequences of noncompliance or details and conditions that may relate to financial risk or loss of opportunity. "The warranty is void if regular service is not obtained" is another example.

The consumer is expected to attend to the message and identify the hazard and/or the needed response to prevent loss, injury, illness, or death in relation to warnings issued whether for a situation (weather alert), product (bicycle helmet), or service (lawn care). Effective actions or precautions depend on consumers' right to be informed as delineated by President Kennedy in the Consumer Bill of Rights. Being informed empowers consumers to take actions in times of emergency (flood, fire, accident), in choice, use, storage, and disposal of products (foods, drugs, household goods), and in selection and use of services (financial, social networks, repairs).

Warnings, as part of a package or label as seen on cigarette packages, ladders, or frozen pizza, describe health and/or safety consequences of use or misuse. Posting of warnings may be required by law (e.g., "employees must wash their hands before returning to work" signs in the restrooms of restaurants). These are often in print or a combination of print and symbols or pictograms (flames indicating flammability; walk/don't walk). Other warnings are in the fine print of agreements and contracts (indicating consequences if conditions are not met), or in signage (limit 65 mph, don't feed the animals, exit). Nonprint warnings are based on human sensory perceptions—visual (warning lights, tire tread indicators, symbols, or pictograms (skull and crossbones)); aural (buzzers, the Emergency Alert System (EAS)); olfactory (distinctive/unusual odors as natural gas); taste (metallic, after taste); or tactile (temperature extremes). Warnings require that recipients have an awareness of the necessary actions to prevent or alleviate the risk or, often on short notice, know where to find information (e.g., owner's manual) or ask questions (poison control center) to best lessen negative or unwanted potentialities associated with the warning.

As vulnerabilities vary, consumers' attention to and response to warnings need to take into account those involved, the situation, and the hazard. Requiring car seats and labeling to assure correct installation of the seats are targeted to adults with responsibility for infants and children. Warnings in relation to vehicle safety have been codified in state laws where noncompliance may result in being charged with violation of a seat belt or child safety restraint law. Warnings must take into account those with sensory impairments (a buzzer and a light for those with either visual or hearing impairments) to ensure the warning will be comprehended.

The expectation in society is, if one is to be safe and secure and lessen risk, consumers must heed warnings provided to them and know the actions to take to protect themselves and others. Likewise, it is hoped that consumers will not increase risks to themselves or others by their actions (removing warning labels) or lack of actions (ignoring product recalls). Continued use of products or acquiring used products may require added diligence on the part of the consumer because the warning labels or information may be obliterated, lost, or inoperable (burned out light).

Warnings are disclosures to improve safety and lessen risk. When not heeded safety is compromised, health and life may be threatened. Warnings may apply to the use of a product or service, its storage (this has implications for data in the virtual world as well), and the disposal of a product or termination of a service. Responsible consumers should attend to a number of practices relevant to warnings:

- Follow product instructions and service conditions.
- Keep warning information available.
- Avoid creating hazards.
- Model and teach best practices for others.
- Pay attention to and be prepared to take appropriate action for general alerts/warnings (natural disaster, closed roads) and the issuance of product recalls.
- Report incidents of products that pose a safety hazard whether an injury is involved under conditions of normal use.

When medical attention is needed for a product-related illness or injury, inform the medical personnel of what occurred Warnings in relation to safety are plentiful in daily life and include those specific to an individual at a given time (taking an aspirin) or those common to a community or society (traffic signals and laws). They may provide information on how to best use a product to avoid risk (don't ingest mouthwash) or they may be codified in law (required licenses for use—autos, guns, pesticide application), with the intent to provide protection to the consumer and reduce risks. Questions remain as to how to increase consumer understanding and attention to warnings, how to reduce loss and injury when warnings are present, and what new and continuing consumer information and education is important to assure safe environments for all.

Carole J. Makela

See also: Caveat Emptor; Caveat Venditor; Consumer Bill of Rights; Consumer Product Safety Commission (CPSC); Kennedy, John F.

References and Additional Readings

Argo, J. J., & Main, K. J. (2004). Meta-analyses of the effectiveness of warning labels. *Journal of Public Policy & Marketing, 23*(2), 193–208.

Cox, A. D., Cox, D., & Zimet, G. (2006). Understanding consumer responses to product risk information. *Journal of Marketing, 70*(1), 79–91.

Laughery, K. R. (2006). Safety communications: Warnings. *Applied Ergonomics, 37*(4), 467–478.

Stewart, D. W., & Martin, I. M. (1994). Intended and unintended consequences of warning messages: A review and synthesis of empirical research. *Journal of Public Policy & Marketing, 13*(1), 1–19.

Wogalter, M. S. (Ed.). (2006). *Handbook of Warnings.* Mahwah, NJ: Lawrence Erlbaum Associates.

Wogalter, M. S., Conzola, V. C., & Smith-Jackson, T. L. (2002). Research-based guidelines for warning design and evaluation. *Applied Ergonomics, 33*(3), 219–230.

Warranties. *See* Extended Warranties; Magnuson–Moss Warranty Act

Warren, Elizabeth. *See* Consumer Financial Protection Bureau; Dodd–Frank Wall Street Reform and Consumer Protection Act

Website Security

Over time, our reliance on using the Internet to communicate and conduct business and financial transactions has led to an increase in the need for website security and an increased need for understanding how consumers perceive a website's security. Before entering information into a website, consumers look for security indicators to increase their feelings of trust in the website. These security indicators include an "s" after http:// (https://) in the browser window, a padlock symbol in the browser window, and the Verisign symbol. The Verisign symbol was renamed the Norton Secured Seal in April 2012, to reflect a partnership between Verisign and Norton.

Entering information into a website that utilizes an https://connection means that information entered is encrypted so other individuals on the network cannot see it or alter it. Clicking on the padlock symbol will allow individuals to verify the identity of the website. Businesses that purchase the Norton Secured Seal are offered data encryption, a website vulnerability assessment, and daily website malware scanning. These offerings assist in data security as well as increasing trust among potential consumers.

An additional means for consumers to gain trust in a website is to have the option to opt out of mailing lists. Regardless of the level of trust an individual has in a website, computer viruses can become problematic when individuals do not practice safe computing practices, such as logging out of websites where they have entered personal information (e.g., financial institution websites, shopping websites) or having passwords that are easily guessed, such as a pet's name or "1234." An individual should keep up-to-date with security patches, have up-to-date virus protection software, and scan his or her computer for viruses weekly. Individuals should have up-to-date malware protection software installed on their computer and scan for malware weekly as well. Malware, such as a keylogger, can negatively affect the security of an individual's personal information they enter into a website as the keylogger will record all keystrokes made and send them to the creator of the keylogger. In addition to having up-to-date virus protection and malware protection, individuals should not engage in online activities where they have to enter personal information when they are on public WiFi networks, as this is a common way computers are infected with viruses and other malware.

Educating children is essential in protecting personal computer from viruses and other malware. "Websites that offer 'cheat' codes to enhance play on video games, video- and music-sharing services, video- and music-sharing services, social interaction, and, unfortunately, pornography are sometimes used by thieves to trick children into downloading software that can put your personal information at risk" (Cullen, 119).

In sum, individuals should look for indicators that a website is trustworthy before entering personal information as well as engage in safe computing practices that include keeping up-to-date on security patches and virus and malware protection software. Additionally, children who have access to a personal computer should be educated about the risks associated with certain types of websites.

Axton E. Betz

See also: Identity Theft; Identity Theft, Child; Privacy: Offline; Privacy: Online

References and Additional Readings

Cullen, T. (2007). *The Wall Street Journal complete identity theft guidebook.* New York: Three Rivers Press.

McCoy, M., & Schmidt, S. (2008). *The silent crime: What you need to know about identity theft.* Des Moines, IA: Twin Lakes Press.

Microsoft. (n.d.a). How to know if an online transaction is secure. Retrieved from http://windows.microsoft.com/en-US/windows7/How-to-know-if-an-online-transaction-is-secure

Microsoft. (n.d.b). HTTPS security improvements in Internet Explorer 7. Retrieved from http://msdn.microsoft.com/en-us/library/bb250503.aspx

Pollach, I. (2007). What's wrong with online privacy policies? *Communications of the ACM, 50*(9), 103–108.

Symantec Corporation. (n.d.a). Compare SSL certificates. Retrieved from http://www.symantec.com/theme.jsp?themeid=compare-ssl-certificates&inid=vrsn_symc_ssl_Compare&mboxSession=1332204644306-718234

Symantec Corporation. (n.d.b). Why verisign? Retrieved from http://www.verisign.com/ssl/why-verisign/index.html

Yenisey, M. M., Ozok, A. A., & Salvendy, G. G. (2005). Perceived security determinants in E-commerce among Turkish university students. *Behavior & Information Technology, 24*(4), 259–274.

Whistleblowing

A whistleblower is someone who reports on a wrongdoer, especially in cases of corporate or government malfeasance. When the term is defined in more detail, the meaning becomes multifaceted. As experts Tom Devine and Tarek Maassarani (2011) explain, "a whistleblower is a person of conscience who uses free-speech rights to challenge abuses of power that betray the public trust and who acts for the good of the public at great personal risk" (p. 316).

History of Legislation to Protect Whistleblowers

The first law passed to protect whistleblowers was the 1863 False Claims Act. The law tried to combat fraud by suppliers of the U.S. government during the Civil War. The act promised whistleblowers a percentage of the money recovered or damages won by the government. The law protected whistleblowers from wrongful dismissal. This is sometimes referred as the Lincoln Law.

The False Claims Act was amended during World War II to respond to requests by military contractors. However, its effectiveness was gradually eroded by Supreme Court decisions. Then in 1986, the law was amended and it has been more effective. Initially, most suits involved Pentagon contracts but there has been a shift to other areas such as health care.

The Lloyd–LaFollette Act of 1912 specifically protects whistleblowers. It guaranteed the right of federal employees to furnish information to the

---

Protecting Whistleblowers

On May 15, 2002, President Bush signed legislation called the No FEAR Act (Notification and Federal Anti-Discrimination and Retaliation Act of 2002). This act, which took effect on October 1, 2003, makes federal agencies individually accountable for violations of antidiscrimination and whistleblower protection laws. Requirements and agency responsibilities under the No FEAR Act include:

- Payments of Settlements and Judgments—Agencies that lose or settle discrimination and whistleblower cases must pay judgments out of their individual budgets.
- Employee Information and Education—Agencies must give their employees, former employees, and applicants for employment written notification of discrimination and whistleblower protection laws. This written notification must include posting the information on the agency's website. Agencies are also required to provide their employees with training regarding the rights and remedies applicable to them under these laws.
- Annual reports to Congress—Each agency must file an annual report with Congress, the Equal Employment Opportunity Commission, and the Attorney General providing information about discrimination and whistleblower cases filed against the agency, including details on how cases were resolved and any disciplinary actions against agency employees resulting from violations of discrimination and whistleblower protection laws.
- Posting of EEO complaint data on the Internet—Each federal agency must post on its public website summary statistical data relating to equal opportunity complaints filed against the agency.

Source: U.S. Department of Commerce. (September 12, 2012). The No FEAR Act. Retrieved from http://www.osec.doc.gov/ocr/nofear/nofear.htm

---

U.S. Congress. Several laws were passed in the 1970s regarding environmental activities and they included some protection for whistleblowers. The laws included the Clean Water Act (1972), Safe Drinking Water Act (1974), Resource Conservation and Recovery Act (1976), Toxic Substances Control Act of 1976, and Energy Reorganization Act of 1974 (through the 1978 amendment to protect nuclear whistleblowers). Other laws passed since the 1970s include the Superfund Law (1980), the Clean Air Act (1990), the Pipeline Safety Improvement Act (2002), and the Sarbanes–Oxley Act of 2002 (for corporate fraud whistleblowers).

The Dodd–Frank Wall Street Reform and Consumer Protection Act (2010) strengthens the whistleblower protection provisions of the False

Claims Act. The Dodd–Frank Act allows whistleblowers to initially report fraud anonymously by filing a claim through an attorney. The act prohibits employers from retaliating against whistleblowers. Employers may not fire, demote, suspend, threaten, harass, or discriminate against a whistleblower.

Recent Examples of Whistleblowing

Tobacco Industry

In 1988, after six months of extensive interviews, Dr. Jeffrey Wigand was hired as vice president of research and development at the Brown & Williamson (B&W) Tobacco Corporation. B&W was part of the world's second-largest tobacco concern. In describing his job, Dr. Wigand wrote "My primary goal was to use the knowledge I had acquired during 20 years of healthcare experience to save lives by developing a 'safer' cigarette and to gain Food and Drug Administration (FDA) approval for tobacco products" (Devine and Maassarani, 2011, xii). While employed at B&W, Dr. Wigand observed, witnessed, and learned about many unethical actions. The actions were unethical because the sole purpose was to maximize profits regardless of lost lives, lost productivity, and exorbitant healthcare costs.

Dr. Wigand was fired by B&W in 1993 because he protested the company's continued efforts to conceal the addictive and toxic nature of cigarettes. The company eliminated its program to develop a safer product. In 1994, Wigand began working with CBS *60 Minutes* to expose the fraud perpetrated by the tobacco industry. His work with *60 Minutes* led to additional investigative work with the FDA on cigarette design, youth addiction, and sustained use of tobacco. The television story for *60 Minutes* led to congressional hearings and Department of Justice investigations of the tobacco industry. Although the overall outcome of Dr. Wigand's whistleblowing of the tobacco industry sounds positive, the effect on Dr. Wigand's personal and professional life were extremely negative. Dr. Wigand's children were threatened, his marriage ended in divorce, he was subjected to a multimillion dollar retaliatory investigation, and he was sued.

Enron

Started in 1985, Enron was a successful energy trading and logistic company. In *Fortune* magazine surveys from 1996 through 2001, Enron was chosen as the most innovative U.S. company—it beat out Apple Computer, eBay, and IBM. However, Enron didn't respond to market signals when it expanded beyond energy into the trading of metals, bandwidth, paper, and other products. Enron entered new markets with little research on industry demand. They used off-balance sheet financing strategies. There was no single moment when Enron quit bending rules and started breaking rules. The company's downfall occurred as a result of a gradual accumulation of offenses encouraged by a corporate culture that was aggressive.

An anonymous Enron employee sent a letter to Chairman Kenneth Lay on August 15, 2001, about the employee's concerns with Enron's accounting practices, specifically the use of Special Purpose Entities (SPEs). The letter said, "I am incredibly nervous that we will implode in a wave of accounting scandals" (Fox, 2003, 247). The letter was written by Sherron Watkins who had bachelors' and master's degrees in accounting from the University of Texas and who had worked for Arthur Andersen before working for Enron. A few days after sending the anonymous letter, Watkins identified herself as the author and met with Chairman Kenneth Lay. To safeguard her employment with Enron, Watkins had asked for a transfer to another department before sending the letter.

A law firm advised Enron that "Texas law does not currently protect corporate whistleblowers" (Fox, 2003, 251). The law firm also recommended that Enron managers not treat Watkins "adversely in any way for having expressed her views" (Fox, 2003, 251). Watkins left Enron in November 2002. Since then she has been giving speeches at management conferences and has cowritten a book about her experiences at Enron and the problems of the U,S, corporate culture.

Government Support for Whistleblowers

There is a government agency to assist employees to speak out about serious problems that they learn about at work. Founded in 1977, the Government Accountability Project (GAP) has helped more than 5,000 whistleblowers. Located in Washington, D.C., the GAP consists of 20 staffs. The GAP conducts an accredited legal clinic for law students and operates an internship program. GAP focuses on the following four day-to-day strategies.

- The GAP represents government and corporate whistleblowers against retaliation. If the GAP does not represent a whistleblower, they offer legal referrals and self-help materials. The GAP *represents* whistleblowers but it does not have the authority to *protect* whistleblowers.

- The GAP conducts investigations of the whistleblower's charges and connects them to the appropriate societal institution. GAP collaborates with news media and other public forums to "reveal, publicize, and galvanize a public response to misconduct that would otherwise be sustained by secrecy" (Devine and Maassarani, 2011, 334).

- The GAP works to strengthen the laws protecting freedom of dissent by helping draft legislation for federal, state, and local laws and for international nongovernment organizations (NGOs) and foreign governments.
- The GAP acts as an expert on occupational free-speech and scientific dissent issues. They do this by speaking, advising, and mentoring for academic and nonacademic publications, agencies, and companies.

Due to budget constraints, GAP is able to help less than 5 percent of the hundreds of cases that come to them. However, people are encouraged to learn more about the GAP and seek help by visiting their website or by calling their office. Their address is Government Accountability Project, 1612 K St. NW, Suite 1100, Washington, D.C., 2006.

Considerations for Potential Whistleblowers

The GAP has three criteria for evaluating potential whistleblower cases. The criteria are as follows. (1) Is the issue substantial enough to warrant the risks of reprisal and the input of resources (both human and financial) needed to expose the issue? (2) Are the allegations reasonable and can they be substantiated? (3) Can the disclosure make a significant difference?

Potential whistleblowers are advised to consider very carefully the effect of any proposed action on their career and their personal life. They suggest that people should project what effect the proposed action will have on their career one year, two years, and five years into the future. They also point out that the person should consider whether they intend to complain anonymously or publicly. GAP states that whistleblowers should not expect that the outcome will produce any of the following: bring them recognition and glory, get revenge, or make money.

Survival tips are necessary for anyone contemplating blowing the whistle. The tips include all of these precautionary actions for a potential whistleblower. The person should confide in family and close friends and obtain their support. The person should discuss the situation with his or her peers at work to be certain that others perceive the situation in the same way. The person should consider and evaluate trying to correct the situation from within. The person should be careful not to overstate his or her case when describing the issue. The person should seek legal and expert advice early in his or her thinking about becoming a whistleblower.

The survival tips continue with the following recommendations for a potential whistleblower. The person should develop a strategic plan (what they hope to accomplish, how they will respond to charges, and what their counter moves will be if challenged). The person should maintain good relations with administrative and support staff on the job. The person should build networks off the job with potential allies such as elected officials and respected journalists. The person should keep a detailed and ongoing record of their activities. The person should secure relevant records before they expose the problem. The potential whistleblower should not use his or her employer's resources to engage in whistleblowing actions such as obtaining evidence. The person should be sure that his or her personal life can stand scrutiny and has a complete copy of the information in his or her personnel file prior to blowing the whistle so that information cannot be placed there later and used against him or her. Finally, the person should maintain a respectful attitude when working with authorities.

Sharon A. DeVaney

Films about Whistleblowing

Enron: the Smartest Guys in the Room is a 2005 documentary film. It is based on the 2003 book by the same name authored by Bethany McLean and Peter Elkind who were reporters for Fortune magazine. The film won the Independent Spirit Award for Best Documentary Feature in 2006 and it was nominated for Best Documentary Feature in 2006.

Erin Brockovich. This was a biographical film about Erin Brockovich who fought against the U.S. West Coast energy corporation Pacific Gas and Electric Company. She was an unemployed mother of three children who lost a personal injury lawsuit. After begging the lawyer to give her a job, she worked as a file clerk in his office. She found files related to the mysterious illness of employees who worked in contaminated ponds. Julia Roberts played the part of Erin Brockovich and received four Best Actress awards. The 2000 film was also nominated for Best Picture and Best Director.

Silkwood. Karen Silkwood was a labor union activist and chemical technician at a nuclear plant in Oklahoma. The 1983 film starred Meryl Streep, Cher, and Kurt Russell. The film received several nominations. Streep, Cher, and Mike Nichols received awards for Best Actress, Best Supporting Actress, and Best Director, respectively.

The Insider is a 1999 film based on the true story of Dr. Jeffrey Wigand who attempted to expose the fraud in the tobacco industry. The movie starred Russell Crowe (in the leading role), Al Pacino, and Christopher Plummer. It was nominated for eight Academy Awards.

See also: Activism; Environmental Protection Agency (EPA); Food and Drug Administration (FDA)

References and Additional Readings

Bianco, A. (2010). *The big lie: Spying, scandal, and ethical collapse at Hewlett-Packard.* New York, NY: Public Affairs.

Coleman-Adebayo, M. (2011). *No fear. A whistleblower's triumph over corruption and retaliation at the EPA.* Chicago, IL: Lawrence Hill Books.

Cooper, C. (2008). *Extraordinary circumstances: The journey of a corporate whistleblower.* Hoboken, NJ: John Wiley & Sons, Inc.

Devine, T., & Maasarrani, T. (2011). *The corporate whistleblower's survival guide.* San Francisco, CA: Berrett-Koehler Publishers.

Domscheit-Berg, D with Tina K. (2011). *Inside WikiLeaks: My time with Julian Assange at the world's most dangerous website.* New York: Crown Publishers.

Fox, Loren. (2003). *Enron: The rise and fall.* Hoboken, NJ: John Wiley & Sons, Inc.

Government Accountability Project. (n.d.). About. Retrieved from http://www.whistleblower.org

McLean, B. (2009). The fall of Fannie Mae. In *Fortune* (Eds.) Scandal! Amazing tales of scandals that shocked the world and shaped modern business (pp. 280–303). New York: Fortune Books.

Schilling, John W. (2008). Undercover: *How I went from company man to FBI spy and exposed the worst health care fraud in history.* New York: American Management Association.

Sweet, William. (June 21, 2010). *Dodd–Frank becomes law.* Harvard Law School Forum on Corporate Governance & Financial Regulation.

Taxpayers Against Fraud. (n.d.). http://www.taf.org/statistics.htm

Wholesome Meat Act

The Wholesome Meat Act became law in 1967, closely followed by the Wholesome Poultry Act of 1968. The Wholesome Meat Act is also known as the "Equal to" law because, following the law, states were required to provide inspection programs that were "at least equal to" federal standards and requirements. If states are unable to meet the standard or choose to discontinue their inspection program, federal oversight will be implemented. This act is overseen by the Department of Agriculture, specifically the Food Safety and Inspection Service (FSIS). The FSIS additionally oversees state inspections performed when meat is sold within the state it is produced. The only exception is when farmers eat the meat they produce and it is not sold; meat in section is not required. Under the Wholesome

Wholesome Meat Act

MEAT STAMPS

Inspection mark on raw meat

Inspection mark on raw poultry

Inspection mark on processed products

QUALITY GRADES:

- **Prime grade** is produced from young, well-fed beef cattle. It has abundant marbling and is generally sold in restaurants and hotels. Prime roasts and steaks are excellent for dry-heat cooking (broiling, roasting, or grilling).

- **Choice grade** is high quality, but has less marbling than Prime. Choice roasts and steaks from the loin and rib will be very tender, juicy, and flavorful and are, like Prime, suited to dry-heat cooking. Many of the less tender cuts, such as those from the rump, round, and blade chuck, can also be cooked with dry heat if not overcooked. Such cuts will be most tender if "braised"—roasted, or simmered with a small amount of liquid in a tightly covered pan.

- **Select grade** is very uniform in quality and normally leaner than the higher grades. It is fairly tender, but, because it has less marbling, it may lack some of the juiciness and flavor of the higher grades. Only the tender cuts (loin, rib, sirloin) should be cooked with dry heat. Other cuts should be marinated before cooking or braised to obtain maximum tenderness and flavor.

- **Standard and Commercial grades** are frequently sold as ungraded or as "store brand" meat.
- **Utility, Cutter, and Canner grades** are seldom, if ever, sold at retail but are used instead to make ground beef and processed products.

Note: Grades such as Prime, Choice, and Select are not acceptable terms for raw cuts of pork or poultry.

Source: USDA Food and Safety Inspection Service. (2012). Production & inspection. Retrieved from http://www.fsis.usda.gov/FACTSheets/Inspection_&_Grading/index.asp

Meat Act, federal–state cooperation for meat inspection was established.

The Wholesome Meat Act is an amendment to the Federal Meat Inspection Act (FMIA) of 1906 which was passed at the same time as the Pure Food and Drug Act. The FMIA aimed to prohibit the sale of adulterated or misbranded meat and products made from meat, as well as, to oversee the slaughtering and processing of meats in slaughter houses. The primary goal was to ensure sanitary conditions.

It is important to note that there is a distinct difference between meat inspection and meat grading. Inspection is required by law and may be done at either the state or federal level. Inspection is funded by public funding. Grading is voluntary, and is based on the

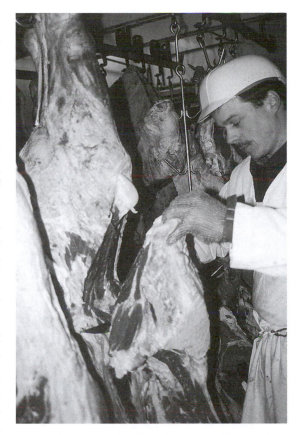

A meat inspector checking for signs of contamination. (Corel)

quality of the meat, including palatability and other attributes. Grading is funded by the meat-packing plants and processors. All meat sold in grocery stores is inspected; most meat is graded USDA Choice, with few exceptions.

Wendy Reiboldt

See also: Department of Agriculture (USDA); Food and Drug Administration (FDA); Food Labeling; Hazard Analysis and Critical Control Point (HACCP)

References and Additional Readings

Department of Agriculture. (2013). Food Safety and Inspection Service (FSIS) Overview. Retrieved from http://www.usda.gov

Federal Drug Administration. (2013). About FDA. Retrieved from http://www.fda.gov

Ray, F. K. (n.d.) Meat inspection and grading. Oklahoma Cooperative Extension Service. Retrieved from http://pods.dasnr.okstate.edu/docushare/dsweb/Get/Document-1950/ANSI-3972web.pdf

Wiley, Harvey

Harvey Washington Wiley was born in the farmlands of Indiana in 1844, his father was the local school teacher. He received his MD from Indiana Medical College, and later he also received a degree in Chemistry from Harvard, after which he served as a professor at the newly founded Purdue University. Subsequently, he spent time working in Germany studying the chemistry of sugar with other noted scientists before returning to his professorship at Purdue. While in Germany, he was elected as a member to the notable German Chemical Society. Dr. Wiley also was one of the founders of the Association of Official Analytic Chemists and wrote multiple book on the subject of food and the adulteration of food.

In 1883, he accepted the job of chief chemist of the Bureau of Chemistry with the Department of Agriculture. In that role, he championed nutrition and food safety for all consumers, noting the presence of adulterated meat, morphine-laced baby medicine, sanded sugar, saw-dusted flour, among others. Despite his public lobbying efforts, many bills relating to pure food sent to Congress were not passed. In an effort to bring more attention to the lack of oversight in food products, in 1902, Dr. Wiley and a team of scientists recruited a group of one dozen healthy men who became known as the Wiley Poison Squad. With the blessing of Congress, and a $5,000 budget, he recruited a new volunteer group every six months to a year who, over a five-year period, willingly ate wholesome meals laced with chemicals and so-called preservatives (e.g., formaldehyde, borax, sulfuric acid, etc.), to test their effects via blood and urine specimens, pulse rate, sweat, weight and height logs, observations

Harvey Wiley, head of the Division of Chemistry of the U.S. Department of Agriculture, predecessor of the Food and Drug Administration, is pictured with his technical staff, ca. 1899. (Food and Drug Administration)

from the attending physician, and so on. The Poison Squad's slogan was "None but the brave can eat the fare." They ate their meals in the basement of the Department of Agriculture's Bureau of Chemistry at what they dubbed "the hygienic table." When the men became sick with headache, nausea, and vomiting, Wiley stopped the experiment. While the direct impact and scientific rigor of his "experiment" was controversial, the attention it garnered was perfectly timed. In 1906, the now infamous book, *The Jungle* by Upton Sinclair was released touting the deplorable conditions in meat-packing plants. A follow-up study by then President Theodore Roosevelt confirmed the conditions reported in the book, and shortly thereafter, Congress passed the Meat Inspection Act and the Pure Food and Drug Act of 1906.

As a result of his efforts and because the Pure Food and Drug Act was largely written by him, Dr. Harvey Wiley was affectionately known as the father of the Pure Food and Drug Act. He worked tirelessly championing the safety of foods, food additives, and food processing. According to most, he was equally hard on his allies and his foes. He was often seen

---

A famous poem by Harvey Wiley about the questionable contents of food:

> We sit at a table delightfully spread,
> And teeming with good things to eat,
> And daintily finger the cream-tinted bread,
> Just needing to make it complete
> A film of the butter so yellow and sweet,
> Well suited to make every minute
> A dread of delight.
> And yet while we eat
> We cannot help asking "What's in it?
> Oh, maybe this bread contains alum and chalk,
> Or sawdust chopped up very fine,
> Or gypsum in powder about which they talk,
> Terra alba just out of the mine.
> And our faith in the butter is apt to be weak,
> For we haven't a good place to pin it
> Annato's so yellow and beef fat so sleek,
> Oh, I wish I could know what is in it?"

Source: Stirling, Dale A. (2002). Harvey W. Wiley. Toxicological Sciences, 67(2). Retrieved from http://toxsci.oxfordjournals.org/content/67/2/157.full

as a bit of a "crank," but he was dutifully focused on the safety and well-being of consumers.

He left his government post after 29 years of service to serve as director of the Good Housekeeping Institute laboratories. The headlines read "WOMEN WEEP AS WATCHDOG OF THE KITCHEN QUITS AFTER 29 YEARS." However, he continued his work with the Good Housekeeping Institute, exposing unsafe products for consumers. Always a man ahead of his time, in the early 1900s, Dr. Wiley wrote for *Good Housekeeping Magazine* on the swindles that were occurring related to "obesity cures," exposing misleading products and fraudulent advertising. He also suspected that tobacco was harmful and postulated that it might promote cancer. As a result of his work in this area, *Good Housekeeping Magazine* stopped accepting advertisements in their magazine from tobacco companies, well before the U.S. Surgeon General reported the dangers of smoking in 1964. He worked for Good Housekeeping for 19 years. Dr. Wiley died in 1930 at the age of 86. He is buried at Arlington Cemetery where he was given a patriot's burial. He preceded his wife in death.

Wendy Reiboldt

See also: Department of Agriculture (USDA); Food and Drug Administration (FDA); Pure Food and Drug Act; *The Jungle*

References and Additional Readings

Arlington National Cemetery. (n.d.) Harvey Washington Wiley. Retrieved from http://arlingtoncemetery.net/hwwiley.htm

Food and Drug Administration. (2006). Harvey W. Wiley: Pioneer consumer activist. *The FDA Consumer Magazine, 40*(1).

Food and Drug Administration. (2013). Harvey W. Wiley. Retrieved from http://www.fda.gov/AboutFDA/WhatWeDo/History/CentennialofFDA/HarveyW.Wiley/default.htm

Francis, F.J. (2000). Harvey W. Wiley: Pioneer in food science and quality. In *A century of food science* (pp. 13–14). Chicago, IL: Institute of Food Technologists.

Lewis, C., & Junod, S.W. (November/December 2002). The 'Poison Squad' and the advent of Food and Drug Regulation. *FDA Consumer Magazine.*

Link, J., & Kidwell, B. (2000). Harvey Wiley: The chemist who led the food safety crusade. *Progressive Farmer, 26*(30).

Weisenberger, B.A. (1996). Doctor Wiley and his poison squad. *American Heritage, 47,* 14–16.

Wireless Local Number Portability (WLNP)

Consumers have been able to keep their land line phone numbers when changing local service providers, but this wasn't the case in the past for cell phones. If a consumer wanted to change their wireless service provider, they were also required to change their cell phone number.

This changed on November 24, 2003, when the Federal Communications Commission's (FCC) passed a ruling allowing consumers to keep their phone number when switching wireless service providers within their same geographical area. This rule also allows consumers to port their existing land line number to a wireless provider.

Wireless Local Number Portability (WLNP) is part of the Telecommunications Act of 1996 that was passed by Congress to stimulate competition in telecommunication services. This act defined and addressed number portability and set an initial compliance date of June 30, 1999, for wireless providers.

Some of the original goals of the act include promoting more competition among service providers leading to more competitive pricing plans, higher quality of services for customers, and encouraging the development of new technologies in order to attract or retain customers.

The act was supported by many in the wireless industry, especially newer wireless providers who wanted to compete with established providers such as Verizon and AT&T. Delays in implementation occurred because the portability rules were challenged by Verizon Wireless and Cellular Telecommunications & Internet Association (CTIA). On June 6, 2003, a ruling by the U.S. Court of Appeals for the District of Columbia Circuit ended the appeals and allowed the FCC to begin implementation of the rules.

Wireless Local Number Portability (WLNP)

Cell phones are obviously important to consumers. Consumer Action (July, 2012) notes that "As consumers increasingly rely on mobile phones and smartphones, these technologies are becoming vital tools for dealing with an emergency. Approximately 70 percent of 911 calls are placed from a mobile phone and 74 percent of consumers have used a mobile phone in an emergency. According to one recent study, 19 percent of consumers had used their mobile phone to get help in an emergency in the last 30 days."

Source: Consumer Action. (July 10, 2012). Using wireless technology before, during, and after emergencies. Retrieved from http://www.consumer-action.org/

When the portability rules first went into effect on November 24, 2003, Verizon Wireless and Nextel Communications gained the most customers, while Cingular and AT&T lost the most customers. Sprint PCS and T-Mobile came out about even.

Initially this rule applied to wireless carriers in the 100 largest Metropolitan areas. For those outside of those areas, the ruling took effect on May 24, 2004. If a consumer wishes to port their service from carrier to another, they must first contact the new company they want to switch to. The new company will initiate the process with the consumer's current company.

The consumer will be responsible for any early termination fees under his or her existing contract with his or her current company as well as any outstanding balances on his or her account. The current company cannot refuse to port the number, even if money is owed to them for an outstanding balance or termination fee. Companies are allowed to charge a fee to recover the costs for number portability. It is important that the consumer inquire about potential fees prior to initiating the change.

Initially the process took four days to complete. In late summer 2010, this was shortened to one business day for simple ports involving one line such as wireless to wireless or landline to wireless. In many instances, porting a number can be completed in a few hours. Other changes may take longer depending on the complexity of the changes with the number of lines involved or adjustments to equipment.

During the day of porting, there may be mixed service for the consumer when they have two telephones with the same number. During this time, 911 emergency service may be affected. The consumer should ask their new company if the one day porting process will affect 911 calls.

In some situations the consumer may be required to purchase new equipment in order to use the services of the new company. The consumer is responsible for inquiring with the new company to determine if his or her current equipment will be compatible.

When a consumer switches from a land line to a wireless line, services provided with his or her land line may no longer be available to them, such as caller ID and call forwarding. The consumer is responsible for inquiring with the new company to find out what services will be available to them after the port. If a consumer has a problem porting their number, they should first try to resolve it with the provider. If that is not possible, the consumer should file a complaint with the FCC. Complaints can be filed online or by phone.

Lisa J. Amos Ledeboer

See also: Federal Communications Commission (FCC)

References and Additional Readings

Associated Press. (2003). Court ok's home-to cell number transfers. Retrieved from http://www.newsmax.com/

Federal Communications Commission. (2011). FCC consumer facts: Keeping your telephone number when you change your service provider. Retrieved from http://www.fcc.gov/guides/portability-keeping-your-phone-number-when-changing-service-providers

Kessing, S.M. (2004).Wireless local number portability: New rules will have broad effects. Retrieved from http://dltr.law.duke.edu/2004/06/09/wireless-local-number-portability-new-rules-will-have-broad-effects/

Workers' Compensation

The following is an excerpt from the National Academy of Social Insurance publication *Workers' Compensation Benefits Coverage and Costs 2009.* Workers' compensation provides medical care, rehabilitation, and cash benefits for workers who are injured on the job or who contract work-related illnesses. It also pays benefits to families of workers who die of work-related causes. Each state regulates its own workers' compensation program, with no standard reporting requirements to any federal agency.

Workers' compensation is an important part of American social insurance. As a source of support for disabled workers, it is surpassed in size only by Social Security Disability Insurance and Medicare. In 2009, Social Security paid $118.3 billion in cash benefits to disabled workers and their dependents, while Medicare paid $70.3 billion for health care for disabled persons under age 65. Workers' compensation programs in the 50 states, the District of Columbia, and federal programs paid $58.3 billion in benefits in 2009. Of the total, $28.9 billion was paid for medical care and $29.4 billion for cash benefits. See Table 37 for more information.

Workers' compensation differs from other disability insurance programs in important ways. Workers' compensation pays for medical care for work-related injuries beginning immediately after the injury occurs; it pays temporary disability benefits after a waiting period of three to seven days; it pays permanent partial and permanent total disability benefits to workers who have lasting consequences of disabilities caused on the job; in most states it pays rehabilitation and training benefits for those unable to return to preinjury careers; and it pays benefits to survivors of workers who die of work-related causes. Social Security, in contrast, pays benefits to workers with long-term disabilities of any cause, but only when the disabilities preclude substantial paid employment. It also encourages return to work and continues to pays benefits even if there is some

Table 37 Workers' Compensation Benefits

Workers' Compensation Benefits*, Coverage, and Costs** in the United States, 2008-2009

Aggregate Amounts	2008	2009	Change In Percent
Covered workers (in thousands)	130,643	124,856	-4.4
Covered wages (in billions)	$5,954	$5,675	-4.7
Workers' compensation benefits paid (in billions)	58.1	58.3	0.4
Medical benefits	29.3	28.9	-1.1
Cash benefits	28.8	29.4	1.9
Employer costs for workers' compensation (in billions)	79.9	73.9	-7.6

Amount per $100 of covered wages	2008	2009	Change In Amount
Benefits paid	$0.98	$1.03	$0.05
Medical payments	0.49	0.51	0.02
Cash payments to workers	0.48	0.52	0.04
Employer costs	1.34	1.30	-0.04

* Benefits are payments in the calendar year to injured workers and to providers of their medical care.

self-employment or "transitional work." Social Security also pays for survivor benefits to families of deceased workers and for rehabilitation services in some circumstances. Social Security Disability Insurance benefits begin no earlier than five months after the disability began; Medicare coverage begins 29 months after the onset of medically verified inability to work. There are typically other state and local disability benefit programs for public employees and particularly for police and firefighters. Paid sick leave, temporary disability benefits, and long-term disability insurance for nonwork-related injuries or diseases are available to some workers through employers or private insurance.

History of Workers' Compensation

Germany enacted the first modern workers' compensation laws, known as Sickness and Accident Laws, in 1884, following their introduction by

Chancellor Otto von Bismarck. The next such laws were adopted in England in 1897. Workers' compensation was the first form of social insurance in the United States. The first workers' compensation law in the United States was enacted in 1908 to cover certain federal civilian workers. The first constitutional state laws were passed in 1911. The adoption of state workers' compensation programs has been called a significant event in the nation's economic, legal, and political history. The adoption of these laws in each state required great efforts by business and labor to reach agreements on the specifics of the benefits to be provided and on which industries and employers would have to provide these benefits. Today, each of the 50 states, the District of Columbia, and U.S. territories has its own program. A separate program covers federal civilian employees. Other federal programs provide benefits to coal miners with black lung disease, Longshore and Harbor workers, employees of overseas contractors with the U.S. government, certain energy employees exposed to hazardous material, workers engaged in the manufacturing of atomic bombs, and veterans injured while on active duty in the armed forces.

Before workers' compensation laws were enacted, an injured worker's only legal remedy for a work-related injury was to bring a tort suit against the employer and prove that the employer's negligence caused the injury. At the time, employers could use three common-law defenses to avoid compensating the worker: assumption of risk (showing, e.g., that the injury resulted from an ordinary hazard of employment); the fellow worker rule (showing that the injury was due to a fellow worker's negligence); and contributory negligence (showing that regardless of any fault of the employer, the worker's own negligence contributed to the accident).

Under the tort system, workers often did not recover damages and experienced delays or high costs when they did. While employers generally prevailed in court, they nonetheless were at risk for substantial and unpredictable losses if the workers' suits were successful. Litigation created friction between employers and workers. Initial reforms took the form of employer liability acts, which eliminated some of the common-law defenses. Nonetheless, employees still had to prove negligence, which remained a significant obstacle to recovery. (As a result, the employers' liability approach was abandoned in all jurisdictions and industries except the railroads, where it still exists.) Ultimately, both employers and employees favored workers' compensation legislation to ensure that a worker who sustained an occupational injury or disease arising out of and in the course of employment would receive predictable compensation without delay, regardless of who was at fault. As a quid pro quo, the employer's liability was limited. Under the exclusive remedy concept, the worker accepts workers' compensation as payment in full and gives up the right to sue. (There are limited exceptions to the exclusive remedy concept in some states, such as when there is an intentional injury of the employee.) Workers' compensation benefits are not subject to federal or state income taxes.

Workers' Compensation Financing and Coverage

Workers' compensation programs vary across states in terms of who is allowed to provide insurance, which injuries or illnesses are compensable, and the level of benefits. Workers' compensation is financed almost exclusively by employers, although economists argue that workers pay for a substantial portion of the costs of the program in the form of lower wages. Workers' compensation coverage is mandatory in all states but Texas. Generally, state laws require employers who wish to self-insure for workers' compensation to obtain approval from the state regulatory authority after demonstrating financial ability to carry their own risk (self-insure). For those employers who purchase insurance, the premiums are based in part on their industry classifications and the occupational classifications of their workers. Many employers are also experience rated, which results in higher (or lower) premiums for employers whose past experience—as evaluated by actuarial formulas that consider injury frequency and aggregate benefit payments—is worse (or better) than the experience of similar employers in the same insurance classification.

Every state except Texas requires almost all private employers to provide workers' compensation coverage. In Texas, coverage is voluntary, but employers not providing coverage are not protected from tort suits. An employee not covered by workers' compensation insurance or an approved self-insurance plan is allowed to file suit claiming the employer is liable for his or her work-related injury or illness in every state. Other states exempt employers from mandatory coverage such as very small firms, certain agricultural farms, household employers, employers of charitable or religious organizations, or employers of some units of state and local government. Employers with fewer than three workers are exempt from mandatory workers' compensation coverage in Arkansas, Georgia, Michigan, New Mexico, North Carolina, Virginia, West Virginia, and Wisconsin. An example of limited coverage of farm workers is Wisconsin, where employers, other than farmers, who usually have less than three employees but who have paid wages of $500 or more in any calendar quarter for work performed within the state are covered the 10th day of the next calendar quarter. Employers with fewer than four workers are exempt in Florida and South Carolina. Those with fewer than five employees are exempt in Alabama, Mississippi, Missouri, and Tennessee. The rules for agricultural workers vary among states. In all except 14 states, farm employers are exempt from mandatory workers' compensation coverage altogether. In other states, coverage is compulsory for some or all farm employers.

Types of Workers' Compensation Benefits

Workers' compensation pays for medical care immediately and pays cash benefits for lost work time after a three- to seven-day waiting period. Most workers' compensation cases do not involve lost work time greater than the waiting period for cash benefits. In these cases, only medical benefits are paid. "Medical only" cases are quite common, but they represent a small share of benefit payments. Medical-only cases accounted for 77 percent of workers' compensation cases, but only 8 percent of all benefits paid for 41 NCCI-covered states for policy years spanning 1998–2006. The remaining 23 percent of cases that involved cash benefits accounted for 92 percent of benefits for cash and medical care combined.

Cash benefits differ according to the duration and severity of the worker's disability. Temporary total disability benefits are paid when the worker is temporarily precluded from performing the preinjury job or another job for the employer that the worker could have performed prior to the injury. Most states pay weekly benefits for temporary total disability that replace two-thirds of the worker's preinjury wage (tax free), subject to a dollar maximum that varies from state to state.

For most lost time injuries, workers fully recover, return to work, and benefits end. In some cases, they return to work before they reach maximum medical improvement, usually with restricted duties and lower pay. In those cases, they receive temporary partial disability benefits in most states. Temporary disability benefits are the most common type of cash benefits. They account for 62 percent of cases involving cash benefits and 17 percent of benefits incurred. If a worker has severe impairments that are judged to be permanent after he or she reaches maximum medical improvement, permanent total disability benefits might be paid. These cases are relatively rare. Permanent total disabilities, together with fatalities, account for one percent of all cases that involve cash benefits, and 17 percent of total cash benefit payments. All these exclude "medical only" cases.

Permanent partial disability benefits are paid when the worker has physical impairments that, although permanent, do not completely limit the worker's ability to work. States differ in their methods for determining whether a worker is entitled to permanent partial benefits, the degree of partial disability, and the amount of benefits to be paid. In some states, the permanent partial disability benefit begins after maximum medical improvement has been achieved. In some cases permanent disability benefits can simply be the extension of temporary disability benefits until the disabled worker returns to employment. Cash benefits for permanent partial disability are frequently limited to a specified duration or an aggregate dollar limit. Permanent partial disabilities account for 37 percent of cases that involve any cash payments and for 66 percent of benefit payments.

Workers' Compensation Benefits and Costs

Total cash benefits to injured workers and medical payments for their health care were $58.3 billion in 2009, a 0.4 percent increase from $58.1 billion in 2008. Medical payments decreased by 1.1 percent to $28.9 billion, and cash benefits to injured workers increased by 1.9 percent to $29.4 billion, from the prior year. Costs to employers fell by a substantial 7.6 percent in 2009 to $73.9 billion.

Costs for self-insured employers are the benefits they pay plus an estimate of their administrative costs. For employers who buy insurance, costs are the premiums they pay in the year plus benefits and administrative costs they pay under deductible arrangements in their insurance policies. From an insurance company's perspective, premiums received in a year are not expected to match up with benefits paid that year. Rather, the premiums are expected to cover all future liabilities for injuries that occur in the year. The National Academy of Social Insurance (NASI) measures of benefits and employer costs are designed to reflect the aggregate experience of two stakeholder groups—workers who rely on compensation for workplace injuries and employers who pay the bills.

For long-term trends, it is useful to consider workers' compensation benefits and employer costs relative to aggregate wages of covered workers. In a steady state, one might expect benefits to keep pace with covered wages. This would be the case with no change in the frequency or severity of injuries and if wage replacement benefits for workers and medical payments to providers tracked the growth of wages in the economy generally. However, in reality, benefits and costs relative to wages vary significantly over time.

In 2009, aggregate wages of covered workers fell by 4.7 percent. When measured relative to the wages of covered workers, workers' compensation benefits rose whereas employer costs fell in 2009 as shown in Table 38.

Table 38 Workers' compensation benefits by type

Workers' Compensation Benefits* by Type of Insurer and Medical Benefits, by State, 2009 (in thousands)

State	Private Carriers		State Funds		Self-Insured[b]				Medical[c]
	Benefits	Percent Share	Benefits	Percent Share	Benefits	Percent Share	Total[g]	Percent Medical	
Alabama	$297,824	47.6			$327,930	52.4	$625,755	67.6	$423,010
Alaska	156,254	73.2			57,119	26.8	213,372	66.4	141,679
Arizona	225,639	34.7	315,649	48.5	109,442	16.8	650,730	62.1	104,103
Arkansas	150,642	69.7			65,574	30.3	216,216	65.8	142,270
California	4,814,138	51.7	1,607,715	17.3	2,895,941	31.1	9,317,794	54.4	5,065,094
Colorado	245,494	27.8	385,554	43.6	252,997	28.6	884,044	50.2	443,790
Connecticut	621,327	74.4			213,347	25.6	834,673	43.5	363,083
Delaware	160,236	77.8			45,736	22.2	205,972	55.1	113,491
District of Columbia	78,046	84.9			13,894	15.1	91,940	37.5	34,477
Florida	1,924,139	64.6			1,053,326	35.4	2,977,465	64.4	1,8917,488
Georgia	1,097,153	73.5			395,543	26.5	1,492,696	49.4	737,392
Hawaii	131,780	53.9	30,571	12.5	82,023	33.6	244,375	43.0	105,1081
Idaho	85,223	32.0	149,948	56.3	31,291	11.7	266,461	61.4	163,607
Illinois	2,256,602	75.7			722,684	24.3	2,979,286	47.9	1,427,078
Indiana	544,868	89.1			66,924	10.9	611,792	71.1	434,984
Iowa	434,115	78.0			122,702	22.0	556,817	54.0	300,681
Kansas	306,423	73.2			112,233	26.8	418,656	59.2	247,844

(Continued)

Table 38 (Continued)

Workers' Compensation Benefits* by Type of Insurer and Medical Benefits, by State, 2009 (in thousands)

State	Private Carriers		State Funds		Self-Insured[b]		Total[g]	Percent Medical	Medical[c]
	Benefits	Percent Share	Benefits	Percent Share	Benefits	Percent Share			
Kentucky	387,820	52.6	116,655	15.8	232,917	31.6	737,392	57.1	421,051
Louisiana	434,395	51.7	135,109	16.1	270,075	32.2	839,580	54.2	455,052
Maine	90,499	34.3	96,250	36.5	76,762	29.1	263,512	46.2	121,742
Maryland	463,558	51.7	210,192	23.5	222,156	24.8	895,905	44.6	399,574
Massachusetts	748,427	78.7			201,963	21.3	950,390	34.2	325,480
Michigan	958,184	63.5			551,697	36.5	1,509,881	35.4	533,944
Minnesota	760,135	70.2	54,046	5.0	268,439	24.8	1,082,620	52.1	564,005
Mississippi	184,327	57.9			134,171	42.1	318,499	59.3	188,870
Missouri	556,200	66.7	84,185	10.1	193,689	23.2	834,075	54.7	456,239
Montana	84,905	33.4	127,934	50.3	41,279	16.2	254,118	56.8	144,339
Nebraska	236,868	77.9			67,287	22.1	304,156	60.5	184,014
Nevada	293,133	67.7			139,557	32.3	432,690	46.1	199,470
New Hampshire	184,713	80.0			46,257	20.0	230,971	41.3	141,585
New Jersey	1,563,464	78.1			439,411	21.9	2,002,875	48.6	973,877
New Mexico	158,641	56.1	36,386	12.9	87,606	31.0	282,633	59.9	169,297
New York	1,797,434	43.3	1,096,455	26.4	1,252,838	30.2	4,146,728	48.0	1,990,429
North Carolina	1,059,199	75.2			349,728	24.8	1,408,926	44.7	629,790
North Dakota[a]			110,526	100.0			110,526	60.5	66,866
Ohio[a]	20,968	0.9	1,925,330	81.8	407,086	17.3	2,353,384	42.4	998,833

Oklahoma	369,263	44.8	262,060	31.8	193,532	23.5	824,855	43.2	356,337
Oregon	237,286	38.1	278,987	44.8	106,822	17.1	623,095	52.0	324,009
Pennsylvania	1,975,878	68.1	310,215	10.7	615,246	21.2	2,901,339	46.0	1,333,716
Rhode Island	56,795	36.0	79,856	50.6	21,069	13.4	157,720	33.4	52,678
South Carolina	651,014	73.0	56,633	6.4	184,183	20.7	891,830	41.3	368,326
South Dakota	90,019	96.2			3,558	3.8	93,578	65.4	61,200
Tennessee	605,574	77.3			178,329	22.7	783,903	53.8	422,524
Texas	917,000	57.5	348,518		329,840	20.7	1,595,358	59.6	950,833
Utah	109,973	37.2	136,676	46.2	48,975	16.6	295,624	69.1	204,276
Vermont	124,564	86.5			19,490	13.5	144,054	49.4	71,163
Virginia	658,203	75.4			215,280	24.6	873,483	57.9	505,747
Washington[a]	19,007	0.8	1,756,175	76.0	537,003	23.2	2,312,186	34.9	807,719
West Virginia[d]	173,769	35.4	271,671	55.4	45,091	9.2	490,531	36.2	177,581
Wisconsin	956,730	85.9			156,511	14.1	1,113,240	68.8	765,593
Wyoming[a]	1,751	1.3	134,764	98.7			136,515	50.9	69,525
Non-federal total	$30,459,597	55.6	$10,118,061	18.5	$14,206,553	25.9	$54,784,211	50.9	$27,900,839

(Continued)

Table 38 *(Continued)*

Workers' Compensation Benefits* by Type of Insurer and Medical Benefits, by State, 2009 (in thousands)

State	Private Carriers		State Funds		Self-Insured[b]		Total[g]	Percent Medical	Medical[c]
	Benefits	Percent Share	Benefits	Percent Share	Benefits	Percent Share			
Federal[e]							3,542,605	29.3	1,039,167
Federal employees[f]							2,763,885	31.3	863,729
TOTAL							$58,326,816	49.6	$28,940,005

*Benefits are payments in the calendar year to injured workers and to providers of their medical care.

a. States with exclusive funds (Ohio, North Dakota, Washington, and Wyoming) may have small amounts of benefits paid in the private carrier category. This results from the fact that some employers doing business in states with exclusive state funds may need to obtain coverage from private carriers under the United States Longshore & Harbor Workers Act or employers liability coverage which the state fund is not authorized to provide. In addition, private carriers may provide excess compensation coverage in some of these states.

b. Self-insurance includes individual self-insurers and group self-insurance.

c. For further details see the Workers' Compensation Benefits Coverage and Costs 2009, www.nasi.org

d. West Virginia completed the transition from monopolistic state fund to competitive insurance status on July 1, 2008.

e. Federal benefits include: those paid under the Federal Employees' Compensation Act for civilian employees; the portion of the Black Lung benefit program that is financed by employers; and a portion of benefits under the Longshore and Harbor Workers' Compensation Act that are not reflected in state data, namely, benefits paid by self-insured employers and by special funds under the LHWCA. See Appendix H for more information about federal programs.

f. Included in the Federal benefits total.

g. These data may not include second injury fund for all states and may be an understatement of total payments data.

Source: Sengupta, R., Reno, V., & Burton, J. REPORT: Workers' Compensation: Benefits, Coverage, and Costs, 2009. Retrieved from http://www.nasi.org/research/2011/report-workers-compensation-benefits-coverage-costs-2009

Total payments on workers' behalf rose by five cents to $1.03 per $100 of covered wages in 2009: medical payments rose by two cents to $0.51 per $100 of wages, while cash benefits rose by four cents per $100 of wages to $0.52. The cost to employers fell by four cents per $100 of covered wages, to $1.30 in 2009 from $1.34 in 2008.

State Trends in Benefits

In 27 states benefit payments declined between 2008 and 2009 and 24 states experienced an increase in their benefit payments in 2009.

Benefits, and how they are recorded and reported, vary within a state from year to year for many reasons, including:

- Changes in workers' compensation statutes, new court rulings, or new administrative procedures;
- Changes in the mix of occupations or industries, because jobs differ in their rates of injury and illness;
- Fluctuations in employment, because more people working means more people at risk of a job-related illness or injury;
- Changes in wage rates to which benefit levels are linked;
- Variations in healthcare practice, which influence the costs of medical care;
- Fluctuations in the number and severity of injuries and illnesses for other reasons (e.g., in a small state, one industrial accident involving many workers in a particular year can show up as a noticeable increase in statewide benefit payments);
- Changes in reporting procedures (e.g., as state agencies update their record-keeping systems, the type of data they are able to report often changes, and new legislation can also affect the data states are able to provide); and
- Changes in the procedures or criteria for reporting lump-sum settlements may affect the amounts in the agreements classified as indemnity payments or medical benefits, thus altering the share of total benefits reported as medical benefits.

Ishita Sengupta

See also: Department of Labor (DOL); Insurance; Social Security

References and Additional Readings

Barth, P., & Niss, M. (1999). *Permanent partial disability benefits: Interstate differences.* Cambridge, MA: Workers Compensation Research Institute.

Burton, J. F. Jr. (2005). Permanent partial disability benefits. In K. Roberts, J. F. Burton, Jr., and M. M. Bodah (Eds.). *In workplace injuries and diseases: Prevention and compensation; essays in honor of Terry Thomason.* Kalamazoo, MI: W.E. Upjohn Institute for Employment Research.

Burton, J. F. Jr., & Mitchell, D. J. B. (2003). Employee benefits and social insurance: The welfare side of employee relations. In Bruce E. Kaufman, Richard A. Beaumont, & Roy B. Helfgot (Eds). *Industrial relations to human resources and beyond.* Armonk, NY: M.E. Sharpe.

Centers for Medicare & Medicaid Services (CMS). (2010). Private data request.

Clayton, A. (2004). Workers' compensation: A background for social security professionals. *Social Security Bulletin, 65*(4).

IAIABC-WCRI. (2011). Workers' Compensation Laws as of January 2010. WC-10-27, 2011.

Leigh, J. P., Markowitz, S., Fahs, M., & Landrigan, P. (2000). *Costs of occupational injuries and illnesses.* Ann Arbor, MI: The University of Michigan Press.

National Council on Compensation Insurance, Inc. (NCCI). (2010). *Annual Statistical Bulletin, 2010 Edition.* Boca Raton, FL: NCCI.

Roberts, K., Burton, Jr., J. F., & Bodah, M. M. (2005). *Diseases: prevention and compensation. Essays in honor of Terry Thomason.* Kalamazoo, MI: W.E. Upjohn Institute for Employment Research.

Social Security Administration (SSA). (2010). Office of Research, Evaluation, and Statistics. The 2009 Annual Report of the Board of Trustees of the Federal Old Age and Survivors Insurance and Disability Insurance Trust Funds. Washington, DC.

Thomason, T., Schmidle, T. P., & Burton, J. F., Jr. (2001). *Workers' compensation: Benefits, costs, and safety under alternative insurance arrangements.* Kalamazoo, MI: W.E. Upjohn Institute for Employment Research.

Working from Home Schemes

"Working from Home" frauds and schemes are offers or ads that falsely lead victims to believe they can easily make large sums of money while the advertiser collects a fee for start-up kits. These advertisers also gather personal information such as social security number, bank account information, or a credit card account number. It is not unusual for a consumer products company to charge a hefty amount for the starter kit or the initial supply of whatever the product may be. The buyer, of course, runs the risk of never selling a thing, never recouping their initial investment. True frauds and schemes are a far more insidious endeavor in that one may never receive any materials they are promised, or worse, may become a victim of identity theft wherein the company about to "hire" drains a bank account or makes illegitimate charges to a credit card belonging to the interested party. A scammer might promise "$2,000 a week" or "$100K potential" for unskilled work that will be completed in the comfort of one's home. The offers are enticing. Fraudsters promise big money with added benefits like "no commuting, no time clock, be your own boss!" Consumers should be wary.

Fraud and scam ads typically use exciting language, are colorful and well placed and sometimes are delivered directly to individuals through telemarketing or the Internet. Working from home frauds and scams are particularly alluring to people looking to make an easy, convenient income on a flexible schedule since the "work" indicated is usually along the lines of stuffing envelopes, doing online surveys or online searches, medical billing, assembly or craft work, rebate processing, or being a secret shopper in one's spare time. Others who are vulnerable to working from home schemes include parents wanting to balance more time with their children, military spouses who pick up and move repeatedly, retirees needing supplemental income, and people with disabilities. Unfortunately, people in desperate financial hardship and those who lack formal workforce training or higher education are often caught in the most outlandish schemes because they offer the quickest fix and the greatest promise of easy money, though an empty promise.

Any ad or offer that seems too good to be true probably is. Any offer that requires potential employees, before learning any of the details of the working arrangement, to disclose personal information such as social security number, bank account information, or credit card number are most likely to be scams. Companies that do not pay a regular salary but instead work by piece rate or commission are questionable. Any offer that mentions an overseas company is almost without a doubt, fraudulent.

Determining whether a working-from-home scenario is legitimate and trustworthy requires research on behalf of the consumer. State Attorney General Offices house consumer protection and consumer fraud records and are a superb place to call and question whether there are any complaints or information on file for a particular company. The Better Business Bureau is another good place to check a company's reputation, however, criminals who are being tracked or who have been prosecuted already are more likely to have a negative report in an Attorney General's Office. A fraudulent company or scheme will only have a Better Business Bureau red flag if someone wronged has taken an additional step after reporting an incident to law enforcement and to the attorney general's fraud department.

The absence of a negative report unfortunately does not guarantee the quality of the company. Many scams go unreported and perpetrators are creative in coming up with new and different solicitations to perpetuate the crime.

The Federal Trade Commission (FTC) is a federal agency working to protect consumers from unfair, deceptive, or fraudulent practices. FTC's Bureau of Consumer Protection can take legal action against companies and people who violate the law. FTC is concerned with all levels of a fraudulent situation: advertising, financial practices, marketing practices, and privacy and identity protection and has expertise and authority to carry out related education, advocacy, law enforcement and litigation to thwart and punish violators.

Some "working from home opportunities" are genuine. However, they are not nearly as plentiful as people would like. Insurance companies and consumer products (personal care, cosmetics, and books) firms, for example, typically are those in which a person maintains a home-based office and covers a certain territory. These are mainly part-time jobs, commission-based, or pay a lump sum for a level of performance, and rarely include health benefits, a pension, or paid leave. It is essential in evaluating an offer for employment of any kind that one recognizes that a requirement for payment up front, before receiving anything, for "certification," "training materials," or a "client list," is cause for great concern. Scammers advertise jobs the same places legitimate employers do, in newspapers, online, and on television. Job seekers who are interested in home employment need to spend time searching for legitimate opportunities, put forth significant effort weeding through scams and give thoughtful contemplation weighing what they really need in the way of income versus the time and personal resources they are willing to put in on the road and perhaps into product.

Some ill-intended companies and con artists will promise a refund if the investor does not succeed; this is part of the deception. A victim will not receive a voluntary refund from a scammer. It is a con artist's mission to collect money and then to disappear. Most scammers regularly trade one company name and one storefront for the next in order to avoid prosecution.

The victim of a working-from-home fraud or scam should contact the nearest law enforcement agency, the FTC and the state Attorney General's Office to report the company, what happened, and the monetary loss. Mail fraud complaints, those relating to advertisements that are received via U.S. Postal mail, can also be filed to the U.S. Postal Inspection Service through the local postmaster. Recovery of lost funds may not be possible, however, reporting the information may help authorities trace the scam, shut it down, and hold the perpetrators accountable according to the law so that others will not fall victim.

Megan J. O'Neil

See also: Attorney General Office (AG); Federal Trade Commission (FTC); Frauds and Scams; Post Office (USPS, United States Postal Service)

References and Additional Readings

Federal Trade Commission. (2013a). Work-at-home & business opportunity scams. Retrieved from http://www.ftc.gov/bcp/edu/microsites/phonefraud/workathome.shtml

Federal Trade Commission. (2013b). Facts for consumers: Work-at-home schemes. Retrieved from http://www.ftc.gov/bcp/edu/pubs/consumer/invest/inv14.shtm

Postal Inspection Service. (2013). Work-at-Home-Schemes. Retrieved from https://postalinspectors.uspis.gov/investigations/MailFraud/fraudschemes/employmentfraud/WorkatHome.aspx

Rayburn, L. (2004). *Work@Home Scams: They just don't pay!* Film/DVD (U.S. Postal Inspection Service).

World Health Organization (WHO)

Following World War II, in 1945, diplomats met to form the United Nations. One priority discussed was to set up a global health organization. Three years later, specifically on April 7, 1948, WHO's constitution became real. Priorities included malaria, tuberculosis, venereal diseases, maternal and child health, sanitary engineering, and nutrition, as well as disease prevention efforts. For example, in the 1960s, WHO promoted a campaign against major pandemics in Asia and Africa. In 1974, it launched a program aimed to vaccinate children worldwide. In the 1990s, WHO focused on developing programs to promote "lifestyle" diseases and prevention of smoking. In 1993, WHO initiated a joint program with the United Nations on HIV/AIDS.

Today, the WHO, as written on their website, "is the directing and coordinating authority for health within the United Nations system." It functions by working in cooperation with other governments to solve global health issues and to promote well-being for all people. Health guidelines and standards are established by WHO experts in English, French, Russian, and Spanish languages for a global population. WHO has six core functions, as written on their website:

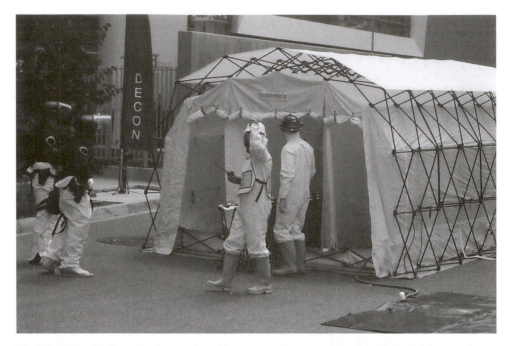

The World Health Organization works with community partners worldwide to achieve and promote the overall safety of consumers. (Loren Rodgers/Shutterstock.com)

April 7, 1948—the date we now celebrate every year as World Health Day

- providing leadership on matters critical to health and engaging in partnerships where joint action is needed;

- shaping the research agenda and stimulating the generation, translation and dissemination of valuable knowledge;

- setting norms and standards and promoting and monitoring their implementation;

- articulating ethical and evidence-based policy options;

- providing technical support, catalyzing change, and building sustainable institutional capacity; and

- monitoring the health situation and assessing health trends.

The organization employs over 8,000 health professionals who work in six regions of the world located in Cairo, New Delhi, Manila, Brazzaville, and Washington, D.C. WHO membership consists of 194 countries plus two associate members that meet annually in Geneva, Switzerland.

Work accomplished at the annual World Health Assembly focuses on setting policy for the Organization and approving the budget. An elected 34-member executive board supports the work of this World Health Assembly. Every five years a director-general for the organization is elected.

The WHO works in conjunction with many agencies to accomplish the health goals of the organization. A good example of a cooperative project with the United Nations occurred in 2000 at the UN Millennium Summit. At that meeting the 191 member nations elected to reduce poverty and improve health by 2015. This effort became known as the UN Millennium Development Goals (MDGs) where optimal health forms the core of the fundamental goals. Many member nations of the WHO have adopted the MDGs and are working on many of these goals within their own countries.

As the needs of global populations change, so do the methods of solving health and related problems change. Using data and other health reports, the objectives of the organization are continuously being realigned to meet the needs of the 21st century. This strategic health-planning process requires the WHO to be flexible in its approach to respond to new and evolving environments.

The three objectives defined at the 64th World Health Assembly in May 24, 2011, and at the May 25, 2011, Executive Board's 129th session for the future include:

- Improved health outcomes, with WHO meeting the expectations of its member states and partners in addressing agreed global health priorities, focused on the actions and areas where the organization has a unique function or comparative advantage, and financed in a way that facilitates this focus.

- Greater coherence in global health, with WHO playing a leading role in enabling the many different actors to play an active and effective role in contributing to the health of all peoples.

- An organization that pursues excellence; one that is effective, efficient, responsive, objective, transparent, and accountable (The World Health Organization).

Since its inception, WHO's commitments to improve global health have made significant impact. By providing information on risk factors for disease; conducting and disseminating research; and developing, implementing and monitoring health-based programs, consumers are better equipped to advocate for themselves and others to not only extend longevity but also to improve quality of life.

Sandra L. Poirier

See also: Department of Health and Human Services (DHS); Health and Health-care; United Nations (UN); World Trade Organization (WTO)

References and Additional Readings

Lee, K. (2008). *World Health Organization* (Vol. 26). London: Routledge.

McCarthy, M. (2002). A brief history of the World Health Organization. *The Lancet*, *360*(9340), 1111–1112.

World Health Organization. (2007). Working for health: An introduction to the World Health Organization. Retrieved from http://www.who.int/about/brochure_en.pdf

World Health Organization. (2009). History of the World Health Organization framework convention on tobacco control. Retrieved from http://www.who.int/fctc/about/history/en/index.html

World Trade Organization (WTO)

The World Trade Organization (WTO), located in Geneva, Switzerland, began in its current form in 1995. The WTO is a member organization that negotiates trade agreements, settles trade disputes, and creates and oversees fair trade rules. Formerly, as early as 1948, the General Agreement on Tariffs and Trade (GATT) set forth rules for the international trade system. GATT focused mainly on trade of goods, while WTO focuses on goods and services, as well as, intellectual property. Commodities such as agriculture, textiles and clothing, banking, and telecommunications are also monitored by the WTO. Over the next 47 years, GATT evolved through several rounds of negotiations. The most recent and largest GATT round of negotiations was the Uruguay Round. That negotiation lasted from 1986 to 1994, and in the end resulted in the WTO's creation in 1995.

An important and significant ministerial meeting was held in Doha, Qatar, in 2001 where members agreed to 21 new priorities, referred to as the Doha Declaration. The agenda included topics such as agriculture, services, intellectual property, transparency in government procurement, trade, and transfer of technology, to name a few. These have yet to be met, and are still a priority for the WTO. More recent meetings have been held in Geneva, Hong Kong, Cancun, and Bali in 2013.

The World Trade Organization (WTO) states:

The trading system should be . . .

- without discrimination—a country should not discriminate between its trading partners (giving them equally "most-favoured-nation" or MFN status); and it should not discriminate between its own and foreign products, services or nationals (giving them "national treatment"). . . .
- freer—barriers coming down through negotiation. . . .
- predictable—foreign companies, investors and governments should be confident that trade barriers (including tariffs and non-tariff barriers) should not be raised arbitrarily; tariff rates and market-opening commitments are "bound" in the WTO. . .
- more competitive—discouraging "unfair" practices such as export subsidies and dumping products at below cost to gain market share. . .
- more beneficial for less developed countries—giving them more time to adjust, greater flexibility, and special privileges.

Source: World Trade Organization. (2013). Principles of the trading system. Retrieved from http://www.wto.org

Members, essentially forums of governments, make decisions based on consensus; power is not delegated to a board like some other member organizations. As of this writing there were 157 member countries. The designated ministers conduct one meeting every one to two years, while ambassadors and delegates meet regularly in Geneva. Conferences are held every two years for technical and training assistance as well as trade negotiations. At that time, the ministers of each member nation convene to settle disputes and to vote on changes to many of the trading agreements. In addition to negotiating new trade agreements, members also assist developing countries by providing technical and training assistance; however, settling trading disputes between member countries is the most important function of the WTO. As a result, agreements often have to be interpreted by the WTO and are generally settled through previous legal agreements.

The WTO provides a forum for governments who experience trade problems with each other. They also provide a set of rules that are agreed upon by a large number of trading nations around the world. These documents provide "ground-rules" for international commerce, according to the WTO website. The overall goal is to allow fair trade while concurrently serving the needs of various populations, free trade as much as possible. In an effort to assure free trade, the WTO promotes liberalization of trade between countries, including removing obstacles to free trade. For developing countries, they provide training and technical assistance related to trade, including courses in Geneva and missions to individual training countries. All trading rules must be understood and applied to all member nations equally so there is transparency and confidence in the multilateral trading system. Naturally, the free trade priority applies when there is no negative effect for economic development of well-being of countries involved. Due to the success of international trade interactions and globalization the production chain may begin in one country and end in another country causing more products to be "Made in the World" rather than "Made in the USA."

Wendy Reiboldt and Sandra L. Poirier

See also: Fair Trade; Made in USA

References and Additional Readings

Bagwell, K., & Staiger, R.W. (2011). What do trade negotiators negotiate about? Empirical evidence from the World Trade Organization. *The American Economic Review, 101*(4), 1238–1273.

Barfield, C.E. (2001). Free trade, sovereignty, democracy: Future of the World Trade Organization. *Chicago Journal of International Law, 2*(2), 403–411.

World Trade Organization. (n.d.a). What is the WTO? Retrieved from www.wto.org

World Trade Organization. (n.d.b) Made in the world. Retrieved from http://www.wto.org/english/res_e/statis_e/miwi_e/miwi_e.htm

World Trade Organization. (n.d.c) Who are we. Retrieved from http://www.wto.org/english/thewto_e/whatis_e/who_we_are_e.htm

World Trade Organization. (n.d.d) WTO organization chart. Retrieved from http://www.wto.org/english/thewto_e/whatis_e/tif_e/org2_e.htm

Primary Source Appendix

The Universal Declaration of Human Rights

Preamble

Whereas recognition of the inherent dignity and of the equal and inalienable rights of all members of the human family is the foundation of freedom, justice and peace in the world,

Whereas disregard and contempt for human rights have resulted in barbarous acts which have outraged the conscience of mankind, and the advent of a world in which human beings shall enjoy freedom of speech and belief and freedom from fear and want has been proclaimed as the highest aspiration of the common people,

Whereas it is essential, if man is not to be compelled to have recourse, as a last resort, to rebellion against tyranny and oppression, that human rights should be protected by the rule of law,

Whereas it is essential to promote the development of friendly relations between nations,

Whereas the peoples of the United Nations have in the Charter reaffirmed their faith in fundamental human rights, in the dignity and worth of the human person and in the equal rights of men and women and have determined to promote social progress and better standards of life in larger freedom,

Whereas Member States have pledged themselves to achieve, in co-operation with the United Nations, the promotion of universal respect for and observance of human rights and fundamental freedoms,

Whereas a common understanding of these rights and freedoms is of the greatest importance for the full realization of this pledge,

Now, Therefore THE GENERAL ASSEMBLY proclaims THIS UNIVERSAL DECLARATION OF HUMAN RIGHTS as a common standard of achievement for all peoples and all nations, to the end that every individual and every organ of society, keeping this Declaration constantly in mind, shall strive by teaching and education to promote respect for these rights and freedoms and by progressive measures, national and international, to secure their universal and effective recognition and observance, both among the peoples of Member States themselves and among the peoples of territories under their jurisdiction.

Article 1

- All human beings are born free and equal in dignity and rights. They are endowed with reason and conscience and should act toward one another in a spirit of brotherhood.

Article 2

- Everyone is entitled to all the rights and freedoms set forth in this declaration, without distinction of any kind, such as race, color, sex, language, religion, political or other opinion, national or social origin, property, birth, or other status. Furthermore, no distinction shall be made on the basis of the political, jurisdictional, or international status of the country or territory to which a person belongs, whether it be independent, trust, nonself-governing, or under any other limitation of sovereignty.

Article 3

- Everyone has the right to life, liberty, and security of person.

Article 4

- No one shall be held in slavery or servitude; slavery and the slave trade shall be prohibited in all their forms.

Article 5

- No one shall be subjected to torture or to cruel, inhuman, or degrading treatment or punishment.

Article 6

- Everyone has the right to recognition everywhere as a person before the law.

Article 7

- All are equal before the law and are entitled without any discrimination to equal protection of the law. All are entitled to equal protection against any discrimination in violation of this declaration and against any incitement to such discrimination.

Article 8

- Everyone has the right to an effective remedy by the competent national tribunals for acts violating the fundamental rights granted him by the constitution or by law.

Article 9

- No one shall be subjected to arbitrary arrest, detention, or exile.

Article 10

- Everyone is entitled in full equality to a fair and public hearing by an independent and impartial tribunal, in the determination of his rights and obligations and of any criminal charge against him.

Article 11

- (1) Everyone charged with a penal offence has the right to be presumed innocent until proved guilty according to law in a public trial at which he has had all the guarantees necessary for his defence.
- (2) No one shall be held guilty of any penal offence on account of any act or omission which did not constitute a penal offence, under national or international law, at the time when it was committed. Nor shall a heavier penalty be imposed than the one that was applicable at the time the penal offence was committed.

Article 12

- No one shall be subjected to arbitrary interference with his privacy, family, home or correspondence, nor to attacks upon his honour and reputation. Everyone has the right to the protection of the law against such interference or attacks.

Article 13

- (1) Everyone has the right to freedom of movement and residence within the borders of each state.
- (2) Everyone has the right to leave any country, including his own, and to return to his country.

Article 14

- (1) Everyone has the right to seek and to enjoy in other countries asylum from persecution.
- (2) This right may not be invoked in the case of prosecutions genuinely arising from non-political crimes or from acts contrary to the purposes and principles of the United Nations.

Article 15

- (1) Everyone has the right to a nationality.
- (2) No one shall be arbitrarily deprived of his nationality nor denied the right to change his nationality.

Article 16

- (1) Men and women of full age, without any limitation due to race, nationality or religion, have the right to marry and to found a family. They are entitled to equal rights as to marriage, during marriage and at its dissolution.
- (2) Marriage shall be entered into only with the free and full consent of the intending spouses.
- (3) The family is the natural and fundamental group unit of society and is entitled to protection by society and the State.

Article 17

- (1) Everyone has the right to own property alone as well as in association with others.
- (2) No one shall be arbitrarily deprived of his property.

Article 18

- Everyone has the right to freedom of thought, conscience and religion; this right includes freedom to change his religion or belief, and freedom, either alone or in community with others and in public or private, to manifest his religion or belief in teaching, practice, worship and observance.

Article 19

- Everyone has the right to freedom of opinion and expression; this right includes freedom to hold opinions without interference and to seek, receive and impart information and ideas through any media and regardless of frontiers.

Article 20

- (1) Everyone has the right to freedom of peaceful assembly and association.
- (2) No one may be compelled to belong to an association.

Article 21

- (1) Everyone has the right to take part in the government of his country, directly or through freely chosen representatives.
- (2) Everyone has the right of equal access to public service in his country.
- (3) The will of the people shall be the basis of the authority of government; this will shall be expressed in periodic and genuine elections which shall be by universal and equal suffrage and shall be held by secret vote or by equivalent free voting procedures.

Article 22

- Everyone, as a member of society, has the right to social security and is entitled to realization, through national effort and international cooperation and in accordance with the organization and resources of each State, of the economic, social and cultural rights indispensable for his dignity and the free development of his personality.

Article 23

- (1) Everyone has the right to work, to free choice of employment, to just and favourable conditions of work and to protection against unemployment.
- (2) Everyone, without any discrimination, has the right to equal pay for equal work.

- (3) Everyone who works has the right to just and favourable remuneration ensuring for himself and his family an existence worthy of human dignity, and supplemented, if necessary, by other means of social protection.
- (4) Everyone has the right to form and to join trade unions for the protection of his interests.

Article 24

- Everyone has the right to rest and leisure, including reasonable limitation of working hours and periodic holidays with pay.

Article 25

- (1) Everyone has the right to a standard of living adequate for the health and well-being of himself and of his family, including food, clothing, housing and medical care and necessary social services, and the right to security in the event of unemployment, sickness, disability, widowhood, old age or other lack of livelihood in circumstances beyond his control.
- (2) Motherhood and childhood are entitled to special care and assistance. All children, whether born in or out of wedlock, shall enjoy the same social protection.

Article 26

- (1) Everyone has the right to education. Education shall be free, at least in the elementary and fundamental stages. Elementary education shall be compulsory. Technical and professional education shall be made generally available and higher education shall be equally accessible to all on the basis of merit.
- (2) Education shall be directed to the full development of the human personality and to the strengthening of respect for human rights and fundamental freedoms. It shall promote understanding, tolerance and friendship among all nations, racial or religious groups, and shall further the activities of the United Nations for the maintenance of peace.
- (3) Parents have a prior right to choose the kind of education that shall be given to their children.

Article 27

- (1) Everyone has the right freely to participate in the cultural life of the community, to enjoy the arts and to share in scientific advancement and its benefits.
- (2) Everyone has the right to the protection of the moral and material interests resulting from any scientific, literary or artistic production of which he is the author.

Article 28

- Everyone is entitled to a social and international order in which the rights and freedoms set forth in this Declaration can be fully realized.

Article 29

- (1) Everyone has duties to the community in which alone the free and full development of his personality is possible.
- (2) In the exercise of his rights and freedoms, everyone shall be subject only to such limitations as are determined by law solely for the purpose of securing due recognition and respect for the rights and freedoms of others and of meeting the just requirements of morality, public order and the general welfare in a democratic society.
- (3) These rights and freedoms may in no case be exercised contrary to the purposes and principles of the United Nations.

Article 30

- Nothing in this Declaration may be interpreted as implying for any State, group or person any right to engage in any activity or to perform any act aimed at the destruction of any of the rights and freedoms set forth herein.

Source: UN General Assembly. *Universal Declaration of Human Rights.* UN General Assembly Resolution 217A (III), A/810 at 71, 1948.

Family and Medical Leave Act (1993)

Adopted on February 5, 1993, the Family and Medical Leave Act requires all employers with 50 or more workers to guarantee unpaid leave to employees who have illness or family responsibilities that will legitimately keep the employees from working. This act attempts to relieve families of the burden of missing work during family medical emergencies.

An Act to grant family and temporary medical leave under certain circumstances.

Be it enacted by the Senate and House of Representatives of the United States of America in Congress assembled,

Section 2. FINDINGS AND PURPOSES.

(a) Findings. Congress finds that—

(1) the number of single-parent households and two-parent households in which the single parent or both parents work is increasing significantly;

(2) it is important for the development of children and the family unit that fathers and mothers be able to participate in early childrearing and the care of family members who have serious health conditions;

(3) the lack of employment policies to accommodate working parents can force individuals to choose between job security and parenting;

(4) there is inadequate job security for employees who have serious health conditions that prevent them from working for temporary periods;

(5) due to the nature of the roles of men and women in our society, the primary responsibility for family caretaking often falls on women, and such responsibility affects the working lives of women more than it affects the working lives of men; and

(6) employment standards that apply to one gender only have serious potential for encouraging employers to discriminate against employees and applicants for employment who are of that gender.

(b) Purposes. It is the purpose of this Act—

(1) to balance the demands of the workplace with the needs of families, to promote the stability and economic security of families, and to promote national interests in preserving family integrity;

(2) to entitle employees to take reasonable leave for medical reasons, for the birth or adoption of a child, and for the care of a child, spouse, or parent who has a serious health condition;

(3) to accomplish the purposes described in paragraphs (1) and (2) in a manner that accommodates the legitimate interests of employers;

(4) to accomplish the purposes described in paragraphs (1) and (2) in a manner that, consistent with the Equal Protection Clause of the Fourteenth Amendment, minimizes the potential for employment discrimination on the basis of sex by ensuring generally that leave is available for eligible medical reasons (including maternity-related disability) and for compelling family reasons, on a gender-neutral basis; and

(5) to promote the goal of equal employment opportunity for women and men, pursuant to such clause.

TITLE I—GENERAL REQUIREMENTS FOR LEAVE
Section 101. DEFINITIONS.
As used in this title:

(1) Commerce. The terms "commerce" and "industry or activity affecting commerce" mean any activity, business, or industry in commerce or in which a labor dispute would hinder or obstruct commerce or the free flow of commerce, and include "commerce" and any "industry affecting commerce", as defined in paragraphs (1) and (3) of section 501 of the Labor Management Relations Act, 1947 (29 U.S.C. 142 (1) and (3)).

(2) Eligible Employee.

(A) In general. The term "eligible employee" means an employee who has been employed—

(i) for at least 12 months by the employer with respect to whom leave is requested under section 102; and

(ii) for at least 1,250 hours of service with such employer during the previous 12-month period.

(B) Exclusions. The term "eligible employee" does not include—

(i) any Federal officer or employee covered under subchapter V of chapter 63 of title 5, United States Code (as added by title II of this Act); or

(ii) any employee of an employer who is employed at a worksite at which such employer employs less than 50 employees if the total number of employees employed by that employer within 75 miles of that worksite is less than 50.

(C) Determination. For purposes of determining whether an employee meets the hours of service requirement specified in subparagraph (A)(ii), the legal standards established under section 7 of the Fair Labor Standards Act of 1938 (29 U.S.C. 207) shall apply.

(3) Employ; Employee; State. The terms "employ", "employee", and "State" have the same meanings given such terms in subsections (c), (e), and (g) of section 3 of the Fair Labor Standards Act of 1938 (29 U.S.C. 203(c), (e), and (g)).

(4) Employer.

(A) In general. The term "employer"—

(i) means any person engaged in commerce or in any industry or activity affecting commerce who employs 50 or more employees for each working day during each of 20 or more calendar workweeks in the current or preceding calendar year;

(ii) includes—

(I) any person who acts, directly or indirectly, in the interest of an employer to any of the employees of such employer; and

(II) any successor in interest of an employer; and

(iii) includes any "public agency", as defined in section 3(x) of the Fair Labor Standards Act of 1938 (29 U.S.C. 203(x)).

(B) Public agency. For purposes of subparagraph (A)(iii), a public agency shall be considered to be a person engaged in commerce or in an industry or activity affecting commerce.

(5) Employment Benefits. The term "employment benefits" means all benefits provided or made available to employees by an employer, including group life insurance, health insurance, disability insurance, sick leave, annual leave, educational benefits, and pensions, regardless of whether such benefits are provided by a practice or written policy of an employer or through an "employee benefit plan", as defined in section 3(3) of the Employee Retirement Income Security Act of 1974 (29 U.S.C. 1002(3)).

(6) Health Care Provider. The term "health care provider" means—

(A) a doctor of medicine or osteopathy who is authorized to practice medicine or surgery (as appropriate) by the State in which the doctor practices; or

(B) any other person determined by the Secretary to be capable of providing health care services.

(7) Parent. The term "parent" means the biological parent of an employee or an individual who stood in loco parentis to an employee when the employee was a son or daughter.

(8) Person. The term "person" has the same meaning given such term in section 3(a) of the Fair Labor Standards Act of 1938 (29 U.S.C. 203(a)).

(9) Reduced Leave Schedule. The term "reduced leave schedule" means a leave schedule that reduces the usual number of hours per workweek, or hours per workday, of an employee.

(10) Secretary. The term "Secretary" means the Secretary of Labor.

(11) Serious Health Condition. The term "serious health condition" means an illness, injury, impairment, or physical or mental condition that involves—

(A) inpatient care in a hospital, hospice, or residential medical care facility; or

(B) continuing treatment by a health care provider.

(12) Son or Daughter. The term "son or daughter" means a biological, adopted, or foster child, a stepchild, a legal ward, or a child of a person standing in loco parentis, who is—

(A) under 18 years of age; or

(B) 18 years of age or older and incapable of self-care because of a mental or physical disability.

(13) Spouse. The term "spouse" means a husband or wife, as the case may be.

Section 102. LEAVE REQUIREMENT.

(a) In general.

(1) Entitlement to Leave. Subject to section 103, an eligible employee shall be entitled to a total of 12 workweeks of leave during any 12-month period for one or more of the following:

(A) Because of the birth of a son or daughter of the employee and in order to care for such son or daughter.

(B) Because of the placement of a son or daughter with the employee for adoption or foster care.

(C) In order to care for the spouse, or a son, daughter, or parent, of the employee, if such spouse, son, daughter, or parent has a serious health condition.

(D) Because of a serious health condition that makes the employee unable to perform the functions of the position of such employee.

(2) Expiration of Entitlement. The entitlement to leave under subparagraphs (A) and (B) of paragraph (1) for a birth or placement of a son or daughter shall expire at the end of the 12-month period beginning on the date of such birth or placement.

(b) Leave taken Intermittently or on a Reduced Leave Schedule.

(1) In general. Leave under subparagraph (A) or (B) of subsection (a) (1) shall not be taken by an employee intermittently or on a reduced leave schedule unless the employee and the employer of the employee agree otherwise. Subject to paragraph (2), subsection (e)(2), and section 103(b)(5), leave under subparagraph (C) or (D) of subsection (a)(1) may be taken intermittently or on a reduced leave schedule when medically necessary. The taking of leave intermittently or on a reduced leave schedule pursuant to this paragraph shall not result in a reduction in the total amount of leave to which the employee is entitled under subsection (a) beyond the amount of leave actually taken.

(2) Alternative Position. If an employee requests intermittent leave, or leave on a reduced leave schedule, under subparagraph (C) or (D) of subsection (a)(1), that is foreseeable based on planned medical treatment, the employer may require such employee to transfer temporarily to an available alternative position offered by the employer for which the employee is qualified and that—

(A) has equivalent pay and benefits; and

(B) better accommodates recurring periods of leave than the regular employment position of the employee.

(c) Unpaid Leave Permitted. Except as provided in subsection (d), leave granted under subsection (a) may consist of unpaid leave. Where an employee is otherwise exempt under regulations issued by the Secretary pursuant to section 13(a)(1) of the Fair Labor Standards Act of 1938 (29 U.S.C. 213(a)(1)), the compliance of an employer with this title by providing unpaid leave shall not affect the exempt status of the employee under such section.

(d) Relationship to Paid Leave.

(1) Unpaid Leave. If an employer provides paid leave for fewer than 12 workweeks, the additional weeks of leave necessary to attain the 12 workweeks of leave required under this title may be provided without compensation.

(2) Substitution of Paid Leave.

(A) In general. An eligible employee may elect, or an employer may require the employee, to substitute any of the accrued paid vacation leave, personal leave, or family leave of the employee for leave provided under subparagraph (A), (B), or (C) of subsection (a)(1) for any part of the 12-week period of such leave under such subsection.

(B) Serious Health Condition. An eligible employee may elect, or an employer may require the employee, to substitute any of the accrued paid vacation leave, personal leave, or medical or sick leave of the employee for leave provided under subparagraph (C) or (D) of subsection (a)(1) for any part of the 12-week period of such leave under such subsection, except that nothing in this title shall require an employer to provide paid sick leave or paid medical leave in any situation in which such employer would not normally provide any such paid leave.

(e) Foreseeable Leave.

(1) Requirement of Notice. In any case in which the necessity for leave under subparagraph (A) or (B) of subsection (a)(1) is foreseeable based on an expected birth or placement, the employee shall provide the employer with not less than 30 days' notice, before the date the leave is to begin, of the employee's intention to take leave under such subparagraph, except that if the date of the birth or placement requires leave to begin in less than 30 days, the employee shall provide such notice as is practicable.

(2) Duties of Employee. In any case in which the necessity for leave under subparagraph (C) or (D) of subsection (a)(1) is foreseeable based on planned medical treatment, the employee—

(A) shall make a reasonable effort to schedule the treatment so as not to disrupt unduly the operations of the employer, subject to the approval of the health care provider of the employee or the health care provider of the son, daughter, spouse, or parent of the employee, as appropriate; and

(B) shall provide the employer with not less than 30 days' notice, before the date the leave is to begin, of the employee's intention to take leave under such subparagraph, except that if the date of the treatment requires leave to begin in less than 30 days, the employee shall provide such notice as is practicable.

(f) Spouses Employed by the Same Employer. In any case in which a husband and wife entitled to leave under subsection (a) are employed by the same employer, the aggregate number of workweeks of leave to which both may be entitled may be limited to 12 workweeks during any 12-month period, if such leave is taken—

(1) under subparagraph (A) or (B) of subsection (a)(1); or

(2) to care for a sick parent under subparagraph (C) of such subsection.

Section 103. CERTIFICATION.

(a) In general. An employer may require that a request for leave under subparagraph (C) or (D) of section 102(a)(1) be supported by a certification issued by the health care provider of the eligible employee or of the son, daughter, spouse, or parent of the employee, as appropriate. The employee shall provide, in a timely manner, a copy of such certification to the employer.

(b) Sufficient Certification. Certification provided under subsection (a) shall be sufficient if it states—

(1) the date on which the serious health condition commenced;

(2) the probable duration of the condition;

(3) the appropriate medical facts within the knowledge of the health care provider regarding the condition;

(4)(A) for purposes of leave under section 102(a)(1)(C), a statement that the eligible employee is needed to care for the son, daughter, spouse, or parent and an estimate of the amount of time that such employee is needed to care for the son, daughter, spouse, or parent; and

(B) for purposes of leave under section 102(a)(1)(D), a statement that the employee is unable to perform the functions of the position of the employee;

(5) in the case of certification for intermittent leave, or leave on a reduced leave schedule, for planned medical treatment, the dates on which such treatment is expected to be given and the duration of such treatment;

(6) in the case of certification for intermittent leave, or leave on a reduced leave schedule, under section 102(a)(1)(D), a statement of the medical necessity for the intermittent leave or leave on a reduced leave schedule, and the expected duration of the intermittent leave or reduced leave schedule; and

(7) in the case of certification for intermittent leave, or leave on a reduced leave schedule, under section 102(a)(1)(C), a statement that the employee's intermittent leave or leave on a reduced leave schedule is necessary for the care of the son, daughter, parent, or spouse who has a serious health condition, or will assist in their recovery, and the expected duration and schedule of the intermittent leave or reduced leave schedule.

(c) Second Opinion.

(1) In general. In any case in which the employer has reason to doubt the validity of the certification provided under subsection (a) for leave under subparagraph (C) or (D) of section 102(a)(1), the employer may require, at the expense of the employer, that the eligible employee obtain the opinion of a second health care provider designated or approved by the employer concerning any information certified under subsection (b) for such leave.

(2) Limitation. A health care provider designated or approved under paragraph (1) shall not be employed on a regular basis by the employer.

(d) Resolution of Conflicting Opinions.

(1) In general. In any case in which the second opinion described in subsection (c) differs from the opinion in the original certification provided under subsection (a), the employer may require, at the expense of the employer, that the employee obtain the opinion of a third health care provider designated or approved jointly by the employer and the employee concerning the information certified under subsection (b).

(2) Finality. The opinion of the third health care provider concerning the information certified under subsection (b) shall be considered to be final and shall be binding on the employer and the employee.

(e) Subsequent Recertification. The employer may require that the eligible employee obtain subsequent recertifications on a reasonable basis.

Section 104. EMPLOYMENT AND BENEFITS PROTECTION.

(a) Restoration to Position.

(1) In general. Except as provided in subsection (b), any eligible employee who takes leave under section 102 for the intended purpose of the leave shall be entitled, on return from such leave—

(A) to be restored by the employer to the position of employment held by the employee when the leave commenced; or

(B) to be restored to an equivalent position with equivalent employment benefits, pay, and other terms and conditions of employment.

(2) Loss of Benefits. The taking of leave under section 102 shall not result in the loss of any employment benefit accrued prior to the date on which the leave commenced.

(3) Limitations. Nothing in this section shall be construed to entitle any restored employee to—

(A) the accrual of any seniority or employment benefits during any period of leave; or

(B) any right, benefit, or position of employment other than any right, benefit, or position to which the employee would have been entitled had the employee not taken the leave.

(4) Certification. As a condition of restoration under paragraph (1) for an employee who has taken leave under section 102(a)(1)(D), the employer

may have a uniformly applied practice or policy that requires each such employee to receive certification from the health care provider of the employee that the employee is able to resume work, except that nothing in this paragraph shall supersede a valid State or local law or a collective bargaining agreement that governs the return to work of such employees.

(5) Construction. Nothing in this subsection shall be construed to prohibit an employer from requiring an employee on leave under section 102 to report periodically to the employer on the status and intention of the employee to return to work.

(b) Exemption Concerning Certain Highly Compensated Employees.

(1) Denial of Restoration. An employer may deny restoration under subsection (a) to any eligible employee described in paragraph (2) if—

(A) such denial is necessary to prevent substantial and grievous economic injury to the operations of the employer;

(B) the employer notifies the employee of the intent of the employer to deny restoration on such basis at the time the employer determines that such injury would occur; and

(C) in any case in which the leave has commenced, the employee elects not to return to employment after receiving such notice.

(2) Affected Employees. An eligible employee described in paragraph (1) is a salaried eligible employee who is among the highest paid 10 percent of the employees employed by the employer within 75 miles of the facility at which the employee is employed.

(c) Maintenance of Health Benefits.

(1) Coverage. Except as provided in paragraph (2), during any period that an eligible employee takes leave under section 102, the employer shall maintain coverage under any "group health plan" (as defined in section 5000(b)(1) of the Internal Revenue Code of 1986) for the duration of such leave at the level and under the conditions coverage would have been provided if the employee had continued in employment continuously for the duration of such leave.

(2) Failure to Return from Leave. The employer may recover the premium that the employer paid for maintaining coverage for the employee under such group health plan during any period of unpaid leave under section 102 if—

(A) the employee fails to return from leave under section 102 after the period of leave to which the employee is entitled has expired; and

(B) the employee fails to return to work for a reason other than—

(i) the continuation, recurrence, or onset of a serious health condition that entitles the employee to leave under subparagraph (C) or (D) of section 102(a)(1); or

(ii) other circumstances beyond the control of the employee.

(3) Certification.

(A) Issuance. An employer may require that a claim that an employee is unable to return to work because of the continuation, recurrence, or onset of the serious health condition described in paragraph (2)(B)(i) be supported by—

(i) a certification issued by the health care provider of the son, daughter, spouse, or parent of the employee, as appropriate, in the case of an employee unable to return to work because of a condition specified in section 102(a)(1)(C); or

(ii) a certification issued by the health care provider of the eligible employee, in the case of an employee unable to return to work because of a condition specified in section 102(a)(1)(D).

(B) Copy. The employee shall provide, in a timely manner, a copy of such certification to the employer.

(C) Sufficiency of Certification.

(i) Leave Due to Serious Health Condition of Employee. The certification described in subparagraph (A)(ii) shall be sufficient if the certification states that a serious health condition prevented the employee from being able to perform the functions of the position of the employee on the date that the leave of the employee expired.

(ii) Leave Due to Serious Health Condition of Family Member. The certification described in subparagraph (A)(i) shall be sufficient if the certification states that the employee is needed to care for the son, daughter, spouse, or parent who has a serious health condition on the date that the leave of the employee expired.

Section 105. PROHIBITED ACTS.

(a) Interference with Rights.

(1) Exercise of Rights. It shall be unlawful for any employer to interfere with, restrain, or deny the exercise of or the attempt to exercise, any right provided under this title.

(2) Discrimination. It shall be unlawful for any employer to discharge or in any other manner discriminate against any individual for opposing any practice made unlawful by this title.

(b) Interference with Proceedings or Inquiries. It shall be unlawful for any person to discharge or in any other manner discriminate against any individual because such individual—

(1) has filed any charge, or has instituted or caused to be instituted any proceeding, under or related to this title;

(2) has given, or is about to give, any information in connection with any inquiry or proceeding relating to any right provided under this title; or

(3) has testified, or is about to testify, in any inquiry or proceeding relating to any right provided under this title.

Section 107. ENFORCEMENT.

(a) Civil Action by Employees.

(1) Liability. Any employer who violates section 105 shall be liable to any eligible employee affected—

(A) for damages equal to—

(i) the amount of—

(I) any wages, salary, employment benefits, or other compensation denied or lost to such employee by reason of the violation; or

(II) in a case in which wages, salary, employment benefits, or other compensation have not been denied or lost to the employee, any actual monetary losses sustained by the employee as a direct result of the violation, such as the cost of providing care, up to a sum equal to 12 weeks of wages or salary for the employee;

(ii) the interest on the amount described in clause (i) calculated at the prevailing rate; and

(iii) an additional amount as liquidated damages equal to the sum of the amount described in clause (i) and the interest described in clause (ii), except that if an employer who has violated section 105 proves to the satisfaction of the court that the act or omission which violated section 105 was in good faith and that the employer had reasonable grounds for believing that the act or omission was not a violation of section 105, such court may, in the discretion of the court, reduce the amount of the liability to the amount and interest determined under clauses (i) and (ii), respectively; and

(B) for such equitable relief as may be appropriate, including employment, reinstatement, and promotion.

(2) Right of Action. An action to recover the damages or equitable relief prescribed in paragraph (1) may be maintained against any employer (including a public agency) in any Federal or State court of competent jurisdiction by any one or more employees for and in behalf of—

(A) the employees; or

(B) the employees and other employees similarly situated.

(3) Fees and Costs. The court in such an action shall, in addition to any judgment awarded to the plaintiff, allow a reasonable attorney's fee, reasonable expert witness fees, and other costs of the action to be paid by the defendant.

(4) Limitations. The right provided by paragraph (2) to bring an action by or on behalf of any employee shall terminate—

(A) on the filing of a complaint by the Secretary in an action under subsection (d) in which restraint is sought of any further delay in the payment of the amount described in paragraph (1)(A) to such employee by an employer responsible under paragraph (1) for the payment; or

(B) on the filing of a complaint by the Secretary in an action under subsection (b) in which a recovery is sought of the damages described in paragraph (1)(A) owing to an eligible employee by an employer liable under paragraph (1), unless the action described in subparagraph (A) or (B) is dismissed without prejudice on motion of the Secretary.

(b) Action by the Secretary.

(1) Administrative Action. The Secretary shall receive, investigate, and attempt to resolve complaints of violations of section 105 in the same manner that the Secretary receives, investigates, and attempts to resolve complaints of violations of sections 6 and 7 of the Fair Labor Standards Act of 1938 (29 U.S.C. 206 and 207).

(2) Civil Action. The Secretary may bring an action in any court of competent jurisdiction to recover the damages described in subsection (a)(1)(A).

(3) Sums Recovered. Any sums recovered by the Secretary pursuant to paragraph (2) shall be held in a special deposit account and shall be paid, on order of the Secretary, directly to each employee affected. Any such sums not paid to an employee because of inability to do so within a period of 3 years shall be deposited into the Treasury of the United States as miscellaneous receipts.

(c) Limitation.

(1) In general. Except as provided in paragraph (2), an action may be brought under this section not later than 2 years after the date of the last event constituting the alleged violation for which the action is brought.

(2) Willful Violation. In the case of such action brought for a willful violation of section 105, such action may be brought within 3 years of the date of the last event constituting the alleged violation for which such action is brought.

(3) Commencement. In determining when an action is commenced by the Secretary under this section for the purposes of this subsection, it shall be considered to be commenced on the date when the complaint is filed.

(d) Action for Injunction by Secretary. The district courts of the United States shall have jurisdiction, for cause shown, in an action brought by the Secretary—

(1) to restrain violations of section 105, including the restraint of any withholding of payment of wages, salary, employment benefits, or other compensation, plus interest, found by the court to be due to eligible employees; or

(2) to award such other equitable relief as may be appropriate, including employment, reinstatement, and promotion.

(e) Solicitor of Labor. The Solicitor of Labor may appear for and represent the Secretary on any litigation brought under this section.

Source: Family and Medical Leave Act of 1993. U.S. Code 29, §§ 2601 et seq.

First session of the 85th Congress of the United States

An Act to provide means of further securing and protecting the civil rights of persons within the jurisdiction of the United States.

Be it enacted by the Senate and House of Representatives of the United States of America in Congress assembled,

PART I. ESTABLISHMENT OF THE COMMISSION ON CIVIL RIGHTS
Section 101.

(a) There is created in the executive branch of the Government a Commission on Civil Rights (hereinafter called the "Commission").

(b) The Commission shall be composed of six members who shall be appointed by the President by and with the advice and consent of the Senate. Not more than three of the members shall at any one time be of the same political party.

(c) The President shall designate one of the members of the Commission as Chairman and one as Vice Chairman. The Vice Chairman shall act as Chairman in the absence or disability of the Chairman, or in the event of a vacancy in that office.

(d) Any vacancy in the Commission shall not affect its powers and shall be filled in the same manner, and subject to the same limitations with respect to party affiliations as the original appointment was made.

(e) Four members of the Commission shall constitute a quorum.

Section 102. Rules of Procedure of the Commission

(a) The chairman or one designated by him to act as Chairman at a hearing of the Commission shall announce in an opening statement the subject of the hearing.

(b) A copy of the Commission's rules shall be made available to the witness before the Commission.

(c) Witnesses at the hearings may be accompanied by their own counsel for the purpose of advising them concerning their constitutional rights.

(d) The Chairman or Acting Chairman may punish breaches of order and decorum and unprofessional ethics on the part of counsel, by censure and exclusion from the hearings.

(e) If the Commission determines that evidence or testimony at any hearing may tend to defame, degrade, or incriminate any person, it shall (1) receive such evidence or testimony in executive session; (2) afford such person an opportunity voluntarily to appear as a witness; and (3) receive and dispose of requests from such person to subpoena additional witnesses.

(f) Except as provided in Sections 102 and 105 (f) of this Act, the Chairman shall receive and the commission shall dispose of requests to subpoena additional witnesses.

(g) No evidence or testimony taken in executive session may be released or used in public sessions without the consent of the Commission. Whoever releases or uses in public without the consent of the Commission evidence or testimony taken in executive session shall be fined not more than $1,000, or imprisoned for not more than one year.

(h) In the discretion of the commission, witnesses may submit brief and pertinent sworn statements in writing for inclusion in the record. The commission is the sole judge of the pertinence of testimony and evidence adduced at its hearings.

(i) Upon payment of the cost thereof, a witness may obtain a transcript copy of his testimony given at a public session or, if given at an executive session, when authorized by the Commission.

(j) A witness attending any session of the Commission shall receive $4 for each day's attendance and for the time necessarily occupied in going to and returning from the same, and 8 cents per mile for going from and returning to his place of residence. Witnesses who attend at points so far removed from their respective residences as to prohibit return thereto from day to day shall be entitled to an additional allowance of $12 per day for expenses of subsistence, including the time necessarily occupied in going to and returning from the place of attendance. Mileage payments shall be tendered to the witness upon service of a subpoena issued on behalf of the Commission or any subcommittee thereof.

(k) The Commission shall not issue any subpoena for the attendance and testimony of witnesses or for the production of written or other matter which would require the presence of the party subpoenaed at a hearing to be held outside of the State, wherein the witness is found or resides or transacts business.

Section 103. Compensation of Members of the Commission

(a) Each member of the Commission who is not otherwise in the service of the Government of the United States shall receive the sum of $50 per day for each day spent in the work of the Commission, shall be reimbursed for actual and necessary travel expenses, and shall receive a per diem allowance of $12 in lieu of actual expenses for subsistence when away from his usual place of residence, inclusive of fees or tips to porters and stewards.

(b) Each member of the Commission who is otherwise in the service of the government of the United States shall serve without compensation in addition to that received for such other service, but while engaged in the work of the commission shall be reimbursed for actual and necessary travel expenses, and shall receive a per diem allowance of $12 in lieu of actual expenses for subsistence when away from his usual place of residence, inclusive of fees or tips to porters and stewards.

Section 104. Duties of the Commission

(a) The Commission shall—

(1) investigate allegations in writing under oath or affirmation that certain citizens of the United States are being deprived of their right to vote and have that vote counted by reason of their color, race, religion, or national origin; which writing, under oath or affirmation, shall set forth the facts upon which such belief or beliefs are based;

(2) study and collect information concerning legal developments constituting a denial of equal protection of the laws under the Constitution; and

(3) appraise the laws and policies of the Federal Government with respect to equal protection of the laws under the constitution.

(b) The Commission shall submit interim reports to the President and to the Congress at such times as either the Commission or the President shall deem desirable, and shall submit to the President and to the Congress a final and comprehensive report of its activities, findings and recommendations not later than two years from the date of the enactment of this Act.

(c) Sixty days after the submission of its final report and recommendations the Commission shall cease to exist.

Section 105. Powers of the Commission

(a) There shall be a full-time staff director for the Commission who shall be appointed by the President by and with the advice and consent of the Senate and who shall receive compensation at a rate, to be fixed by the President, not in excess of $22,500 a year. The President shall consult with the Commission before submitting the nomination of any person for appointment to the position of staff director. Within the limitations of its appropriations, the Commission may appoint such other personnel as it deems advisable, in accordance with the civil service and classification laws, and may procure services as authorized by section 15 of the Act of August 2, 1946 (60 Stat. 810; 5 U.S.C. 55a), but at rates for individuals not in excess of $50 per diem.

(b) The commission shall not accept or utilize services of voluntary or uncompensated personnel, and the term "whoever" as used in paragraph

(g) of section 102 hereof shall be construed to mean a person whose services are compensated by the United States.

(c) The Commission may constitute such advisory committees within States composed of citizens of that State and may consult with governors, attorneys general, and other representatives of State and local governments, and private organizations, as it deems advisable.

(d) Members of the Commission, and members of advisory committees constituted pursuant to subsection (c) of this section, shall be exempt from the operation of sections 281, 283, 284, 434, and 1914 of title 18 of the United States Code, and section 190 of the Revised Statutes (5 U.S.C. 99).

(e) All Federal agencies shall cooperate fully with the Commission to the end that it may effectively carry out its functions and duties.

(f) The Commission, or on the authorization of the Commission any subcommittee of two or more members, at least one of whom shall be of each major political party, may, for the purpose or carrying out the provisions of this Act, hold such hearings and act at such times and places as the Commission or such authorized subcommittee may deem advisable. Subpoenas for the attendance and testimony of witnesses or the production of written or other matter may be issued in accordance with the rules of the Commission as contained in section 102 (j) and (k) of this Act, over the signature of the Chairman of the Commission or of such subcommittee, and may be served by any person designated by such Chairman.

(g) In case of contumacy or refusal to obey a subpoena, any district court of the United States or the United States court of any Territory or possession, or the District Court of the United States for the District of Columbia, within the jurisdiction of which the inquiry is carried on or within the jurisdiction of which said person guilty of contumacy or refusal to obey is found or resides or transacts business, upon application by the Attorney General of the United States shall have jurisdiction to issue to such person an order requiring such person to appear before the Commission or a subcommittee thereof, there to produce evidence is so ordered, or there to give testimony touching the matter under investigation; and any failure to obey such order of the court may be punished by said court as a contempt thereof.

Section 106. Appropriations

There is hereby authorized to be appropriated, out of any money in the Treasury not otherwise appropriated, so much as may be necessary to carry out the provisions of this Act.

PART II. TO PROVIDE FOR AN ADDITIONAL ASSISTANT ATTORNEY GENERAL

Section 111.

There shall be in the Department of Justice one additional Assistant Attorney General, who shall be appointed by the President, by and with the advice and consent of the Senate, who shall assist the Attorney General in the performance of his duties, and who shall receive compensations at the rate prescribed by law for other Assistant Attorneys General.

PART III. TO STRENGTHEN THE CIVIL RIGHTS STATUTES, AND FOR OTHER PURPOSES

Section 121.

Section 1343 of title 28, United States Code, is amended as follows:

(a) Amend the catch line of said section to read: "Section 1343. Civil Rights and elective franchise"

(b) Delete the period at the end of paragraph (3) and insert in lieu thereof a semicolon.

(c) Add a paragraph as follows: "(4) to recover damages or to secure equitable or other relief under any Act of Congress providing for the protection of civil rights, including the right to vote."

Section 122.

Section 1989 of the Revised Statutes (42 U.S.C. 1993) is hereby repealed.

PART IV. TO PROVIDE MEANS OF FURTHER SECURING AND PROTECTING THE RIGHT TO VOTE

Section 131.

Section 2004 of the Revised statutes (42 U.S.C. 1971), is amended as follows:

(a) Amend the catch line of said section to read, "Voting rights".

(b) Designate its present text with the subsection symbol "(a)".

(c) Add, immediately following the present text, four new subsections to read as follows:

"(b) No person, whether acting under color of law or otherwise, shall intimidate, threaten coerce, or attempt to intimidate, threaten or coerce any other person for the purpose of interfering with the right of such other person to vote or to vote as he may choose, or of causing such other person to vote for, or not to vote for, any candidate for the office of President, Vice President, presidential elector, Member of the Senate, or Member of the house of Representatives, Delegates or Commissioners from the Territories or possessions, at any general special, or primary election held solely or in part for the purpose of selecting or electing any such candidate."

"(c) whenever any person has engaged or there are reasonable grounds to believe that any person is about to engage in any act or practice which would deprive any other person of any right or privilege secured by a subsection (a) or (b), the Attorney General may institute for the United States, or in the name of the United States, a civil action or other proper proceeding for preventive relief, including an application for a permanent or temporary injunction, restraining order, or other order. In any proceeding hereunder the United States shall be liable for costs the same as a private person."

"(d) the district courts of the United States shall have jurisdiction of the proceedings instituted pursuant to this section and shall exercise the same without regard to whether the party aggrieved shall have exhausted any administrative or other remedies that may be provided by law."

"(e) Any person cited for an alleged contempt under this Act shall be allowed to make his full defense by counsel learned in the law; and the court before which he is cited or tried, or some judge thereof, shall immediately, upon his request, assign to him such counsel, not exceeding two, as he may desire, who shall have free access to him at all reasonable hours. He shall be allowed, in his defense to make any proof that he can produce by lawful witnesses, and shall have the like process of the court to compel his witnesses to appear at his trial or hearing, as is usually granted to compel witnesses to appear on behalf of the prosecution. If such person shall be found by the court to be financially unable provide for such counsel, it shall be the duty of the court to provide such counsel."

PART V. TO PROVIDE TRIAL BY JURY FOR PROCEEDINGS TO PUNISH CRIMINAL CONTEMPTS OF COURT GROWING OUT OF CIVIL RIGHTS CASES AND TO AMEND THE JUDICIAL CODE RELATING TO FEDERAL JURY QUALIFICATIONS.

Section 151.

All cases of criminal contempt arising under the provisions of this Act, the accused, upon conviction, shall be punished by fine or imprisonment or both: Provided however, That in case the accused is a natural person the fine to be paid shall not exceed the sum of $1,000, nor shall imprisonment exceed the term of six months: Provided Further, that in any such proceeding for criminal contempt, at the discretion of the judge, the accused may be tried with or without a jury: Provided further, however, That in the event such proceeding for a criminal contempt be tried before a judge without a jury and the sentence of the court upon conviction is a fine in excess of the sum of $30 or imprisonment in excess of forty-five days, the accused in said proceeding, upon demand therefore, shall be entitled to a trial de novo before a jury which shall conform as near as may be to the practice in other criminal cases.

This section shall not apply to contempts committed in the presence of the court or so near thereto as to interfere directly with the administration of justice nor to the misbehavior, misconduct, or disobedience, of any officer of the court in respect to the writs, orders, or process of the court.

Nor shall anything herein or in any other provision of law be construed to deprive courts of their power, by civil contempt proceedings, without a jury, to secure compliance with or to prevent obstruction of, as distinguished from punishment for violations of, any lawful writ, process, order, rule, decree, or command of the court in accordance with the prevailing usages of law equity, including the power of detention.

Section 152.

Section 1861, title 28, of the United States Code is hereby amended to read as follows:

Section 1861. Qualifications of Federal jurors. Any citizen of the United States who has attained the age of twenty-one years and who has resided for a period of one year within the judicial district, is competent to serve as a grand or petit juror unless—

(1) he has been convicted in a State or Federal court of record of a crime punishable by imprisonment for more than one year and his civil rights have not been restored by pardon or amnesty.

(2) He is unable to read, write, speak, and understand the English language.

(3) He is incapable, by reason of mental or physical infirmities to render efficient jury service.

Section 161.

This Act may be cited as the "Civil Rights Act of 1957".

Source: Civil Rights Act of 1957. Public Law 85–315. 71 *U.S. Statutes at Large* 634 (1957).

Identity Theft and Assumption Deterrence Act

SECTION 001. Short Title.

This Act may be cited as the "Identity Theft and Assumption Deterrence Act of 1998".

SEC. 002. Constitutional Authority to Enact this Legislation.

The constitutional authority upon which this Act rests is the power of Congress to regulate commerce with foreign nations and among the several States, and the authority to make all laws which shall be necessary and proper for carrying into execution the powers vested by the Constitution in the Government of the United States or in any department or officer thereof, as set forth in article I, section 8 of the United States Constitution.

SEC. 003. Identity Theft.

(a) Establishment of Offense.—Section 1028(a) of title 18, United States Code, is amended—

(1) in paragraph (5), by striking "or" at the end;

(2) in paragraph (6), by adding "or" at the end;

(3) in the flush matter following paragraph (6), by striking "or attempts to do so,"; and

(4) by inserting after paragraph (6) the following: "(7) knowingly transfers or uses, without lawful authority, a means of identification of another person with the intent to commit, or to aid or abet, any unlawful activity that constitutes a violation of Federal law, or that constitutes a felony under any applicable State or local law;"

(b) Penalties.—Section 1028(b) of title 18, United States Code, is amended—

(1) in paragraph (1)—

(A) in subparagraph (B), by striking "or" at the end;

(B) in subparagraph (C), by adding "or" at the end; and

(C) by adding at the end the following: "(D) an offense under paragraph (7) of such subsection that involves the transfer or use of 1 or more means of identification if, as a result of the offense, any individual committing the offense obtains anything of value aggregating $1,000 or more during any 1-year period;"

(2) in paragraph (2)—

(A) in subparagraph (A), by striking "or transfer of an identification document or" and inserting ", transfer, or use of a means of identification, an identification document, or a"; and

(B) in subparagraph (B), by inserting "or (7)" after "(3)";

(3) by amending paragraph (3) to read as follows:

"(3) a fine under this title or imprisonment for not more than 20 years, or both, if the offense is committed—

"(A) to facilitate a drug trafficking crime (as defined in section 929(a) (2));

"(B) in connection with a crime of violence (as defined in section 924(c) (3)); or

"(C) after a prior conviction under this section becomes final;";

(4) in paragraph (4), by striking "and" at the end;

(5) by redesignating paragraph (5) as paragraph (6); and

(6) by inserting after paragraph (4) the following: "(5) in the case of any offense under subsection (a), forfeiture to the United States of any personal property used or intended to be used to commit the offense; and".

(c) Circumstances.—Section 1028(c) of title 18, United States Code, is amended by striking paragraph (3) and inserting the following:

"(3) either—

"(A) the production, transfer, possession, or use prohibited by this section is in or affects interstate or foreign commerce; or

"(B) the means of identification, identification document, false identification document, or document-making implement is transported in the mail in the course of the production, transfer, possession, or use prohibited by this section."

(d) Definitions—Subsection (d) of section 1028 of title 18, United States Code, is amended to read as follows:

"(d) In this section—

"(1) the term 'document-making implement' means any implement, impression, electronic device, or computer hardware or software, that is specifically configured or primarily used for making an identification document, a false identification document, or another document-making implement;

"(2) the term 'identification document' means a document made or issued by or under the authority of the United States Government, a State, political subdivision of a State, a foreign government, political subdivision of a foreign government, an international governmental or an international quasi-governmental organization which, when completed with information concerning a particular individual, is of a type intended or commonly accepted for the purpose of identification of individuals;

"(3) the term 'means of identification' means any name or number that may be used, alone or in conjunction with any other information, to identify a specific individual, including any—

"(A) name, social security number, date of birth, official State or government issued driver's license or identification number, alien registration number, government passport number, employer or taxpayer identification number;

"(B) unique biometric data, such as fingerprint, voice print, retina or iris image, or other unique physical representation;

"(C) unique electronic identification number, address, or routing code; or

"(D) telecommunication identifying information or access device (as defined in section 1029(e));

"(4) the term 'personal identification card' means an identification document issued by a State or local government solely for the purpose of identification;

"(5) the term 'produce' includes alter, authenticate, or assemble; and

"(6) the term 'State' includes any State of the United States, the District of Columbia, the Commonwealth of Puerto Rico, and any other commonwealth, possession, or territory of the United States."

(e) Attempt and Conspiracy.—Section 1028 of title 18, United States Code, is amended by adding at the end the following: "(f) Attempt and

Conspiracy.—Any person who attempts or conspires to commit any offense under this section shall be subject to the same penalties as those prescribed for the offense, the commission of which was the object of the attempt or conspiracy."

(f) Forfeiture Procedures.—Section 1028 of title 18, United States Code, is amended by adding at the end the following: "(g) Forfeiture Procedures.— The forfeiture of property under this section, including any seizure and disposition of the property and any related judicial or administrative proceeding, shall be governed by the provisions of section 413 (other than subsection (d) of that section) of the Comprehensive Drug Abuse Prevention and Control Act of 1970 (21 U.S.C. 853)."

(g) Rule of Construction.—Section 1028 of title 18, United States Code, is amended by adding at the end the following:"(h) Rule of Construction.— For purpose of subsection (a)(7), a single identification document or false identification document that contains 1 or more means of identification shall be construed to be 1 means of identification."

(h) Conforming Amendments.—Chapter 47 of title 18, United States Code, is amended—

(1) in the heading for section 1028, by adding "and information" at the end; and

(2) in the table of sections at the beginning of the chapter, in the item relating to section 1028, by adding "and information" at the end.

SEC. 004. Amendment of Federal Sentencing Guidelines for Offenses Under Section 1028.

(a) In General—Pursuant to its authority under section 994(p) of title 28, United States Code, the United States Sentencing Commission shall review and amend the Federal sentencing guidelines and the policy statements of the Commission, as appropriate, to provide an appropriate penalty for each offense under section 1028 of title 18, United States Code, as amended by this Act.

(b) Factors for Consideration—In carrying out subsection (a), the United States Sentencing Commission shall consider, with respect to each offense described in subsection (a)—

(1) the extent to which the number of victims (as defined in section 3663A(a) of title 18, United States Code) involved in the offense, including harm to reputation, inconvenience, and other difficulties resulting from the offense, is an adequate measure for establishing penalties under the Federal sentencing guidelines;

(2) the number of means of identification, identification documents, or false identification documents (as those terms are defined in section 1028(d)

of title 18, United States Code, as amended by this Act) involved in the offense, is an adequate measure for establishing penalties under the Federal sentencing guidelines;

(3) the extent to which the value of the loss to any individual caused by the offense is an adequate measure for establishing penalties under the Federal sentencing guidelines;

(4) the range of conduct covered by the offense;

(5) the extent to which sentencing enhancements within the Federal sentencing guidelines and the court's authority to sentence above the applicable guideline range are adequate to ensure punishment at or near the maximum penalty for the most egregious conduct covered by the offense;

(6) the extent to which Federal sentencing guidelines sentences for the offense have been constrained by statutory maximum penalties;

(7) the extent to which Federal sentencing guidelines for the offense adequately achieve the purposes of sentencing set forth in section 3553(a)(2) of title 18, United States Code; and

(8) any other factor that the United States Sentencing Commission considers to be appropriate.

SEC. 005. Centralized Complaint and Consumer Education Service for Victims of Identity Theft.

(a) In General—Not later than 1 year after the date of enactment of this Act, the Federal Trade Commission shall establish procedures to—

(1) log and acknowledge the receipt of complaints by individuals who certify that they have a reasonable belief that 1 or more of their means of identification (as defined in section 1028 of title 18, United States Code, as amended by this Act) have been assumed, stolen, or otherwise unlawfully acquired in violation of section 1028 of title 18, United States Code, as amended by this Act;

(2) provide informational materials to individuals described in paragraph (1); and

(3) refer complaints described in paragraph (1) to appropriate entities, which may include referral to—

(A) the 3 major national consumer reporting agencies; and

(B) appropriate law enforcement agencies for potential law enforcement action.

(b) Authorization of Appropriations—There are authorized to be appropriated such sums as may be necessary to carry out this section.

SEC. 006. Technical Amendments to Title 18, United States Code.

(a) Technical Correction Relating to Criminal Forfeiture Procedures.—Section 982(b)(1) of title 18, United States Code, is amended to read as follows: "(1) The forfeiture of property under this section, including any seizure and disposition of the property and any related judicial or administrative proceeding, shall be governed by the provisions of section 413 (other than subsection (d) of that section) of the Comprehensive Drug Abuse Prevention and Control Act of 1970 (21 U.S.C. 853)."

(b) Economic Espionage and Theft of Trade Secrets as Predicate Offenses for Wire Interception.—Section 2516(1)(a) of title 18, United States Code, is amended by inserting "chapter 90 (relating to protection of trade secrets)," after "to espionage)."

SEC. 007. Redaction of Ethics Reports Filed by Judicial Officers and Employees.

Section 105(b) of the Ethics in Government Act of 1978 (5 U.S.C. App.) is amended by adding at the end the following new paragraph:

"(3)(A) This section does not require the immediate and unconditional availability of reports filed by an individual described in section 109(8) or 109(10) of this Act if a finding is made by the Judicial Conference, in consultation with United States Marshall Service, that revealing personal and sensitive information could endanger that individual.

"(B) A report may be redacted pursuant to this paragraph only—

"(i) to the extent necessary to protect the individual who filed the report; and

"(ii) for as long as the danger to such individual exists.

"(C) The Administrative Office of the United States Courts shall submit to the Committees on the Judiciary of the House of Representatives and of the Senate an annual report with respect to the operation of this paragraph including—

"(i) the total number of reports redacted pursuant to this paragraph;

"(ii) the total number of individuals whose reports have been redacted pursuant to this paragraph; and

"(iii) the types of threats against individuals whose reports are redacted, if appropriate.

"(D) The Judicial Conference, in consultation with the Department of Justice, shall issue regulations setting forth the circumstances under which redaction is appropriate under this paragraph and the procedures for redaction.

"(E) This paragraph shall expire on December 31, 2001, and apply to filings through calendar year 2001."

Approved October 30, 1998.

Source: Identity Theft and Assumption Deterrence Act of 1998. Public Law 105–318, 112 *U.S. Statutes at Large* 3007 (1999).

The Sherman Anti-Trust Act (1890)

Fifty-first Congress of the United States of America, At the First Session,
Begun and held at the City of Washington on Monday, the second day of December, one thousand eight hundred and eighty-nine.

An act to protect trade and commerce against unlawful restraints and monopolies.

Be it enacted by the Senate and House of Representatives of the United States of America in Congress assembled,

Sec. 1. Every contract, combination in the form of trust or otherwise, or conspiracy, in restraint of trade or commerce among the several States, or with foreign nations, is hereby declared to be illegal. Every person who shall make any such contract or engage in any such combination or conspiracy, shall be deemed guilty of a misdemeanor, and, on conviction thereof, shall be punished by fine not exceeding five thousand dollars, or by imprisonment not exceeding one year, or by both said punishments, at the discretion of the court.

Sec. 2. Every person who shall monopolize, or attempt to monopolize, or combine or conspire with any other person or persons, to monopolize any part of the trade or commerce among the several States, or with foreign nations, shall be deemed guilty of a misdemeanor, and, on conviction thereof; shall be punished by fine not exceeding five thousand dollars, or by imprisonment not exceeding one year, or by both said punishments, in the discretion of the court.

Sec. 3. Every contract, combination in form of trust or otherwise, or conspiracy, in restraint of trade or commerce in any Territory of the United States or of the District of Columbia, or in restraint of trade or commerce between any such Territory and another, or between any such Territory or Territories and any State or States or the District of Columbia, or with foreign nations, or between the District of Columbia and any State or States or foreign nations, is hereby declared illegal. Every person who shall make any such contract or engage in any such combination or conspiracy, shall be deemed guilty of a misdemeanor, and, on conviction thereof, shall be punished by fine not exceeding five thousand dollars, or by imprisonment not exceeding one year, or by both said punishments, in the discretion of the court.

Sec. 4. The several circuit courts of the United States are hereby invested with jurisdiction to prevent and restrain violations of this act; and it shall be the duty of the several district attorneys of the United States, in their respective districts, under the direction of the Attorney-General, to institute proceedings in equity to prevent and restrain such violations. Such proceedings may be by way of petition setting forth the case and praying that such violation shall be enjoined or otherwise prohibited. When the parties complained of shall have been duly notified of such petition the court shall proceed, as soon as may be, to the hearing and determination of the case; and pending such petition and before final decree, the court may at any time make such temporary restraining order or prohibition as shall be deemed just in the premises.

Sec. 5. Whenever it shall appear to the court before which any proceeding under section four of this act may be pending, that the ends of justice require that other parties should be brought before the court, the court may cause them to be summoned, whether they reside in the district in which the court is held or not; and subpoenas to that end may be served in any district by the marshal thereof.

Sec. 6. Any property owned under any contract or by any combination, or pursuant to any conspiracy (and being the subject thereof) mentioned in section one of this act, and being in the course of transportation from one State to another, or to a foreign country, shall be- forfeited to the United States, and may be seized and condemned by like proceedings as those provided by law for the forfeiture, seizure, and condemnation of property imported into the United States contrary to law.

Sec. 7. Any person who shall be injured in his business or property by any other person or corporation by reason of anything forbidden or declared to be unlawful by this act, may sue therefore in any circuit court of the United States in the district in which the defendant resides or is found, without respect to the amount in controversy, and shall recover three fold the damages by him sustained, and the costs of suit, including a reasonable attorney's fee.

Sec. 8. That the word "person," or "persons," wherever used in this act shall be deemed to include corporations and associations existing under or authorized by the laws of either the United States, the laws of any of the Territories, the laws of any State, or the laws of any foreign country.

Approved, July 2, 1890.

Source: The Sherman Antitrust Act. 26 U.S. Statutes at Large 209 (1890).

Selected Bibliography

Aaker, D. A. & Day, G. S. (1982). *Consumerism: Search for the consumer interest.* New York: The Free Press.

Albaum, G., & Wiley, J. (2010). Consumer perceptions of extended warranties and service providers. *Journal of Consumer Marketing, 27*(6), 516–523.

Alper, J. S., Alper, J. K., & Natowicz, M. R. (1996). EEOC Compliance Manual for the ADA and Genetic Discrimination. *American Journal of Medical Genetics, 61*(1), 95–95.

American Bar Association. Section of Antitrust Law. (2004). *Consumer protection handbook.* Chicago, IL: American Bar Association.

Anderson, M. H., & Raymond, J. (2010) Perspectives on payday loans: The evidence from Florida. *Review of Business Research, 10*(5), 154–161.

Anderson, M. H., & Jaggia, S. (2012). Return, purchase, or skip? Outcome, duration, and consumer behavior in the rent-to-own market. *Empirical Economics*, 1–22.

Anderson, W., Block, W., DiLorenzo, T., & Westley, C. (2001). The Microsoft Corporation in collision with antitrust law. *Journal of Social, Political, and Economic Studies, 26*(1), 287–302.

Asher, A. (1998). Going global: a new paradigm for consumer protection. *Journal of Consumer Affairs, 32*(2), 183–1183.

Bagwell, K., & Staiger, R. W. (2011). What do trade negotiators negotiate about? Empirical evidence from the World Trade Organization. *The American Economic Review, 101*(4), 1238–1273.

Barfield, C. E. (2001). Free trade, sovereignty, democracy: Future of the World Trade Organization. *Chicago Journal of International Law, 2*, 403.

Bar-Gill, O. (2012). *Seduction by contract: Law, economics, and psychology in consumer markets.* Oxford: Oxford University Press.

Barnett, R. E. (2010). *The Oxford introductions to US law: Contracts.* Oxford, United Kingdom: Oxford University Press.

Belmas, G. I., & Larson, B. N. (2007). Clicking away your speech rights: The enforceability of gagwrap licenses. *Communication Law and Policy, 12*(1), 37–89.

Ben-Shahar, O., & Posner, E. A. (2011). The right to withdraw in contract law. *The Journal of Legal Studies, 40*(1), 115–148.

Bertola, G., Disney, R., & Grant, C. (2008). *The economics of consumer credit* (Vol. 1). Cambridge, MA: The MIT Press.

Bevans, N. R. (2011). *Consumer law & protection: A practical approach for paralegals and the public.* Durham, NC: Carolina Academic Press.

Bircher, J. (2005). Towards a dynamic definition of health and disease. *Medicine, Health Care and Philosophy, 8*(3), 335–341.

Border, R. (2003). *Your consumer rights: Pocket lawyer.* Portland, OR: Taylor & Francis Group.

Bradsher, K. (2004). *High and mighty: The dangerous rise of the SUV.* New York: PublicAffairs.

Brobeck, S., Mayer, R. N., & Herrmann, R. O. (1997). *Encyclopedia of the consumer movement.* Santa Barbara, CA: ABC-CLIO.

Carson, R. (2002). *Silent spring.* Boston, MA: Mariner Books.

Chen, K., & Fadlalla, A. (2008). *Online consumer protection: Theories of human relativism.* Information Science Reference—Imprint of IGI Publishing.

Coleman-Adebayo, M. (2011). *No fear: A whistleblower's triumph over corruption and retaliation at the EPA.* Chicago, IL: Lawrence Hill Books.

Collins, J. M. (2006). *Investigating identity theft: A guide for businesses, law enforcement, and victims.* Hoboken, NJ: Wiley.

Consumer Reports. (May 1995). Is lawsuit reform good for consumers? *Consumer Reports, 312.*

Cook, G. G. (March 1995). The case for (some) regulation. *Washington Monthly,* 34.

Cooper, C. (2009). *Extraordinary circumstances: The journey of a corporate whistleblower.* Hoboken, NJ: Wiley.

Cunningham, D. (2004). *There's something happening here: The new left, the Klan, and FBI counterintelligence.* Berkeley, CA: University of California Press.

Cunningham, M. H. (2009). In safe hands: True stories about the men and women of United States customs and border protection. Bloomington, IN: Xlibris Corp.

D'Agostino, D. M., Mark, A., Camarillo, Y., Harms, N., Kmetz, L., Perdue, C., & Widhagen, J. (2011). *Observations on the costs and benefits of an increased Department of Defense role in helping to secure the southwest land border.* Washington, DC: Government Accountability Office.

David, R. (2010). *Mortgage confidential: What you need to know that your lender won't tell you.* New York, NY: AMACOM.

Dilger, R. J. (2003). *American transportation policy*. Westport, CT: Praeger Publishers.

Dobalian, A., Callis, R., & Davey, V. J. (2011). Evolution of the Veterans Health Administration's role in emergency management since September 11, 2001. *Disaster Medicine and Public Health Preparedness, 5*(Suppl 2), S182.

Donohue, J. M., Cevasco, M., & Rosenthal, M. B. (2007). A decade of direct-to-consumer advertising of prescription drugs. *New England Journal of Medicine, 357*(7), 673–681.

Dowd, A. R. (1997). Protect your privacy: A money investigation reveals the five biggest threats to your privacy and how you can safeguard yourself against the most serious types of snooping. *Money, 1*, 104–107.

Eisenberg, T., & Miller, G. P. (2004). Attorney fees in class action settlements: An empirical study. *Journal of Empirical Legal Studies, 1*(1), 27–78.

Erbe, N. D. (2006). Appreciating mediation's global role in promoting good governance. *Harvard Negotiation Law Review, 11*, 355.

Erbe, N. (2011). *Negotiation alchemy*. Berkeley, CA: Public Policy Press.

Federal Reserve Bank of Atlanta Economic Review, First and Second Quarters. (2007). *Some further thoughts about the road to safer banking* (1st and 2nd quarters). Atlanta, GA: Kaufman, George.

French, G., & Bond, M. (2010). Caveat Venditor. *Information Security Technical Report, 15*, 28–32.

Friedman, D. A. (2012). Explaining 'bait-and-switch' regulation. 4 Wm. & Mary Bus. L. Rev. 575

Gallant, P. (2011). *Discounted telephone service for low income consumers*. Washington, DC: Universal Service Administrative Company.

Gallo, N. R. (2009). *Elder law*. Clifton Park, NY: Delmar.

Garman, E. T., & Forgue, R. (2011). *Personal finance*. Mason, OH: South-Western Pub.

Gaynor, T. (2009). *Midnight on the Line: The Secret Life of the US-Mexico Border*. New York, NY: Thomas Dunne Books.

Goldsmith, E. B. (2009). *Consumer economics: issues and behaviors*. Upper Saddle River, NJ: Pearson Education.

Green, R. K., & Wachter, S. M. (2005). The American mortgage in historical and international context. *The Journal of Economic Perspectives, 19*(4), 93–114.

Hart, D. K. (2011). Contract law now—reality meets legal fictions. *University of Baltimore Law Review, 41,*(1), 1–82. Retrieved from http://law.ubalt.edu/downloads/law_downloads/5_Hart.41.1.pdf

Hicks, J. (2010). State department planning and real estate: We don't pick our markets either. *Corporate Real Estate Journal, 1*(1), 53–66.

Hogue, C. (2006). Change in the air. *Chemical and Engineering News, 84*(51), 15.

Holder, K., Manuel, K., & Clerk, L. (2007). Predatory lending: A comparison of state laws to the Federal Home Ownership and Equity Protection Act. Congressional Research Service Report RL32784.

Holmberg, J., & Bruzzese, D. (2008). *The teen's guide to personal finance: Basic concepts in personal finance that every teen should know.* The teen's guide.

Hynes, R.M., & Walt, S.D. (2010). Why banks are not allowed in bankruptcy. *Washington and Lee Law Review, 67,* 985.

Investment Company Institute v. Camp, 401 U.S. 617, 634 (1971).

Isaacs, P., & Whittaker, J.M. (2011) *Unemployment insurance: Programs and benefits, congressional research service.* CreateSpace Independent Publishing Platform. http://greenbook.waysandmeans.house.gov/sites/green book.waysandmeans.house.gov/files/images/RL33362_gb.pdf

Jasper, M.C. (1997). *Consumer rights law* (pp. 23–25). Dobbs Ferry, NY: Oceana Publications.

Jiang, B., & Zhang, X. (2011). How does a retailer's service plan affect a manufacturer's warranty? *Management Science, 57*(4), 727–740.

Kallet, A. (1935). *One hundred million guinea pigs: Dangers in everyday foods, drugs, & cosmetics (getting and spending).*United States: Grosset and Dunlap.

Kemper, V. (1995). A citizen for all seasons. *Common Cause Magazine,* 12–17.

Kilian, B., Jones, C., Pratt, L., & Villalobos, A. (2006). Is sustainable agriculture a viable strategy to improve farm income in Central America? A case study on coffee. *Journal of Business Research, 59*(3), 322–330.

Koh, H.H. (2012). The State Department Legal Adviser's Office: Eight decades in peace and war. *Georgetown Law Journal, 100,* 1747–1829.

Lande, R., & Averitt, N. (1997). Consumer sovereignty: A unified theory of antitrust and consumer protection law. *Antitrust Law Journal, 65,* 713.

Laughery, K.R. (2006). Safety communications: Warnings. *Applied Ergonomics, 37*(4), 467–478.

Lear, L. (1998). *Rachel Carson: Witness for nature.* New York; NY: Holt Paperbacks.

Lewis, J. (1988). Looking backward: A historical perspective on environmental regulations. *Environmental Protection Agency Journal, 14,* 26.

Light, P.C. (1993). *Monitoring government: Inspectors general and the search for accountability.* Washington, DC: Brookings Institution Press.

Ling, Peter J. (2002). *Martin Luther King, Jr.* New York, NY: Routledge Publishing.

Lipscomb, T. (2011). *Re-made in the USA: How we can restore jobs, retool manufacturing, and compete with the world.* Hoboken, NJ: Wiley.

Mallery, S. (2009). Beyond Seinfeld's Good Samaritan Debacle: Protecting citizens who render care at the scene of an accident from civil liability. *McGeorge Law Review, 41,* 647.

Mallin, C. A. (2009). *Corporate social responsibility: A case study approach.* Northampton, MS: Edward Elgar Publishing.

Manheimer, A. S. (2005). *Martin Luther King Jr: Dreaming of equality.* Minneapolis, MN: Twenty-First Century Books.

Martin, M. E. (2011). *Introduction to human services. Through the eyes of practice settings* (2nd ed.). Boston, MA: Allyn and Bacon.

Mayer, R. N. (1989). *The consumer movement: Guardians of the marketplace* (pp. 25–58). Boston, MA: Twayne Publishers.

Mayer, R. N. (1998). Thoughts on women's contributions to the modern consumer movement. *Advancing the Consumer Interest, 10*(2), 5–13.

McCloud, L., & Dwyer, R. E. (2011). The fragile American: hardship and financial troubles in the 21st century. *The Sociological Quarterly, 52*(1), 13–35.

Mertus, J. A. (2009). *The United Nations and human rights: A guide for a new era* (Vol. 33). London, UK: Routledge.

Mervis, J. (2012). What would wiping out the Commerce Department mean for science? *Science Insider.* American Association for the Advancement of Science.

Nader, R. (1965). Unsafe at any speed. The designed-in dangers of the American automobile. New York, NY: Grossman Publishers.

Nelson, J. P. (2006). Cigarette advertising regulation: A meta-analysis. *International Review of Law and Economics, 26*(2), 195–226.

Nyachuba, D. G. (2010). Foodborne illness: Is it on the rise? *Nutrition reviews, 68*(5), 257–269.

Parham, M. A. (Ed.) (2009). *Mass marketing and consumer fraud: Background, issues and data.* New York: Nova Science Publishers, Inc.

Peterson, E., Conkling, W., & Friedman, M. (1996). Restless: The memoirs of labor and consumer activist Esther Peterson. *Journal of Consumer Affairs, 30*(2), 499–501.

Peterson, P. E. (2010). *Saving schools: From Horace Mann to virtual learning.* Cambridge, MA: Harvard University Press.

Plunkett, T., & Mierzwinski, E. (2009). Consumer Federation of America: U.S. Public Interest Research Group (U.S. PIRG). *Congressional Digest, 88,* 176–190.

Poon, M. (2009). From new deal institutions to capital markets: Commercial consumer risk scores and the making of subprime mortgage finance. *Accounting, Organizations and Society, 34*(5), 654–674.

Portman, J., & Stewart, M. (2012). *Every Tenant's Legal Guide.* Berkeley, CA: Nolo.

Powell, W. W., & Steinberg, R. (Eds.). (2006). *The nonprofit sector: A research handbook.* New Haven, CT: Yale University Press.

Radin, B. A. (2010). When is a health department not a health department? The case of the U.S. department of health and human services. *Social Policy & Administration, 44,* 142–154.

Rustad, M. (2007). *Everyday law for consumers.* Suginami, Tokyo:Paradigm Pub.

Sachs, B. (2009). Consumerism and information privacy: How Upton Sinclair can again save us from ourselves. *Virginia Law Review, 95,* 205.

Saucer, C. (March 1998) Small group, big impact. *Best's Review,* 50.

Schmitz, A., Moss, C. B., & Schmitz, T. G. (2010). *Agricultural policy, agribusiness, and rent-seeking behaviour.* Toronto, Canada: University of Toronto Press.

Schmitz, A. (Ed.). (2011). *The economics of alternative energy sources and globalization.* Bentham Science Publishers.

Schmidt, S. W., & McCoy, M. R. (2008). *The silent crime: What you need to know about identity theft.* Twin Lakes, WI: Twin Lakes Press.

Sinclair, U. (1906). *The Jungle.* New York: Doubleday, Jabber, and Co.

Sindell, K. (2009). *Managing your money all-in-one for dummies.* Indianapolis, IN: Wiley Publishing.

Singer, N. (2005). Labels can hide the presence of phthalates. *New York Times.*

Smith, S. S., Roberts, J. M., & Vander Wielen, R. J. (2011). *The American Congress.* Cambridge, MA: Cambridge University Press.

Stern, L. (2010). Should you cosign for your child? *Money.* Retrieved at http://money.cnn.com/2010/11/04/pf/cosign_for_your_kid.money mag/index.htm

Sullivan, B. (2004). *Your evil twin: Behind the identity theft epidemic.* Hoboken, NJ: John Wiley & Sons.

Sullivan, N. P. (2008). *Cell phones provide significant economic gains for low-income American households.* Washington, DC: New Millennium Research Council.

Sun, W., Stewart, J., & Pollard, D. (2010). *Reframing corporate social responsibility: Lessons from the global financial crisis.* West Yorkshire, England: Emerald Group Publishing Limited.

Taylor, M. R. (2011). Will the Food Safety Modernization Act help prevent outbreaks of foodborne illness?. *New England Journal of Medicine, 365*(9).

Zelenak, M., & Reiboldt, W. (2009). *Consumer economics: The consumer in our society.* Scottsdale, AZ: Holcomb Hathaway Publishers.

United States Department of Housing and Urban Development. (May 18, 2007). HUD historical background. Web. August 6, 2012.

United States Department of Housing and Urban Development. (2011). Frequently asked questions about HUD's reverse mortgages. Web. August 6, 2012.

U.S. Bureau of Labor Statistics. (2011). Consumer Expenditure Survey, 2010. *Focus on Prices and Spending*, 2(12), 1–5.

U.S. Securities and Exchange Commission. (2006). Affinity fraud: How to avoid investment scams that target groups. Retrieved from http://www.sec.gov/investor/pubs/affinity.htm (December 11, 2011).

Wang, P. (1992). A consumer warning on new rip-offs. *Money*, 21(3), 34.

Warne, C.E., Morse, R.L., & Snyder, F.E. (1993). *The consumer movement: Lectures.* Manhattan, KS: Family Economics Trust Press.

Warner, R. (2012). *Everybody's guide to small claims court.* Berkeley, Ca: Nolo.

Warren, E. (2008). Product safety regulation as a model for financial services regulation. *Journal of Consumer Affairs*, 42(3), 452–460.

Winerman, M. (2003). Origins of the FTC: Concentration, cooperation, control, and competition. *Antitrust Law Journal*, 71, 1.

Zegart, A.B. (2009). *Spying blind: The CIA, the FBI, and the origins of 9/11.* Princeton, NJ: Princeton University Press.

Editors and Contributors

Editors

Wendy Reiboldt, PhD, is professor of consumer affairs and chair of the Department of Family and Consumer Sciences at California State University, Long Beach. Her teaching interests are in the areas of consumer protection, consumer in the legal and economic environment, consumer and family resource management, as well as, research methods and statistics. Her published works include a textbook, *Consumer Economics: The Consumer in Our Society,* and refereed journal articles in *Family and Consumer Sciences Research Journal, The Journal of Consumer Education, The Journal of Elder Abuse and Neglect, The Journal of Family and Consumer Sciences,* among others. Reiboldt holds a doctorate in consumer economics from the Ohio State University.

Melanie Horn Mallers, PhD, is assistant professor in the Department of Human Services and the Masters in Gerontology Program at California State University, Fullerton. Her teaching interests are in the areas of leadership, policy, program planning, aging, and health. Her published works include refereed journal articles in *Psychology and Health, The Gerontologist, Archives in Gerontology and Geriatrics,* and *Developmental Psychology.* She also has numerous book chapters and conference proceedings related to the health and well-being of individuals. Her research has also been featured on CNN Live. Mallers is currently coauthoring a textbook, *An Overview of Human Services.* Mallers holds a doctorate in family studies and human development from the University of Arizona, Tuscon.

Contributors

Melissa K. Afable, BS
Veterans Emergency Management Evaluation Center
Boston University

Mariné Aghekyan-Simonian, PhD
California State University, Long Beach

Trena T. Anastasia, PhD
QDG Consulting
Colorado State University
University of Wyoming

Michael H. Anderson, PhD
University of Massachusetts, Dartmouth

Joanne Bankston, PhD
Kentucky State University

Stephen Barrett, MD
Quackwatch

Zoran K. Basich, JD
Nursin Home Solutions
Basich Family Affairs
American International Financial Group

Andrea H. Beller, PhD
University of Illinois at Urbana-Champaign, Emerita
Affiliate Institute of Government and Public Affairs

Genelle I. Belmas, PhD
California State University, Fullerton

Henning Best, PhD
Gesis-Leibniz Institute for the Social Sciences

Axton Betz, PhD
Eastern Illinois University

Marie Botkin, PhD
California State University, Long Beach

Michael K. Botts, JD
Attorney at Law

John R. Burton, PhD
University of Utah, Emeritus

Diane E. Carson, PhD
California State University, Long Beach

Andrew T. "Andy" Carswell, PhD
University of Georgia

Yunhee Chang, PhD
University of Mississippi

Erin S. Cikanek, MA
Northwestern University

Maria Claver, PhD
California State University, Long Beach

Brenda J. Cude, PhD
University of Georgia

Sharon A. DeVaney, PhD
Purdue University, Emerita

Dara Duguay, MA
Duguay & Associates

Jason M. Duquette-Hoffman, MS
The University of Vermont

Karen E. Edwards, JD
University of South Carolina

Zoe Bryan Engstrom, EdD
California State University, Long Beach

Nancy D. Erbe, JD
California State University, Dominguez Hills

Patti J. Fisher, PhD
Virginia Tech

Robert L. FitzPatrick, BA
Pyramid Scheme Alert

Angela Fontes, PhD
Illinois State University

Monroe Friedman, PhD
Eastern Michigan University, Emeritus

Martie Gillen, PhD
University of Florida

Casey Goeller, MS, MA
California State University, Long Beach

Shuyi Guan, MS
SUNY at Albany

Elowin Harper, MA
Middle Tennessee State

Celia Ray Hayhoe, PhD
Virginia Tech

Deborah C. Haynes, PhD
Montana State University

Pastor Herrera Jr., BA
California State University, Northridge

Kevin C. Heslin, PhD
Veterans Emergency Management Evaluation Center

Cynthia R. Jasper, PhD
University of Wisconsin–Madison

Mary Jane "M.J." Kabaci, PhD
University of Georgia

Kristi Kanel, PhD
California State University, Fullerton

Nicole Kelly, BS
Illinois State University

Jane Kolodinsky, PhD
The University of Vermont

Lisa J. Amos Ledeboer, MS
Mt. San Antonio College

Irene Leech, PhD
Virginia Tech
Consumer Federation of America
Board

Laurie A. Lucas, JD
Oklahoma State University

Laura B. Lucas, BS
Eastern Illinois University

Valerie Lucus-McEwen, MS
California State University, Long Beach

Carole J. Makela, PhD
Colorado State University

Robert N. Mayer, PhD
University of Utah

Jean Memken, PhD
Northwest Missouri State University

Jon P. Nelson, PhD
Pennsylvania State University,
University Park, Emeritus

Mary Niemczyk, PhD
Arizona State University

Megan J. O'Neil, MPS
The University of Maryland Extension

Aleta Ostlund, MA
California State University,
Long Beach
Ostlund Insurance

Whitney Paul, MAG
Eastern Illinois University

Rebecca Perley, MHA
California State University, Long Beach

Ross D. Petty, JD
Babson College

Sandra L. Poirier, EdD
Middle Tennesee State

Susan Reichelt, PhD
Winthrop University

Rigoberto Reyes, BA
California Consumer Affairs
Association

Dolores Robles, MA
California State University, Long
Beach

James R. Ruby, PhD
California State University, Fullerton

Lorna Saboe-Wounded Head, PhD
South Dakota State University

Cynthia Schlesinger, MSG
California State University, Northridge

Andrew Schmitz, PhD
University of Florida, Gainesville

Troy G. Schmitz, PhD
Arizona State University

David L. Schult, MS
California State University, Long Beach

Jayna Seidel, BS
California State University, Fullerton

Ishita Sengupta, PhD
National Academy of Social Insurance

Joyce Serido, PhD
The University of Arizona

Linda Sherry
Consumer Action

Linda Simpson, PhD
Eastern Illinois University

Tony Sinay, PhD
California State University, Long Beach

Don Soifer, BA
Lexington Institute
Consumer Postal Council

Jeff Sovern, JD
St. John's University School of Law

Ann M. Stahl, MA
California State University, Northridge

George Richard-Thomas Stahle, BS
US Airways Group, Inc.

Monica Steinisch, BA
Consumer Action

Jasmine V. Tucker, MPA
National Academy of Social Insurance

Esiquio Ramos Uballe, EdD
California State University, Fullerton

Virginia B. Vincenti, PhD
University of Wyoming

Whitney Walters, BS
Eastern Illinois University

Amy Widman, JD
Northern Illinois University College of Law

Zheng Yan, EdD
SUNY at Albany

Stewart M. Young, JD
University of Wyoming

Olivia Zavala, BS
California State University, Fullerton

Mel J. Zelenak, PhD
University of Missouri-Columbia

Index

Note: Page numbers in **boldface** reflect main entries in the book.